Connections
Reading, Writing, and Thinking

Connections
Reading, Writing, and Thinking

Robert DiYanni
Pace University

BOYNTON/COOK PUBLISHERS, INC.
UPPER MONTCLAIR, NEW JERSEY 07043

Acknowledgments

ATHENEUM PUBLISHERS, INC. "Adam's Task," in *The Night Mirror* by John Hollander. Copyright © 1971 by John Hollander. "Crise de Coeur," in *Types of Shape* by John Hollander. Copyright © 1969 by John Hollander. Both reprinted with permission of the publisher.

CONGDON & WEED, INC. Chapter One from *Growing Up* by Russell Baker. Copyright © 1982 by Russell Baker. Reprinted by permission of the publisher.

DOUBLEDAY & COMPANY, INC. "The Waking" from *The Collected Poems of Theodore Roethke*. Copyright 1953 by Theodore Roethke. Reprinted by permission of the publisher.

RUTH EISENBERG "Jocasta" and "Writing Jocasta" by Ruth Eisenberg. Copyright by Ruth Eisenberg.

FABER AND FABER PUBLISHERS "A Study of Reading Habits" from *The Whitsun Weddings* by Philip Larkin. Reprinted by permission of the publisher.

FARRAR, STRAUS & GIROUX, INC. "Sestina" from *The Complete Poems 1927–1979* by Elizabeth Bishop. Copyright © 1956, 1969 by Elizabeth Bishop. Copyright © 1983 by Alice Helen Methfessel. Reprinted by permission of the publisher.

THE GUARDIAN "What the Executioner Actually Faces" by Michael Lake in *The Guardian,* April 9, 1973. Reprinted by permission of the publisher.

HARCOURT BRACE JOVANOVICH, INC. "A Hanging" from *Shooting an Elephant and Other Stories* by George Orwell, copyright 1950 by Sonia Brownell Orwell; renewed 1968 by Sonia Brownell Orwell. "The Meaning of a Poem" from *The Collected Essays, Journalism and Letters of*

Library of Congress Cataloging in Publication Data

DiYanni, Robert
   Connections: writing, reading, and reasoning.

   1. College readers. I. Title.
PE1122.D55   1984   808'.0427   84-16825
ISBN 0-86709-049-9

Copyright © 1985 by Boynton/Cook Publishers, Inc.
All rights reserved. No part of this book may be used or reproduced in any manner without written permission except in the case of brief quotations embodied in critical articles and reviews.

For information address Boynton/Cook Publishers, Inc., 52 Upper Montclair Plaza, P.O. Box 860, Upper Montclair, NJ 07043

Printed in the United States of America
85 86 87 88   10 9 8 7 6 5 4 3 2 1

Acknowledgments (cont.)

George Orwell, Volume 2, copyright © 1968 by Sonia Brownell Orwell. *The Oedipus Rex of Sophocles*: An English Version by Dudley Fitts and Robert Fitzgerald, copyright 1949 by Harcourt Brace Jovanovich, Inc.; renewed 1977 by Cornelia Fitts and Robert Fitzgerald. All reprinted by permission of the publisher.

HARVARD UNIVERSITY PRESS Poems 435 and 1078 from *The Poems of Emily Dickinson,* edited by Thomas H. Johnson, Cambridge, MA: The Belknap Press of Harvard University Press, copyright © 1955, 1979, 1983 by the President and fellows of Harvard College. Reprinted by permission of the publishers and the Trustees of Amherst College.

HOLT, RINEHART AND WINSTON, PUBLISHERS "When I Was One-and-Twenty" from "A Shropshire Lad"—Authorized Edition—from *The Collected Poems of A. E. Housman.* Copyright 1939, 1940, © 1965 by Holt, Rinehart and Winston. Copyright © 1967, 1968 by Robert E. Symons "Departmental" and "Design" from *The Poetry of Robert Frost* edited by Edward Connery Lathem. Copyright © 1969 by Holt, Rinehart and Winston. Copyright © 1936 by Robert Frost. Copyright © 1964 by Lesley Frost Ballantine. All reprinted by permission of the publisher.

HOUGHTON MIFFLIN COMPANY "Cinderella" from *Transformations* by Anne Sexton. Copyright © 1971 by Anne Sexton. Reprinted by permission of the publisher.

ALFRED A. KNOPF, INC. "Summer Sestina" from *Admit Impediment* by Marie Ponsot. Copyright 1977 by Marie Ponsot. "Peter Quince at the Clavier," "Thirteen Ways of Looking at a Blackbird," and "The House Was Quiet and the World Was Calm" from *The Collected Poems of Wallace Stevens.* Copyright 1923, 1947 and renewed 1951 by Wallace Stevens. All reprinted by permission of the publisher.

MACMILLAN PUBLISHING COMPANY "Down by the Salley Gardens" from *The Poems of W. B. Yeats* edited by Richard J. Finneran. Reprinted with permission of the publisher.

NEW DIRECTIONS PUBLISHING CORPORATION "In Dreams Begin Responsibilities" from *In Dreams Begin Responsibilities* by Delmore Schwartz. Copyright © 1978 by New Directions Publishing Corporation. "Do Not Go Gentle into That Good Night" from *Poems of Dylan Thomas.* Copyright 1952 by Dylan Thomas. Both reprinted by permission of the publisher.

W. W. NORTON & COMPANY, INC. Part II, Chapter IX of *Madame Bovary* by Gustave Flaubert, translated by Paul DeMan, a Norton Critical Edition. Copyright © 1965 by W. W. Norton & Company, Inc. Reprinted by permission of the publisher.

OXFORD UNIVERSITY PRESS "Cinderella" from *The Classic Fairy Tales* by Iona and Peter Opie (1974). Copyright © Iona and Peter Opie, 1974. "Felix Randal" from *Poems of Gerard Manley Hopkins.* Both reprinted by permission of the publisher.

Acknowledgments (cont.)

PENGUIN BOOKS LTD. "People" from *Selected Poems* by Yevgeny Yevtushenko, translated by Robin Milner-Gulland and Peter Levi (Penguin Modern European Poets 1962) pp. 85–86. Copyright © Robin Milner-Gulland and Peter Levi, 1962. Reprinted by permission of the publisher.

RANDOM HOUSE, INC. "The Kugelmass Episode" from *Side Effects* by Woody Allen. Copyright © 1977 by Woody Allen. "Continuity of Parks" from *End of the Game and Other Stories* by Julio Cortázar. Copyright © 1967 by Random House, Inc. "The Flow of the River" from *The Immense Journey* by Loren Eiseley. Copyright 1953 by Loren Eiseley. Chapter 1 of *The Duke of Deception* by Geoffrey Wolff. Copyright © 1979 by Geoffrey Wolff. "Continuity of Parks" is reprinted by permission of Pantheon Books, a division of Random House, Inc. The others are reprinted by permission of Random House, Inc.

SCIENTIFIC AMERICAN, INC. "Multistability in Perception" by Fred Attneave, from the December, 1977, *Scientific American,* p. 64. Copyright © 1977 by Scientific American, Inc. Reprinted by permission of W. H. Freeman and Company.

SIMON & SCHUSTER, INC. "Company Man" and "Blame the Victim" from *Close to Home* by Ellen Goodman. Copyright © 1979 by The Washington Post Company. Excerpt from *Old Glory* (pp. 317–18) by Jonathan Raban. Copyright © 1981 by Jonathan Raban. All reprinted by permission of the publisher.

HELEN THURBER "The Owl Who Was God" and "The Little Girl and the Wolf" from *Fables for Our Time* by James Thurber. Copyright © 1940 by James Thurber. Copyright © 1968 by Helen Thurber. Published by Harper & Row. Reprinted by permission of Helen Thurber.

VISUAL ARTISTS AND GALLERIES ASSOCIATION, INC. "Relativity," "Day and Night" and "Circle Limit IV" by M. C. Escher. Collection Haags Gemeentamuseum—The Hague. Copyright © Beeldrecht, Amsterdam/VAGA, New York. Reprinted by permission of VAGA.

VIKING PENGUIN INC. Excerpt from "Benjamin Franklin" from *Studies in Classic American Literature* by D. H. Lawrence. Copyright 1923 by Thomas Seltzer, Inc. Copyright renewed 1950 by Frieda Lawrence. "Piano" from *The Complete Poems of D. H. Lawrence,* collected and edited by Vivian de Sola Pinto and F. Warren Roberts. Copyright © 1964, 1971 by Angelo Ravagli and C. M. Weekley, executors of the Estate of Frieda Lawrence Ravagli. "Autonomy" from *Lives of a Cell* by Lewis Thomas. Copyright © 1972, 1974 by Lewis Thomas. All reprinted by permission of the publisher.

Preface

> Literacy is not merely the capacity to understand the conceptual content of writings and utterances, but the ability to participate fully in a set of social and intellectual practices. It is not passive but active; not imitative but creative, for participation in the speaking and writing of language is participation in the activities it makes possible.
>
> James Boyd White

Connections is rooted in the idea that all learning involves making connections, linking new information and experience with what we have previously learned and, in the process, readjusting our understanding of what we know. From this standpoint, learning is less a matter of accumulating information and adding one bit to another than a way of re-envisioning and re-conceptualizing our knowledge. This understanding of how we learn has something in common with T. S. Eliot's explanation of how a literary tradition emerges: as a new work of art is created, it adds to the body of art that previously existed; but it also alters the relationships among all the works that antedate it. *Connections* is based on the related idea that learning proceeds by a similar revision and reconstruction of what was previously known.

Another principle governing the book is that reading, writing, and thinking proceed in cyclical, not linear fashion. A dialectic occurs between reading and writing, writing and thinking, and thinking and reading, with all three processes working together reinforcing and stimulating each other. Because they reinforce and stimulate each other, reading, writing, and thinking should be taught together. *Connections* tries to capitalize on their interrelationships by allying them as much as possible. Parts I and III can be taught as *Writing*-Reading and Thinking sections; Parts II and IV as *Reading*-Thinking and Writing sections.

Part I is a set of invention exercises, discovery procedures, thinking games designed to introduce students to the process of how they make meaning. Part III includes exercises and guidelines for style, with analysis and imitation as central features. Readings include sample sentences and an occasional poem which is appropriated to make some specific point about how language works. Part II invites the making of connections between sets of readings, usually paired, sometimes grouped. The readings play off against one another in different ways, with students guided to the connections between and among them by headnotes, exercises, and questions (entitled *Considerations* to highlight their emphasis on thinking rather than on finding the "right" answer). These paired readings are introduced by a brief discussion of the process of reading and responding with accompanying demonstrations and guidelines. Part IV offers a potpourri of readings (essays mostly, with a few stories, poems, and letters). Students are encouraged throughout this section to keep making their own connections. Following the selections here, as in Part II, are invitations to think (the Considerations) and encouragements to respond—often in writing (the Exercises). Also, as in Part II the selections in Part IV are prefaced by brief headnotes which attempt to whet students' appetites to chew, savor, and digest what they read.

Connections encourages and invites students to compose; it assures them that they already know things useful in developing their ability to read, write, and think. The reading and writing questions and exercises invite students to participate, to *do* things rather than vegetate. Students are urged to become active respondents in dialogues with the text, with one another, and with themselves. Many of the exercises are inductive; some are not. Most can be done without the assistance of the instructor. Almost all contain open-ended questions that can be dealt with in a variety of ways. Designed to stimulate students to observe, infer, connect, and conclude (at least tentatively), the Considerations and Exercises ask them to make *sense* of what they read and to *make* sense in what they write. They invite students to construe texts, construct them, and make meaning—over and over, again and again.

Connections is not a reader, an anthology, or a rhetoric-handbook, though it shares features with all of these. It is, instead, an invention-centered, response-oriented reading, writing, and thinking book.

For help in developing the book, for believing in it and in me, I want to thank Bob Boynton—editor, publisher, and friend—whose support and advice have been incomparably valuable. I would also like to thank Peter Stillman, whose intelligent criticism, scrupulous editing, and collaborative assistance (particularly in Part IV) have done much to improve the book. Thanks also to my friends and colleagues who read an earlier version and offered much wise counsel: Robert Lyons and Sandra Schor of Queens College and Susan Gannon of Pace University. And finally, thanks to Anita Cimina and Vicki Gannon for their gracious assistance with clerical tasks.

Contents

Preface

PART I

Getting Started: Writing as Discovery and Revision   1

    Fears about Writing 1
    Annotating 3
    Listing 6
    Questioning 6
        In Dreams Begin Responsibilities 9
            Delmore Schwartz
    Lateral Thinking 19
        What Is the Grass? 20
            Walt Whitman
        Thirteen Ways of Looking at a Blackbird 22
            Wallace Stevens
        Much Madness Is Divinest Sense 24
            Emily Dickinson
        A Meditation upon a Broomstick 26
            Jonathan Swift
    Perception 28
        Multistability in Perception 29
            Fred Attneave
        Woodcuts 32, 33, 35
            M. C. Escher
        The Wives of the Dead 36
            Nathaniel Hawthorne
        Design 41
            Robert Frost
    Revision 41
        Myths about Revision 43
            The Piano 44
                D. H. Lawrence

PART II
Reading and Responding: Getting Involved with Texts   47

Principles and Guidelines 47
A Hanging 48
<small>George Orwell</small>
People 55
<small>Yevgeny Yevtushenko</small>
Michael Lake Describes What the Executioner Actually Faces 56
Felix Randal 57
<small>Gerard Manley Hopkins</small>
The Meaning of a Poem 58
<small>George Orwell</small>

Double-Entry Notebook 61
from *Life on the Mississippi* 62
<small>Mark Twain</small>

Paired and Grouped Readings 65
1. Fables 65
    The Wolf and the Mastiff 65
    <small>Aesop</small>
    The Owl Who Was God 65
    <small>James Thurber</small>
    The Fox and the Grapes 67
    <small>Aesop</small>
    The Little Girl and the Wolf 68
    <small>James Thurber</small>
2. Parables 68
    Muddy Road 68
    <small>Zen</small>
    Learning to Be Silent 69
    <small>Zen</small>
    The Good Samaritan 69
    <small>Jesus</small>
    The Sower and the Seed 70
    <small>Jesus</small>
    The Tares and the Wheat 71
    <small>Jesus</small>
3. The Character 71
    The Gross Man 71
    <small>Theophrastus</small>
    The Company Man 73
    <small>Ellen Goodman</small>
4. Fairy Tales 74
    Cinderella 74
    <small>Anne Sexton</small>
    Cinderella 77
    <small>The Fairy Tale</small>
5. Two Versions of the Susanna Story 82
    The Story of Susanna 82
    <small>The Bible</small>

Peter Quince at the Clavier 85
  Wallace Stevens
6. Living and Dying: Two Villanelles 88
    The Waking 88
      Theodore Roethke
    Do Not Go Gentle into That Good Night 89
      Dylan Thomas
7. Two Sestinas 90
    Summer Sestina 90
      Marie Ponsot
    Sestina 91
      Elizabeth Bishop
8. Two Versions of a Poem 93
    A Noiseless Patient Spider 93
      Walt Whitman
    The Soul, Reaching, Throwing Out for Love 94
      Walt Whitman
9. Innocence and Experience 94
    The Chimney Sweeper I and II 94
      William Blake
    Nurse's Song I and II 96
      William Blake
10. Two Shapes 96
    Crise de Coeur 97
      John Hollander
    The Altar 98
      George Herbert
11. Two Views of Perfection 98
    Arriving at Perfection 99
      Benjamin Franklin
    Benjamin Franklin 102
      D. H. Lawrence
12. Remembering Parents 105
    from *Growing Up* 105
      Russell Baker
    from *The Duke of Deception* 111
      Geoffrey Wolff
13. Two Studies in Entomology 115
    Departmental 116
      Robert Frost
    The Battle of the Ants 117
      Henry David Thoreau
14. The River as Teacher 119
    from *Life on the Mississippi* 119
      Mark Twain
    from *Old Glory* 126
      Jonathan Raban
15. Two Views of the River 128
    from *Huckleberry Finn* 128
      Mark Twain
    from *Life on the Mississippi* 130
      Mark Twain

16. The Fish 132
    Remembering Agassiz 132
        Samuel Scudder
    from *The Autobiography of Nathaniel Shaler* 136
17. Owning Land 137
    Buying a Farm 138
        Henry David Thoreau
    Hamatreya 140
        Ralph Waldo Emerson
18. Three Readings on Reading 142
    The House Was Quiet and the World Was Calm 142
        Wallace Stevens
    Continuity of Parks 143
        Julio Cortázar
    A Study of Reading Habits 144
        Philip Larkin
19. Five Short Poems: Stephen Crane 146
20. Poe on Poe 147
    The Black Cat 147
        Edgar Allan Poe
    from *The Imp of the Perverse* 155
        Edgar Allan Poe
21. Madame Bovary Revisited 158
    from *Madame Bovary* 158
        Gustave Flaubert
    The Kugelmass Episode 165
        Woody Allen
22. Oedipus and Jocasta 173
    Oedipus Rex 174
        Sophocles
    Jocasta 214
        Ruth Eisenberg
    Two Versions of *Jocasta, Part I* 222
    Writing Jocasta 224
        Ruth Eisenberg

PART III
Playing With Language: Words, Sentences, and Punctuation 229

    Words 230
        Police! Police! 231
            Lisa Bogdonoff
        Jabberwocky 235
            Lewis Carroll
        Adam's Task 236
            John Hollander
    Etymology 237
    Metaphor 238
        A _____ Is a Collection of Half-injustices 241
            Stephen Crane
    Cliché 242

The Mister Queens College Contest 243
   Anthony Litwinko
   The Bustle in a House 244
   Emily Dickinson
Jargon 244
Sound and Sense 245
   Rhyme, Alliteration, Simulation 248
   Assonance, Consonance, Dissonance 249
Sentences 250
   The Cumulative Sentence 251
   The Periodic Sentence 251
   The Parallel and Antithetical Sentence 252
   The Questioning Sentence 254
   The Fragmentary Sentence 255
   The Inverted Sentence 256
   The Interrupted Sentence 257
   Sentence Length 258
Punctuation 259
   Colon 259
   Dash 260
   Double Dash and Parentheses 262
   Hyphen 263
   Semicolon 263
   Comma 264

PART IV

Making Connections: The Discovery of Relationships   267

Jonah 268
   The Bible
Meditation XVII 272
   John Donne
Of Revenge 274
   Francis Bacon
Letter to His Son 276
   Lord Chesterfield
Letter to His Son 277
   Alexander Boswell
Hints Toward an Essay on Conversation 280
   Jonathan Swift
On the Pleasures of Painting 286
   William Hazlitt
Tom Pry 295
   Charles Lamb
Tom Pry's Wife 296
   Charles Lamb
Fra Lippo Lippi 298
   Robert Browning
A Mystery of Heroism 308
   Stephen Crane

War Is Kind 315
    Stephen Crane
When I Was One-and-Twenty 316
    A. E. Housman
Down by the Salley Gardens 317
    William Butler Yeats
Corn-Pone Opinions 318
    Mark Twain
The Advocate 322
    Herman Melville
Blame the Victim 326
    Ellen Goodman
Autonomy 328
    Lewis Thomas
The Flow of the River 331
    Loren Eiseley

for Ruth

PART I

Getting Started
Writing as Discovery and Revision

Before there is meaning there has to occur some personal act of vision.
Eudora Welty

A writer is not so much someone who has something to say as he is someone who has found a process that will bring about new things he would not have thought of if he had not started to say things.
William Stafford

We often come into possession of an idea or feeling precisely through the expression of it, the process required to make it intelligible to others.
Barbara H. Smith

The craftsman writes by rewriting . . . and rewrites by re-seeing and re-thinking.
Donald Murray

FEARS ABOUT WRITING

For many student writers, and for many professionals as well, the hardest thing about writing is getting started. There's something intimidating, even petrifying about confronting a blank page. Perhaps the main reason for both the existence and the intensity of this fear is a lack of assurance about what to say. These writers believe that you have to know what you're going to say before you say it, that writing is a simple transcription onto the page of what's in your mind. But writing rarely happens that way. Ideas don't come fully formed, perfectly clarified, beautifully phrased—even for professionals. They usually find form and focus during the process of writing, not before.

Many writers don't know what they're going to write until they've actually written it. E. M. Forster, the modern essayist and novelist, put it this way: "How do I know what I think until I see what I say?" Writing stimulates thinking and helps to clarify it. So the answer to at least one of your possible fears about writing is this: don't worry at the start about the clarity, logic, or strength of your ideas. Don't worry if at the beginning you can't even call your fuzzy thinking "ideas" at all. Instead, concentrate on writing, on putting words on paper. You'll find that one sentence leads to another, that one thought or phrase, sometimes only a word, sets something going in your consciousness—or taps your subconscious. And before you realize what's happening, you're writing and thinking together.

A second fear that might inhibit your writing is the fear of criticism. You're afraid, perhaps, that what you write may not be good, that others won't be interested or impressed, that it will make you look bad. There's no solution to this problem. Perhaps simply to acknowledge it and to accept the risks that writing often involves will help for a start. It will also help if you think of your writing both as something in process and as something capable of being improved. Finally, try to get a few readers to respond to what you write. Good readers can help you see whether you've said what you've tried to say; they can also help you find ways to say it more clearly and forcefully.

Besides uncertainty about your ideas and fear of criticism, you might also be afraid that your control of fundamentals is weak. Perhaps you make errors in grammar, spell words incorrectly, and violate accepted norms of language usage. There are at least two ways to deal with such fears. One is simply to learn the conventions of grammar, spelling, and usage—not through memorizing lists of menacing rules, but through reading and writing regularly. Through sustained work in reading and writing, you'll make gradual but significant progress. The other thing is to remember that neither grammar nor spelling is writing. If you try to learn all you need to know about them before you write, you may never get to do any real writing. Concentrate first on learning to write. Let the mechanical elements of composition take their place in support of learning to compose.

This is not to suggest that grammar is unimportant, that spelling accuracy doesn't count. The way you spell and punctuate and the grammatical competence you display reveal something of your confidence and control as a writer. They also reveal your concern about what you're saying. But in order to improve these mechanical elements you have to care about what you're writing. You must want to improve them because grammatical problems, for example, distract your readers from looking at what you're saying. But the first thing is to have (discover) something to say, and then care enough about it to want to say it well.

Before going any further in this chapter, pick up your pen. If you have no paper handy, write in the margins or on a blank page. Write out your reactions to what you've read so far. How much applies directly to your writing experience? What doesn't? Provide an example from your experience to illustrate one of the "fears" discussed above. Or perhaps explain why such fears have never bothered you—or how you've overcome them.

Another way to respond is to think of what you *do* when you write. What do you do, for example, when you have to write a paper for a course assignment or when you write a letter? What do you do when you're faced with writing something you'd rather not write? Still another way of responding to the suggestions above is to explain *why* you write, or why you don't.

ANNOTATING

If you found yourself writing in the margins of *Connections,* you were probably "annotating." To annotate means simply to make notes alongside what you're reading. When you annotate a text, you record your reactions, usually in abbreviated form, letting your thoughts spill out onto the page. In doing this, you set up a dialogue, first with what you're reading, later with yourself as you make connections between your annotations.

No one can tell you exactly what to write in the margins as you read. No one has to, for you should simply react, putting down quickly what you think and feel. Your annotations will depend on what you're reading and why you're reading it. You'll annotate a chapter of a history text differently from a newspaper editorial. And you'll very likely annotate a work that you're reading as a course assignment more fully if you're also planning to write about it.

Here are two brief passages with sample annotations:

each species of whale each and *every* individual whale??	Each whale has its own characteristic song; the highly complex patterns are repeated over and over again with great faithfulness. No scientific fact that I have learned in the last decade struck me with more force than Payne's report that the length of some songs may extend for more than half an hour. I have never been able to memorize the five-minute first Kyrie of the B-minor Mass (and not for	
		more like a symphony than a song
the relativity of experience Proportion: 1:30	want of trying); how could a whale sing for thirty minutes and then repeat itself accurately? Of what possible use is a thirty-minute repeat cycle—far too long for a human to recognize: we would never grasp it as a single song (without Payne's recording machinery and much study after the fact). But then I remembered the whale's metabolic rate, the enormously slow pace of its life compared with ours. What do we know about a whale's	

perception of thirty minutes? A humpback may scale the world to its own metabolic rate: its half-hour song may be our minute waltz. From any point of view, the song is spectacular; it is the most elaborate single display so far discovered in any animal. I merely urge the whale's point of view as an appropriate perspective.

Stephen Jay Gould
"Our Allotted Lifetimes"

> what's the whale song for?? Mating? Communicating? Pure joy?

> a good question—what *do* we know about a whale's perception (of time or of anything else)?

Re-vision—the act of looking back, of seeing with fresh eyes, of entering an old text from a new critical direction—is for us more than a chapter in cultural history: it is an act of survival. Until we can understand the assumptions in which we are drenched we cannot know ourselves. And this drive to self-knowledge, for woman, is more than a search for identity: it is part of her refusal of the destructiveness of male-dominated society. A radical critique of literature, feminist in its impulse, would take the work first of all as a clue to how we live, how we have been living, how we have been led to imagine ourselves, how our language has trapped as well as liberated us; and how we can begin to see—and therefore live—afresh. A change in the concept of sexual identity is essential if we are not to see the old political order reassert itself in every new revolution. We need to know the writing of the past, and know it differently than we have ever known it; not to pass on a tradition but to break its hold over us.

Adrienne Rich
"When We Dead Awaken: Writing as Revision"

> feminizing revision

> Is Rich really re-envisioning? Or is she mouthing predictable clichés?

> knowing as a matter of understanding cultural assumptions

> a political vision; connects vision with action

> doesn't she oversimplify relation to tradition? conserving and preservative as well as subversive?

> what kind of change?

Since many of your ideas derive directly from your reading, annotating can help you read with greater comprehension and more enjoyment. In addition, you'll discover that as you annotate someone else's ideas, you'll be thinking for yourself, stimulated both by the ideas of the text and by your responses as you write in the margins. You'll end up in a double dialogue—with the text and with yourself.

Before going on to the annotation exercise below, why not simply annotate what I've said here about annotation. Or make your own annotations of the two passages I've annotated as examples, perhaps even annotating my annotations—arguing, disagreeing, extending what the texts and the annotations imply.

Exercise

Annotate one or more of the following passages. React as fully as you can.

> Americans are at last realizing that the acquisition of goods is not the whole of life. Consumption, on one level, is turning insipid, especially as the quality of the artifacts themselves seems to be deteriorating. On another level, consumption is turning sour. There is a growing guilt about the masses of discarded junk—rusting automobiles and refrigerators and washing machines and dehumidifiers—that it is uneconomical to recycle. Indestructible plastic hasn't even the grace to undergo chemical change. America, the world's biggest consumer, is the world's biggest polluter. Awareness of this is a kind of redemptive grace, but it doesn't appreciably lead to repentance and a revolution in consumer habits. Citizens of Los Angeles are horrified by that daily pall of golden smog, but they don't noticeably clamor for a decrease in the number of owner-vehicles. There is no worse neurosis than that which derives from a consciousness of guilt and an inability to reform.
>
> *Anthony Burgess*
> *"Is America Falling Apart?"*

> Composing—putting things together—is a continuum, a process that continues without any sharp breaks. Making sense of the world is composing. It includes being puzzled, being mistaken, and then suddenly seeing things for what they probably are; making wrong—unproductive, unsatisfactory, incorrect, inaccurate—identifications and assessments and correcting them or giving them up and getting some new ones. And all these things happen when we write: writing is like the composing we do all the time when we respond to the world, make up our minds, try to figure out things again. We aren't born knowing how to write, but we are born knowing how to know.
>
> *Ann E. Berthoff*
> *Forming/Thinking/Writing*

> We communicate an extraordinary range of meanings just through tone of voice. Listen to yourself talk to listeners—babies, dogs, cats—who can't understand concepts but who respond to intonation. You are talking a language of pure attitude, of love, reassurance, frustration, fatigue. This emotional overdubbing can color any event, make a laughingstock of the most sublime poetry, salvage the most banal cliché. It can tell you to seek out dirty innuendo or launder your mind. The distance between the line on the page and the line read represents precisely the distance between the play in the book and the play in the theater. To read prose aloud is to perform it, literally bring it to life. And life is no neutral place.
>
> *Richard Lanham*
> *Analyzing Prose*

LISTING

So far you've been generating ideas about writing through annotations and informal responses. Another quick way to begin putting words on paper is to make a list. Since listing is familiar to you from other contexts, it should form an easy carry-over to writing. Remember, however, that a list is not a formal outline. It's less rigid, more random. Unlike an outline, a list is a place to start from, a point of departure rather than a map of a preconceived route. Listing is a way to begin writing, to jot down thoughts as they come—without worrying about whether you'll retain or reject them, or how you'll organize and develop them. (Those things come later.) In addition, listing is a way to record ideas before they get away.

Exercise

Make a list of things you like or dislike. Write for five minutes, jotting down whatever comes to mind, however silly or insignificant it may seem. Don't be concerned if some of the items don't fit in with others. In creating the list, your purpose is to see what emerges, to discover connections between two or more items. When you've generated a list of perhaps ten items, go back over it looking for the most promising and most interesting ones. Select two or three of these and write a few sentences in response to each.

In addition to seeking connections, you might look for ways in which items lead in different directions. By exploring some of these possibilities you'll be playing off against each other two techniques for generating ideas: listing and responding. And you may find, further, that out of your responses will come still another list, another set of items that could be explored in additional responses. These two techniques, then, can be used together, alternately to stimulate your thinking, to get you started writing.

Besides lists and responses, you may find other ways to generate ideas helpful in getting started. The remainder of this section of *Connections* explains some additional techniques to help you generate ideas. They include asking questions, using lateral thinking, sharpening your powers of perception, and finally, revising. You'll find that some of the suggestions overlap. They're presented as alternative ways to begin thinking and writing rather than as a systematic program to be followed one technique after the next. In fact, you'll probably discover that some of the suggestions work far better for you than others. Those you find helpful, use; those you don't, ignore.

QUESTIONING

To probe your ideas more thoroughly than you might be able to do with either informal responses or with lists, you can ask questions. Learning to ask questions is an essential skill for reading, writing, and thinking. It's as important to learn how to *ask* questions as it is to know how to *answer* them. (Perhaps more important—at least for generating ideas—because you can't answer questions you haven't asked.)

One way of using questions is to work with them in sets or blocks. The journalist's questions, for example, can provide a handy way to begin probing a subject. Journalists routinely ask and answer the following questions: Who? What? Where? When? Why? How? We can pair the questions this way: What happened and to whom? Where and When did it happen? How and Why?

Generally a reporter will answer these questions in the opening paragraph of a news story. The questions serve as guidelines to the reporter (and reader) for the kinds of information the news account provides. But the journalist's questions can also be used to probe a subject, to explore it thoroughly. In answering a "Who" question, for example, your concern might be more than merely to identify the person involved; it might instead be to think hard about what you know about "who" and to research what you don't know. Whether you're writing an autobiographical essay about an experience in your life, an analysis of the character of Huckleberry Finn, or a research paper on the trial of Sacco and Vanzetti, you can use the journalist's first question as a starting point for your thinking. Identifying the "who" means more than simply pointing; it involves a thoughtful effort to understand, to account for the behavior, feelings, attitudes of the "who" you write about.

The same is true of the other journalistic questions. To indicate where and when an event occurred is only a first step in exploring and explaining the importance of time and place. If you're writing about a personal experience, you can ask yourself why it happened when and where it did. You might speculate about whether it could have happened earlier or later in your life, or in another place. And you could raise similar questions about time and place in thinking through the action of a story like "In Dreams Begin Responsibilities" (p.9) or in researching a historical event.

In using the journalist's questions, you shouldn't worry initially about whether you'll organize your paper around them. Nor should you be concerned if your answers seem to overlap or if one question generates more promising responses and information than others. Follow the lead of the promising questions. Let one question lead into the others. Use them to get started, to begin, not end your thinking and writing.

Another set of traditional questions you can use in getting started offers perspectives on and general approaches to almost any subject. But as with the journalist's questions, they won't all lead you equally well to ideas about a given subject. Here are these traditional questions, or commonplaces of invention, as they are sometimes called:

Definition: What is it? How can I define or describe it?

Comparison: What's it like? What can I compare (and contrast) it with? How will related things help me to better understand it and explain it?

Classification: What is it a kind or type of? How can I classify or categorize it?

Causal Analysis: Why is it like this? What will be its effects in the future? What will happen if it . . . ?

Illustration: What examples can clarify it? How many and what kind of examples will best illustrate what I want to say about it?

In using either the journalist's questions or the traditional commonplaces of invention, keep these things in mind:

1) These are places to begin, not end, your thinking. 2) Although they've been separated and distinguished from one another, in real writing they overlap and intersect. 3) Use the questions to stimulate your thinking. They're aids to thinking and writing, not formats or plans for organizing essays.

Besides using journalistic and traditional questions, you may find helpful a less systematic, less formalized technique: random questioning. In random questioning you simply ask questions about your subject as they occur to you—without either the benefits or the limitations of systematic questions that "cover" the subject. A good way to prompt yourself to do such free questioning would be to begin by thinking: "I wonder if . . . " Or: "What would happen if . . ." Or: "If so and so, then what?" Such hypothetical questions often open up your thinking, sending it off in surprising, rewarding directions. Moreover, if you question your subject from a variety of angles rather than from a single perspective, you'll discover more about it (and what you think about it). You'll be in a better position to decide what to include and what to leave out of your writing to suit your audience, your occasion, and your purpose.

Another way to use questions in writing is to ask questions of your statements. Frequently one of your ideas presented as a simple statement of attitude or information can be expanded by imagining and answering questions readers might ask about what you've written. You'll discover where you can fruitfully ask such questions of your writing as you revise. You need not actually write the questions into your paper, though it might be helpful to jot them in the margins or between the lines. You can then develop answers to flesh out your writing with additional information, ideas, and examples. And finally, you'll probably discover when you begin to raise questions that one question leads to another, and that your questions multiply. So much the better, for your purpose in questioning your writing is to stimulate additional thinking, which in turn will give you more to say.

Before moving on to still other ways to generate ideas, try out the strategies discussed so far by reading and responding to the following story, "In Dreams Begin Responsibilities." As you can see, the story is divided into six numbered sections. The first two have been annotated and provided with descriptive headings. Provide your own annotations and headings for the remaining sections. And as you read and annotate, look for connections between one section and another.

IN DREAMS BEGIN RESPONSIBILITIES

Delmore Schwartz

1

[An Awkward Visit]

<aside>a provocative title— how are dreams related to responsibilities? What kind of dreams?</aside>

I think it is the year 1909. I feel as if I were in a motion picture theater, the long arm of light crossing the darkness and spinning, my eyes fixed on the screen. This is a silent picture as if an old Biograph one, in which the actors are dressed in ridiculously old-fashioned clothes, and one flash succeeds another with sudden jumps. The actors too seem to jump about and walk too fast. The shots themselves are full of dots and rays, as if it were raining when the picture was photographed. <aside>time and place established: Brooklyn 1909</aside> The light is bad.

It is Sunday afternoon, June 12th, 1909, and my father is walking down the quiet streets of Brooklyn on his way to visit my mother. His clothes are newly pressed and his tie is too tight in his high collar. He jingles the coins in his pockets, thinking of the witty things he will say. I feel as if I had by now relaxed entirely in the soft darkness of the theater; the organist peals out the obvious and approximate emotions on which the audience rocks unknowingly. I am anonymous, and I have forgotten myself. It is always so when one goes to the movies, it is, as they say, a drug. <aside>narrator thinking about his father as a young man— pictures him. Something most people would like to do—see their parents as they were during courtship?</aside>

My father walks from street to street of trees, lawns and houses, once in a while coming to an avenue on which a streetcar skates and gnaws, slowly progressing. The conductor, who has a handle-bar mustache, helps a young lady wearing a hat like a bowl with feathers on to the car. She lifts her long skirts slightly as she mounts the steps. He leisurely makes change and rings his bell. It is obviously Sunday, for everyone is wearing Sunday clothes, and the streetcar's noises emphasize the quiet of the holiday. Is not Brooklyn the City of

Churches? The shops are closed and their shades drawn, but for an occasional stationery store or drug-store with great green balls in the window.

My father has chosen to take this long walk because he likes to walk and think. He thinks about himself in the future and so arrives at the place he is to visit in a state of mild exaltation. He pays no attention to the houses he is passing, in which the Sunday dinner is being eaten, nor to the many trees which patrol each street, now coming to their full leafage and the time when they will room the whole street in cool shadow. An occasional carriage passes, the horse's hooves falling like stones in the quiet afternoon, and once in a while an automobile, looking like an enormous upholstered sofa, puffs and passes.

My father thinks of my mother, of how nice it will be to introduce her to his family. But he is not yet sure that he wants to marry her, and once in a while he becomes panicky about the bond already established. He reassures himself by thinking of the big men he admires who are married: William Randolph Hearst, and William Howard Taft, who has just become President of the United States.

My father arrives at my mother's house. He has come too early and so is suddenly embarrassed. My aunt, my mother's sister, answers the loud bell with her napkin in her hand, for the family is still at dinner. As my father enters, my grandfather rises from the table and shakes hands with him. My mother has run upstairs to tidy herself. My grandmother asks my father if he has had dinner, and tells him that Rose will be downstairs soon. My grandfather opens the conversation by remarking on the mild June weather. My father sits uncomfortably near the table, holding his hat in his hand. My grandmother tells my aunt to

time: the narrator has opened a window on the past. His father—in that past—thinks about the future.

story of past action— the father's visit is presented in the present tense. Why?

The narrator not only sees the action. He also can see into his father's mind & heart. He knows what his father thought & how he felt.

take my father's hat. My uncle, twelve years old, runs into the house, his hair tousled. He shouts a greeting to my father, who has often given him a nickel, and then runs upstairs. It is evident that the respect in which my father is held in this household is tempered by a good deal of mirth. He is impressive, yet he is very awkward.

> The narrator shows his father as both impressive and somewhat ridiculous. How far does this look into the past reflect the narrator's present attitudes & feelings?

2

[Of Novels and Money]

Finally my mother comes downstairs, all dressed up, and my father being engaged in conversation with my grandfather becomes uneasy, not knowing whether to greet my mother or continue the conversation. He gets up from the chair clumsily and says "hello" gruffly. My grandfather watches, examining their congruence, such as it is, with a critical eye, and meanwhile rubbing his bearded cheek roughly, as he always does when he reflects. He is worried; <u>he is afraid that my father will not make a good husband for his oldest daughter.</u> At this point something happens to the film, just as my father is saying something funny to my mother; I am awakened to myself and my unhappiness just as my interest was rising. The audience begins to clap impatiently. Then the trouble is cared for but the film has been returned to a portion just shown, and once more I see my grandfather rubbing his bearded cheek and pondering my father's character. It is difficult to get back into the picture once more and forget myself, but as my mother giggles at my father's words, <u>the darkness drowns me.</u>

My father and mother depart from the house, my father shaking hands with my mother once more, out of some unknown uneasiness. I stir uneasily also, slouched in the hard chair of the theatre. Where is the older uncle, my mother's older bro-

> In part one the narrator said he had forgotten himself (par. 2). Here he is jolted out of his reverie. Why does he say he is unhappy?

> Is this something the narrator <u>knows</u> or is it something he imagines? Is it perhaps what he himself feels

> This sounds ominous; as if the darkness of the theatre is symbolic—but of what? He <u>drowns</u>? Why?

a startling juxtaposition of past & present

ther? He is studying in his bedroom upstairs, studying for his final examination at the College of the City of New York, having been dead of rapid pneumonia for the last twenty-one years. My mother and father walk down the same quiet streets once more. My mother is holding my father's arm and telling him of the novel which she has been reading; and my father utters judgments of the characters as the plot is made clear to him. This is a habit which he very much enjoys, for he feels the utmost superiority and confidence when he approves and condemns the behavior of other people. At times he feels moved to utter a brief "Ugh,"—whenever the story becomes what he would call sugary. This tribute is paid to his manliness. My mother feels satisfied by the interest which she has awakened; she is showing my father how intelligent she is, and how interesting.

Is the narrator's attitude here approving? Condemnatory?

They reach the avenue, and the streetcar leisurely arrives. They are going to Coney Island this afternoon, although my mother considers that such pleasures are inferior. She has made up her mind to indulge only in a walk on the boardwalk and a pleasant dinner, avoiding the riotous amusements as being beneath the dignity of so dignified a couple.

My father tells my mother how much money he has made in the past week, exaggerating an amount which need not have been exaggerated. But my father has always felt that actualities somehow fall short. Suddenly I begin to weep. The determined old lady who sits next to me in the theatre is annoyed and looks at me with an angry face, and being intimidated, I stop. I drag out my handkerchief and dry my face, licking the drop which has fallen near my lips. Meanwhile I have missed something, for here are my mother and father alighting at the last stop, Coney Island.

Is the narrator judging his father here? Is this in criticism of one of his father's weaknesses?

The narrator weeps. Why?

3

They walk toward the boardwalk, and my father commands my mother to inhale the pungent air from the sea. They both breathe in deeply, both of them laughing as they do so. They have in common a great interest in health, although my father is strong and husky, my mother frail. Their minds are full of theories of what is good to eat and not good to eat, and sometimes they engage in heated discussions of the subject, the whole matter ending in my father's announcement, made with a scornful bluster, that you have to die sooner or later anyway. On the boardwalk's flagpole, the American flag is pulsing in an intermittent wind from the sea.

My father and mother go to the rail of the boardwalk and look down on the beach where a good many bathers are casually walking about. A few are in the surf. A peanut whistle pierces the air with its pleasant and active whine, and my father goes to buy peanuts. My mother remains at the rail and stares at the ocean. The ocean seems merry to her; it pointedly sparkles and again and again the pony waves are released. She notices the children digging in the wet sand, and the bathing costumes of the girls who are her own age. My father returns with the peanuts. Overhead the sun's lightning strikes and strikes, but neither of them are at all aware of it. The boardwalk is full of people dressed in their Sunday clothes and idly strolling. The tide does not reach as far as the boardwalk, and the strollers would feel no danger if it did. My mother and father lean on the rail of the boardwalk and absently stare at the ocean. The ocean is becoming rough; the waves come in slowly, tugging strength from far back. The moment before they somersault, the moment when they arch their backs so beautifully, showing green and white veins amid the black, that moment is intolerable. They finally crack, dashing fiercely upon the sand, actually driving, full force downward, against the sand, bouncing upward and forward, and at last petering out into a small stream which races up the beach and then is recalled. My parents gaze absentmindedly at the ocean, scarcely interested in its harshness. The sun overhead does not disturb them. But I stare at the terrible sun which breaks up sight, and the fatal, merciless, passionate ocean, I forget my parents. I stare fascinated and finally, shocked by the indifference of my father and mother, I burst out weeping once more. The old lady next to me pats me on the shoulder and says "There, there, all of this is only a movie, young man, only a movie," but I look up once more at the terrifying sun and the terrifying ocean, and being unable to control my tears, I get up and go to the men's room, stumbling over the feet of the other people seated in my row.

4

When I return, feeling as if I had awakened in the morning sick for lack of sleep, several hours have apparently passed and my parents are riding on the merry-go-round. My father is on a black horse, my mother on a white one, and they seem to be making an eternal circuit for the single purpose of snatching nickel rings which are attached to the arm of one of the posts. A hand-organ is playing; it is one with the ceaseless circling of the merry-go-round.

For a moment it seems that they will never get off the merry-go-round because it will never stop. I feel like one who looks down on the avenue from the 50th story of a building. But at length they do get off; even the music of the hand-organ has ceased for a moment. My father has acquired ten rings, my mother only two, although it was my mother who really wanted them.

They walk along on the boardwalk as the afternoon descends by imperceptible degrees into the incredible violet of dusk. Everything fades into a relaxed glow, even the ceaseless murmuring from the beach, and the revolutions of the merry-go-round. They look for a place to have dinner. My father suggests the best one on the boardwalk and my mother demurs, in accordance with her principles.

However they do go to the best place, asking for a table near the window, so that they can look out on the boardwalk and the mobile ocean. My father feels omnipotent as he places a quarter in the waiter's hand as he asks for a table. The place is crowded and here too there is music, this time from a kind of string trio. My father orders dinner with a fine confidence.

As the dinner is eaten, my father tells of his plans for the future, and my mother shows with expressive face how interested she is, and how impressed. My father becomes exultant. He is lifted up by the waltz that is being played, and his own future begins to intoxicate him. My father tells my mother that he is going to expand his business, for there is a great deal of money to be made. He wants to settle down. After all, he is twenty-nine, he has lived by himself since he was thirteen, he is making more and more money, and he is envious of his married friends when he visits them in the cozy security of their homes, surrounded, it seems, by the calm domestic pleasures, and by delightful children, and then, as the waltz reaches the moment when all the dancers swing madly, then, then with awful daring, then he asks my mother to marry him, although awkwardly enough and puzzled, even in his excitement, at how he had arrived at the proposal, and she, to make the whole business worse, begins to cry, and my father looks nervously about, not knowing at all what to do now, and my mother says: "It's all I've wanted from the moment I saw you," sobbing, and he finds all of this very difficult, scarcely to his taste, scarcely as he had thought it would be, on his long walks over Brooklyn Bridge in the revery of a fine cigar, and it was then that I stood up in the theatre and shouted: "Don't do it. It's not too late to change your minds, both of you. Nothing good will come of it, only remorse, hatred, scandal, and two children whose characters are monstrous." The whole audience turned to look at me, annoyed, the usher came hurrying down the aisle flashing his searchlight, and the old lady next to me tugged me down into my seat, saying: "Be quiet. You'll be put out, and you paid thirty-five cents to come in." And so I shut my eyes because I could not bear to see what was happening. I sat there quietly.

5

But after awhile I begin to take brief glimpses, and at length I watch again with thirsty interest, like a child who wants to maintain his sulk although offered the bribe of candy. My parents are now having their picture taken in a photographer's booth along the boardwalk. The place is shadowed in the mauve light which is apparently necessary. The camera is set to the side on its tripod and looks like a Martian man. The photographer is instructing my parents in how to pose. My father has his arm over my mother's shoulder, and both of them smile emphatically. The photographer brings my mother a bouquet of flowers to hold in her hand but she holds it at the wrong angle. Then the photographer covers himself with the black cloth which drapes the camera and all that one sees of him is one protruding arm and his hand which clutches the rubber ball which he will squeeze when the picture is finally taken. But he is not satisfied with their appearance. He feels with certainty that somehow there is something wrong in their pose. Again and again he issues from his hidden place with new directions. Each suggestion merely makes matters worse. My father is becoming impatient. They try a seated pose. The photographer explains that he has pride, he is not interested in all of this for the money, he wants to make beautiful pictures. My father says: "Hurry up will you? We haven't got all night." But the photographer only scurries about apologetically, and issues new directions. The photographer charms me. I approve of him with all my heart, for I know just how he feels, and as he criticizes each revised pose according to some unknown idea of rightness, I become quite hopeful. But then my father says angrily: "Come on, you've had enough time, we're not going to wait any longer." And the photographer, sighing unhappily, goes back under his black covering, holds out his hand, says: "One, two, three, Now!", and the picture is taken, with my father's smile turned to a grimace and my mother's bright and false. It takes a few minutes for the picture to be developed and as my parents sit in the curious light they become quite depressed.

6

They have passed a fortune-teller's booth, and my mother wishes to go in, but my father does not. They begin to argue about it. My mother becomes stubborn, my father once more impatient, and then they begin to quarrel, and what my father would like to do is walk off and leave my mother there, but he knows that that would never do. My mother refuses to budge. She is near to tears, but she feels an uncontrollable desire to hear what the palm-reader will say. My father consents angrily, and they both go into a booth which is in a way like the photographer's, since it is draped in black cloth and its light is shadowed. The place is too warm, and my father keeps saying this is all nonsense, pointing to the crystal ball on the table. The fortune-teller, a fat, short woman, garbed in what is supposed to be Oriental robes, comes into the room from the back and greets them, speaking with an accent. But suddenly my father feels that the whole thing is intolerable; he tugs at my mother's arm, but my mother refuses to budge. And then, in terrible anger, my father lets go of my mother's arm and strides out, leaving my mother stunned. She moves to go after my father, but the fortune-teller holds her arm tightly and begs her not to do so, and I in my seat am shocked more than can ever be said, for I feel as if I were walking a tight-rope a hundred feet over a circus-audience and suddenly the rope is showing signs of breaking, and I get up from my seat and begin to shout once more the first words I can think of to communicate my terrible fear and once more the usher comes hurrying down the aisle flashing his searchlight, and the old lady pleads with me, and the shocked audience has turned to stare at me, and I keep shouting: "What are they doing? Don't they know what they are doing? Why doesn't my mother go after my father? If she does not do that, what will she do? Doesn't my father know what he is doing?"—But the usher has seized my arm and is dragging me away, and as he does so, he says: "What are *you* doing? Don't you know that you can't do whatever you want to do? Why should a young man like you, with your whole life before you, get hysterical like this? Why don't you *think* of what you're doing? You can't act like this even if other people aren't around! You will be sorry if you do not do what you should do, you can't carry on like this, it is not right, you will find that out soon enough, everything you do matters too much," and he said that dragging me through the lobby of the theatre into the cold light, and I woke up into the bleak winter morning of my 21st birthday, the windowsill shining with its lip of snow, and the morning already begun.

Exercises

1. Make up five questions you'd like to ask another reader about the story. Ask them.

2. Answer two of them in a paragraph each.

3. Explain the narrator's behavior at the end of the story. Also explain the significance of the following: the narrator's feeling that he is walking a tightrope; the usher's comments to the narrator; the "cold light" and "bleak winter morning" of the narrator's 21st birthday; the title.

LATERAL THINKING

Besides the techniques for discovering ideas that have been discussed so far, there are other ways to generate ideas. One of these is to use lateral thinking,* a strategy for seeing things in new and unexpected ways. Providing an alternative to logical thinking, lateral thinking complements rather than contradicts logic. Lateral thinking is creative; you play with ideas, not worrying about their "correctness" or their logicality. You can gain a sense of what lateral thinking is by doing the following exercises.

Exercises

1. Set yourself a quota of alternatives for a problem such as improving your grades or saving time. Before making up your own problem and set of solutions, try three of these. For each, make a list of "X ways of dealing with Y."

Four ways to learn a foreign language
Five ways to lose weight (or gain it)
Six ways to fly a kite
Three ways to define "tree"

---

*The discussion of lateral thinking is derived from the work of Edward de Bono. Two of his books are especially important: *New Think* (New York: Avon, 1968) and *Lateral Thinking* (New York: Harper & Row, 1970).

Seven ways to get a date
Eight ways of looking at a tomato
Four ways to read a book
Six ways to eat spaghetti

2. Divide each of these squares into four equal parts. Do it a different way each time.

3. Divide the following figure into four equal parts. See how many ways you can do this. Then divide it into four *un*equal parts. Try doing that three ways.

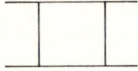

4. Look at the figure in #3 as something familiar, a table, for example, or a crosswalk. Try to see it at least three different ways.

5. Use the following figures as the basis for a simple drawing. Extend the lines to form a figure or image. See what you can turn them into.

6. Explain the connection between the following paired terms. Then fill in the blanks for the incomplete pairs.

poet—architect	passion—fire	_____—dinosaur
athlete—warrior	woman—rose	_____—eagle
hatred—poison	child—lamb	teacher—_____
		beauty—_____

7. Read the following excerpt from Walt Whitman's "Song of Myself." How many ways of seeing and thinking about the grass has Whitman included? Jot down at least two others.

> A child said, What is the grass? fetching it to me with
>   full hands;
> How could I answer the child? .... I do not know
>   what it is any more than he.
>
> I guess it must be the flag of my disposition, out of
>   hopeful green stuff woven.
>
> Or I guess it is the handkerchief of the Lord,
> 5 A scented gift and remembrancer designedly dropped,
> Bearing the owner's name someway in the corners,
>   that we may see and remark, and say Whose?

> Or I guess the grass is itself a child . . . . the produced babe of the vegetation.
>
> Or I guess it is a uniform hieroglyphic,
> And it means, Sprouting alike in broad zones and narrow zones,
> 10 Growing among black folks as among white,
> Kanuck, Tuckahoe, Congressman, Cuff, I give them the same, I receive the same.
>
> And now it seems to me the beautiful uncut hair of graves.

In logical thinking you begin with a single approach to a problem and then proceed step-by-step, sequentially, until you solve it. In lateral thinking, on the other hand, you generate more than one approach to a problem and often more than one solution as well. In fact, you should try to generate as many approaches and solutions as you can. Lateral thinking offers you a chance to shift gears and change directions as you think. It encourages you to let your mind wander around a problem or a subject without worrying about knowing for sure where you'll arrive. Part of the excitement of thinking laterally is in avoiding predictable directions of thought and in coming upon something unexpected.

This table highlights the essential differences between logical and lateral thinking:

Logical Thinking	*Lateral Thinking*
1. Selective, restrictive	1. Generative, open-minded
2. Moves in a single direction—usually the most likely one.	2. Moves in many directions, some of them unlikely ones.
3. Analytical	3. Provocative
4. Sequential	4. Non-sequential
5. Correctness essential at every stage.	5. Judgments about correctness held off till the end.
6. Excludes the irrelevant.	6. Includes anything, excludes nothing as irrelevant.

In using lateral thinking to generate ideas for writing, you can concentrate on the following techniques:

1. *Establishing a quota of alternatives.* If you decide, for example, that you need three or four examples to make a point, you can set yourself a goal of perhaps ten examples from which you will select the three or four you need. If you choose from among more examples than you need, the chances of discovering something effective are greater than if you work with only the first or second thing that comes to mind. Establishing a quota of alternatives is a way to challenge yourself to think in a more wide-ranging way. It's a way to push yourself to see things differently and see different things.

Exercises

1. The following problem can be solved in more than one way. Once you've solved it, don't quit. Look for a second, third, even fourth solution. Then discuss your ideas with your classmates.

Each weekday morning a man takes the elevator in his office building to the tenth floor. He gets out there and walks up to the sixteenth floor, where his office is. After work he enters the elevator on the sixteenth floor and rides down to the first floor, exits, and heads home. What might the man be up to?*

2. The following poem by Wallace Stevens is grounded in a series of alternative perceptions of the blackbird. Without worrying about making sense of all thirteen stanzas, try to see the poem as an imaginative act in which the writer keeps turning over the idea of blackbird again and again and again—thirteen times.

**THIRTEEN WAYS OF
LOOKING AT A BLACKBIRD**

I

Among twenty snowy mountains,
The only moving thing
Was the eye of the blackbird.

II

I was of three minds,
5 Like a tree
In which there are three blackbirds.

III

The blackbird whirled in the autumn winds.
It was a small part of the pantomime.

IV

A man and a woman
10 Are one.
A man and a woman and a blackbird
Are one.

V

I do not know which to prefer,
The beauty of inflections
15 Or the beauty of innuendos,
The blackbird whistling
Or just after.

---

*This problem and others like it can be found in Edward de Bono's *The Mechanism of Mind* (New York: Simon and Schuster, 1969).

VI

Icicles filled the long window
With barbaric glass.
The shadow of the blackbird
Crossed it, to and fro.
The mood
Traced in the shadow
An indecipherable cause.

VII

O thin men of Haddam,
Why do you imagine golden birds?
Do you not see how the blackbird
Walks around the feet
Of the women about you?

VIII

I know noble accents
And lucid, inescapable rhythms;
But I know, too,
That the blackbird is involved
In what I know.

IX

When the blackbird flew out of sight,
It marked the edge
Of one of many circles.

X

At the sight of blackbirds
Flying in a green light,
Even the bawds of euphony
Would cry out sharply.

XI

He rode over Connecticut
In a glass coach.
Once, a fear pierced him,
In that he mistook
The shadow of his equipage
For blackbirds.

XII

The river is moving.
The blackbird must be flying.

XIII

It was evening all afternoon.
It was snowing

> and it was going to snow.
> The blackbird sat
> In the cedar-limbs.

As a further exercise in establishing a quota of alternatives, imagine that the poem has become "*Twenty* Ways of Looking at a Blackbird." Write at least four more stanzas, thinking of the blackbird in other contexts and from other perspectives. (Don't worry about matching the poet's meter.)

2. *Reversing relationships.* A second technique of lateral thinking useful for generating ideas is reversing relationships. In this technique you take two things that are related in one way and think of their relationship in an opposite way. For example, instead of thinking of fire warming the air, think of the air cooling off the fire; or instead of thinking of table legs supporting the top, think of them hanging from the top. In the following poem Emily Dickinson reverses relationships when she thinks of "madness" in terms of "sense" and "sense" in terms of "madness."

> Much Madness is divinest Sense—
> To a discerning Eye—
> Much Sense—the starkest Madness—
> 'Tis the Majority
> In this, as All, prevail—
> Assent—and you are sane—
> Demur—you're straightway dangerous—
> And handled with a Chain—

Exercises

1. Think of some specific things that you might plug into Dickinson's poem that are generally thought of as sane or insane but which can be thought of in the opposite way. For each, decide what the conventional view is, and then write a few sentences justifying the opposite view. Some possibilities:

> saving money
> speed reading
> being on time
> lying
> majoring in computer science or accounting or engineering

2. Think of two things which are normally considered opposite. Then write sentences in which you suggest a non-conventional, unorthodox view of their relationship. An example: truths—lies: Some truths are the basest lies, some lies the most astonishing truths. (Does that make any "sense"? Why or why not?) Some possibilities:

> devils—angels
> darkness—light
> weakness—strength

courage—cowardice
objectivity—subjectivity
hatred—love
speech—silence
fire—ice

Try writing sentences for four or five pairs such as these. Then choose one of your pairs and the sentence you wrote for it and develop it further by explaining what your unconventional statement means.

3. *Cross-Fertilization.* With this technique you apply the ways of thinking about one kind of activity to something else. For example, you might use the vocabulary of football to talk about business—or the vocabulary of war to talk about love. (We already use the language of war to talk about football: *blitz* and *bomb* are two of many words that do service in both worlds. Can you think of others?) Or you might take terms and concepts from the graphic arts—color, line, texture, pattern—and apply them to music or literature or cooking.

Cross-fertilization is a special type of analogical thinking, a way of seeing relationships between things that are normally not seen as being related. Cross-fertilization, like the other techniques of lateral thinking, involves an act of the imagination. And as in any type of analogical thinking you look for connections between things, deliberately seeking them in places where you might least expect to find them.

Exercises

1. One way to begin to gain a sense of the generative power of analogical thinking is to set up a series of analogies as topics. In the first part of the exercise you are given both parts of the analogy. In the second part you are given the X term and you have to supply the Y term—the second half of the analogy. In the third section you have to invent both the X and Y terms. For all, write a brief explanation of how the analogy works—of what it means.

Section I
School as an adventure
School as a prison
Life as a journey
Life as a dream
Home as a heaven
Home life as a nightmare

Section II
Reading as a form of _____
Writing as a form of _____
Sky diving as a form of _____
Watching television as a form of _____
Shopping as a form of _____
Eating as a form of _____
Sleeping as a form of _____

Section III
X as a form of Y

2. The following "meditation" by Jonathan Swift employs analogical thinking to make a point about human beings.

A MEDITATION UPON A BROOMSTICK:

According to

The Style and Manner of the Honourable Robert Boyle's Meditations

This single Stick, which you now behold ingloriously lying in that neglected Corner, I once knew in a flourishing State in a Forest: It was full of Sap, full of Leaves, and full of Boughs: But now, in vain does the busy Art of Man pretend to vye with Nature, by tying that withered Bundle of Twigs to its sapless Trunk: It is now at best but the Reverse of what it was; a Tree turned upside down, the Branches on the Earth, and the Root in the Air: It is now handled by every dirty Wench, condemned to do her Drudgery; and by a capricious Kind of Fate, destined to make other Things clean, and be nasty it self. At length, worn to the Stumps in the Service of the Maids, it is either thrown out of Doors, or condemned to its last Use of kindling a Fire. When I beheld this, I sighed, and said within my self SURELY MORTAL MAN IS A BROOMSTICK; Nature sent him into the World strong and lusty, in a thriving Condition, wearing his own Hair on his Head, the proper Branches of this reasoning Vegetable; till the Axe of Intemperance has lopped off his Green Boughs, and left him with a withered Trunk: He then flies to Art, and puts on a *Perriwig*; valuing himself upon an unnatural Bundle of Hairs, all covered with Powder, that never grew on his Head: But now, should this our *Broom-stick* pretend to enter the Scene, proud of those *Birchen* Spoils it never bore, and all covered with Dust, though the Sweepings of the finest Lady's Chamber; we should be apt to ridicule and despise its Vanity. Partial Judges that we are of our own Excellence, and other Mens Defaults!

Considerations

1. Swift develops two analogies: between broomstick and tree, between broomstick and man. Explain what point he makes with each. List the details he uses to flesh out his analogies. How close are the parallels between man and broomstick? How plausible do they sound? What object other than broomstick might figure in such an analogy today?

2. Swift returns to an image from the beginning of the essay when he reaches the end (broomstick as upside-down tree). But he develops a new idea from this same basic analogy. What is this idea?

3. Write your own meditation upon an _____. Try to see your subject, your X, as something other than what it really is.

4. *Shifting Attention.* Sometimes in thinking and writing, you run up against a problem or run out of ideas because you are too sharply focused on only one element of the problem or one area of the subject. Often a deliberate shift of attention away from the dominant element to something else may lead you to additional, useful ideas.

Here's an example that shows how a shift of attention can lead to the solution of a problem:

While changing a tire, a man lost the lugs when they vanished down a sewer drain. Since he didn't have any extras, he decided to leave his car jacked up and hitch a ride to obtain help. As he was about to thumb a lift, a boy walked by and asked what the problem was. When the man told him, he said, "Oh, you don't have to leave the car. Just take one nut off each of the other wheels and that should get you where you're going."

Exercise

The following story presents a problem that can be solved by a shift of attention.*

A merchant had the misfortune of owing a large sum to an old and ugly moneylender who was attracted to the merchant's beautiful young daughter. Proposing a bargain, the moneylender said he would cancel the merchant's debt if he could have the girl instead.

Both the merchant and his daughter were horrified at the proposal. Suggesting that they let chance determine, the moneylender told them that he would put a black pebble and a white one into an empty moneybag from which the girl would have to pick a pebble. If she picked the black pebble, she would become his wife and her father's debt would be cancelled. If she picked the white pebble, she would stay with her father and the debt would still be cancelled. But if she refused to pick out a pebble, her father would be thrown into jail.

The merchant and his daughter agreed. They were standing on a pebble-strewn path in the merchant's garden. When the moneylender bent down to pick up the two pebbles, the girl saw that he had chosen two black ones rather than one black and one white as they had agreed. After putting them into the bag, he asked her to pick out the pebble that was to decide her fate and her father's.

What should she do?

One of the most important things you can learn from lateral thinking is not to be critical of your ideas too soon. Often, an inexperienced writer rejects an idea before it has had a chance to develop. With lateral thinking you don't reject "bad" ideas right away; nor do you decide on "good" ones. You reserve judgment for later, generating as many ideas and alternatives as you can. Eventually, of course, you'll discard some ideas, and retain and modify still others. Eventually, you'll have to evaluate your ideas, judging them to

---

*Adapted from Edward de Bono, *New Think.*

see which ones hold up under logical scrutiny, which you can make the most of. But that can come later, after you've given yourself time to explore your ideas and experiment with them, after they've had a chance to develop. If you judge too soon, you may end up having too few ideas to work with; you may cut off some potentially good ideas before they have the opportunity to mature.

PERCEPTION

The renowned art historian, E. H. Gombrich, has noted that "we can never neatly separate what we see from what we know." This is so for two related, complementary reasons. First, because we can't know more than we can see. We can't understand something until we "see" it, either literally or metaphorically (as when you "grasp" or "see" an idea). Second, because our ability to see something is grounded in prior experience; it is based on our knowledge and the expectations that grow out of it, and on the conceptual categories we use to "think" with. Our ability to see something, anything, derives largely from seeing it in a context, from seeing it "as" something, and from connecting it with other things we already know (from things we've already "seen" either with the eye or the mind).

Seeing, also, is a kind of thinking, as another art historian, Rudolf Arnheim, has argued. For Arnheim, "observation is also invention": when you see something, you make sense of it by making inferences about it, guessing about what it is and adjusting those guesses to conform to your changing perceptions. Seeing, moreover, is an active, selective, interpretive enterprise. When you see something, an editing process occurs. Your brain highlights particular features of what you are looking at and suppresses others. Without the brain's editing of visual stimuli, you couldn't make sense of what you see—which amounts to not being able to see it at all. By selecting, classifying, and relating details, the brain allows you to see *some*thing rather than a jumble of confused *no*-things. If, for example, you don't see a tree as a *kind* of *some*thing, you don't see it at all. If your brain didn't isolate and highlight particular features of what you look at, you would register, in the famous phrase of psychologist William James, "a blooming, buzzing confusion."

Furthermore, when you see, you start with an instantaneous generalization about what you are looking at. You then move from that to a guess about the kind of thing it appears to be, with an increasing sense of distinction and discrimination. You begin, in other words, to see it more clearly, to be more certain as to precisely what kind of something it is. Unless, of course, your initial guess is wrong. In that case, you see it as something else. You refine or correct your initial guess until you get it "right."

Something similar happens when you read. You assign to the words you read a provisional category or genre (detective story, fairy tale, lyric poem, e.g.). Then you test your intuitive sense of the kind of thing you think you're reading against the details that follow. It's something like putting together a jig-saw puzzle: you work both toward and from your intuitive sense of the whole, checking and correcting yourself along the way. In reading, as in writing, you structure your discourses retrospectively and projectively together. You turn back in thought to what you've already read or written to help you go forward in making sense. In the same manner you also project ahead, anticipating what is to come based on what you have already read or written.

These ideas about perception are illustrated in the essay excerpts and the exercises that follow. Read the selection and then respond to the questions and pictures.

MULTISTABILITY IN PERCEPTION
Fred Attneave

It is the business of the brain to represent the outside world. Perceiving is not just sensing but rather an effect of sensory input on the representational system. An ambiguous figure provides the viewer with an input for which there are two or more possible representations that are quite different and about equally good, by whatever criteria the perceptual system employs. When alternative representations or descriptions of the input are equally good, the perceptual system will sometimes adopt one and sometimes another. In other words, the perception is multistable. There are a number of physical systems that have the same kind of multistable characteristics, and a comparison of multistability in physical and perceptual situations may yield some significant clues to the basic processes of perception. First, however, let us consider several kinds of situations that produce perceptual multistability.

Reversible Goblet was introduced by Edgar Rubin in 1915 and is still a favorite demonstration of figure-ground reversal. Either a goblet or a pair of silhouetted faces is seen.

Figure-ground reversal has long been used in puzzle pictures. It is often illustrated by a drawing that can be seen as either a goblet or a pair of faces. This figure was introduced by the Danish psychologist Edgar Rubin. Many of the drawings and etchings of the Dutch artist Maurits C. Escher are particularly elegant examples of figure-ground reversal. These examples are somewhat misleading because they suggest that the components of a figure-ground reversal must be familiar objects. Actually you can make a perfectly good reversing figure by scribbling a meaningless line down the middle of a circle. The line will be seen as a contour or a boundary, and its appearance is quite different depending on which side of the contour is seen as the inside and which as the outside. The difference is so fundamental that if a person first sees one side of the contour as the object or figure, the probability of his recognizing the same contour when it is shown as part of the other half of the field is little better than if he had never seen it at all; this was demonstrated by Rubin in a classic study of the figure-ground dichotomy.

Note that it is quite impossible to see both sides of the contour as figures at the same time. Trying to think of the halves as two pieces of a jigsaw puzzle that fit together does not help; the pieces are still seen alternately and not simultaneously. . . .

Some of the most striking and amusing ambiguous figures are pictures (which may or may not involve figure-ground reversal) that can be seen as either of two familiar objects, for example, a duck or a rabbit, a young girl or an old woman, and a man or a girl. What is meant by "familiar" in this context is that the visual inputs can be matched to some acquired or learned schemata of classes of objects. Just what such class schemata consist of—whether they are like composite photographs or

Rabbit-Duck Figure was used in 1900 by psychologist Joseph Jastrow as an example of rival-schemata ambiguity. When it is a rabbit, the face looks to the right; when it is a duck, the face looks to the left. It is difficult to see both duck and rabbit at the same time.

Young Girl-Old Woman was brought to the attention of psychologists by Edwin G. Boring in 1930. Created by cartoonist W. E. Hill, it was originally published in *Puck* in 1915 as "My Wife and My Mother-in-law." The young woman's chin is the old woman's nose.

like lists of properties—remains a matter of controversy. In any case the process of identification must involve some kind of matching between the visual input and a stored schema. If two schemata match the visual input about equally well, they compete for its perceptual interpretation; sometimes one of the objects is seen and sometimes the other. Therefore one reason ambiguity exists is that a single input can be matched to different schemata.

Exercises

1. Provide a title for the following picture. Describe in writing why the title is appropriate and what adjustments of a visual nature you made in order to understand it the way you did.

M. C. Escher

2. Make up at least three titles for this work, and briefly explain why you chose them.

Do the white or the black figures dominate the work? Can you see both sets of figures simultaneously, or do you have to shift between them?

Divide the work into sections and explain the basis of your division.

M. C. Escher

3. Describe what you see in the numbered drawings below. If you start with drawing #1, at what point do you no longer see the figure? If you begin with drawing #8, what do you see? Where do you lose sight of this figure?

4. This last visual work is an exercise in perspective. What kinds of adjustments do you have to make as you look at it?

Two remarks by the artist might be worth thinking about with respect to this work: a) "Are you sure that a floor cannot also be a ceiling?" b) "Are you absolutely certain that you go up when you walk up a staircase?"

M. C. Escher

The following story, Nathaniel Hawthorne's "The Wives of the Dead," involves an ambiguity similar to the kind we've been exploring with pictures. Read it and explain what you think happens at the end. See if you can also offer an alternative account of what happens.

THE WIVES OF THE DEAD

The following story, the simple and domestic incidents of which may be deemed scarcely worth relating, after such a lapse of time, awakened some degree of interest, a hundred years ago, in a principal seaport of the Bay Province. The rainy twilight of an autumn day; a parlor on the second floor of a small house, plainly furnished, as beseemed the middling circumstances of its inhabitants, yet decorated with little curiosities from beyond the sea, and a few delicate specimens of Indian manufacture—these are the only particulars to be premised in regard to scene and season. Two young and comely women sat together by the fireside, nursing their mutual and peculiar sorrows. They were the recent brides of two brothers, a sailor and a landsman, and two successive days had brought tidings of the death of each, by the chances of Canadian warfare and the tempestuous Atlantic. The universal sympathy excited by this bereavement drew numerous condoling guests to the habitation of the widowed sisters. Several, among whom was the minister, had remained till the verge of evening, when, one by one, whispering many comfortable passages of Scripture that were answered by more abundant tears, they took their leave, and departed to their own happier homes. The mourners, though not insensible to the kindness of their friends, had yearned to be left alone. United, as they had been, by the relationship of the living, and now more closely so by that of the dead, each felt as if whatever consolation her grief admitted were to be found in the bosom of the other. They joined their hearts, and wept together silently. But after an hour of such indulgence, one of the sisters, all of whose emotions were influenced by her mild, quiet, yet not feeble character, began to recollect the precepts of resignation and endurance which piety had taught her, when she did not think to need them. Her misfortune, besides, as earliest known, should earliest cease to interfere with her regular course of duties; accordingly, having placed the table before the fire, and arranged a frugal meal, she took the hand of her companion.

"Come, dearest sister; you have eaten not a morsel today," she said. "Arise, I pray you, and let us ask a blessing on that which is provided for us."

Her sister-in-law was of a lively and irritable temperament, and the first pangs of her sorrow had been expressed by shrieks and passionate lamentation. She now shrunk from Mary's words, like a wounded sufferer from a hand that revives the throb.

"There is no blessing left for me, neither will I ask it!" cried Margaret, with a fresh burst of tears. "Would it were His will that I might never taste food more!"

Yet she trembled at these rebellious expressions, almost as soon as they were uttered, and, by degrees, Mary succeeded in bringing her sister's mind nearer to the situation of her own. Time went on, and their usual hour of repose arrived. The brothers and their brides, entering the married state with no more than the slender means which then sanctioned such a step, had confederated themselves in one household, with equal rights to the parlor, and claiming exclusive privileges in two sleeping rooms contiguous to it. Thither the widowed ones retired, after heaping ashes upon the dying embers of their fire, and placing a lighted lamp upon the hearth. The doors of both chambers were left open, so that a part of the interior of each, and the beds, with their unclosed curtains, were reciprocally visible. Sleep did not steal upon the sisters at one and the same time. Mary experienced the effect often consequent upon grief quietly borne, and soon sunk into temporary forgetfulness; while Margaret became more disturbed and feverish, in proportion as the night advanced with its deepest and stillest hours. She lay listening to the drops of rain that came down in monotonous succession, unswayed by a breath of wind, and a nervous impulse continually caused her to lift her head from the pillow, and gaze into Mary's chamber and the intermediate apartment. The cold light of the lamp threw the shadows of the furniture up against the wall, stamping them immovably there, except when they were shaken by a sudden flicker of the flame. Two vacant armchairs were in their old positions on opposite sides of the hearth, where the brothers had been wont to sit in young and laughing dignity, as heads of families; two humbler seats were near them, the true thrones of that little empire, where Mary and herself had exercised in love a power that love had won. The cheerful radiance of the fire had shone upon the happy circle, and the dead glimmer of the lamp might have befitted their reunion now. While Margaret groaned in bitterness, she heard a knock at the street door.

"How would my heart have leapt at that sound but yesterday!" thought she, remembering the anxiety with which she had long awaited tidings from her husband. "I care not for it now; let them begone, for I will not arise."

But even while a sort of childish fretfulness made her thus resolve, she was breathing hurriedly, and straining her ears to catch a repetition of the summons. It is difficult to be convinced of the death of one whom we have deemed another self. The knocking was now renewed in slow and regular strokes, apparently given with the soft end of a doubled fist, and was accompanied by words, faintly heard through several thicknesses of wall. Margaret looked to her sister's chamber, and beheld her still lying in the depths of sleep. She arose, placed her foot upon the floor, and slightly arrayed herself, trembling between fear and eagerness as she did so.

"Heaven help me!" sighed she. "I have nothing left to fear, and methinks I am ten times more a coward than ever."

Seizing the lamp from the hearth, she hastened to the window that overlooked the street door. It was a lattice, turning upon hinges; and having thrown it back, she stretched her head a little way into the moist atmosphere. A lantern was reddening the front of the house, and melting its light in the neighboring puddles, while a deluge of darkness overwhelmed every other object. As the window grated on its hinges, a man in a broad-brimmed hat and blanket coat stepped from under the shelter of the projecting story, and looked upward to discover whom his application had aroused. Margaret knew him as a friendly innkeeper of the town.

"What would you have, Goodman Parker?" cried the widow.

"Lackaday, is it you, Mistress Margaret?" replied the innkeeper. "I was afraid it might be your sister Mary; for I hate to see a young woman in trouble, when I haven't a word of comfort to whisper her."

"For Heaven's sake, what news do you bring?" screamed Margaret.

"Why, there has been an express through the town within this half hour," said Goodman Parker, "traveling from the eastern jurisdiction with letters from the Governor and council. He tarried at my house to refresh himself with a drop and a morsel, and I asked him what tidings on the frontiers. He tells me we had the better in the skirmish you wot of, and that thirteen men reported slain are well and sound, and your husband among them. Besides, he is appointed of the escort to bring the captivated Frenchers and Indians home to the province jail. I judged you wouldn't mind being broke of your rest, and so I stepped over to tell you. Good night."

So saying, the honest man departed; and his lantern gleamed along the street, bringing to view indistinct shapes of things, and the fragments of a world, like order glimmering through chaos, or memory roaming over the past. But Margaret stayed not to watch these picturesque effects. Joy flashed into her heart, and lighted it up at once; and breathless, and with winged steps, she flew to the bedside of her sister. She paused, however, at the door of the chamber, while a thought of pain broke in upon her.

"Poor Mary!" said she to herself. "Shall I waken her, to feel her sorrow sharpened by my happiness? No; I will keep it within my own bosom till the morrow."

She approached the bed, to discover if Mary's sleep were peaceful. Her face was turned partly inward to the pillow, and had been hidden there to weep; but a look of motionless contentment was now visible upon it, as if her heart, like a deep lake, had grown calm because its dead had sunk down so far within. Happy is it, and strange, that the lighter sorrows are those from which dreams are chiefly fabricated.

Margaret shrunk from disturbing her sister-in-law, and felt as if her own better fortune had rendered her involuntarily unfaithful, and as if altered and diminished affection must be the consequence of the disclosure she had to make. With a sudden step she turned away. But joy could not long be repressed, even by circumstances that would have excited heavy grief at another moment. Her mind was thronged with delightful thoughts, till sleep stole on, and transformed them to visions, more delightful and more wild, like the breath of winter (but what a cold comparison!) working fantastic tracery upon a window.

When the night was far advanced, Mary awoke with a sudden start. A vivid dream had latterly involved her in its unreal life, of which, however, she could only remember that it had been broken in upon at the most interesting point. For a little time, slumber hung about her like a morning mist, hindering her from perceiving the distinct outline of her situation. She listened with imperfect consciousness to two or three volleys of a rapid and eager knocking; and first she deemed the noise a matter of course, like the breath she drew; next, it appeared a thing in which she had no concern; and lastly, she became aware that it was a summons necessary to be obeyed. At the same moment, the pang of recollection darted into her mind; the pall of sleep was thrown back from the face of grief; the dim light of the chamber, and the objects therein revealed, had retained all her suspended ideas, and restored them as soon as she unclosed her eyes. Again there was a quick peal upon the street door. Fearing that her sister would also be disturbed, Mary wrapped herself in a cloak and hood, took the lamp from the hearth, and hastened to the window. By some accident, it had been left unhasped, and yielded easily to her hand.

"Who's there?" asked Mary, trembling as she looked forth.

The storm was over, and the moon was up; it shone upon broken clouds above, and below upon houses black with moisture, and upon little lakes of the fallen rain, curling into silver beneath the quick enchantment of a breeze. A young man in a sailor's dress, wet as if he had come out of the depths of the sea, stood alone under the window. Mary recognized him as one whose livelihood was gained by short voyages along the coast; nor did she forget that, previous to her marriage, he had been an unsuccessful wooer of her own.

"What do you seek here, Stephen?" said she.

"Cheer up Mary, for I seek to comfort you," answered the rejected lover. "You must know I got home not ten minutes ago, and the first thing my good mother told me was the news about your husband. So, without saying a word to the old woman, I clapped on my hat, and ran out of the house. I couldn't have slept a wink before speaking to you, Mary, for the sake of old times."

"Stephen, I thought better of you!" exclaimed the widow, with gushing tears and preparing to close the lattice, for she was no whit inclined to imitate the first wife of Zadig.

"But stop, and hear my story out," cried the young sailor. "I tell you we spoke to a brig yesterday afternoon, bound in from Old England. And whom do you think I saw standing on deck, well and hearty, only a bit thinner than he was five months ago?"

Mary leaned from the window, but could not speak.

"Why, it was your husband himself," continued the generous seaman. "He and three others saved themselves on a spar, when the 'Blessing' turned bottom upwards. The brig will beat into the bay by daylight, with this wind, and you'll see him here tomorrow. There's the comfort I bring you, Mary, and so good night."

He hurried away, while Mary watched him with a doubt of waking reality, that seemed stronger or weaker as he alternately entered the shade of the houses, or emerged into the broad streaks of moonlight. Gradually, however, a blessed flood of conviction swelled into her heart, in strength enough to overwhelm her, had its increase been more abrupt. Her first impulse was to rouse her sister-in-law, and communicate the newborn gladness. She opened the chamber door, which had been closed in the course of the night, though not latched, advanced to the bedside, and was about to lay her hand upon the slumberer's shoulder. But then she remembered that Margaret would awake to thoughts of death and woe, rendered not the less bitter by their contrast with her own felicity. She suffered the rays of the lamp to fall upon the unconscious form of the bereaved one. Margaret lay in unquiet sleep, and the drapery was displaced around her; her young cheek was rosy-tinted, and her lips half opened in a vivid smile; an expression of joy, debarred its passage by her sealed eyelids, struggled forth like incense from the whole countenance.

"My poor sister! you will waken too soon from that happy dream," thought Mary.

Before retiring, she set down the lamp, and endeavored to arrange the bedclothes so that the chill air might not do harm to the feverish slumberer. But her hand trembled against Margaret's neck, a tear also fell upon her cheek, and she suddenly awoke.

Considerations

1. Separate fact from fancy, dream from reality, in this story, using any or all of the tools and methods so far described.

2. Suppose the story had ended with its next-to-last paragraph. Would that alter your sense of it? Why or why not?

3. Look again at the final paragraph, especially at the final sentence. Whose hand trembled? Whose tear fell? Upon whose cheek? And which sister awoke?

4. Is there any advantage to the author's not specifying exactly what happened at the end? What are the implications of the ending if it is Mary who awakes? If it is Margaret?

5. What comparisons and contrasts does Hawthorne establish between Mary and Margaret? Why and how are their similarities and differences in behavior significant?

An illustration of the connections among reading/writing, seeing, and thinking can be made with the following Robert Frost poem.

DESIGN

I found a dimpled spider, fat and white,
On a white heal-all, holding up a moth
Like a white piece of rigid satin cloth—
Assorted characters of death and blight
5 Mixed ready to begin the morning right,
Like the ingredients of a witches' broth—
A snow-drop spider, a flower like a froth,
And dead wings carried like a paper kite.

What had that flower to do with being white,
10 The wayside blue and innocent heal-all?
What brought the kindred spider to that height,
Then steered the white moth thither in the night?
What but design of darkness to appall?—
If design govern in a thing so small.

The poem begins with observation, with details of sight; it ends in speculation. In its movement from the specific to the general, "Design" imitates meaning-making. The poem describes how the speaker looks at spider, moth, and flower; from that initial seeing, the narrator moves into speculative thinking. Early in the poem, however, before he gets to the larger philosophical question on which the poem turns—the question of the design of the universe—the speaker, in his seeing, is also thinking. The three elements—flower, moth, and spider—are seen in relationship to one another and in relationship to other things. The speaker specifies them; he classifies and analogizes them. The poet stands behind all this. And he designs his poem to reflect and embody this movement of the mind from seeing to thinking by organizing the poem as a two-part structure. The first part records the speaker's literal observations; the second raises broader questions about the meaning of what is described in the first part. Seeing is itself part of the thinking and knowing, not just a triggering mechanism. We don't know whether Frost actually saw the scene he describes in the poem, but we do know that he conceived it out of possibilities his experience had stored and that he wanted his readers to see the "design of darkness" his speaker sees and questions.

REVISION

So far we've been emphasizing how you can generate ideas, how you can make connections between what you see and think, between what you read and write. Implicit in the discussion, especially in the sections on perception and lateral thinking, has been a concern with another important aspect of composing: revision. Revision is literally that—a re-envisioning of what you're saying when you think and write. Revision is simply a re-seeing and re-making of the sense you make all along as you write—and as you read. It's not a stage or step you perform after you've finished. Rather it's an act of continuous re-imagining.

But why should you be concerned about re-envisioning what you see, think, and write? Why revise your writing at all? Because revising is an essential part of writing—not an added burden, not a luxury, but an inevitable, necessary part of the process. As W. H. Auden notes, "your first idea is not always your best." For E. B. White it may be less a matter of going after a new and better idea than of clarifying the idea he began with. White puts it this way: "I rewrite a good deal to make it clear.... The least I can do is to make it as easy as possible for [a reader] to find what I'm trying to get at."

These two comments suggest that the reason for writing and rewriting is to make something clear for oneself and for a reader. They also suggest that you will, more than likely, not clarify that something on the first try, or perhaps on the fourth try. And they suggest further that when you revise, you reconsider your thinking as well as your wording. Rather than simply cleaning up a messy first draft, revision requires that you clarify, modify, qualify your ideas, that you re-view and re-think them both for yourself (to see exactly what you think) and for your readers (so they can understand what you're saying).

Revising is as important as getting started. In fact, it's a way of getting re-started. As such, revising needs to be thought of as more than a form of first aid (or last aid) for injured writing. Try to avoid thinking of revision as a kind of patching or fixing up of writing in need of repair. This is to reduce revision to its least important element—editing. Revision is far more than editing (although it includes editing). Synonymous, fundamentally, with writing, revising is an ongoing attempt to discover and re-think your ideas, to find satisfying form for those ideas, to adjust image and idea, word and phrase and sentence, all in an effort to make meaning. And you do these things together, for these aspects of composing can't be separated. When you re-think an idea, for example, you also alter the way you express it, the way it takes shape in your mind and on the page. Analogously, when you adjust the phrasing and tone of your writing, you simultaneously clarify and qualify your meaning. You find meaning in making it.

Such a conception of revising can become a formative principle. It can help you see that writing, essentially, is re-writing, that the process goes on continuously, and that change—of idea, form, style—is a natural part of the process. It can help you see, also, that all writing, from scribbled notes to final draft, is writing-in-process, work-in-progress. Finally, this view of revision might prompt you to reconsider (to revise) your own writing habits, adjusting them to give revision the central place it deserves.

Myths about Revision

Before going on to look more closely at revision, we should briefly consider four common myths about it that have done much to promote misunderstanding of what writing really involves.

Myth #1: "Revision isn't necessary." A writer who believes that says something like this: "My readers will know what I mean. They'll be able to figure it out. Besides, don't readers have to do some work too?" The answer to the second part of this, of course, is that readers certainly should work at understanding what they read, but not more than they have to. The answer to the first part is that readers will only understand what is clear. And to achieve clarity, most writers have to revise most of the time.

Myth #2: "Revision will destroy the natural flow and the real sense of my writing. What comes naturally in the first writing is the genuine, unadulterated me. Any tampering will destroy the authenticity and the honesty of my ideas and feelings. Besides, sometimes I feel inspired, and I wouldn't want to destroy what I write under such inspiration."

The answer to this is more complicated than the response to the first myth. Let's suppose that you do produce some inspired writing. Isn't it true that with a second look and a second effort you'll see ways to increase the effectiveness of what you wrote in the initial burst of inspiration? There's also the possibility that what came to you as inspired writing may not be very good after all, that after you distance yourself from it you'll see flaws. And finally, in response to the first part of this myth, consider that the reflective, deliberative you looking back at something you've written is just as much "you" as the writer who poured out the ideas initially. This critical you is just as honest and authentic as the creative you.

Myth #3: "Revision is only for students; real writers don't revise. For professionals, writing is an easy succession of perfect pages." The simplest and probably the most persuasive way to counter this argument is to let a few writers speak for themselves.

W. H. Auden: "I do an enormous amount of revising. . . . I revise if I feel the language is prolix or obscure."

Leo Tolstoy: "I can't understand how anyone can write without rewriting everything over and over again. I scarcely ever reread my published writing, but if by chance I come across a page, it always strikes me, all this must be rewritten."

John Hersey: "To be a writer is to throw away a good deal, not to be satisfied, to type again and again, and once more, and over and over."

Myth #4: "Revision is a form of punishment; it means I've done something wrong." Not so. Revision is a necessary part of a process you're doing right. You simply have to see revision as part of an ongoing effort to make meaning instead of as a "correction" procedure for "mistakes" you made in your initial writing.

One way to gain insight into revision is to study the drafts of a work. Here are two versions of a poem by D. H. Lawrence. As you compare them, notice how Lawrence, in going from the early to the later version, revised chiefly by leaving things out—revision by excision. What does he leave out and why? What other changes do you notice? How do you account for them? Look especially at the way each poem begins and ends, and look also at the characters in each.

[Early Version]

THE PIANO

Somewhere beneath that piano's superb sleek black
Must hide my mother's piano, little and brown, with the back
That stood close to the wall, and the front's faded silk both torn,
And the keys with little hollows, that my mother's fingers had worn.

5 Softly, in the shadows, a woman is singing to me.
Quietly, through the years I have crept back to see
A child sitting under the piano, in the boom of the shaking strings
Pressing the little poised feet of the mother who smiles as she sings.

The full throated woman has chosen a winning, living song
10 And surely the heart that is in me must belong
To the old Sunday evenings, when darkness wandered outside
And hymns gleamed on our warm lips, as we watched mother's fingers glide.

Or this is my sister at home in the old front room
Singing love's first surprised gladness, alone in the gloom.
15 She will start when she sees me, and blushing, spread out her hands
To cover my mouth's raillery, till I'm bound in her shame's heart-spun bands.

A woman is singing me a wild Hungarian air
And her arms, and her bosom, and the whole of her soul is bare,
And the great black piano is clamouring as my mother's never could clamour
20 And my mother's tunes are devoured of this music's ravaging glamour.

[Later Version]

Softly, in the dusk, a woman is singing to me;
Taking me back down the vista of years, till I see
A child sitting under the piano, in the boom of the tingling strings
And pressing the small, poised feet of a mother who smiles as she sings.

5 In spite of myself, the insidious mastery of song
Betrays me back, till the heart of me weeps to belong
To the old Sunday evenings at home, with winter outside
And hymns in the cosy parlour, the tinkling piano our guide.

So now it is vain for the singer to burst into clamour
10 With the great black piano appassionato. The glamour
Of childish days is upon me, my manhood is cast
Down in the flood of remembrance, I weep like a child for the past.

Try to think of your writing as work-in-progress. Even if you've written and revised a piece half a dozen times and are favorably disposed toward it, think of it as "finished-for-now," as a work tentatively at rest, but not finished. You might keep in mind a remark of the modern French poet, Paul Valéry: "A poem is never finished. It is only abandoned."

Before you abandon your writing, however, you can re-envision it enough so that it's worthy of being abandoned. Even though you may not be finished with a piece, you can submit it for others to read while giving yourself some distance from it. Put it aside for awhile. When you return to it and after you hear other readers' responses, you'll be in a better position to know what's strong or weak. In addition, you might keep in mind the following questions:

1. Are you saying as honestly as you can what you want to say? Do you believe it? And, do you care about what you're saying?
2. Why do you think readers will care about it? What is there about it that demands thoughtful response rather than token assent? Is there anything in it that will make reading it a pleasure rather than a duty?
3. What are you trying to do? How do you want your readers to respond? How do you want to affect them? If you had more time to rework your piece, what would you do to make yourself more satisfied with it?
4. What is there about it that might not be clear to readers, perhaps because it really isn't completely clear to you? This is probably the point at which you should ask a few readers for their honest responses to what you've written. It can be immensely helpful to know that readers are amused, confused, baffled or delighted at specific points in your work.

Much of what I've been saying about writing and revising is true also for reading. Both reading and writing involve what I. A. Richards calls a "continuing audit of meaning," a revisionary openness to an emerging text, whether it's created on your page as you write or recreated in your mind as you read. The next section of *Connections,* while focusing on the reading process—especially on what you *do* as you read—also continues to stress the connections between reading/writing and seeing and thinking that already have been established.

PART II

Reading and Responding
Getting Involved with Texts

Reading startles into life those parts of us which might otherwise have remained dormant.... It reminds us of something we knew but did not know we knew.

Holbrook Jackson

Learning to write may be a part of learning to read.... Both reading and writing are experiences—lifelong—in the course of which we who encounter words used in certain ways are persuaded by them to be brought mind and heart within the presence, the power of the imagination.

Eudora Welty

Principles and Guidelines

"Once upon a time there was a fine young king who was married to the loveliest of queens." You've probably never read this exact line before, yet it should sound strongly familiar, as if you had heard it again and again. It's the first line of a fairy tale, not that you had to be told. When a piece of writing begins with "Once upon a time" and features kings and queens, few readers over eight will have any difficulty identifying what type of literature it is or even guessing fairly closely about what will probably happen to the king and queen before the story is over.

Fairy tales never begin with lines like "The door of Henry's lunchroom opened and two men came in." What kind of story *might* start with such a line? Although you can't be sure, it's likely that this brief sentence suggested something about what kind of material this is—whether or not it's fiction, modern or premodern, American or foreign, for example—and even faintly about why the two men are entering Henry's and whether the events that unfold around this situation will probably be funny, sad, grim, frightening or whatever. (To find out what *does* happen, read Ernest Hemingway's short story, "The Killers.")

When we read, we naturally, and most often unconsciously, identify the text as a certain kind of discourse, whether it's a fairy tale, gothic novel, science fiction story, or editorial. This ability to orient oneself is an important aspect of reading, chiefly because it allows us to bring quickly to bear on the reading all of our past experiences with the mode and subject of the discourse. Thus, we rarely come at a reading "cold," without a prior sense of it, a familiarity with its shape, an existing body of feelings, insights, facts to color our responses. Reading isn't only a matter of *extracting* information—meaning—but of each reader's bringing something uniquely her own to the material. We'll all understand the fairy tale's story line—the particulars of its plot—pretty much the same way, but past that, our responses will differ. Mine won't be "better" or "smarter" than yours, only different. We're both making sense of the text, but our "senses" aren't, thank goodness, identical.

You should become aware (to the extent that it's possible) of how you make sense as you read—how *you* figure in the meaning-making process. This is meant to be the main function of Part II, which begins with an exercise of sorts in reading. The selection has been printed with intervening commentary and questions. You can read it that way, one section at a time with commentary, or you can read it as its author intended, without interruptions, and save the commentary for a second reading.

As you read, annotate "A Hanging," jotting brief observations in the margins. You should also annotate the intervening material, responding to the observations made there. As you read both the essay and the commentary, keep making connections between them and your ideas and feelings about them. Don't worry about being "right," or about finding something important-sounding to jot; just annotate.

A HANGING
George Orwell

1 It was in Burma, a sodden morning of the rains. A sickly light, like yellow tinfoil, was slanting over the high walls into the jail yard. We were waiting outside the condemned cells, a row of sheds fronted with double bars, like small animal cages. Each cell measured about ten feet by ten and was quite bare within except for a plank bed and a pot for drinking water. In some of them brown silent men were squatting at the inner bars, with their blankets draped round them. These were the condemned men, due to be hanged within the next week or two.

1. What do you think you're reading? A story? A news account? An essay? What makes you think so? What do you know once you've read this opening paragraph? What details stand out in your mind? What, if any, associations form for you? What do you expect to come next?

2 One prisoner had been brought out of his cell. He was a Hindu, a puny wisp of a man, with a shaven head and vague liquid eyes. He had a thick, sprouting moustache, absurdly too big for his body, rather like the moustache of a comic man on the films. Six tall Indian warders were guarding him and getting him ready for the gallows. Two of them stood by with rifles and fixed bayonets, while the others handcuffed him, passed a chain through his handcuffs and fixed it to their belts, and lashed his arms tight to his sides. They crowded very close about him, with their hands always on him in a careful, caressing grip, as though all the while feeling him to make sure he was there. It was like men handling a fish which is still alive and may jump back into the water. But he stood quite unresisting, yielding his arms limply to the ropes, as though he hardly noticed what was happening.

2. Does this paragraph confirm your expectations? Does it seem a natural follow-up to the opening paragraph? What is the center of interest here? What is your impression of the prisoner? On what do you think your impression is based? What is suggested by the comparison with the fish? Does it seem appropriate that the guards—six of them—take the precautions they do?

3 Eight o'clock struck and a bugle call, desolately thin in the wet air, floated from the distant barracks. The superintendent of the jail, who was standing apart from the rest of us, moodily prodding the gravel with his stick, raised his head at the sound. He was an army doctor, with a gray toothbrush moustache and a gruff voice. "For God's sake hurry up, Francis," he said irritably. "The man ought to have been dead by this time. Aren't you ready yet?"

4 Francis, the head jailer, a fat Dravidian in a white drill suit and gold spectacles, waved his black hand. "Yes sir, yes sir," he bubbled. "All iss satisfactorily prepared. The hangman iss waiting. We shall proceed."

5 "Well, quick march, then. The prisoners can't get their breakfast till this job's over."

3, 4, and 5. After the opening paragraph, which presents the location and background of the action, and after the second, which centers on the prisoner and his guards, we encounter two additional characters, Francis and the superintendent. Explain your impression of each. What does their language reveal about them?

6 We set out for the gallows. Two warders marched on either side of the prisoner, with their rifles at the slope; two others marched close against him, gripping him by arm and shoulder, as though at once pushing and supporting him. The rest of us, magistrates and the like, followed behind. Suddenly, when we had gone ten yards, the procession stopped short without any order or warning. A dreadful thing had happened—a dog,

come goodness knows whence, had appeared in the yard. It came bounding among us with a loud volley of barks, and leapt round us wagging its whole body with glee at finding so many human beings together. It was a large woolly dog, half Airedale, half pariah. For a moment it pranced round us, and then, before anyone could stop it, it had made a dash for the prisoner and, jumping up, tried to lick his face. Everyone stood aghast, too taken aback even to grab at the dog.

6. The march to the scaffold begins here and is stopped almost as soon as it starts—by a bounding, barking dog. What is the relationship between the dog's action and the actions of the men? Why do you think Orwell included this detail? By now you have probably formed at least a tentative impression of the narrator. What sort of person is he? Do you like him? Dislike him? Explain.

7 "Who let that bloody brute in here?" said the superintendent angrily. "Catch it, someone!"

8 A warder, detached from the escort, charged clumsily after the dog, but it danced and gamboled just out of his reach, taking everything as part of the game. A young Eurasian jailer picked up a handful of gravel and tried to stone the dog away, but it dodged the stones and came after us again. Its yaps echoed from the jail walls. The prisoner, in the grasp of the two warders, looked on incuriously, as though this was another formality of the hanging. It was several minutes before someone managed to catch the dog. Then we put my handkerchief through its collar and moved off once more, with the dog still straining and whimpering.

7 and 8. Of course, they have to catch the dog and get on with their business. But notice the irritability in the superintendent's voice. And notice too how the dog takes everything, including their pursuit of him, as part of the game. The action is incongruous, out of keeping with the seriousness the superintendent wants to maintain in the proceedings. Moreover, the incongruity of the dog's gamboling about is heightened by the fact that the men don't catch it right away.

9 It was about forty yards to the gallows. I watched the bare brown back of the prisoner marching in front of me. He walked clumsily with his bound arms, but quite steadily, with that bobbing gait of the Indian who never straightens his knees. At each step his muscles slid neatly into place, the lock of hair on his scalp danced up and down, his feet printed themselves on the wet gravel. And once, in spite of the men who gripped him by each shoulder, he stepped slightly aside to avoid a puddle on the path.

9. This is an important paragraph. Orwell returns here to a description of the prisoner: how as he walks his muscles slide into place, his hair dances on his scalp, his feet print the wet gravel. What for you is the cumulative effect of these details? What do you think of and how do you feel about this man at this point? And why do you think Orwell includes the detail about the prisoner stepping aside to avoid a puddle? What does this suggest about the condemned man?

10   It is curious, but till that moment I had never realized what it means to destroy a healthy, conscious man. When I saw the prisoner step aside to avoid the puddle I saw the mystery, the unspeakable wrongness, of cutting a life short when it is in full tide. This man was not dying, he was alive just as we are alive. All the organs of his body were working—bowels digesting food, skin renewing itself, nails growing, tissues forming—all toiling away in solemn foolery. His nails would still be growing when he stood on the drop, when he was falling through the air with a tenth of a second to live. His eyes saw the yellow gravel and the gray walls, and his brain still remembered, foresaw, reasoned—reasoned even about puddles. He and we were a party of men walking together, seeing, hearing, feeling, understanding the same world; and in two minutes, with a sudden snap, one of us would be gone—one mind less, one world less.

10. Paragraph 10 intensifies and makes explicit what has been implied in the preceding paragraph. Orwell explains "what it means to destroy a healthy, conscious man." He explains what the side-step of the puddle means, and he indicates how he feels about it. Notice how Orwell implicates himself—and us—by writing: "he was alive just as *we* are alive." And again: "He and *we* were a party of *men* . . . understanding the *same* world . . . one of *us* would be gone."

Notice too the particular details Orwell employs to convey the fact of the man's "aliveness." He mentions that his bodily organs are operating—that his bowels digest food, that his skin and nails grow. And he uses "ing" verbs (present participles) to do this, so he can emphasize that the man's bodily processes were functioning at that precise moment. Then, to intensify the feelings we're experiencing, Orwell reminds us that these processes would all be going on as the prisoner falls through the air, up to the split-second before his death. He clinches this point with a reminder that the prisoner's brain—his seeing, thinking, remembering organ—is as alive and active as the rest of his body. Finally, in the last sentence of the paragraph, Orwell emphasizes our common humanity by stressing our kinship with the prisoner ("we" and "us"), and by cataloguing, in a series of "ing" verbs, human life in action. Once he has driven all this home, he snaps the sentence shut with a powerful idea: when a man dies, a whole world—his individual world—dies with him. What conclusions and reactions do you think Orwell expects from his readers at this point? Why?

11 The gallows stood in a small yard, separate from the main grounds of the prison, and overgrown with tall prickly weeds. It was a brick erection like three sides of a shed, with planking on top, and above that two beams and a crossbar with the rope dangling. The hangman, a gray-haired convict in the white uniform of the prison, was waiting beside his machine. He greeted us with a servile crouch as we entered. At a word from Francis the two warders, gripping the prisoner more closely than ever, half led, half pushed him to the gallows and helped him clumsily up the ladder. Then the hangman climbed up and fixed the rope around the prisoner's neck.

11. If this were an essay opposing capital punishment, it could end at this point, leaving us to imagine the details of the hanging. But it's also a report, a narrative account of what happened, whether imaginary or actual. Therefore, after stopping the narrative movement to make an implied argument against capital punishment (paragraphs 9-10), Orwell continues the march to the gallows. What do the details of paragraph 11 reveal about the hangman? About the warders?

12 We stood waiting, five yards away. The warders had formed in a rough circle round the gallows. And then, when the noose was fixed, the prisoner began crying out to his god. It was a high, reiterated cry of "Ram! Ram! Ram! Ram!" not urgent and fearful like a prayer or cry for help, but steady, rhythmical, almost like the tolling of a bell. The dog answered the sound with a whine. The hangman, still standing on the gallows, produced a small cotton bag like a flour bag and drew it down over the prisoner's face. But the sound, muffled by the cloth, still persisted, over and over again: "Ram! Ram! Ram! Ram!"

13 The hangman climbed down and stood ready, holding the lever. Minutes seemed to pass. The steady, muffled crying from the prisoner went on and on, "Ram! Ram! Ram!" never faltering for an instant. The superintendent, his head on his chest, was slowly poking the ground with his stick; perhaps he was counting the cries, allowing the prisoner a fixed number—fifty, perhaps, or a hundred. Everyone had changed color. The Indians had gone gray like bad coffee, and one or two of the bayonets were wavering. We looked at the lashed, hooded man on the drop, and listened to his cries—each cry another second of life; the same thought was in all our minds: oh, kill him quickly, get it over, stop that abominable noise!

12 and **13.** These two paragraphs show the prisoner on the scaffold, ready momentarily to be hanged. How do you respond to the prisoner's cries: "Ram! Ram! Ram!"? What other sounds does Orwell mention and what do they contribute to the tone of the paragraph? Notice also that different forms of the word "cry" occur ("cries" and "crying" par. 7) and that "Ram" is repeated twelve times. Are these repetitions necessary? If so, why?

14 Suddenly the superintendent made up his mind. Throwing up his head he made a swift motion with his stick. "Chalo!" he shouted almost fiercely.

14. This paragraph is brief—abrupt. Why?

15 There was a clanking noise, and then dead silence. The prisoner had vanished, and the rope was twisting on itself. I let go of the dog, and it galloped immediately to the back of the gallows; but when it got there it stopped short, barked, and then retreated into a corner of the yard, where it stood among the weeds, looking timorously out at us. We went round the gallows to inspect the prisoner's body. He was dangling with his toes pointed straight downward, very slowly revolving, as dead as a stone.

15. The actual hanging over, Orwell focuses our attention on the rope. Why? Then he highlights the actions of the dog. Again, why? Finally, he describes the man's toes pointing down, and his body "very slowly revolving, as dead as a stone."

16 The superintendent reached out with his stick and poked the bare brown body; it oscillated slightly. "*He's* all right," said the superintendent. He backed out from under the gallows, and blew out a deep breath. The moody look had gone out of his face quite suddenly. He glanced at his wrist watch. "Eight minutes past eight. Well, that's all for this morning, thank God."

16. Why does the superintendent poke the body? What does he mean by saying, "*He's* all right"? Why does he blow out a deep breath? How much time has elapsed during all the action? And what is the effect of his remark: "Well that's all for this morning, thank God"?

17 The warders unfixed bayonets and marched away. The dog, sobered and conscious of having misbehaved itself, slipped after them. We walked out of the gallows yard, past the condemned cells with their waiting prisoners, into the big central yard of the prison. The convicts, under the command of warders armed with lathis, were already receiving their breakfast. They squatted in long rows, each man holding a tin pannikin, while two warders with buckets marched round ladling out rice; it seemed quite a homely, jolly scene after the hanging. An enormous relief had come upon us now that the job was done. One felt an impulse to sing, to break into a run, to snigger. All at once everyone began chattering gaily.

17. This paragraph contrasts two groups: the prisoners waiting in the condemned cells with the convicts. How are the two groups described? Why is everyone, even Orwell, chattering gaily? This response certainly isn't appropriate but is it psychologically plausible? Why or why not?

18   The Eurasian boy walking beside me nodded toward the way we had come, with a knowing smile: "Do you know, sir, our friend [he meant the dead man] when he heard his appeal had been dismissed, he pissed on the floor of his cell. From fright. Kindly take one of my cigarettes, sir. Do you not admire my new silver case, sir? From the boxwalah, two rupees eight annas. Classy European style."

19   Several people laughed—at what, nobody seemed certain.

20   Francis was walking by the superintendent, talking garrulously: "Well, sir, all hass passed off with the utmost satisfactoriness. It was all finished—flick! like that. It iss not always so—oah, no! I have known cases where the doctor was obliged to go beneath the gallows and pull the prissoner's legs to ensure decease. Most disagreeable!"

21   "Wriggling about, eh? That's bad," said the superintendent.

22   "Ach, sir, it iss worse when they become refractory! One man, I recall, clung to the bars of hiss cage when we went to take him out. You will scarcely credit, sir, that it took six warders to dislodge him, three pulling at each leg. We reasoned with him. 'My dear fellow,' we said, 'think of all the pain and trouble you are causing to us!' But no, he would not listen! Ach, he wass very troublesome!"

23   I found that I was laughing quite loudly. Everyone was laughing. Even the superintendent grinned in a tolerant way. "You'd better all come out and have a drink," he said quite genially. "I've got a bottle of whiskey in the car. We could do with it."

24   We went through the big double gates of the prison into the road. "Pulling at his legs!" exclaimed a Burmese magistrate suddenly, and burst into a loud chuckling. We all began laughing again. At that moment Francis' anecdote seemed extraordinarily funny. We all had a drink together, native and European alike, quite amicably. The dead man was a hundred yards away.

18–24. What is the point of each of the remarks made after the hanging is over? What is the point of the final sentence? What would be lost if it were omitted, and why?

In reading "A Hanging," you've been doing these things: observing details, making inferences about them, and drawing conclusions based on these acts. That's what reading amounts to. Singling out its aspects here is only for our purposes of discussion; in reality, the observing-connecting-inferring-concluding aren't discrete, fully conscious acts but are fused into one process—reading.

Part of the meaning of "A Hanging," as I suggested earlier, is the *experience* you underwent as you read it—the way the text created expectations for you, elicited responses that belong to you and no one else. This doesn't mean that Orwell's intent is of no consequence—that meaning is whatever you want to make of it. "A Hanging" is not an essay about how funny executions are, and if you think it is, you may be somewhat unbalanced. You and the text are reciprocal sources of its meaning.

"People" is by the contemporary Russian poet, Yevgeny Yevtushenko. Respond to it, both intellectually and emotionally; that is, don't only seek to explain it to yourself, but also to discover how you feel about it, what associations (connections) it helps you form, what its imagery may evoke in you and why. For example, will you react more strongly to "books and bridges/ and painted canvas and machinery," or "In any man who dies there dies with him/his first snow and kiss and fight"? (And how can you account for the reaction?) Annotate the poem, providing at least a brief gloss for each stanza. Also, compare the central idea with that advanced in paragraphs 9 and 13 of "A Hanging."

PEOPLE

No people are uninteresting.
Their fate is like the chronicle of planets.

Nothing in them is not particular,
and planet is dissimilar from planet.

5 And if a man lived in obscurity
making his friends in that obscurity
obscurity is not uninteresting.

To each his world is private,
and in that world one excellent minute.

10 And in that world one tragic minute.
These are private.

In any man who dies there dies with him
his first snow and kiss and fight.
It goes with him.

15 They are left books and bridges
and painted canvas and machinery.

Whose fate is to survive.
But what has gone is also not nothing:

by the rule of the game something has gone.
20 Not people die but worlds die in them.

Whom we knew as faulty, the earth's creatures.
Of whom, essentially, what did we know?

Brother of a brother? Friend of friends?
Lover of lover?

25 We who knew our fathers
in everything, in nothing.

>   They perish. They cannot be brought back.
>   The secret worlds are not regenerated.
>
>   And every time again and again
> 30 I make my lament against destruction.

Exercises

1. The following news report, which appeared in a British newspaper, is an eyewitness account of a hanging. It shares some details with Orwell's essay but it's also quite different. Make a list of similarities and differences between the two pieces. Consider the purpose and point of each; the intended or implied audience; the number and kinds of details included; the differing voices and styles.

MICHAEL LAKE DESCRIBES
WHAT THE EXECUTIONER ACTUALLY FACES
Guardian 9 April, 1973

It is doubtful if those who seek the reintroduction of capital punishment have ever seen a hanging. It is a grim business, far removed from the hurly burly of Parliament, from the dusty gloom of the Old Bailey and a million light years away from the murder.

In New Zealand hangings were always in the evening. There were never any crowds, but three journalists were always summoned to witness the hanging. Their names were published later that night, along with those of the sheriff, the coroner and others, in the Official Gazette. I watched the last hanging in New Zealand.

Walter James Bolton was a farmer from the west coast of the North Island. He had poisoned his wife. He was 62, and the oldest and heaviest man ever hanged in New Zealand. They had to make sure they got the length of rope right so the drop wouldn't tear off his head.

I arrived at Mt Eden Gaol, Auckland, at 6 o'clock on a Monday evening. With the other witnesses I was led through the main administrative block, down some steps, and along a wing which, it turned out, was a sort of Death Row.

We were led to the foot of the scaffold in a yard immediately at the end of the wing. The sky was darkening and a canvas canopy over the yard flapped gently in the breeze.

After a long time, there was a murmuring. Into view came a strange procession; the deputy governor of the prison, leading four warders and among them, walked or rather shambled the hulking figure of Bolton. His arms were pinioned by ropes to his trunk.

Behind him walked a parson reading aloud. It was with disbelief and shock that I recognised the Burial Service from the Book of Common Prayer.

High upon the scaffold, 17 steps away, the executioner stood immobile. He wore a black broad-brimmed hat, a black trench coat, and heavy boots, and he was masked. Only the slit for his eyes and his white hands gleamed in the light.

Bolton was helped up the steps by the warders, who bound his ankles together. The sheriff then asked him if he had anything to say before sentence was carried out.

Bolton mumbled. After a few seconds mumbling the parson, apparently unaware that the prisoner was talking, interrupted with further readings from the Burial Service.

I checked my shorthand notes with the other reporters. One, an elderly man who had witnessed 19 hangings, had heard nothing. The other man's shorthand outlines matched my own. He had said: 'The only thing I want to say is . . . .'

The warders did all the work. They bound him and put a white canvas hood over his head as he stood there, swaying in their grasp. Then they dropped the loop over his head, with the traditional hangman's knot, tidied it up, and stepped back.

The sheriff lifted his hand and lowered it. The executioner moved for the first and only time. He pulled a lever, and stepped back. Bolton dropped behind a canvas screen. The rope ran fast through the pulley at the top, and then when the Turk's Head knotted in the end jammed in the pulley, the block clanged loudly up against the beam to which it was fixed. The rope quivered, and that was the end of Walter James Bolton.

A doctor repaired behind the screen which hid the body from us. A hanged man usually ejaculates and evacuates his bowels. In New Zealand, at any rate, he also hanged for an hour. Bolton hung while we sat back in the deputy governor's office drinking the whiskey traditionally provided by the Government for these occasions—'Who's for a long drop,' asked some macabre wit.

The city coroner, Mr. Alf Addison, an old friend of mine, called us across to his office where we duly swore we had seen the sentence of the court carried out.

I went back to my newspaper office and wrote three paragraphs. No sensations, I told the night editor, the bloke hadn't made a fuss. Then I went home with a sense of loss and corruption I have never quite shed.

2. In this exercise you'll read and write about two selections, a poem and an essay about it. Read the poem slowly, two or three times at least, both silently and aloud. In annotating, consider the possible differences in response to the different readings. Ask a classmate to read the poem to you and list your responses to this experience.

FELIX RANDAL
Gerard Manley Hopkins

Felix Randal the farrier, O is he dead then? my duty all ended,
Who have watched his mould of man, big-boned and hardy-handsome
Pining, pining, till time when reason rambled in it and some
Fatal four disorders, fleshed there, all contended?

5 Sickness broke him. Impatient he cursed at first, but mended
Being anointed and all; though a heavenlier heart began some
Months earlier, since I had our sweet reprieve and ransom
Tendered to him. Ah well, God rest him all road ever he offended!

This seeing the sick endears them to us, us too it endears.
10 My tongue had taught thee comfort, touch had quenched thy tears,
Thy tears that touched my heart, child, Felix, poor Felix Randal;

How far from then forethought of, all thy more boisterous years,
When thou at the random grim forge, powerful amidst peers,
Didst fettle for the great gray drayhorse his bright and battering sandal!

Considerations

1. What is actually going on in the poem? What do you understand its dramatic situation to be?

2. What "duty" has ended for the speaker, and why? What are the particulars of such a duty as Hopkins describes them? As you understand them? Do you and Hopkins generally agree?

3. What's Felix Randal like? How do you know? What lines establish his person? Beyond what they tell you, how do you know about Randal's nature?

4. We know of Felix only through the speaker, a priest. But in detailing the farrier and his fate, he also reveals much of himself. What kind of person does he seem to be? Don't settle for such stock terms as *nice, religious, sincere,* etc. If he emerges as a person, he is more than a loosely fitting label or two. Account for his rather worn, priestly figures of speech, his "Ah well, God rest him . . . ," for example. Argue that the poem is as much about the speaker as it is about the title character.

5. What for you are the connotations of *mould, rambled, anointed, boisterous, battering* within the context of this poem? Is there significant connotative difference between *farrier* and *blacksmith*? between *healed* and *mended*? Explain.

Here is George Orwell's response to "Felix Randal." As you read it, write out your reactions in the margins. When you're done, jot down your impressions of the whole. Interpret Orwell's interpretations and comment on whether or not it was at all valuable in helping you understand Hopkins's poem.

from
"THE MEANING OF A POEM"

. . . It is what people call a "difficult" poem—I have reason for choosing a difficult poem, which I will come back to in a moment—but no doubt the general drift of its meaning is clear enough. Felix Randal is a blacksmith—a farrier. The poet, who is also his priest, has known him in the prime of life as a big powerful man, and then he has seen him dying, worn out by disease and weeping on his bed like a child. That is all there is to it, so far as the "story" of the poem goes.

But now to come back to the reason why I deliberately chose such an obscure and one might say mannered poem. Hopkins is what people call a writer's writer. He writes in a very strange, twisted style—perhaps it is a bad style, really: at any rate, it would be a bad one to imitate—which is not at all easy to understand but which appeals to people who are professionally interested in points of technique. In criticisms of Hopkins, therefore, you will usually find all the emphasis laid on his use of language and his subject-matter very lightly touched on. And in any criticism of poetry, of course, it seems natural to judge primarily by the ear. For in verse the words—the sounds of words, their associations, and the harmonies of sound and association that two or three words together can set up—obviously matter more than they do in prose. Otherwise there would be no reason for writing in metrical form. And with Hopkins, in particular, the strangeness of his language and the astonishing beauty of some of the sound-effects he manages to bring off seem to overshadow everything else.

The best touch, one might say the especial touch, in this poem is due to a verbal coincidence. For the word that pins the whole poem together and gives it finally an air of majesty, a feeling of being tragic instead of merely pathetic, is that final word "sandal," which no doubt only came into Hopkins' mind because it happened to rhyme with Randal. I ought perhaps to add that the word "sandal" is more impressive to an English reader than it would be to an Oriental, who sees sandals every day and perhaps wears them himself. To us a sandal is an exotic thing, chiefly associated with the ancient Greeks and Romans. When Hopkins describes the cart-horse's shoe as a sandal, he suddenly converts the cart-horse into a magnificent mythical beast, something like a heraldic animal. And he reinforces that effect by the splendid rhythm of the last line—"Didst fettle for the great gray drayhorse his bright and battering sandal"—which is actually a hexameter, the same meter in which Homer and Vergil wrote. By a combination of sound and association he manages to lift an ordinary village death on to the plane of tragedy.

But that tragic effect cannot simply exist in the void, on the strength of a certain combination of syllables. One cannot regard a poem as simply a pattern of words on paper, like a sort of mosaic. This poem is moving because of its sound, its musical qualities, but it is also moving because of an emotional content which could not be there if Hopkins's philosophy and beliefs were different from what they were. It is the poem, first of all, of a Catholic, and secondly of a man living at a particular moment of time, the latter part of the nineteenth century, when the old English agricultural way of life—the old Saxon village community—was finally passing away. The whole feeling of the poem is Christian. It is about death, and the attitude toward death varies in the great religions of the world. The Christian attitude towards death is not that it is something to be welcomed, or that it is something to be met with stoical indifference, or that it is something to be avoided as long as possible; but that it is something profoundly tragic which has to be gone through with. A Christian, I suppose, if he were offered the chance of everlasting life on this earth would refuse it, but he would still feel that death is profoundly sad. Now this feeling conditions Hopkins's use of words. If it were not for his special relationship as priest it would not, probably, occur to him to address the dead blacksmith as "child." And he could not, probably, have evolved that phrase . . . "all thy more boisterous years", if he had not the special Christian vision of the necessity and the sadness of death. But, as I have said, the poem is also conditioned by the fact that Hopkins lived at the latter end of the nineteenth century. He had lived in rural communities when they were still distinctly similar to what they had been in Saxon times, but when they were just beginning to break up under the impact of the railway. Therefore he can see a type like Felix Randal, the small independent village craftsman, in perspective, as one can only see something when it is passing away. He can admire him, for instance, as an earlier writer probably could not have done. And that is why in speaking of his work he can evolve phrases like "the random grim forge" and "powerful amidst peers".

But one comes back to the technical consideration that a subject of this kind is very much helped by Hopkins's own peculiar style. English is a mixture of several languages, but mainly Saxon and Norman French, and to this day, in the country districts, there is a class distinction between the two. Many agricultural laborers speak almost pure Saxon. Now, Hopkins's own language is very Saxon, he tends to string several English words together instead of using a single long Latin one, as most people do when they want to express a complicated thought, and he deliberately derived from the early English poets, the ones who come before Chaucer. In this poem, he even uses several dialect words, "road" for way, and "fettle" for fix. The special power he has of re-creating the atmosphere of an English village would not belong to him if it were not for the purely technical studies he had made, earlier in his life, of the old Saxon poets. It will be seen that the poem is a synthesis—but more than a synthesis, a sort of growing together—of a special vocabulary and a special religious and social outlook. The two fuse together, inseparably, and the whole is greater than the parts.

I have tried to analyze this poem as well as I can in a short period, but nothing I have said can explain, or explain away, the pleasure I take in it. That is finally inexplicable, and it is just because it *is* inexplicable that detailed criticism is worthwhile. Men of science can study the life-process of a flower, or they can split it up into component elements, but any scientist will tell you that a flower does not become less wonderful, it becomes more wonderful, if you know all about it.

Considerations

1. Does Orwell's "story" outline coincide generally with yours? Do you agree with the essayist that the poem is "difficult," "obscure," "mannered"? Why or why not?

2. Hopkins frequently did with a line or phrase something like what the Globetrotters do with a basketball: seemingly impossible things, quirky, beautiful things, unforgettable things. It's not unusual for students with only the faintest interest in poetry to pick up and carry with them through life some arrestingly lovely Hopkins line, even if they don't fully understand what it means. Orwell suggests that in a way this is a problem—that Hopkins's "sound effects" outshout his meanings, or at least become irresistible distractions. On the basis of this poem and possibly other Hopkins works you may be familiar with, do you agree? What lines, if any, in "Felix Randal" seem to you to challenge the conventions of grammar, produce "strangenesses," "astonishing beauty"? Does the word *sandal* "[pin] the whole poem together" for you? "[Give] it . . . an air of majesty, a feeling of being tragic instead of merely pathetic"? Or does this seem to you to be overstating the value and power of the word as the poet uses it? Why or why not? Did the word initially strike you as being "exotic"? Did it make the drayhorse seem "mythical"? If so, was it for the reason Orwell gives? Explain.

3. In his last paragraph Orwell indicates that he can explain everything about the poem but the pleasure he takes in it. Do you agree with him that pleasure, delight, wonder—these "inexplicable" responses—increase with one's knowledge about a subject? Or are you persuaded, along with Mark Twain in a forthcoming selection, that close study of an object eliminates its mysteries, but along with them its romance and beauty? Argue the matter from one side or the other, using your own experiences in support of your position.

DOUBLE-ENTRY NOTEBOOK

You've been reading and writing about texts by responding to them informally in writing and conversation, but asking and answering questions, by making comparisons and connections of various sorts. An additional technique useful for reading and writing in response to texts is the "double-entry notebook."* This is a notation system in which you reserve separate facing pages for different things: on one side you "take notes" (or "make notes"), summarizing and paraphrasing what you read and reacting to it; on the other side you jot down questions, ideas, responses to your notes and to the piece. On this reacting side of the notebook, you can go beyond the text and your original response by questioning or criticizing them and by relating them to other things you know, think, and feel. The important thing is to get a dialogue going, both with the texts and with your own responses. When you read, try to think of the words on the page as the voice of a person with

---

*Credit for the idea of the double-entry notebook goes to Ann E. Berthoff, from whose book on writing it is adapted. See her *Forming/Thinking/Writing*. (Upper Montclair, NJ: Boynton/Cook Publishers, 1978).

something to say and a particular way of saying it. Think of your reactive comments as a kind of talking to the author, and also a kind of talking to yourself.

You can try out the double-entry notebook technique on any of the reading selections in *Connections*. Set up your page so that it looks like this:

Reactions and Questions	*Observations and Notes*
A set of reactions to the idea and its expression and to your first response. You can include things you notice about the selection's language, length, examples, details, structure, tone, voice, even things that seem to be missing. You can also make connections between the selection and other things you've read or experienced. You might also raise some questions about what you thought before—about things suggested but not directly included in the text.	Here you summarize or paraphrase the idea(s) of the selection. That is, put the author's idea(s) into your own words. Single out what you think is the point, the central idea. You might try doing this without looking at the selection. And you might also begin reacting to the text.

Here's an example of the double-entry notebook technique used in response to a paragraph from Mark Twain's *Life on the Mississippi*. First, the passage:

> It turned out to be true. The face of the water in time became a wonderful book—a book that was a dead language to the uneducated passenger but which told its mind to me without reserve, delivering its most cherished secrets as clearly as if it uttered them with a voice. And it was not a book to be read once and thrown aside, for it had a new story to tell every day. Throughout the long twelve hundred miles there was never a page that was void of interest, never one that you could leave unread without loss, never one that you would want to skip, thinking you could find higher enjoyment in some other thing. There never was so wonderful a book written by man, never one whose interest was so absorbing, so unflagging, so sparklingly renewed with every reperusal. The passenger who could not read it was charmed with a peculiar sort of faint dimple on its surface (on the rare occasions when he did not overlook it altogether) but to the pilot that was an italicized passage; indeed it was more than that, it was a legend of the largest capitals with a string of shouting exclamation points at the end of it, for it meant that a wreck or a rock was buried there that could tear the life out of the strongest vessel that ever floated. It is the faintest and simplest expression the water ever makes, and the most hideous to a pilot's eye. In truth, the passenger who could not read this book saw nothing but all manner of pretty pictures in it, painted by the sun and shaded by the

clouds, whereas to the trained eye these were not pictures at all, but the grimmest and most dead-earnest of reading-matter.

Reactions and Questions	*Observations and Notes*
The emphasis here is on the dangers of the river. Does Twain de-romanticize it? Is he saying something about the terror of nature along with its beauty—that beauty and terror exist together?	Twain makes an analogy between reading and interpreting a book and interpreting or "reading" a river. He distinguishes between the passengers, who can't read, and the pilot who can (and the cub pilot who's learning to read). Twain suggests that the passengers see only the pretty, romantic qualities of the river while the pilot sees beyond and beneath to what the details mean for the safety of his passage. Learning to read in this way is made a condition for survival. Book knowledge and life knowledge coalesce—both require observing and drawing out implications of observations.
Seeing is important here—knowing how to see—knowing what to look for and knowing how to make sense of what is noticed.	
The pilot's seeing is based on knowledge, on experience. He has a different set of expectations than the "uneducated" or uninitiated passengers.	
How does such knowledge of the river affect the young pilot's view of it? Can he still see its beauty? Or is that beauty (which probably drew him to the river in the first place) now destroyed?	A complication: the river's story is constantly changing. An implication of this: it's easier to read a book than a river. Another: like a good book, it requires more than one reading.
	Also: How far should the river-book analogy be taken?

So far we have spoken of the double-entry notebook as a technique to improve your reading. But it can also stimulate your thinking and enhance your powers of observation. In making notes on what you observe or read, you prime yourself to look more carefully; in recording your responses, you clarify what you think, how you feel, and why. Moreover, the double-entry notebook is a useful memory aid.

In the *Notes and Observations* part you can also record quotations, jotting down passages you would like to hold onto, perhaps for use in an academic paper, or simply for your private enjoyment. You might want to set them off in some way from your other notes and observations. If you collect enough quotations you will develop within your double-entry notebook an additional book-within-a-book, a "commonplace" book in which passages you find meaningful are collected in a common place. Perhaps also, when you look through your collected quotations, you will discover connections among them, which you can then explore in the response side of your notebook or in a more formal paper.

Besides these connections, you can also think about connections between the notes you make in response to one selection, and those you make elsewhere. You can look for and explore connections between different works by the same author. Mark Twain, for example, makes multiple appearances in this book. You should be alert for connections between the subjects and ideas of these selections, and for connections between the Twain selections and others similar in subject or method.

Seeing, thinking, writing. Reading, noting, connecting. Observing, reacting, questioning. Use the double-entry notebook regularly for these and you'll develop both your competence and confidence as a reader and writer. Cultivate the habit of getting a dialogue going between yourself and what you read and also between one response and another. You'll end up talking with texts rather than just listening to them.

□   □   □

Throughout this discussion of reading and writing, we have been highlighting the connections that exist between them. In the selections that follow, you'll be invited to continue making connections, usually by playing one work off against another. The selections vary in the amount of editorial assistance provided. For almost every set of readings, however, you've been given headnotes, questions, and writing suggestions. As you work on them, keep in mind the principles and techniques of reading, writing, and thinking explained in the first part of the book. Ideally, you should annotate each work, however briefly. For the more complex ones and those you may be writing about more extensively, you should write double-entry notebook responses. If you keep a double-entry notebook of your reading throughout this section, you'll discover all kinds of connections among the selections and your responses to them.

You're being offered paired (and occasionally grouped) selections here, not to make things neatly symmetrical, but to emphasize a major theme: the following works appear mostly in two's because they argue for connections—because they represent different ways of looking at essentially similar things, usually with equal authority and conviction. This kind of arranging should encourage a greater latitude of response than you may be used to: How, for example, are you to react to two dissimilar fables with the same moral? To a classical fairy tale and a modern poem built on the same plot? You'll be pressed here to *reconsider,* not occasionally but at every turning, what you believe about literature.

The pairings are designed to help you focus your attention on some common features of the texts. By studying their comparative or contrasting elements side by side, you'll be able to see each more sharply. One will shed light on the other; you'll notice details about each that you might overlook without the presence of the other. This comparative method, by the way, is central to all learning, and is especially useful in both science and literature, as Ezra Pound has noted in *The ABC of Reading*. "The proper METHOD for studying poetry and good letters is the method of contemporary biologists, that is, careful firsthand examination of the matter, and continual COMPARISON of one 'slide' or specimen with another." Here are our first "slides."

Paired and Grouped Texts

1. FABLES

One of the oldest and most venerable literary forms is the fable. Here's an example:

THE WOLF AND THE MASTIFF

A Wolf, who was almost skin and bone—so well did the dogs of the neighborhood keep guard—met, one moonshiny night, a sleek Mastiff, who was, moreover, as strong as he was fat. Bidding the Dog good-night very humbly, he praised his good looks. "It would be easy for you," replied the Mastiff, "to get as fat as I am if you liked." "What shall I have to do?" asked the Wolf. "Almost nothing," answered the Dog. They trotted off together, but, as they went along, the Wolf noticed a bare spot on the Dog's neck. "What is that mark?" said he. "Oh, the merest trifle," answered the Dog; "the collar which I wear when I am tied up is the cause of it." "Tied up!" exclaimed the Wolf, with a sudden stop; "tied up? Can you not always then run where you please?" "Well, not quite always," said the Mastiff; "but what can that matter?" "It matters much to me," rejoined the Wolf, and, leaping away, he ran once more to his native forest.

Moral: Better starve free, than be a fat slave.

Aesop

Compare the modern fable below with the one you just read. Listen especially to the tone and voice of each. What differences in attitude and intention do you discern? What do the two fables share? Don't be satisfied with the obvious—that they're both (a) short, (b) didactic, and (c) use animals for characters. What other qualities do they share beyond these?

THE OWL WHO WAS GOD

Once upon a starless midnight, there was an owl who sat on the branch of an oak tree. Two ground moles tried to slip quietly by, unnoticed. "You!" said the owl. "Who?" they quavered, in fear and astonishment, for they could not believe it was possible for anyone to see them in that thick darkness. "You two!" said the owl. The moles hurried away and told the other creatures of the field and forest that the owl was the greatest and wisest of all animals because he could see in the dark and because he could answer any question. "I'll see about that," said a secretary bird, and he called on the owl one night when it was again very dark. "How many claws am I holding up?" said the secretary bird, "Two," said the owl, and that was right. "Can you give me another expression for 'that is to say' or 'namely'?" asked the secretary bird. "To wit," said the owl. "Why does a lover call on his love?" asked the secretary bird. "To woo," said the owl.

The secretary bird hastened back to the other creatures and reported that the owl was indeed the greatest and wisest animal in the world because he could see in the dark and because he could answer any question. "Can he see in the daytime, too?" asked a red fox. "Yes," echoed a dormouse and a French poodle. "Can he see in the daytime, too?" All the other creatures laughed loudly at this silly question, and they set upon the red fox and his friends and drove them out of the region. Then they sent a messenger to the owl and asked him to be their leader.

When the owl appeared among the animals it was high noon and the sun was shining brightly. He walked very slowly, which gave him an appearance of great dignity, and he peered about him with large, staring eyes, which gave him an air of tremendous importance. "He's God!" screamed a Plymouth Rock hen. And the others took up the cry "He's God!" So they followed him wherever he went and when he began to bump into things they began to bump into things, too. Finally he came to a concrete highway and he started up the middle of it and all the other creatures followed him. Presently a hawk, who was acting as outrider, observed a truck coming toward them at fifty miles an hour, and he reported to the secretary bird and the secretary bird reported to the owl. "There's danger ahead," said the secreatry bird. "To wit?" said the owl. The secretary bird told him. "Aren't you afraid?" He asked. "Who?" said the owl calmly, for he could not see the truck. "He's God!" cried all the creatures again, and they were still crying "He's God!" when the truck hit them and ran them down. Some of the animals were merely injured, but most of them, including the owl, were killed.

Moral: You can fool too many of the people too much of the time.

James Thurber

Considerations

Argue either side of the assertion that a fable's moral is no more nor less than what you're often assigned to root out of more complex literary forms: the work's central *theme*, a truth that can be abstracted from, say, a Shakesperian tragedy, a lyric poem, a novel, a movie, an ancient myth.

Exercises

1. It's interesting to speculate about how fables get written: whether it's a matter of first creating the moral and then writing a fable in support of it; or whether it typically works the other way around. Consider briefly which approach seems more natural to you. Then go ahead and write a fable of your own. You should observe conventions, of course: fables are short, sometimes no longer than a paragraph, and therefore have uncomplicated plots. Furthermore, there are usually only two main characters, whose points of view and lifestyles are opposed. (Consider, for example, the tortoise and the hare, the lion and the mouse, the fox and the crane.) Fables are never written in first person, are only casually concerned with setting (deep in a forest, by a pond in the woods, etc.), and deal in stereotypes rather than distinctive characters, e.g., foxes are sly and cunning, donkeys stupid, roosters vain.

This is all you need to know to write a fable. If you end up stuck for a moral (all fables have morals; otherwise they would be something else), offer your work to other readers. Have them jot down a truism evidenced by the fable and broadly applicable to life itself.

2. Take the moral from either of these fables, or any other that comes to mind, and without pondering its implications very deeply, sketch a fable to support it. No mastiffs, wolves or owls this time; the specifics of your fable must be markedly different from those offered here.

3. Re-see any one of these fables with two human characters rather than animals. Imagine them in a drawing room or barber shop or wherever, and perceive the fable's dramatic situation as part of something larger—an episode from a soap opera, a scene in a short story or novel, the core of a half-hour TV melodrama. Rough out what preceded and what will follow this segment. (You're encouraged to take this all the way to finished form, although you're expected to produce only enough detail to enable another reader to read between the lines and develop a general sense of what you have in mind.)

4. As a final fabulous exercise, read the following fables and make up morals to fit them. Provide at least two morals for each of the fables.

THE FOX AND THE GRAPES

A famished Fox saw some clusters of ripe black grapes hanging from a trellised vine. She resorted to all her tricks to get at them, but wearied herself in vain, for she could not reach them. At last she turned away, beguiling herself of her disappointment and saying: "The Grapes are sour, and not ripe as I thought."

Moral:

Aesop

THE LITTLE GIRL AND THE WOLF

One afternoon a big wolf waited in a dark forest for a little girl to come along carrying a basket of food to her grandmother. Finally a little girl did come along and she was carrying a basket of food. "Are you carrying that basket to your grandmother?" asked the wolf. The little girl said yes, she was. So the wolf asked her where her grandmother lived and the little girl told him and he disappeared into the wood.

When the little girl opened the door of her grandmother's house she saw that there was somebody in bed with a nightcap and nightgown on. She had approached no nearer than twenty-five feet from the bed when she saw that it was not her grandmother but the wolf, for even in a nightcap a wolf does not look any more like your grandmother than the Metro-Goldwyn lion looks like Calvin Coolidge. So the little girl took an automatic out of her basket and shot the wolf dead.

Moral:

James Thurber

2. PARABLES

Related to the fable is the parable. Both fable and parable tell stories. Both include morals, with the moral of the parable implied and the moral of the fable stated explicitly. But the major difference between the two is in subject and tone. Fables emphasize human nature and character, especially human failings. Most often they use animals as characters. Their tone is satirical; that is, they point out *human* foibles. Parables are stories through which a religious or ethical point is conveyed. Their purpose is instruction, their tone usually serious. Here are two Zen parables. Explain the meaning of each. What connections do you see between the two? What thematic and stylistic features do they share?

MUDDY ROAD

Tanzan and Ekido were once traveling together down a muddy road. A heavy rain was still falling.

Coming around a bend, they met a lovely girl in a silk kimono and sash, unable to cross the intersection.

"Come on, girl," said Tanzan at once. Lifting her in his arms, he carried her over the mud.

Ekido did not speak again until that night when they reached a lodging temple. Then he no longer could restrain himself. "We monks don't go near females," he told Tanzan, "especially not young and lovely ones. It is dangerous. Why did you do that?"

"I left the girl there," said Tanzan. "Are you still carrying her?"

LEARNING TO BE SILENT

The pupils of the Tendai school used to study meditation before Zen entered Japan. Four of them who were intimate friends promised one another to observe seven days of silence.

On the first day all were silent. Their meditation had begun auspiciously, but when night came and the oil lamps were growing dim one of the pupils could not help exclaiming to a servant: "Fix those lamps."

The second pupil was surprised to hear the first one talk. "We are not supposed to say a word," he remarked.

"You two are stupid. Why did you talk?" asked the third.

"I am the only one who has not talked," concluded the fourth pupil.

You're probably familiar with this parable of Jesus from the New Testament.

THE GOOD SAMARITAN

And, behold, a certain lawyer stood up, and tempted him, saying, Master, what shall I do to inherit eternal life? He said unto him, What is written in the law? how readest thou? And he answering said, Thou shalt love the Lord thy God with all thy heart, and with all thy soul, and with all thy strength, and with all thy mind; and thy neighbor as thyself. And he said unto him, Thou hast answered right: this do, and thou shalt live. But he, willing to justify himself, said unto Jesus, And who is my neighbor? And Jesus answering said, A certain man went down from Jerusalem to Jericho, and fell among thieves, which stripped him of his raiment, and wounded him, and departed, leaving him half dead. And by chance there came down a certain priest that way: and when he saw him, he passed by on the other side. And likewise a Levite, when he was at the place, came and looked on him, and passed by on the other side. But a certain Samaritan, as he journeyed, came where he was: and when he saw him, he had compassion on him, and went to him, and bound up his wounds, pouring oil and wine, and set him on his own beast, and brought him to an inn, and took care of him. And on the morrow when he departed, he took out two pence, and gave them to the host, and said unto him, Take care of him; and whatsoever thou spendest more, when I come again, I will repay thee. Which now of these three, thinkest thou, was neighbor unto him that fell among the thieves? And he said, He that shewed mercy on him. Then said Jesus unto him, Go, and do thou likewise.

Considerations

1. As you can see, the moral of "The Good Samaritan" is woven into the story rather than tacked on at the end. Furthermore, it is somewhat different in kind from the morals typically found at the bottoms of fables, which are more likely to be generalized observations about life rather than

moral imperatives. What is it that we are meant to "Go, and do . . . likewise"? Only give aid to injured strangers? Put this parable's moral into your own words and discuss its implications in today's world.

2. That Christ employed parables in his teaching has suggested to some scholars that this form provided a way to deal with sensitive subjects without openly defying the law. This is an interesting theory and serves to remind us that to succeed in his mission, Christ had to be not only an inspired leader but also a shrewd student of the political and religious climate in which he lived.

"The Sower and the Seed" parable offers a hint that Christ did indeed employ the parable form for reasons beyond its direct and memorable narrative appeal (although this too)—that it was a way to address a religious subject without openly preaching about it. (Note that even Christ's disciples are puzzled by the parable.) What is it that the listener was meant to take away? What can you assume about Christ's audience from the parable's specifics? From its general tone?

THE SOWER AND THE SEED

And when much people were gathered together, and were come to him out of every city, he spake by a parable: A sower went out to sow his seed: and as he sowed, some fell by the way side; and it was trodden down, and the fowls of the air devoured it. And some fell upon a rock; and as soon as it was sprung up, it withered away, because it lacked moisture. And some fell among thorns; and the thorns sprang up with it, and choked it. And other fell on good ground, and sprang up, and bare fruit an hundredfold. And when he had said these things, he cried, He that hath ears to hear, let him hear. And his disciples asked him, saying, What might this parable be? And he said, Unto you it is given to know the mysteries of the kingdom of God: but to others in parables; that seeing they might not see, and hearing they might not understand. Now the parable is this: The seed is the word of God. Those by the way side are they that hear; then cometh the devil, and taketh away the word out of their hearts, lest they should believe and be saved. They on the rock are they, which, when they hear, receive the word with joy; and these have no root, which for a while believe, and in time of temptation fall away. And that which fell among thorns are they, which, when they have heard, go forth, and are choked with cares and riches and pleasures of this life, and bring no fruit to perfection. But that on the good ground are they, which in an honest and good heart, having heard the word, keep it, and bring forth fruit with patience.

3. Would the fable (an established form long before Christ's time) have served his purposes as well? Why or why not? That is, what is there about the parable that might have made it particularly powerful as a Christian medium?

4. The next parable, "The Tares and the Wheat," is also *allegorical*: its objects are metaphorical; each stands for something else, has a symbolic

equivalent. The parable's meaning can be worked out by a decoding process like that which Christ used with his disciples—by determining what each significant object or detail stands for. What are the equivalences of the master, the enemy, the tares (weeds), the wheat, the barn, the harvest, the fire?

THE TARES AND THE WHEAT

Another parable put he forth unto them, saying, The kingdom of heaven is likened unto a man which sowed good seed in his field: but while men slept, his enemy came and sowed tares among the wheat, and went his way. But when the blade was sprung up, and brought forth fruit, then appeared the tares also. So the servants of the householder came and said unto him, Sir, didst not thou sow good seed in thy field? from whence then hath it tares? He said unto them, An enemy hath done this. The servants said unto him, Wilt thou then that we go and gather them up? But he said, Nay; lest while ye gather up the tares, ye root up also the wheat with them. Let both grow together until the harvest: and in the time of harvest I will say to the reapers, Gather ye together first the tares, and bind them in bundles to burn them: but gather the wheat into my barn.

Exercise

Write a parable. You can make your parable one of general symbolic import, like "The Good Samaritan", or you can make it allegorical, by working out a series of one-to-one correspondences between the details and their symbolic meanings, as in "The Sower and the Seed" or "The Tares and the Wheat." Or you can strive for the design and tone of the Zen parables.

3. THE CHARACTER

Although the parable is a decidedly religious literary form, it also has extra-religious literary characteristics. In "The Good Samaritan," for instance, we are given a character type—the person who practices the spirit of the religion he professes to believe in and live by. A very different form of "character" is presented in the following piece by the Greek writer, Theophrastus. Compare the way the character of the central figure in "The Gross Man" is built up with the way the character is presented in "The Good Samaritan."

THE GROSS MAN

Grossness is such neglect of one's person as gives offense to others. The gross man is one who goes about with an eczema, or white eruption, or diseased nails, and says that these are congenital ailments; for his father had them, and his grandfather, too, and it would be hard to foist an outsider upon their family. He's very apt to have sores on his shins and bruises on his toes, and to neglect these things so that they grow worse.

His armpits are hairy like an animal's for a long distance down his sides; his teeth are black and decayed. As he eats, he blows his nose with his fingers. As he talks, he drools, and has no sooner drunk wine than up it comes. After bathing he uses rancid oil to anoint himself; and when he goes to marketplace, he wears a thick tunic and a thin outer garment disfigured with spots of dirt.

When his mother goes to consult the soothsayer, he utters words of evil omen; and when people pray and offer sacrifices to the gods he lets the goblet fall, laughing as though he had done something amusing. When there's playing on the flute, he alone of the company claps his hands, singing an accompaniment and upbraiding the musician for stopping so soon.

Often he tries to spit across the table,—only to miss the mark and hit the butler.

"The Gross Man," a portrait of a character type, was written more than twenty-five hundred years ago. How might a modern, updated portrait of today's gross man compare with that drawn by Theophrastus?

Exercise

Write a "character" in the general manner of Theophrastus. Here are some possible topics:

The Baseball (or Hockey or Tennis or Football) Fan
The Jock
The Flirt
The Flatterer
The Weightlifter
The Cheerleader
The Hardhat
The Politician
The Salesman
The Video Junkie
The Glutton
The Preppie
The Backseat Driver
The Armchair Quarterback

The following essay, written as a syndicated newspaper column, illustrates another kind of character, this one more familiar, perhaps, than "The Gross Man." Yet both pieces offer stereotypes, profiles not only of individuals, but of entire subspecies of the human animal. Which of these two seems more a generalized picture, less recognizable as an individual? Does anyone come to mind when you read either of these selections?

THE COMPANY MAN
Ellen Goodman

He worked himself to death, finally and precisely, at 3:00 A.M. Sunday morning.

The obituary didn't say that, of course. It said that he died of a coronary thrombosis—I think that was it—but everyone among his friends and acquaintances knew it instantly. He was a perfect Type A, a workaholic, a classic, they said to each other and shook their heads—and thought for five or ten minutes about the way they lived.

This man who worked himself to death finally and precisely at 3:00 A.M. Sunday morning—on his day off—was fifty-one years old and a vice-president. He was, however, one of six vice-presidents, and one of three who might conceivably—if the president died or retired soon enough—have moved to the top spot. Phil knew that.

He worked six days a week, five of them until eight or nine at night, during a time when his own company had begun the four-day week for everyone but the executives. He worked like the Important People. He had no outside "extracurricular interests," unless, of course, you think about a monthly golf game that way. To Phil, it was work. He always ate egg salad sandwiches at his desk. He was, of course, overweight, by 20 or 25 pounds. He thought it was okay, though, because he didn't smoke.

On Saturdays, Phil wore a sports jacket to the office instead of a suit, because it was the weekend.

He had a lot of people working for him, maybe sixty, and most of them liked him most of the time. Three of them will be seriously considered for his job. The obituary didn't mention that.

But it did list his "survivors" quite accurately. He is survived by his wife, Helen, forty-eight years old, a good woman of no particular marketable skills, who worked in an office before marrying and mothering. She had, according to her daughter, given up trying to compete with his work years ago, when the children were small. A company friend said, "I know how much you will miss him." And she answered, "I already have."

"Missing him all these years," she must have given up part of herself which had cared too much for the man. She would be "well taken care of."

His "dearly beloved" eldest of the "dearly beloved" children is a hardworking executive in a manufacturing firm down South. In the day and a half before the funeral, he went around the neighborhood researching his father, asking the neighbors what he was like. They were embarrassed.

His second child is a girl, who is twenty-four and newly married. She lives near her mother and they are close, but whenever she was alone with her father, in a car driving somewhere, they had nothing to say to each other.

The youngest is twenty, a boy, a high-school graduate who has spent the last couple of years, like a lot of his friends, doing enough odd jobs to stay in grass and food. He was the one who tried to grab at his father, and tried to mean enough to him to keep the man at home. He was his father's favorite. Over the last two years, Phil stayed up nights worrying about the boy.

The boy once said, "My father and I only board here."

At the funeral, the sixty-year-old company president told the forty-eight-year-old widow that the fifty-one-year-old deceased had meant much to the company and would be missed and would be hard to replace. The widow didn't look him in the eye. She was afraid he would read her bitterness and, after all, she would need him to straighten out the finances—the stock options and all that.

Phil was overweight and nervous and worked too hard. If he wasn't at the office, he was worried about it. Phil was a Type A, a heart-attack natural. You could have picked him out in a minute from a lineup.

So when he finally worked himself to death, at precisely 3:00 A.M. Sunday morning, no one was really surprised.

By 5:00 P.M. the afternoon of the funeral, the company president had begun, discreetly of course, with care and taste, to make inquiries about his replacement. One of three men. He asked around: "Who's been working the hardest?"

Exercise

Write an imitation of "The Company Man." In selecting the details for your character, try to catch Goodman's ironic tone. You might also use some of her techniques, such as repeating words and phrases, or giving general titles rather than specific names to other figures involved with the "character."

4. FAIRY TALES

One of the most popular of story forms is the fairy tale, and one of the best-known is "Cinderella." Anne Sexton, a contemporary American poet, has written a transformed version of the story in her poem of the same title. The fairy tale is printed after Sexton's poem so you can see how she has used it and for what purposes.

CINDERELLA

You always read about it:
the plumber with twelve children
who wins the Irish Sweepstakes.
From toilets to riches.
5 That story.

Or the nursemaid,
some luscious sweet from Denmark
who captures the oldest son's heart.

From diapers to Dior.
10 That story.

Or a milkman who serves the wealthy,
eggs, cream, butter, yogurt, milk,
the white truck like an ambulance
who goes into real estate
15 and makes a pile.
From homogenized to martinis at lunch.

Or the charwoman
who is on the bus when it cracks up
and collects enough from the insurance.
20 From mops to Bonwit Teller.
That story.

Once
the wife of a rich man was on her deathbed
and she said to her daughter Cinderella:
25 Be devout. Be good. Then I will smile
down from heaven in the seam of a cloud.
The man took another wife who had
two daughters, pretty enough
but with their hearts like blackjacks.
30 Cinderella was their maid.
She slept on the sooty hearth each night
and walked around looking like Al Jolson.
Her father brought presents home from town,
jewels and gowns for the other women
35 but the twig of a tree for Cinderella.
She planted that twig on her mother's grave
and it grew to a tree where a white dove sat.
Whenever she wished for anything the dove
would drop it like an egg upon the ground.
40 The bird is important, my dears, so heed him.

Next came the ball, as you all know.
It was a marriage market.
The prince was looking for a wife.
All but Cinderella were preparing
45 and gussying up for the big event.
Cinderella begged to go too.
Her stepmother threw a dish of lentils
into the cinders and said: Pick them
up in an hour and you shall go.
50 The white dove brought all his friends;
all the warm wings of the fatherland came,
and picked up the lentils in a jiffy.

No, Cinderella, said the stepmother,
you have no clothes and cannot dance.
55 That's the way with stepmothers.

Cinderella went to the tree at the grave
and cried forth like a gospel singer:
Mama! Mama! My turtledove,
send me to the prince's ball!
60 The bird dropped down a golden dress
and delicate little gold slippers.
Rather a large package for a simple bird.
So she went. Which is no surprise.
Her stepmother and sisters didn't
65 recognize her without her cinder face
and the prince took her hand on the spot
and danced with no other the whole day.

As nightfall came she thought she'd better
get home. The prince walked her home
70 and she disappeared into the pigeon house
and although the prince took an axe and broke
it open she was gone. Back to her cinders.
These events repeated themselves for three days.
However on the third day the prince
75 covered the palace steps with cobbler's wax
and Cinderella's gold shoe stuck upon it.

Now he would find whom the shoe fit
and find this strange dancing girl for keeps.
He went to their house and the two sisters
80 were delighted because they had lovely feet.
The eldest went into a room to try the slipper on
but her big toe got in the way so she simply
sliced it off and put on the slipper.
The prince rode away with her until the white dove
85 told him to look at the blood pouring forth.
That is the way with amputations.
They don't just heal up like a wish.
The other sister cut off her heel
but the blood told as blood will.
90 The prince was getting tired.
He began to feel like a shoe salesman.
But he gave it one last try.
This time Cinderella fit into the shoe
like a love letter into its envelope.

95 At the wedding ceremony
the two sisters came to curry favor

and the white dove pecked their eyes out.
Two hollow spots were left
like soup spoons.
100 Cinderella and the prince
lived, they say, happily ever after,
like two dolls in a museum case
never bothered by diapers or dust,
never arguing over the timing of an egg,

never telling the same story twice,
105 never getting a middle-aged spread,
their darling smiles pasted on for eternity.
Regular Bobbsey Twins.
That story.

CINDERELLA
or, The Little Glass Slipper

There was once upon a time a gentleman who married for his second wife the proudest and most haughty woman that ever was known. She had been a widow, and had by her former husband two daughters of her own humor, who were exactly like her in all things. He had also by a former wife a young daughter, but of an unparalleled goodness and sweetness of temper, which she took from her mother, who was the best creature in the world.

No sooner were the ceremonies of the wedding over, but the mother-in-law began to display her ill humor; she could not bear the good qualities of this pretty girl; and the less, because they made her own daughters so much the more hated and despised. She employed her in the meanest of work of the house, she cleaned the dishes and stands, and scrubbed Madam's chamber, and those of the young Madams her daughters: she lay on the top of the house in a garret, upon a wretched straw bed, while her sisters lay in fine rooms, with floors all inlaid, upon beds of the newest fashion, and where they had looking-glasses so large that they might see themselves at their full length, from head to foot. The poor girl bore all patiently, and dared not tell her father, who would have rattled her off; for his wife governed him entirely. When she had done her work, she used to go into the chimney corner, and sit down upon the cinders, which made her commonly be called in the house *Cinderbreech*: but the youngest, who was not so rude and uncivil as the eldest, called her *Cinderella*. However, Cinderella, notwithstanding her poor clothes, was a hundred times handsomer than her sisters, though they wore the most magnificent apparel.

Now, it happened that the King's son gave a ball, and invited all persons of quality to it: our young ladies were also invited; for they made a very great figure. They were very well pleased thereat, and were very busy in choosing out such gowns, petticoats, and head-clothes as might become them best. This was a new trouble to Cinderella; for it was she that ironed her sisters' linen, and plaited their ruffles; they talked all day long of nothing but how they should be dressed. For my part, said the eldest, I'll wear my red velvet suit, with French trimming. And I, said the youngest, will have my common petticoat; but then, to make amends for that, I'll put on my gold flowered manteau, and my diamond stomacher, which is not the most indifferent in the world. They sent for the best tirewoman they could get, to dress their heads, and adjust their double pinners, and they had their red brushes and patches from Mrs. De la Poche.

Cinderella advised them the best in the world, and offered herself to dress their heads; which they were very willing she should do. As she was doing this, they said to her, Cinderella, would you not be glad to go to the ball? Ah! said she, you only banter me; it is not for such as I am to go thither. You are in the right of it, said they, it would make the people laugh to see a Cinderbreech at a ball. Any one but Cinderella would have dressed their heads awry; but she was very good, and dressed them perfectly well. They were almost two days without eating, so much were they transported with joy: they broke above a dozen of laces in trying to be laced up close, that they might have a fine slender shape, and they were continually at their looking-glass. At last the happy day came; they went to court, and Cinderella followed them with her eyes as long as she could, and when she had lost sight of them, she fell a crying.

Her godmother, who saw her all in tears, asked her what was the matter? I wish I could ____, I wish I could ____; she could not speak the rest, her tears interrupting her. Her godmother, who was a Fairy, said to her, Thou wishest thou couldst go to the ball, is it not so? Y____es, said Cinderella, with a great Sob. Well, said her godmother, be but a good girl, and I'll contrive thou shalt go. Then she took her into her chamber, and said to her, go into the garden, and bring me a pumpkin; Cinderella went immediately to gather the finest she could get, and brought it to her Godmother, not being able to imagine how this pumpkin could make her go to the ball: her godmother scooped out all the inside of it, having left nothing but the rind; she struck it with her wand, and the pumpkin immediately was turned into a fine coach, gilt all over with gold. After that, she went to look into her mouse-trap, where she found six mice all alive; she ordered Cinderella to lift up a little trap door, and she gave every mouse that went out a stroke with her wand, and the mouse was that moment turned into a fine horse, which all together made a very fine set of six horses, of a beautiful mouse-colored dapple grey. As she was at a loss for a coachman, I'll go and see, says Cinderella, if there be never a rat in the rat-trap, we'll make a coachman of him. You are in the right, said her godmother, go and see. Cinderella brought the trap to her, and in it there were three huge rats: the Fairy made choice of one of the three, which had the largest beard, and having touched him with her wand, he was turned into a fat jolly coachman, that had the finest whiskers as ever were seen.

After that, she said to her, Go into the garden, and you will find six lizards behind the watering-pot, bring them to me; she had no sooner done so, but her godmother turned them into six footmen, who skipped up immediately behind the coach, with their liveries all bedaubed with gold and silver, and clung so close behind one another, as if they had done nothing else all their lives. The Fairy then said to Cinderella, Well, you see here an equipage fit to go to the ball with; are you not pleased with it? O yes, said she, but must I go thither as I am, with these ugly nasty clothes? Her godmother only just touched her with her wand, and at the same instant her clothes were turned into cloth of gold and silver, all beset with jewels: after this, she gave her a pair of glass slippers, the finest in the world. Being thus dressed out she got into her coach; but her godmother, above all things, commanded her not to stay behind twelve o'clock at night; telling her at the same time, that if she stayed at the ball one moment longer, her coach would be a pumpkin again, her horses mice, her footmen lizards, and her clothes resume their old form.

She promised her godmother she would not fail of leaving the ball before midnight, and then departed not a little joyful at her good fortune. The King's son, who was informed that a great Princess, whom they did not know, was come, ran out to receive her; he gave her his hand as she alighted out of the coach, and led her into the hall where the company was: there was a great silence; they left off dancing, and the violins ceased to play, so attentive was everybody to contemplate the extraordinary beauties of this unknown person: there was heard nothing but a confused noise of ha! how handsome she is, ha! how handsome she is. The King himself, as old as he was, could not help looking at her, and telling the Queen in a low voice, that it was a long time since he had seen so beautiful and lovely a creature. All the ladies were busied in considering her clothes and head-dress, that they might have some made the next day after the same pattern, supposing they might get such fine materials, and as able hands to make them.

The King's son showed her to the most honorable place, and afterwards took her out to dance with him: she danced with so much gracefulness, that they more and more admired her. A fine collation was served up, of which the young Prince ate nothing, so much was he taken up in looking at her. She went and set herself down by her sisters, and showed them a thousand civilities: she gave them some of the oranges and lemons that the Prince had presented her with; which very much surprised them; for they did not know her. While the company was thus employed, Cinderella heard the clock go eleven and three quarters; upon which she immediately made a courtesy to the company; and went away as fast as she could.

As soon as she came home, she went to find out her godmother, and after having thanked her, she told her, she could not but heartily wish to go the next day to the ball, because the King's son had desired her. As she was busy in telling her godmother every thing that had passed at the ball, her two sisters knocked at the door. Cinderella went and opened it. You have stayed a long while, said she, gaping, rubbing her eyes, and stretching herself as if she had been just awaked out of her sleep; she had however no manner of inclination to sleep since they went from home. If thou hadst been at the ball, said one of her sisters, thou wouldst not have been tired with it: there came thither the most beautiful Princess, the most beautiful that ever was seen; she showed us a thousand civilities, and gave us oranges and lemons. Cinderella seemed indifferent; she asked them the name of that Princess; but they told her they did not know it, and that the King's son was very uneasy on her account, and would give all the world to know where she was. At this Cinderella smiled, and said, she must then be very handsome indeed; Lord how happy have you been, could not I see her? Ah! good Madam Charlotte, lend me your yellow suit of clothes that you wear every day. Undoubtedly, said Madam Charlotte, lend my clothes to such a Cinderbreech as you are, who is fool then? Cinderella was very glad of the refusal, for she would have been sadly put to it if her sister had lent her clothes.

The next day the two sisters were at the ball, and so was Cinderella, but dressed more richly than she was at first. The King's son was always by her, and saying abundance of tender things to her; the young lady was no ways tired, and forgot what her godmother had recommended to her, so that she heard the clock begin to strike twelve, when she thought it was only eleven, she then rose up and fled as nimble as a deer: the Prince followed her, but could not catch hold of her; she dropped one of her glass slippers, which the Prince took up very carefully; Cinderella came home quite out of breath, without coach or footmen, and in her old ugly clothes; she had nothing left her of all her finery, but one of the little slippers, fellow to that she dropped. The guards at the palace gate were asked if they had not seen a Princess go out, who said, they had seen nobody go out but a young woman very badly dressed, and who had more the air of a poor country wench than a lady.

When the two sisters returned from the ball, Cinderella asked them if they had been well diverted, and if the fine lady had been there; they told her, Yes, but that she flew away as soon as it had struck twelve o'clock, and with so much haste that she dropped one of her little glass slippers, the prettiest in the world, and which the King's son had taken up, that he did nothing but look at her all the time of the ball, and that certainly he was very much in love with the beautiful person who owned the little slipper. What they said was very true; for a few days after, the King's son caused it to be proclaimed by sound of trumpet, that he would marry her whose foot this slipper would just fit. They began to try it on upon the princesses, then the dutchesses, and all the court, but in vain; it was brought to the two sisters, who did all they possibly could to thrust their foot into the slipper, but they could not effect it. Cinderella, who saw all this, and knew the slipper, said to them laughing, Let me see if it will not fit me; her sisters burst out laughing and, began to banter her. The gentleman who was sent to try the slipper looked earnestly at Cinderella, and finding her very handsome, said, it was but just that she should try, and that he had orders to let everybody do so. He made Cinderella sit down, and putting the slipper to her foot, he found it went in very easily, and fitted her, as if it had been made of wax. The astonishment her two sisters were in was very great; but much greater, when Cinderella pulled out of her pocket the other slipper, and put it upon her foot. Upon this her godmother came in, who having touched with her wand Cinderella's clothes, made them more rich and magnificent than ever they were before.

And now, her two sisters found her to be that fine beautiful lady that they had seen at the ball. They threw themselves at her feet to beg pardon for all the ill treatment they had made her undergo. Cinderella took them up, and told them, as she embraced them, that she forgave them with all her heart, and desired them always to love her. She was conducted to the young Prince dressed as she was: he thought her more beautiful than ever, and a few days after married her. Cinderella, who was as good as handsome, gave her two sisters lodgings in the palace and married them the same day to two great lords of the court.

Considerations

1. What reactions did the poem's title trigger in you? What anticipations did you bring to the reading? How did they shape your response? (We nearly always approach a piece of writing with predispositions, expectations of our own. If we didn't, we'd all respond in the same way—an appalling notion.)

2. You've probably heard it said that there aren't any truly new stories, that it's a matter of dressing ancient plots in new or different clothing. (A Chinese version of "Cinderella" is nearly 1000 years old.) In what ways (and by what means) is Sexton's poem both a proof of and a commentary on this observation?

3. There's a good chance that the last movie or TV drama you saw contained some "Cinderella" plot elements and character types. Explain and describe them. Take this a step further: What modern movie, play, or novel is generally faithful to the "Cinderella" plot?

4. Although Sexton's version of the story is reasonably close to the original, some things about it are strikingly different. How would you characterize the differences? What are the tonal effects of phrases like "From diapers to Dior," "hearts like blackjacks," "gussying up for the big event"? How has Sexton made them work with such lines as "I will smile/down from heaven in the seam of a cloud" and "it grew to a tree where a white dove sat"?

Exercises

1. The Cinderella story isn't finished. Stories rarely are, as you know. There's always a question or two left unanswered (which soap opera writers discovered years ago), a curiosity about what will happen to a story's characters after the last page. You're invited to narrate—in poem, song, story, even film—(a) whatever happened to Cinderella's sisters; (b) what dark event shattered the marriage of the insipidly good Cinderella and her equally boring prince; or (c) the after-effects of being reduced in a twinkling from a jolly coachman back to a rat.

2. Take another well-known fairytale and re-see it in another form. You needn't tackle an entire work; a famous scene revised and cast in another form or with a different twist is enough. (How might Woody Allen, or you, approach the princess's kissing the toad to free the handsome prince?)

5. TWO VERSIONS OF THE SUSANNA STORY

The Biblical story of Susanna inspired the modern poem, "Peter Quince at the Clavier," by Wallace Stevens. Read both selections more than once and consider *how* the poet has borrowed from the Bible, what he ignores or adds, and how and why he has altered the story to suit another medium and even another intent.

THE STORY OF SUSANNA

There once lived in Babylon a man named Joakim. He married a wife named Susanna, the daughter of Hilkiah, a very beautiful and pious woman. Her parents also were upright people and instructed their daughter in the Law of Moses. Joakim was very rich, and he had a fine garden adjoining his house; and the Jews used to come to visit him because he was the most distinguished of them all.

That year two of the elders of the people were appointed judges—men of the kind of whom the Lord said,

"Lawlessness came forth from Babylon, from elders who were judges, who were supposed to guide the people."

These men came constantly to Joakim's house, and all who had cases to be decided came to them there. And it happened that when the people left at midday, Susanna would go into her husband's garden and walk about. So the two elders saw her every day, as she went in and walked about, and they conceived a passion for her. So their thoughts were perverted and they turned away their eyes, so as not to look up to heaven or consider justice in giving judgment. They were both smitten with her, but they could not disclose their passion, for they desired to have relations with her, and they watched jealously every day for a sight of her. And they said to one another,

"Let us go home, for it is dinner-time."

So they went out of the garden and parted from one another; then they turned back and encountered one another. And when they cross-questioned one another as to the explanation, they admitted their passion. Then they agreed together upon a time when they would be able to find her alone.

Now it happened, as they were watching for an opportunity, that she went in one day as usual with no one but her two maids, and wished to bathe in the garden, as it was very hot. And there was no one there except the two elders who had hidden themselves and were watching her. And she said to her maids,

"Bring me olive oil and soap, and close the doors of the garden, so that I can bathe."

And they did as she told them, and shut the doors of the garden, and went out at the side doors to bring what they had been ordered to bring, and they did not see the elders, for they were hidden. And when the maids went out, the two elders got up and ran to her and said,

"Here the doors of the garden are shut, and no one can see us, and we are in love with you, so give your consent and lie with us. If you do not, we will testify against you that there was a young man with you, and that was why you dismissed your maids."

And Susanna groaned and said,

"I am in a tight place. For if I do this, it means my death; but if I refuse, I cannot escape your hands. I had rather not do it and fall into your hands than commit sin in the Lord's sight!"

Then Susanna gave a loud scream, and the two elders shouted against her. And one of them ran and opened the garden doors. And when the people in the house heard the shouting in the garden, they rushed through the side doors to see what had happened to her. And when the elders told their story, her slaves were deeply humiliated, for such a thing had never been said about Susanna.

The next day, when the people came together to her husband, Joakim, the two elders came, full of their wicked design to put Susanna to death. And they said before the people,

"Send for Susanna, the daughter of Hilkiah, Joakim's wife."

And they did so. And she came, with her parents and her children, and all her relatives. Now Susanna was accustomed to luxury and was very beautiful. And the lawbreakers ordered her to be unveiled, for she was wearing a veil, so that they might have their fill of her beauty. And the people with her and all who saw her wept. And the two elders stood up in the midst of the people and laid their hands on her head, and she wept and looked up to heaven, for her heart trusted in the Lord. And the elders said,

"As we were walking by ourselves in the garden, this woman came in with two maids, and shut the doors of the garden and dismissed her maids, and a young man, who had been hidden, came to her, and lay down with her. And we were in the corner of the garden, and when we saw this wicked action, we ran up to them, and though we saw them together, we could not hold him, because he was stronger than we, and opened the doors and rushed out. But we laid hold of this woman and asked her who the young man was; and she would not tell us. This is our testimony."

Then the assembly believed them, as they were elders of the people and judges, and they condemned her to death. But Susanna uttered a loud cry, and said,

"Eternal God, you who know what is hidden, who know all things before they happen, you know that what they have testified to against me is false, and here I am to die when I have done none of the things they have so wickedly charged me with."

And the Lord heard her cry, and as she was being led away to be put to death, God stirred up the holy spirit of a young man named Daniel, and he loudly shouted,

"I am clear of the blood of this woman."

And all the people turned to him and said,

"What does this mean, that you have said?"

And he took his stand in the midst of them and said,

"Are you such fools, you Israelites, that you have condemned a daughter of Israel without any examination or ascertaining of the truth? Go back to the place of trial. For these men have borne false witness against her."

So all the people hurried back. And the elders said to him,

"Come, sit among us and inform us, for God has given you the right to do so."

And Daniel said to them,

"Separate them widely from one another, and I will examine them."

And when they were separated from each other, he called one of them to him, and said to him,

"You ancient of wicked days, how your sins have overtaken you, that you committed before, making unjust decisions, condemning the innocent and acquitting the guilty, although the Lord said, 'You shall not put an innocent and upright man to death.' So now, if you saw this woman, tell us, Under which tree did you see them meet?"

He answered,

"Under a mastic tree."

And Daniel said,

"You have told a fine lie against your own life, for already the angel of God has received the sentence from God, and he will cut you in two."

And he had him removed and ordered them to bring in the other. And said to him,

"You descendant of Canaan and not of Judah, beauty has beguiled you, and desire has corrupted your heart! This is how you have been treating the daughters of Israel, and they yielded to you through fear, but a daughter of Judah would not endure your wickedness. So now tell me, Under which tree did you catch them embracing each other?"

And he said,
"Under a liveoak tree."
And Daniel said to him,
"You have also told a fine lie against your own life! For the angel of God is waiting with his sword to saw you in two, to destroy you both."

And the whole company uttered a great shout and blessed God who saves those who hope in him. And they threw themselves upon the two elders, for Daniel had convicted them out of their own mouths of having borne false witness, and treated them as they had wickedly planned to treat their neighbor; they obeyed the Law of Moses and killed them. And innocent blood was saved that day.

And Hilkiah and his wife praised God for their daughter Susanna and so did Joakim her husband and all her relatives, because she had done nothing immodest. And from that day onward, Daniel had a great reputation in the eyes of the people.

PETER QUINCE AT THE CLAVIER
Wallace Stevens

I

Just as my fingers on these keys
Make music, so the selfsame sounds
On my spirit make a music, too.

Music is feeling, then, not sound;
5 And thus it is that what I feel,
Here in this room, desiring you,

Thinking of your blue-shadowed silk,
Is music. It is like the strain
Waked in the elders by Susanna.

10 Of a green evening, clear and warm,
She bathed in her still garden, while
The red-eyed elders watching, felt

The basses of their beings throb
In witching chords, and their thin blood
15 Pulse pizzicati of Hosanna.

II

In the green water, clear and warm,
Susanna lay.
She searched
The touch of springs,
20 And found
Concealed imaginings.
She sighed,
For so much melody.

Upon the bank, she stood
25 In the cool
of spent emotions.
She felt, among the leaves,
The dew
Of old devotions.

30 She walked upon the grass,
Still quavering.
The winds were like her maids,
On timid feet,
Fetching her woven scarves,
35 Yet wavering.

A breath upon her hand
Muted the night.
She turned—
A cymbal crashed,
40 And roaring horns.

III

Soon, with a noise like tambourines,
Came her attendant Byzantines.

They wondered why Susanna cried
Against the elders by her side;

45 And as they whispered, the refrain
Was like a willow swept by rain.

Anon, their lamps' uplifted flame
Revealed Susanna and her shame.

And then, the simpering Byzantines
50 Fled, with a noise like tambourines.

IV

Beauty is momentary in the mind—
The fitful tracing of a portal;
But in the flesh it is immortal.

The body dies; the body's beauty lives.
55 So evenings die, in their green going,
A wave, interminably flowing.
So gardens die, their meek breath scenting
The cowl of winter, done repenting.
So maidens die, to the auroral
60 Celebration of a maiden's choral.

Susanna's music touched the bawdy strings
Of those white elders; but escaping,
Left only Death's ironic scraping.

Now, in its immortality, it plays
65 On the clear viol of her memory,
And makes a constant sacrament of praise.

Considerations

A poem such as this one may seem too opaque, too riddlesomely complicated to justify the time and effort spent figuring out exactly what the poet had in mind. But while a decent poem is never empty of meaning, it's not necessarily a matter of there being only one narrow way to respond to it, understand it. A poem is a door ajar, not a locked one that can only be opened with one key. It asks that you bring yourself into the reading, not that you rely solely on others' understandings. If you've been taught otherwise, much good poetry will prove frustrating and finally discouraging. If you develop a relaxed and open-minded stance, however—if you allow for a dozen possibilities, not one—even if you let yourself delight in a line or stanza because of its sound alone, without coming to any conclusions about its literal meaning—you'll like poetry more.

"Peter Quince at the Clavier" is rich in possibilities. Respond to all of the following questions and you still won't have an "answer" to the poem. No book or instructor can tell you the one thing it means because, depending on how you choose to look at it, it has many meanings.

1. Begin with Peter Quince himself. What kind of fellow does he seem to be? Knowing him becomes a way to sense what he's musing about, why Susanna enters his thoughts, why she quickly replaces the "you" in "blue-shadowed silk." Or does she? The Susanna story has been the subject for many paintings. Does one of them depict her in "blue-shadowed silk," and is it this image of her the "you" the speaker addresses? Could be.

2. Does Quince, while he plinks away at the clavier (an instrument somewhat like a harpsichord), slide into an erotic revery, and is Susanna its object? Take another look at lines 16 through 35.

3. How is the Susanna story we find in the poem different from the original? The changes themselves provide one way to make sense of the poem, even if the understanding is incomplete.

4. Poetry isn't music, but has Stevens attempted here a close approximation of music? Could each stanza represent a symphonic movement, and are we meant perhaps more to *listen* to the poem rather than simply to read it? From what you know of classical music, identify the movements by name. Which, for instance, is possibly an *andante,* which a *scherzo*? Jot down or at least note the musical terms the poem incorporates. How do their specific meanings bear on possible interpretations of the lines and stanzas in which they appear? Consider too why Quince is playing a clavier rather than a piano. What is this perhaps meant to indicate?

5. Is this possibly meant to be a humorous poem? This is what one critic makes of it. Where are there elements of humor? How about lines 10 through 15? Is there anything funny to be found in the Susanna story, even if just a small scene?

6. Is the poem deeply romantic, or is it, as another critic judges it, symbolic of an earlier, Eastern approach to sexual desire, without the theme of romantic love as we know it today?

7. Then there's the Peter Quince who lives outside the poem. Stevens borrowed not only from the Bible, but from Shakespeare too. Quince is a character in *A Midsummer Night's Dream,* a play whose theme is chastity and the joys of marriage. That is, he is in the play, but yet he isn't. We find him involved in a play within the play. Did Stevens mean to suggest by the name "Peter Quince" only that there is a story within the poem as clearly enough there is? Or is he also slyly directing us to the *subject* of the play within the play, which deals with the Pyramus and Thisbe legend on which Shakespeare also based his *Romeo and Juliet*? (Remember that Romeo stole into Juliet's garden and that the elders accused Susanna of entertaining a lover in *her* garden. What do you make of that? Was the poet suggesting that there is more than one way to understand the Susanna story? If so, what's another way?) Also, are we possibly meant to react to the original Quince's being a comic character and the inner play's being an overblown, clumsy parody?

8. Finally, there's your ear for attractive lines. Literal significance aside, what lines are distinctly beautiful, memorable for their imagery, sound, shape?

6. LIVING AND DYING: TWO VILLANELLES

Both of these poems comment on that broadest of subjects, *life,* although in tone, point of view, and other particulars they differ considerably. Use both annotation and the double-entry notebook to respond to these villanelles—to discover what they mean and how and why much of their meaning comes from you.

THE WAKING
Theodore Roethke

I wake to sleep, and take my waking slow.
I feel my fate in what I cannot fear.
I learn by going where I have to go.

We think by feeling. What is there to know?
5 I hear my being dance from ear to ear.
I wake to sleep, and take my waking slow.

Of those so close beside me, which are you?
God bless the Ground! I shall walk softly there,
And learn by going where I have to go.

10 Light takes the Tree; but who can tell us how?
The lowly worm climbs up a winding stair;
I wake to sleep, and take my waking slow.

Great Nature has another thing to do
To you and me; so take the lively air,
15 And, lovely, learn by going where to go.

This shaking keeps me steady. I should know.
What falls is always. And is near.
I wake to sleep, and take my waking slow.
I learn by going where I have to go.

DO NOT GO GENTLE
INTO THAT GOOD NIGHT
Dylan Thomas

Do not go gentle into that good night,
Old age should burn and rave at close of day;
Rage, rage against the dying of the light.

Though wise men at their end know dark is right,
5 Because their words had forked no lightning they
Do not go gentle into that good night.

Good men, the last wave by, crying how bright
Their frail deeds might have danced in a green bay,
Rage, rage against the dying of the light.

10 Wild men who caught and sang the sun in flight,
And learn, too late, they grieved it on its way,
Do not go gentle into that good night.

Grave men, near death, who see with blinding sight
Blind eyes could blaze like meteors and be gay,
15 Rage, rage against the dying of the light.

And you, my father, there on the sad height,
Curse, bless, me now with your fierce tears, I pray.
Do not go gentle into that good night.
Rage, rage against the dying of the light.

Considerations

1. What are you able to observe about the two poems' points of view through close consideration of the following lines?

> . . . so take the lively air,
> And, lovely, learn by going where to go.
>   and
> Do not go gentle into that good night.
> Rage, rage against the dying of the light.

2. Both poems employ strongly ironic, even paradoxical, ideas and imagery. For example, How is it possible for ideas to dance in a bay? How can one wake to sleep? What other examples can you find? How, for you, do

these seemingly contradictory elements become reasonable, even powerful, in the poems' contexts? Or if they don't, why don't they?

Exercises

1. What's a villanelle? Without consulting other sources, determine the villanelle's formal characteristics. Note rhyme scheme, meter and stanza pattern. From these particulars you should be able to write up a description of the villanelle form that will make its distinctions clear to yourself and other readers. (There's no reason why this should be a solo project. It's an ideal subject for small-group investigation.)

2. Write a villanelle, either alone or in collaboration with one or two classmates.

7. TWO SESTINAS

Like the pair of poems in section 6 the following pair shares a common form, the intricate and beautiful sestina. By examining the way the six words at the ends of lines in the first stanza are repeated throughout the poems, you can discover the general form of the sestina. This spiraling quality is nicely illustrated in the two examples below.

SUMMER SESTINA
for Rosemary
Marie Ponsot

Her daylilies are afloat on evening
As their petals, lemon- or melon-colored,
Dim and lift in the loosening grip of light
Until their leaves lie like their shadows, there
5 Where she had hid dry corms of them, in earth
She freed of stones, weeded, and has kept rich.

With dusk, the dense air rises unmixed, rich,
Around our bodies dim with evening;
Creek air pours up the cliff to her tilled earth
10 And we swim in cool, our thoughts so colored
They can haunt each other, speechless, there
Where bubbles of birdsong burst like mental light.

Among the isles of lilies soaked with light.
We wait for moonrise that may make us rich
15 With the outsight of insight, spilling there
On her meadow when the moon ends evening
And brings back known shapes, strangely uncolored,
To this earthly garden, this gardened earth.

Deep deep go these dug fertile beds of earth
20 Where mystery prepares the thrust for light.
Years of leaffall, raked wet and discolored

With winter kitchen scraps, make the mix rich;
The odds against such loam are evening,
Worked on by her intentions buried there.

25 Why she does it is neither here nor there—
Why would anyone choose to nurture earth,
Kneel to its dayneeds, dream it at evening,
Plan and plant according to soil and light,
Apple, basil, snowpea, each season rich—
30 What counts isn't that her world is colored

Or that by it our vision is colored,
But that the gardener who gardens there
Has been so gardened by her garden: grown rich,
Grown fruitful, grown to stand upon the earth
35 In answer to the ordering of light
She lends to us this August evening.

By her teaching there we are changed, colored,
Made ready for evening, reconciled to earth,
Gardened to richness by her spendthrift light.

SESTINA
Elizabeth Bishop

September rain falls on the house.
In the failing light, the old grandmother
sits in the kitchen with the child
beside the Little Marvel Stove,
5 reading the jokes from the almanac,
laughing and talking to hide her tears.

She thinks that her equinoctial tears
and the rain that beats on the roof of the house
were both foretold by the almanac,
10 but only known to a grandmother.
The iron kettle sings on the stove.
She cuts some bread and says to the child,

It's time for tea now; but the child
is watching the teakettle's small hard tears
15 dance like mad on the hot black stove,
the way the rain must dance on the house.
Tidying up, the old grandmother
hangs up the clever almanac

on its string. Birdlike, the almanac
20 hovers half open above the child,
hovers above the old grandmother
and her teacup full of dark brown tears.

She shivers and says she thinks the house
feels chilly, and puts more wood in the stove.

25 *It was to be,* says the Marvel Stove.
I know what I know, says the almanac.
With crayons the child draws a rigid house
and a winding pathway. Then the child
puts in a man with buttons like tears
30 and shows it proudly to the grandmother.

But secretly, while the grandmother
busies herself about the stove,
the little moons fall down like tears
from between the pages of the almanac
35 in the flower bed the child
has carefully placed in the front of the house.

Time to plant tears, says the almanac.
The grandmother sings to the marvellous stove
and the child draws another inscrutable house.

Considerations

1. In "Sestina," notice how the imagery undergoes transformation: rain and boiling water become tears. In what other guises do tears appear, and who is crying and why? Notice, too, the italicized phrases in lines 13, 25, 26, and 37. The first is literal and the last metaphorical. Why do you suppose it is "time to plant tears"? And why is the image of *planting* tears appropriate? Also, how do the phrases "It was to be" and "I know what I know" help you to understand the situation the poem implies. Finally, attend to the elaborate repetitions. Explain how the end-words of lines 1–6 recur.

2. In "Summer Sestina," notice how the poet has used long, flowing sentences to create a lulling slowness of time and to convey the subtly shifting elements of light and shapes. Notice too the intricate word-play (freed . . . weeded, earthly garden . . . gardened earth), and how the poet has managed to focus on garden and gardener as if they are inseparable, even somehow synonymous. Finally, consider the symbolic implications of the poem, especially in the last three stanzas. What do they mean to you?

3. The shifting repetition of end-line words is not merely a mechanical convention of the sestina, but more importantly it's a way to reiterate and strengthen meaning. Note that all six words in "Summer Sestina" form from stanza to stanza an image that mixes earth, light, and color in ways that change pleasingly, yet also stay the same, somewhat like the relationship of earth, light, and color itself. Jot down the end-words from each stanza in order. Which six-word arrangement seems to you closest to the poem's central meaning? Which is most pleasing to your ear and eye? (Is your choice the same as most of the others? Do you feel that you have to justify it? Why or why not?)

4. Try finding in the first lines of the stanzas an inner poem. Rearrange the order of the lines until you find one that is particularly satisfying, meaningful. Or work with second lines or third lines, etc. What do the results suggest about the sestina? About poetry? About the functions and significances of form in shaping meaning?

Exercise

You're encouraged to write a sestina, but if this seems too ambitious or time-consuming, compose a briefer work of similar design, either alone or with a partner or two. Make it three or four six-line (or even five-line) stanzas, each using the same end-words, in shifting order.

Make note of the ways you approach the writing, too, and compare them with others' ways. Did you, for example, settle on six words that seemed promising and then, line by line, fit them to some central meaning? Or did you work from the other direction, first developing a stanza that had some meaning for you, without concerning yourself about what word ended each line? Or what?

8. TWO VERSIONS OF A POEM: REVISION

Here are two versions of a poem by Walt Whitman. The one immediately below appeared in Whitman's *Leaves of Grass*; the other version is an earlier draft. Consider (and use the speculative tools I've urged on you) whether the distinctions between the two are more suggestive of stylistic polishing or revisions in the poet's understanding of the poem's meaning. Try to determine too whether there are clear distinctions between *reshaping* and *rethinking*, and if so, what they are.

A NOISELESS PATIENT SPIDER

A noiseless patient spider,
I mark'd where on a little promontory it stood isolated,
Mark'd how to explore the vacant vast surrounding,
It launch'd forth filament, filament, filament, out of itself,
5   Ever unreeling them, ever tirelessly speeding them.
And you O my soul where you stand,
Surrounded, detached, in measureless oceans of space,
Ceaselessly musing, venturing, throwing, seeking the spheres to
    connect them,
Till the bridge you will need be form'd, till the ductile anchor hold,
10 Till the gossamer thread you fling catch somewhere, O my soul.

Considerations

1. Although there is no stanza division, the poem falls into two parts. With what line does the second part begin? By what metaphor are the two parts connected?

2. What words in the second part parallel those in the first part? The spider, in line 2, for example, is described as "isolated." What word(s) in lines 5–10 suggest a similar situation? What additional connections can you make between specific words and phrases of the two parts?

3. In the version below, Whitman's use of the spider is less effective. Specifically why (unless you disagree) does it work less well? What other symbol does Whitman stress here? What single phrase has it been reduced to in the version above?

4. Newer versions of a work aren't necessarily more effective than earlier ones (but don't take this as an argument against revision). Here, however, it seems rather obvious that there is dramatic improvement from one version to another. In a five-minute mini-lecture or brief paper, deal with a particular change and comment on its contribution to the later version as a whole.

THE SOUL, REACHING, THROWING OUT FOR LOVE

The Soul, reaching, throwing out for love,
As the spider, from some little promontory, throwing out filament after filament, tirelessly out of itself, that one at least may catch and form a link, a bridge, a connection
O I saw one passing along, saying hardly a word—yet full of love I detected him, by certain signs
O eyes wishfully turning! O silent eyes!
For then I thought of you o'er the world,
O latent oceans, fathomless oceans of love!
O waiting oceans of love! yearning and fervid! and of you sweet souls perhaps in the future, delicious and long:
But Death, unknown on the earth—ungiven, dark here, unspoken, never born:
You fathomless latent souls of love—you pent and unknown oceans of love!

9. INNOCENCE AND EXPERIENCE

The two poems by William Blake below were published respectively in collections titled *Songs of Innocence* and *Songs of Experience.* It will be readily clear why, although you may find that your connotations of "innocence" and "experience" differ somewhat from Blake's.

THE CHIMNEY SWEEPER

When my mother died I was very young,
And my father sold me while yet my tongue,
Could scarcely cry weep weep weep weep.
So your chimneys I sweep & in soot I sleep.

5 Theres little Tom Dacre, who cried when his head
That curl'd like a lambs back, was shav'd, so I said.

Hush Tom never mind it, for when your head's bare,
You know that the soot cannot spoil your white hair.

And so he was quiet, & that very night,
10 As Tom was a sleeping he had such a sight,
That thousands of sweepers Dick, Joe, Ned & Jack
Were all of them lock'd up in coffins of black

And by came an Angel who had a bright key,
And he opened the coffins & set them all free.
15 Then down a green plain leaping laughing they run
And wash in a river and shine in the Sun.

Then naked & white, all their bags left behind,
They rise upon clouds, and sport in the wind.
And the Angel told Tom if he'd be a good boy,
20 He'd have God for his father & never want joy.

And so Tom awoke and we rose in the dark
And got with our bags & our brushes to work.
Tho' the morning was cold, Tom was happy and warm,
So if all do their duty, they need not fear harm.

THE CHIMNEY SWEEPER

A little black thing among the snow:
Crying weep, weep, in notes of woe!
Where are thy father & mother? say?
They are both gone up to the church to pray.

Because I was happy upon the heath,
And smil'd among the winters snow:
They clothed me in the clothes of death,
And taught me to sing the notes of woe.

And because I am happy, & dance & sing,
They think they have done me no injury:
And are gone to praise God & his Priest & King
Who make up a heaven of our misery.

Considerations

1. What broad distinctions between innocence and experience are implied in these poems? By what particular and general means has Blake conveyed the distinctions? Do you think the speaker in both poems is the same?

2. Which, for you, is the more effective poem? What does "effective" mean to you? (Consider your probable response to each had you not read the other.)

3. Which of the following paired poems was included in *Songs of Innocence* and which in *Songs of Experience*? Explain how you decided. In both pairs of poems, what has happened to change the tone of the songs?

NURSE'S SONG

When the voices of children, are heard on the green
And whisperings are in the dale:
The days of my youth rise fresh in my mind,
My face turns green and pale.

Then come home my children, the sun is gone down
And the dews of night arise
Your spring & your day, are wasted in play
And your winter and night in disguise.

NURSE'S SONG

When the voices of children are heard on the green
And laughing is heard on the hill,
My heart is at rest within my breast
And everything else is still.

5 Then come home my children, the sun is gone down
And the dews of night arise
Come come leave off play, and let us away
Till the morning appears in the skies.

No no let us play, for it is yet day
10 And we cannot go to sleep
Besides in the sky, the little birds fly
And the hills are all covered with sheep.

Well well go & play till the light fades away
And then go home to bed
15 The little ones leaped & shouted & laugh'd
And all the hills ecchoed.

Exercise

Choose any two poems, not necessarily by the same poet, and in a brief paper explain how and why one touches on the theme of innocence, the other on experience. Or comment in writing about a poem that examines both themes. You probably won't have to look far; the fall from innocence is one of the most pervasive themes in literature.

10. TWO SHAPES

Poetry comes in many shapes, and although we may not be deeply conscious of its functions, shape can enhance meaning and heighten a reader's pleasure. Sometimes, as with these next poems, shape not only aids meaning, it becomes an essential aspect of it.

CRISE DE COEUR
John Hollander

                        Help me
                    O help me for only
                 a brief while ago I hung red
              and yet erect in the world of wide
           white reticent backgrounds against which
         I registered Correctly placed as if pointing
        out a direction downwards towards which all must
       fall I stood firm I beat out the cut time which we
      always hope we have to count on More surely than as an
     emblem cut into a thick-skinned tree transfixed by a dart
    perhaps I shone and signified Being all crimson and heraldic
    as I was and near-kin to the promiscuous scarlet pips of cards
   I was unyielding and if conventional then surely constant But as
  I stood in my round-shouldered pride you struck Some fell impulse
 seized me as if for a moment the surface I clung to had gone blank
like that As if a glimpse of folded arm or breast or thigh curved
 under itself plunging deep into its own shadow had unhung me quite
  Or as if some loss as of dry leaves blown across marble corridors
   was felt for an instant even while unseen I fell tripping over a
    minute lapse in lifes surface I fell heavily ah indeed flipped
     over and now I lie bleeding on my sheet a sick valentine who
      short of breath can barely sigh BE MINE before I fail for
       even the short while that will be forever Lying here I
        have blackened some and paled Yet recognizable for
         what I am and unable to leap I rest uneasy Fever
          warms me up towards evening after failure of
           nerve has made a noon too bright to bear
            bringing in place of sleep a sense
              of something wrong something
                 half-unbroken   Like
                       a heart

Considerations

1. In "Crise de Coeur" (crisis of the heart), we're asked to accept the idea of a heart that speaks. But that's not all. Beyond this, what does Hollander request of the reader?

2. What does the speaker's problem seem to boil down to? What are its causes? To whom are the cries for help directed?

3. Is the poem's tone humorous, mock-tragic, sad, maudlin, or what? What made you decide what you decided?

4. Is the poem, in part, at least, a spoof of the figurative qualities we associate with this organ? At what points does this possibility suggest itself? Could the poem's Valentine shape be part of the spoof? If so, how?

THE ALTAR
George Herbert

    A broken **ALTAR**, Lord, thy servant rears,
    Made of a heart, and cemented with tears:
    Whose parts are as thy hand did frame;
    No workman's tool hath touched the same.
        A **HEART** alone
        Is such a stone,
        As nothing but
        Thy pow'r doth cut.
        Wherefore each part
        Of my hard heart
        Meets in this frame,
        To praise thy name.
    That, if I chance to hold my peace,
    These stones to praise thee may not cease.
    O let thy blessed **SACRIFICE** be mine,
    And sanctify this **ALTAR** to be thine.

Considerations

1. Although both poems deal emphatically with the heart, Herbert's work is more complex than Hollander's. In the first two lines the speaker has figuratively made an altar "of a heart." Why is the altar "broken"? How would the meaning of the lines change if "broken" modified "heart" instead of "ALTAR"? Or would it? In line 3 does "parts" refer to the altar or to the heart? What is it that "No workman's tool hath touched"?

2. How are we meant to understand line 5? Does "alone" mean *isolated* or *only*? How do lines 7 and 8 help to answer this question? In line 10 does "hard heart" mean *cold, insensitive* or *stone-like*? In line 11, to what does "frame" refer: the bodily frame? the framed shape of the altar? the frame of the poem itself? And how does line 14 help to suggest which?

3. Which of the two shapes is for you the more significantly related to the poem's meaning? Why?

Exercises

1. As you have worked it out, put the meaning of "The Altar" in a single sentence.

2. Try a shaped poem of your own (the point being to have fun in the process).

11. TWO VIEWS OF PERFECTION

Benjamin Franklin was a conscious perfectionist. The following passage from his autobiography details his determination to arrive at moral perfection. In reading about Franklin's "bold and arduous Project," consider what qualities of character he reveals, whether you agree with his choices of "Virtues" (what would you add, delete?), and whether the plan he outlines seems reasonable.

The Franklin piece is followed by a response to it by English writer D. H. Lawrence. Provide a set of annotations and a double-entry notebook reaction, first to Franklin, then to Lawrence.

ARRIVING AT PERFECTION

It was about this time that I conceiv'd the bold and arduous Project of arriving at moral Perfection. I wish'd to live without committing any Fault at any time; I would conquer all that either Natural Inclination, Custom, or Company might lead me into. As I knew, or thought I knew, what was right and wrong, I did not see why I might not *always* do the one and avoid the other. But I soon found I had undertaken a Task of more Difficulty than I had imagined: While my Care was employ'd in guarding against one Fault, I was often surpriz'd by another. Habit took the Advantage of Inattention. Inclination was sometimes too strong for Reason. I concluded at length, that the mere speculative Conviction that it was our Interest to be compleatly virtuous, was not sufficient to prevent our Slipping, and that the contrary Habits must be broken and good Ones acquired and established, before we can have any Dependance on a steady uniform Rectitude of Conduct. For this purpose I therefore contriv'd the following Method.

In the various Enumerations of the moral Virtues I had met with in my Reading, I found the Catalogue more or less numerous, as different Writers included more or fewer Ideas under the same Name. Temperance, for Example, was by some confin'd to Eating and Drinking, while by others it was extended to mean the moderating every other Pleasure, Appetite, Inclination or Passion, bodily or mental, even to our Avarice and Ambition. I propos'd to myself, for the sake of Clearness, to use rather more Names with fewer Ideas annex'd to each, than a few Names with more Ideas; and I included after Thirteen Names of Virtues all that at that time occurr'd to me as necessary or desirable, and annex'd to each a short Precept, which fully express'd the Extent I gave to its Meaning.

These Names of Virtues with their Precepts were

1. *Temperance.* Eat not to Dulness. Drink not to Elevation.
2. *Silence.* Speak not but what may benefit others or your self. Avoid trifling conversation.
3. *Order.* Let all your Things have their Places. Let each Part of your Business have its Time.
4. *Resolution.* Resolve to perform what you ought. Perform without fail what you resolve.
5. *Frugality.* Make no Expence but to do good to others or yourself: i.e. Waste nothing.

6. *Industry.* Lose no Time. Be always employ'd in something useful. Cut off all unnecessary Actions.
7. *Sincerity.* Use no hurtful Deceit. Think innocently and justly; and, if you speak; speak accordingly.
8. *Justice.* Wrong none, by doing Injuries or omitting the Benefits that are your Duty.
9. *Moderation.* Avoid Extreams. Forbear resenting Injuries so much as you think they deserve.
10. *Cleanliness.* Tolerate no Uncleanness in Body, Cloaths or Habitation.
11. *Tranquility.* Be not disturbed at Trifles, or at Accidents common or unavoidable.
12. *Chastity.* Rarely use Venery but for Health or Offspring; Never to Dulness, Weakness, or the Injury of your own or another's Peace or Reputation.
13. *Humility.* Imitate Jesus and Socrates.

My intention being to acquire the *Habitude* of all these Virtues, I judg'd it would be well not to distract my Attention by attempting the whole at once, but to fix it on one of them at a time, and when I should be Master of that, then to proceed to another, and so on till I should have gone thro' the thirteen. And as the previous Acquisition of some might facilitate the Acquisition of certain others, I arrang'd them with that View as they stand above. *Temperance* first, as it tends to procure that Coolness and Clearness of Head, which is so necessary where constant Vigilance was to be kept up, and Guard maintained, against the unremitting Attraction of ancient Habits, and the Force of perpetual Temptations. This being acquir'd and establish'd, *Silence* would be more easy, and my Desire being to gain Knowledge at the same time that I improv'd in Virtue, and considering that in Conversation it was obtain'd rather by the Use of the Ears than of the Tongue, and therefore wishing to break a Habit I was getting into of Prattling, Punning and Joking, which only made me acceptable to trifling Company, I gave *Silence* the second Place. This, and the next, *Order,* I expected would allow me more Time for attending to my Project and my Studies; RESOLUTION once become habitual, would keep me firm in my Endeavors to obtain all the subsequent Virtues; *Frugality* and *Industry,* by freeing me from my remaining Debt, and producing Affluence and Independance would make more easy the Practice of *Sincerity* and *Justice,* etc. etc. Conceiving then that agreable to the Advice of Pythagoras in his Golden Verses, daily examination would be necessary, I contriv'd the following Method for conducting that Examination.

I made a little Book in which I allotted a Page for each of the Virtues. I rul'd each Page with red Ink so as to have seven Columns, one for each Day of the Week, marking each Column with a Letter for the Day. I cross'd these Columns with thirteen red Lines, marking the Beginning of each Line with the first Letter of one of the Virtues, on which Line and in its proper Column I might mark by a little black Spot every Fault I found upon Examination, to have been committed respecting that Virtue upon that Day.

	TEMPERANCE					
	Eat not to Dulness. *Drink not to Elevation.*					
	S	M	T	W	T	F	S
T							
S	••	•		•		•	
O	•	•	•		•	•	•
R			•		•		
F		•			•		
I			•				
S							
J							
M							
Cl.							
T							
Ch.							
H							

I determined to give a Week's strict Attention to each of the Virtues successively. Thus in the first Week my great Guard was to avoid every the least Offence against Temperance, leaving the other Virtues to their ordinary Chance, only marking every Evening the faults of the Day. Thus if in the first Week I could keep my first Line marked T clear of Spots, I suppos'd the Habit of that Virtue so much strengthen'd and its opposite weaken'd, that I might venture extending my Attention to include the next, and for the following Week keep both Lines clear of Spots. Proceeding thus to the last, I could go thro' a Course compleat in Thirteen Weeks, and four Courses in a Year. And like him who having a Garden to weed, does not attempt to eradicate all the bad Herbs at once, which would exceed his Reach and his Strength, but works on one of the Beds at a time, and having accomplish'd the first proceeds to a second; so I should have, (I hoped) the encouraging Pleasure of seeing on my Pages the Progress I made in Virtue, by clearing successively my Lines of their Spots, till in the End by a Number of Courses,

I should be happy in viewing a clean Book after a thirteen Weeks daily Examination. . . .

Here is Lawrence's response, which appeared originally in his *Studies in Classic American Literature.* It will be clear from the start that Lawrence is on the attack, but is it only Franklin he is after, or something more? Is his response, as he says, only a matter of having fun (at Franklin's expense)? Why or why not?

BENJAMIN FRANKLIN

The Perfectibility of Man! Ah heaven, what a dreary theme! The perfectibility of the Ford car! The perfectibility of which man? I am many men. Which of them are you going to perfect? I am not a mechanical contrivance.

Education! Which of the various me's do you propose to educate, and which do you propose to suppress?

Anyhow, I defy you. I defy you, oh society, to educate me or to suppress me, according to your dummy standards.

The ideal man! And which is he, if you please? Benjamin Franklin or Abraham Lincoln? The ideal man! Roosevelt or Porfirio Díaz?

There are other men in me, besides this patient ass who sits here in a tweed jacket. What am I doing, playing the patient ass in a tweed jacket? Who am I talking to? Who are you, at the other end of this patience?

Who are you? How many selves have you? And which of these selves do you want to be?

Is Yale College going to educate the self that is in the dark of you, or Harvard College?

The ideal self! Oh, but I have a strange and fugitive self shut out and howling like a wolf or a coyote under the ideal windows. See his red eyes in the dark? This is the self who is coming into his own.

The perfectibility of man, dear God! When every man as long as he remains alive is in himself a multitude of conflicting men. Which of these do you choose to perfect, at the expense of every other?

Old Daddy Franklin will tell you. He'll rig him up for you, the pattern American. Oh, Franklin was the first downright American. He knew what he was about, the sharp man. He set up the first dummy American.

At the beginning of his career this cunning little Benjamin drew up for himself a creed that should "satisfy the professors of every religion, but shock none". . . .

Man is a moral animal. All right. I am a moral animal. And I'm going to remain such. I'm not going to be turned into a virtuous little automaton as Benjamin would have me. "This is good, that is bad. Turn the little handle, and let the good tap flow," saith Benjamin, and all America with him. "But first of all extirpate those savages who are always turning on the bad tap."

I am a moral animal. But I am not a moral machine. I don't work with a little set of handles or levers. The Temperance-silence-order-resolution-frugality-industry-chastity-humility keyboard is not going to get me going. I'm really not just an automatic piano with a moral Benjamin getting tunes out of me.

Here's my creed, against Benjamin's. This is what I believe:

"That I am I."

"That my soul is a dark forest."

"That my known self will never be more than a little clearing in the forest."

"That gods, strange gods, come forth from the forest into the clearing of my known self, and then go back."

"That I must have the courage to let them come and go."

"That I will never let mankind put anything over me, but that I will try always to recognize and submit to the gods in me and the gods in other men and women."

There is my creed. He who runs may read. He who prefers to crawl, or to go by gasoline, can call it rot.

Then for a "list." It is rather fun to play at Benjamin.

1

TEMPERANCE

Eat and carouse with Bacchus, or munch dry bread with Jesus, but don't sit down without one of the gods.

2

SILENCE

Be still when you have nothing to say; when genuine passion moves you, say what you've got to say, and say it hot.

3

ORDER

Know that you are responsible to the gods inside you and to the men in whom the gods are manifest. Recognize your superiors and your inferiors, according to the gods. This is the root of all order.

4

RESOLUTION

Resolve to abide by your own deepest promptings, and to sacrifice the smaller thing to the greater. Kill when you must, and be killed the same: the *must* coming from the gods inside you, or from the men in whom you recognize the Holy Ghost.

5
Frugality

Demand nothing; accept what you see fit. Don't waste your pride or squander your emotion.

6
Industry

Lose no time with ideals; serve the Holy Ghost; never serve mankind.

7
Sincerity

To be sincere is to remember that I am I, and that the other man is not me.

8
Justice

The only justice is to follow the sincere intuition of the soul, angry or gentle. Anger is just, and pity is just, but judgment is never just.

9
Moderation

Beware of absolutes. There are many gods.

10
Cleanliness

Don't be too clean. It impoverishes the blood.

11
Tranquillity

The soul has many motions, many gods come and go. Try and find your deepest issue, in every confusion, and abide by that. Obey the man in whom you recognize the Holy Ghost; command when your honour comes to command.

12
Chastity

Never "use" venery at all. Follow your passional impulse, if it be answered in the other being; but never have any motive in mind, neither offspring nor health nor even pleasure, nor even service. Only know that "venery" is of the great gods. An offering-up of yourself to the very great gods, the dark ones, and nothing else.

13
Humility

See all men and women according to the Holy Ghost that is within them. Never yield before the barren.

There's my list. I have been trying dimly to realize it for a long time, and only America and old Benjamin have at last goaded me into trying to formulate it. . . .

Considerations

1. Consider that a century and a half, as well as an ocean, separate Franklin and Lawrence. In this light, could it be said that Lawrence's response is thus narrow-mindedly neglectful of cultural and historical change? Or is Franklin's "Project" so priggish and simplistic that, regardless of time and distance, its author is fairly called to account for it? Did *you* view Franklin more unfavorably after reading Lawrence? Or more favorably? If either, account for your change of heart.
2. Whose "creed" better suits the human condition as you know it to be, Lawrence's or Franklin's? Why?
3. Human perfectibility is not a uniquely American idea, of course, but it does find strong and continuing expression in our nation's institutions and beliefs. List specific examples of this theme (the self-made man, for example), and comment on their possible connections with Franklin's piece.
4. What does Lawrence probably mean in maxims 1, 3, 4, 8? How do they compare with Franklin's versions?

Exercise

Write your own "bold and arduous" plan for self-improvement, commenting briefly on its salient points, as Franklin and Lawrence do. (You don't have to be serious about your "Project." If a parody seems suitable, then parody.)

12. REMEMBERING PARENTS

The two selections that follow are both first chapters of books. Russell Baker, in his autobiography, *Growing Up,* remembers his mother near the end of her life. And Geoffrey Wolff describes his father in a biography, *The Duke of Deception.* For each piece use annotation or the double-entry notebook to record your observations and responses.

from
GROWING UP

At the age of eighty my mother had her last bad fall, and after that her mind wandered free through time. Some days she went to weddings and funerals that had taken place half a century earlier. On others she presided over family dinners cooked on Sunday afternoons for children who were now gray with age. Through all this she lay in bed but moved across time, traveling among the dead decades with a speed and ease beyond the gift of physical science.

"Where's Russell?" she asked one day when I came to visit at the nursing home.

"I'm Russell," I said.

She gazed at this improbably overgrown figure out of an inconceivable future and promptly dismissed it.

"Russell's only this big," she said, holding her hand, palm down, two feet from the floor. That day she was a young country wife with chickens in the backyard and a view of hazy blue Virginia mountains behind the apple orchard, and I was a stranger old enough to be her father.

Early one morning she phoned me in New York. "Are you coming to my funeral today?" she asked.

It was an awkward question with which to be awakened. "What are you talking about, for God's sake?" was the best reply I could manage.

"I'm being buried today," she declared briskly, as though announcing an important social event.

"I'll phone you back," I said and hung up, and when I did phone back she was all right, although she wasn't all right, of course, and we all knew she wasn't.

She had always been a small woman—short, light-boned, delicately structured—but now, under the white hospital sheet, she was becoming tiny. I thought of a doll with huge, fierce eyes. There had always been a fierceness in her. It showed in that angry, challenging thrust of the chin when she issued an opinion, and a great one she had been for issuing opinions.

"I tell people exactly what's on my mind," she had been fond of boasting. "I tell them what I think, whether they like it or not." Often they had not liked it. She could be sarcastic to people in whom she detected evidence of the ignoramus or the fool.

"It's not always good policy to tell people exactly what's on your mind," I used to caution her.

"If they don't like it, that's too bad," was her customary reply, "because that's the way I am."

And so she was. A formidable woman. Determined to speak her mind, determined to have her way, determined to bend those who opposed her. In that time when I had known her best, my mother had hurled herself at life with chin thrust forward, eyes blazing, and an energy that made her seem always on the run.

She ran after squawking chickens, an axe in her hand, determined on a beheading that would put dinner in the pot. She ran when she made beds, ran when she set the table. One Thanksgiving she burned herself badly when, running up from the cellar oven with the ceremonial turkey, she tripped on the stairs and tumbled back down, ending at the bottom in the debris of giblets, hot gravy, and battered turkey. Life was combat, and victory was not to the lazy, the timid, the slugabed, the drugstore cowboy, the libertine, the mushmouth afraid to tell people exactly what was on his mind whether people liked it or not. She ran.

But now the running was over. For a time I could not accept the inevitable. As I sat by her bed, my impulse was to argue her back to reality. On my first visit to the hospital in Baltimore, she asked who I was.

"Russell," I said.

"Russell's way out west," she advised me.

"No, I'm right here."

"Guess where I came from today?" was her response.

"Where?"

"All the way from New Jersey."

"When?"

"Tonight."

"No. You've been in the hospital for three days," I insisted.

"I suggest the thing to do is calm down a little bit," she replied. "Go over to the house and shut the door."

Now she was years deep into the past, living in the neighborhood where she had settled forty years earlier, and she had just been talking with Mrs. Hoffman, a neighbor across the street.

"It's like Mrs. Hoffman said today: The children always wander back to where they come from," she remarked.

"Mrs. Hoffman has been dead for fifteen years."

"Russ got married today," she replied.

"I got married in 1950," I said, which was the fact.

"The house is unlocked," she said.

So it went until a doctor came by to give one of those oral quizzes that medical men apply in such cases. She failed catastrophically, giving wrong answers or none at all to "What day is this?" "Do you know where you are?" "How old are you?" and so on. Then, a surprise.

"When is your birthday?" he asked.

"November 5, 1897," she said. Correct. Absolutely correct.

"How do you remember that?" the doctor asked.

"Because I was born on Guy Fawkes Day," she said.

"Guy Fawkes?" asked the doctor. "Who is Guy Fawkes?"

She replied with a rhyme I had heard her recite time and again over the years when the subject of her birth date arose:

> "Please to remember the Fifth of November,
> Gunpowder treason and plot.
> I see no reason why gunpowder treason
> Should ever be forgot."

Then she glared at this young doctor so ill informed about Guy Fawkes' failed scheme to blow King James off his throne with barrels of gunpowder in 1605. She had been a schoolteacher, after all, and knew how to glare at a dolt. "You may know a lot about medicine, but you obviously don't know any history," she said. Having told him exactly what was on her mind, she left us again.

The doctors diagnosed a hopeless senility. Not unusual, they said. "Hardening of the arteries" was the explanation for laymen. I thought it was more complicated than that. For ten years or more the ferocity with which she had once attacked life had been turning to a rage against the weakness, the boredom, and the absence of love that too much age had brought her. Now, after the last bad fall, she seemed to have broken chains that imprisoned her in a life she had come to hate and to return to a time inhabited by people who loved her, a time in which she was needed. Gradually I understood. It was the first time in years I had seen her happy.

She had written a letter three years earlier which explained more than "hardening of the arteries." I had gone down from New York to Baltimore, where she lived, for one of my infrequent visits and, afterwards, had written her with some banal advice to look for the silver lining, to count her blessings instead of burdening others with her miseries. I suppose what it really amounted to was a threat that if she was not more cheerful during my visits I would not come to see her very often. Sons are capable of such letters. This one was written out of a childish faith in the eternal strength of parents, a naive belief that age and wear could be overcome by an effort of will, that all she needed was a good pep talk to recharge a flagging spirit. It was such a foolish, innocent idea, but one thinks of parents differently from other people. Other people can become frail and break, but not parents.

She wrote back in an unusually cheery vein intended to demonstrate, I suppose, that she was mending her ways. She was never a woman to apologize, but for one moment with the pen in her hand she came very close. Referring to my visit, she wrote: "If I seemed unhappy to you at times—" Here she drew back, reconsidered, and said something quite different:

"If I seemed unhappy to you at times, I am, but there's really nothing anyone can do about it, because I'm just so very tired and lonely that I'll just go to sleep and forget it." She was then seventy-eight.

Now, three years later, after the last bad fall, she had managed to forget the fatigue and loneliness and, in these free-wheeling excursions back through time, to recapture happiness. I soon stopped trying to wrest her back to what I considered the real world and tried to travel along with her on those fantastic swoops into the past. One day when I arrived at her bedside she was radiant.

"Feeling good today," I said.

"Why shouldn't I feel good?" she asked. "Papa's going to take me up to Baltimore on the boat today."

At that moment she was a young girl standing on a wharf at Merry Point, Virginia, waiting for the Chesapeake Bay steamer with her father, who had been dead sixty-one years. William Howard Taft was in the White House, Europe still drowsed in the dusk of the great century of peace, America was a young country, and the future stretched before it in beams of crystal sunlight. "The greatest country on God's green earth," her father might have said, if I had been able to step into my mother's time machine and join him on the wharf with the satchels packed for Baltimore.

I could imagine her there quite clearly. She was wearing a blue dress with big puffy sleeves and long black stockings. There was a ribbon in her hair and a big bow tied on the side of her head. There had been a childhood photograph in her bedroom which showed all this, although the colors of course had been added years later by a restorer who tinted the picture.

About her father, my grandfather, I could only guess, and indeed, about the girl on the wharf with the bow in her hair, I was merely sentimentalizing. Of my mother's childhood and her people, of their time and place, I knew very little. A world had lived and died, and though it was part of my blood and bone I knew little more about it than I knew of the world of the pharaohs. It was useless now to ask for help from my mother. The orbits of her mind rarely touched present interrogators for more than a moment.

Sitting at her bedside, forever out of touch with her, I wondered about my own children, and their children, and children in general, and about the disconnections between children and parents that prevent them from knowing each other. Children rarely want to know who their parents were before they were parents, and when age finally stirs their curiosity there is no parent left to tell them. If a parent does lift the curtain a bit, it is often only to stun the young with some exemplary tale of how much harder life was in the old days.

I had been guilty of this when my children were small in the early 1960s and living the affluent life. It galled me that their childhoods should be, as I thought, so easy when my own had been, as I thought, so hard. I had developed the habit, when they complained about the steak being overcooked or the television being cut off, of lecturing them on the harshness of life in my day.

"In my day all we got for dinner was macaroni and cheese, and we were glad to get it."

"In my day we didn't have any television."

"In my day . . ."

"In my day . . ."

At dinner one evening a son had offended me with an inadequate report card, and as I leaned back and cleared my throat to lecture, he gazed at me with an expression of unutterable resignation and said, "Tell me how it was in your days, Dad."

I was angry with him for that, but angrier with myself for having become one of those ancient bores whose highly selective memories of the past become transparently dishonest even to small children. I tried to break the habit, but must have failed. A few years later my son was referring to me when I was out of earshot as "the old-timer." Between us there was a dispute about time. He looked upon the time that had been my future in a disturbing way. My future was his past, and being young, he was indifferent to the past.

As I hovered over my mother's bed listening for muffled signals from her childhood, I realized that this same dispute had existed between her and me. When she was young, with life ahead of her, I had been her future and resented it. Instinctively, I wanted to break free, cease being a creature defined by her time, consign her future to the past, and create my own. Well, I had finally done that, and then with my own children, I had seen my exciting future become their boring past.

These hopeless end-of-the-line visits with my mother made me wish I had not thrown off my own past so carelessly. We all come from the past, and children ought to know what it was that went into their making, to know that life is a braided cord of humanity stretching up from time long gone, and that it cannot be defined by the span of a single journey from diaper to shroud.

I thought that someday my own children would understand that. I thought that, when I am beyond explaining, they would want to know what the world was like when my mother was young and I was younger, and we two relics passed together through strange times. I thought I should try to tell them how it was to be young in the time before jet planes, superhighways, H-bombs, and the global village of television. I realized I would have to start with my mother and her passion for improving the male of the species, which in my case took the form of forcing me to "make something of myself."

Lord, how I hated those words. . . .

Considerations

Some literature, despite what you may have been taught to think, says only what it seems to say, without hidden meanings or complicated messages. The Baker piece falls into this category (although you may find in it meanings that I missed): a well-known writer writes about his failing mother with wit and grace, tolerance and affection, then turns to reflecting on the need for maintaining connections among the generations, about "the braided cord of humanity" that should hold us all together. Rather than consider closely the technical qualities of the work, then, comment instead on what this piece may have suggested to you:

1. What do you want *your* children to know about you? About the age you grew up in and what about it was beautiful, miserable, confusing, terribly difficult?

2. What has been your response to someone lecturing to you on the theme of "When I was your age . . ."? Do you believe that life in your parents' or grandparents' time *was* tougher, that it took more grit than your generation possesses? Have the implications of "Make something of yourself" changed since your parents' time? If so, how?

3. What are the disadvantages, personal and cultural, of throwing off one's past "so carelessly"? Do you detect signs that we are becoming a dangerously future-oriented society?

4. Mark Twain once said something like, "When I was seventeen, my father was terribly ignorant. It's amazing to me how much he had learned by the time I reached twenty-one." Regardless of how old you are now, do you think there's a chance for your parents? Or for you?

from
THE DUKE OF DECEPTION

I listen for my father and I hear a stammer. This was explosive and unashamed, not a choking on words but a spray of words. His speech was headlong, edgy, breathless: there was neither room in his mouth nor time in the day to contain what he burned to utter. I have a remnant of that stammer, and I wish I did not; I stammer and blush, my father would stammer and grin. He depended on a listener's good will. My father depended excessively upon people's good will.

As he spoke straight at you, so did he look at you. He could stare down anyone, though this was a gift he rarely practiced. To me, everything about him seemed outsized. Doing a school report on the Easter Islanders I found in an encyclopedia pictures of their huge sculptures, and there he was, massive head and nose, nothing subtle or delicate. He was in fact (and how diminishing those words, *in fact,* look to me now) an inch or two above six feet, full bodied, a man who lumbered from here to there with deliberation. When I was a child I noticed that poeple were respectful of the cubic feet my father occupied; later I understood that I had confused respect with resentment.

I recollect things, a gentleman's accessories, deceptively simple fabrications of silver and burnished nickle, of brushed Swedish stainless, of silk and soft wool and brown leather. I remember his shoes, so meticulously selected and cared for and used, thin-soled, with cracked uppers, older than I was or could ever be, shining dully and from the depths. Just a pair of shoes? No: I knew before I knew any other complicated thing that for my father there was nothing he possessed that was "just" something. His pocket watch was not "just" a timepiece, it was a miraculous instrument with a hinged front and a representation on its back of porcelain ducks rising from a birch-girt porcelain pond. It struck the hour unassertively, musically, like a silver tine touched to a crystal glass, no hurry, you might like to know it's noon.

He despised black leather, said black shoes reminded him of black attaché cases, of bankers, lawyers, look-before-you-leapers anxious not to offend their clients. He owned nothing black except his dinner jacket and his umbrella. His umbrella doubled as a shooting-stick, and one afternoon at a polo match at Brandywine he was sitting on it when a man asked him what he would do if it rained, sit wet or stand dry? I laughed. My father laughed also, but tightly, and he did not reply; nor did he ever again use this quixotic contraption. He took things, *things*, seriously.

My father, called Duke, taught me skills and manners; he taught me to shoot and to drive fast and to read respectfully and to box and to handle a boat and to distinguish between good jazz music and bad jazz music. He was patient with me, led me to understand for myself why Billie Holiday's understatements were more interesting than Ella Fitzgerald's complications. His codes were not novel, but they were rigid, the rules of decorum that Hemingway prescribed. A gentleman kept his word, and favored simplicity of sentiment; a gentleman chose his words with care, as he chose his friends. A gentleman accepted responsibility for his acts, and welcomed the liberty to act unambiguously. A gentleman was a stickler for precision and punctilio; life was no more than an inventory of small choices that together formed a man's character, entire. A gentleman was this, and not that; a *man* did, did not, said, would not say.

My father could, however, be coaxed to reveal his bona fides. He had been schooled at Groton and passed along to Yale. He was just barely prepared to intimate that he had been tapped for "Bones," and I remember his pleasure when Levi Jackson, the black captain of Yale's 1948 football team, was similarly honored by that secret society. He was proud of Skull and Bones for its hospitality toward the exotic. He did sometimes wince, however, when he pronounced Jackson's Semitic Christian name, and I sensed that his tolerance for Jews was not inclusive; but I never heard him indulge express bigotry, and the first of half a dozen times he hit me was for having called a neighbor's kid a guinea.

There was much luxury in my father's affections, and he hated what was narrow, pinched, or mean. He understood exclusion, mind you, and lived his life believing the world to be divided between a few *us's* and many *thems*, but I was to understand that aristocracy was a function of taste, courage, and generosity. About two other virtues—candor and reticence—I was confused, for my father would sometimes proselytize the one, sometimes the other.

If Duke's preoccupation with bloodlines was finite, this did not cause him to be unmindful of his ancestors. He knew whence he had come, and whither he meant me to go. I saw visible evidence of this, a gold signet ring which I wear today, a heavy bit of business inscribed arsy-turvy with lions and flora and a motto, *nulla vestigium retrorsit.* "Don't look back" I was told it meant.

After Yale—class of late nineteen-twenty something, or early nineteen-thirty something—my father batted around the country, living a high life in New York among school and college chums, flying as a test pilot, marrying my mother, the daughter of a rear admiral. I was born a year after the marriage, in 1937, and three years after that my father went to England as a fighter pilot with Eagle Squadron, a group of American volunteers in the Royal Air Force. Later he transferred to the OSS, and was in Yugoslavia with the partisans; just before the Invasion he was parachuted into Normandy, where he served as a sapper with the Resistance, which my father pronounced *ray-zee-staunce*.

His career following the war was for me mysterious in its particulars; in the service of his nation, it was understood, candor was not always possible. This much was clear: my father mattered in the world, and was satisfied that he mattered, whether or not the world understood precisely why he mattered.

A pretty history for an American clubman. Its fault is that it was not true. My father was a bullshit artist. True, there were many boarding schools, each less pleased with the little Duke than the last, but none of them was Groton. There was not Yale, and by the time he walked from a room at a mention of Skull and Bones I knew this, and he knew that I knew it. No military service would have him; his teeth were bad. So he had his teeth pulled and replaced, but the Air Corps and Navy and Army and Coast Guard still thought he was a bad idea. The ring I wear was made according to his instructions by a jeweler two blocks from Schwab's drugstore in Hollywood, and was never paid for. The motto, engraved backwards so that it would come right on a red wax seal, is dog Latin and means in fact "leave no trace behind," but my father did not believe me when I told him this.

My father was a Jew. This did not seem to him a good idea, and so it was his notion to disassemble his history, begin at zero, and re-create himself. His sustaining line of work till shortly before he died was as a confidence man. If I now find his authentic history more surprising, more interesting, than his counterfeit history, he did not. He would not make peace with his actualities, and so he was the author of his own circumstances, and indifferent to the consequences of this nervy program.

There were some awful consequences, for other people as well as for him. He was lavish with money, with others' money. He preferred to stiff institutions: jewelers, car dealers, banks, fancy hotels. He was, that is, a thoughtful buccaneer, when thoughtfulness was convenient. But people were hurt by him. Much of his mischief was casual enough. I lost a tooth when I was six, and the Tooth Fairy, "financially inconvenienced" or "temporarily out of pocket," whichever was then his locution, left under my pillow an IOU, a sight draft for two bits, or two million.

I wish he hadn't selected from among the world's possible disguises the costume and credentials of a yacht club commodore. Beginning at scratch he might have reached further, tried something a bit more bold and odd, a bit less inexorably conventional, a bit less calculated to please. But it is true, of course, that a confidence man who cannot inspire confidence in his marks is nothing at all, so perhaps his tuneup of his bloodline, educational *vita,* and war record was merely the price of doing business in a culture preoccupied with appearances.

I'm not even now certain what I wish he had made of himself: I once believed that he was most naturally a fictioneer. But for all his preoccupation with make-believe, he never tried seriously to write it. A confidence man learns early in his career that to commit himself to paper is to court trouble. The successful bunco artist does his game, and disappears himself: Who was that masked man? No one, no one at all, *nulla vestigium* [sic] *retrorsit* [sic], not a trace left behind.

Well, I'm left behind. One day, writing about my father with no want of astonishment and love, it came to me that I am his creature as well as his get. I cannot now shake this conviction, that I was trained as his instrument of perpetuation, put here to put him into the record. And that my father knew this, calculated it to a degree. How else explain his eruption of rage when I once gave up what he and I called "writing" for journalism? I had taken a job as the book critic of *The Washington Post,* was proud of myself; it seemed then like a wonderful job, honorable and enriching. My father saw it otherwise: "You have failed me," he wrote, "you have sold yourself at discount" he wrote to me, his prison number stamped below his name.

He was wrong then, but he was usually right about me. He would listen to anything I wished to tell him, but would not tell me only what I wished to hear. He retained such solicitude for his clients. With me he was strict and straight, except about himself. And so I want to be strict and straight with him, and with myself. Writing to a friend about this book, I said that I would not now for anything have had my father be other than what he was, except happier, and that most of the time he was happy enough, cheered on by imaginary successes. He gave me a great deal, and not merely life, and I didn't want to bellyache; I wanted, I told my friend, to thumb my nose on his behalf at everyone who had limited him. My friend was shrewd, though, and said that he didn't believe me, that I couldn't mean such a thing, that if I followed out its implications I would be led to a kind of ripe sentimentality, and to mere piety. Perhaps, he wrote me, you would not have wished him to lie to himself, to lie about being a Jew. Perhaps you would have him fool others but not so deeply trick himself. "In writing about a father," my friend wrote me about our fathers, "one clambers up a slippery mountain, carrying the balls of another in a bloody sack, and whether to eat them or worship them or bury them decently is never cleanly decided."

So I will try here to be exact. I wish my father had done more headlong, more elegant inventing. I believe he would respect my wish, be willing to speak with me seriously about it, find some nobility in it. But now he is dead, and he had been dead two weeks when they found him. And in his tiny flat at the edge of the Pacific they found no address book, no batch of letters held with a rubber band, no photograph. Not a thing to suggest that he had ever known another human being.

Considerations

1. Which of the two people in these pieces is for you more a flesh and blood character? Why?

2. Baker and Wolff are both deft writers, and furthermore these brief chapters are in many ways quite similar. Which writer do you like better? Account for your choice.

3. Wolff's father is a liar, a cheat, a fraud. How does the author save him from being merely vile (or does he)? What do these lines indicate to you about the man? About Wolff himself? "There was nothing he possessed that was 'just' something"; "He took things, *things,* seriously"; "He would not make peace with his actualities, and so he was the author of his own circumstances . . ."; "I wish my father had done more headlong, more elegant inventing."

Exercises

1. We're all made up of a myriad of particulars, and when a writer depicts a character, he sorts through the particulars and selects the ones he feels will create a portrait he wants us to see. The reader, not the writer, assembles the pieces, the particulars, into a whole. Neither Baker nor Wolff fully describes his parent. It would be impossible. Instead they offer us a few small pieces: Baker's mother recites a childhood rhyme, makes a bizarre phone call, falls downstairs. Wolff spends two paragraphs detailing "gentleman's accessories," quotes his father's Tooth Fairy notes, twice considers the inscription on the signet ring, etc. Write the same way about someone you know. That is, without attempting to put the whole person on the pages, but instead considering as you write who seems to be emerging and what few, well-chosen details will strengthen the image that begins to show.

Show a draft to a classmate, or better, to a group of them. Find out who they see emerging. It may be someone other than you intended. This kind of discovery should not be at all discouraging. (Get discouraged—frustrated, anyhow—only if nobody emerges for your reader.)

2. What do you think you found out about yourself in writing this piece? Write another one discussing those findings.

13. TWO STUDIES IN ENTOMOLOGY

The following pieces, the first by Robert Frost, the second by Henry David Thoreau, describe the behavior of ants. While both selections include information about the insect, neither is meant to be a guide to ant behavior; instead, these close detailings seem to direct us eventually to examinations of *our* world, not just that of ants.

DEPARTMENTAL

An ant on the tablecloth
Ran into a dormant moth
Of many times his size.
He showed not the least surprise.
His business wasn't with such.
He gave it scarcely a touch,
And was off on his duty run.
Yet if he encountered one
Of the hive's enquiry squad
Whose work is to find out God
And the nature of time and space,
He would put him onto the case.
Ants are a curious race;
One crossing with hurried tread
The body of one of their dead
Isn't given a moment's arrest —
Seems not even impressed.
But he no doubt reports to any
With whom he crosses antennae,
And they no doubt report
To the higher up at court.
Then word goes forth in Formic:
"Death's come to Jerry McCormic,
Our selfless forager Jerry.
Will the special Janizary
Whose office it is to bury
The dead of the commissary
Go bring him home to his people.
Lay him in state on a sepal.
Wrap him for shroud in a petal.
Embalm him with ichor of nettle.
This is the word of your Queen."
And presently on the scene
Appears a solemn mortician:
And taking formal position
With feelers calmly atwiddle,
Seizes the dead by the middle,
And heaving him high in the air,
Carries him out of there.
No one stands round to stare.
It is nobody else's affair.

It couldn't be called ungentle.
But how thoroughly departmental.

THE BATTLE OF THE ANTS

.. One day when I went out to my wood-pile, or rather my pile of stumps, I observed two large ants, the one red, the other much larger, nearly half an inch long, and black, fiercely contending with one another. Having once got hold they never let go, but struggled and wrestled and rolled on the chips incessantly. Looking farther, I was surprised to find that the chips were covered with such combatants, that it was not a *duellum,* but a *bellum,* a war between two races of ants, the red always pitted against the black, and frequently two red ones to one black. The legions of these Myrmidons covered all the hills and vales in my wood-yard, and the ground was already strewn with the dead and dying, both red and black. It was the only battle which I have ever witnessed, the only battle-field I ever trod while the battle was raging; internecine war; the red republicans on the one hand, the black imperialists on the other. On every side they were engaged in deadly combat, yet without any noise that I could hear, and human soldiers never fought so resolutely. I watched a couple that were fast locked in each other's embraces, in a little sunny valley amid the chips, now at noonday prepared to fight till the sun went down, or life went out. The smaller red champion had fastened himself like a vise to his adversary's front, and through all the tumblings on that field never for an instant ceased to gnaw at one of his feelers near the root, having already caused the other to go by the board; while the stronger black one dashed him from side to side, and, as I saw on looking nearer, had already divested him of several of his members. They fought with more pertinacity than bulldogs. Neither manifested the least disposition to retreat. It was evident that their battle-cry was "Conquer or die." In the meanwhile there came along a single red ant on the hillside of this valley, evidently full of excitement, who either had dispatched his foe, or had not yet taken part in the battle; probably the latter, for he had lost none of his limbs; whose mother had charged him to return with his shield or upon it. Or perchance he was some Achilles, who had nourished his wrath apart, and had now come to avenge or rescue his Patroclus. He saw this unequal combat from afar,—for the blacks were nearly twice the size of the red,— he drew near with rapid pace till he stood on his guard within half an inch of the combatants; then, watching his opportunity, he sprang upon the black warrior, and commenced his operations near the root of his right fore leg, leaving the foe to select among his own members; and so there were three united for life, as if a new kind of attraction had been invented which put all other locks and cements to shame. I should not have wondered by this time to find that they had their respective musical bands stationed on some eminent chip, and playing their national airs the while, to excite the slow and cheer the dying combatants. I was myself excited somewhat even as if they had been men. The more you think of it, the less the difference. And certainly there is not the fight recorded in Concord history, at least, if in the history of America, that will bear a moment's comparison with this, whether for the numbers engaged in it, or for the patriotism and heroism displayed. For numbers and for carnage it was an Austerlitz or Dresden. Concord fight! Two killed on the patriot's side, and Luther Blanchard wounded! Why here every ant was a Buttrick,—"Fire, for God's sake fire!"—and thousands shared the fate of Davis and Hosmer. There was not one hireling there. I have no doubt that it was a principle they fought for, as much as our ancestors, and not to avoid a three-penny tax on their tea; and the results of this battle will be as important and memorable to those whom it concerns as those of the battle of Bunker Hill, at least.

I took up the chip on which the three I have particularly described were struggling, carried it into my house, and placed it under a tumbler on my window-sill, in order to see the issue. Holding a microscope to the first-mentioned red ant, I saw that, though he was assiduously gnawing at the near fore leg of his enemy, having severed his remaining feeler, his own breast was all torn away, exposing what vitals he had there to the jaws of the black warrior, whose breastplate was apparently too thick for him to pierce; and the dark carbuncles of the sufferer's eyes shone with ferocity such as war only could excite. They struggled half an hour longer under the tumbler, and when I looked again the black soldier had severed the heads of his foes from their bodies, and the still living heads were hanging on either side of him like ghastly trophies at his saddle-bow, still apparently as firmly fastened as ever, and he was endeavoring with feeble struggles, being without feelers and with only the remnant of a leg, and I know not how many other wounds, to divest himself of them; which at length, after half an hour more, he accomplished. I raised the glass, and he went off over the window-sill in that crippled state. Whether he finally survived that combat, and spent the remainder of his days in some Hôtel des Invalides, I do not know; but I thought that his industry would not be worth much thereafter. I never learned which party was victorious, nor the cause of the war; but I felt for the rest of that day as if I had had my feelings excited and harrowed by witnessing the struggle, the ferocity and carnage of a human battle before my door.

Considerations

1. As Frost uses the term, what does "departmental" mean? In human society, "Whose work is [it] to find out God/And the nature of time and space"? What departmental conventions make this work "nobody else's affair"?

2. Thoreau, like Frost, finds tempting similarities between ant and human behavior. How does he humanize the scene he witnesses by his woodpile? What does he read into its circumstances? What is your response to the lines beginning "I was myself excited somewhat even as if they had been men," and continuing through the end of the paragraph? Does the passage seem credible, exaggerated, or what?

3. Comparisons between ants and humans are common enough; we've all made them. There are two ways to look at this link between species, though: we can either see ants as being people-like, or view the connection the other way around. Which does Frost do? Which of the two pieces makes you feel less comfortable about the assumed preeminence of the human species, and why?

4. Physician-scientist-writer Lewis Thomas asks that we view the ant-human analogy more than casually, figuratively. In *The Lives of a Cell,* Thomas observes that an ant by itself is not viable, that "There is really no such creature as a single individual; he has no more life of his own than a cast-off cell marooned from the surface of your skin." Only in groups, masses, do ants become a "whole beast," capable of constructive, intelligent-seeming activity. Here is a connection, says Thomas, that we don't like to make: that people, like ants, may be viewed as interdependent parts of a "conjoined intelligence," that there is perhaps a largely-ignored biological circuitry that links *us,* and not just other highly social species such as ants. It may be that our business, together, amounts to building an ant hill of sorts. "The circuitry seems to be there," writes Thomas, "even if the current is not always on."

What "circuitry" is Thomas possibly referring to? Where are its evidences? How can it be argued that we are "more attached to each other, more inseparable in our behavior than bees [or ants]"? What ant-hill are we busy building? If it is discomfiting to think of our species this way, why is it?

Exercise

Describe some facet of human behavior that people generally ignore. Find a way to re-see it for its possible significance. The writing need not be in essay form. You're encouraged to try a poem, even a mock lab report.

14. THE RIVER AS TEACHER

The two passages below deal with the Mississippi. The first is from Mark Twain's *Life on the Mississippi,* and the second is from *Old Glory,* a book that recounts Jonathan Raban's recent voyage down the same river that Twain navigated both in literature and life more than a century before. Note how the river is portrayed in these writings—how the writers differ in their responses to it, their feelings about it. Just as importantly, be aware of your responses to their responses.

from
LIFE ON THE MISSISSIPPI

At the end of what seemed a tedious while, I had managed to pack my head full of islands, towns, bars, "points," and bends, and a curiously inanimate mass of lumber it was, too. However, inasmuch as I could shut my eyes and reel off a good long string of these names without leaving out more than ten miles of river in every fifty, I began to feel that I could take a boat down to New Orleans if I could make her skip those little gaps. But of course my complacency could hardly get start enough to lift my nose a trifle into the air, before Mr. Bixby would think of something to fetch it down again. One day he turned on me suddenly with this settler:

"What is the shape of Walnut Bend?"

He might as well have asked me my grandmother's opinion of protoplasm. I reflected respectfully and then said I didn't know it had any particular shape. My gunpowdery chief went off with a bang, of course, and then went on loading and firing until he was out of adjectives.

I had learned long ago that he only carried just so many rounds of ammunition and was sure to subside into a very placable and even remorseful old smooth-bore as soon as they were all gone. That word "old" is merely affectionate; he was not more than thirty-four. I waited. By and by he said:

"My boy, you've got to know the *shape* of the river perfectly. It is all there is left to steer by on a very dark night. Everything else is blotted out and gone. But mind you, it hasn't the same shape in the night that it has in the daytime."

"How on earth am I ever going to learn it, then?"

"How do you follow a hall at home in the dark? Because you know the shape of it. You can't see it."

"Do you mean to say that I've got to know all the million trifling variations in shape in the banks of this interminable river as well as I know the shape of the front hall at home?"

"On my honor, you've got to know them *better* than any man ever did know the shapes of the halls in his own house."

"I wish I was dead!"

"Now I don't want to discourage you, but—"

"Well, pile it on me; I might as well have it now as another time."

"You see, this has got to be learned, there isn't any getting around it. A clear starlight night throws such heavy shadows that, if you didn't know the shape of a shore perfectly, you would claw away from every bunch of timber, because you would take the black shadow of it for a solid cape, and you see you would be getting scared to death every fifteen minutes by the watch. You would be fifty yards from shore all the time when you ought to be within fifty feet of it. You can't see a snag in one of those shadows but you know exactly where it is, and the shape of the river tells you when you are coming to it. Then there's your pitch-dark night; the river is a very different shape on a pitch-dark night from what it is on a star-light night. All shores seem to be straight lines then, and mighty dim ones too, and you'd *run* them for straight lines, only you know better. You boldly drive your boat right into what seems to be a solid, straight wall (you knowing very well that in reality there's a curve there) and that wall falls back and makes way for you.

Then there's your gray mist. You take a night when there's one of these grisly, drizzly, gray mists, and then there isn't *any* particular shape to a shore. A gray mist would tangle the head of the oldest man that ever lived. Well, then, different kinds of *moonlight* change the shape of the river in different ways. You see—"

"Oh, don't say any more, please! Have I got to learn the shape of the river according to all these five hundred thousand different ways? If I tried to carry all that cargo in my head it would make me stoop-shouldered."

"*No!* you only learn *the* shape of the river, and you learn it with such absolute certainty that you can always steer by the shape that's *in your head* and never mind the one that's before your eyes."

"Very well, I'll try it; but, after I have learned it, can I depend on it? Will it keep the same form and not go fooling around?"

Before Mr. Bixby could answer, Mr. W. came in to take the watch, and he said:

"Bixby, you'll have to look out for President's Island and all that country clear away up above the Old Hen and Chickens. The banks are caving and the shape of the shores changing like everything. Why, you wouldn't know the point above 40. You can go up inside the old sycamore snag, now."

So that question was answered. Here were leagues of shore changing shape. My spirits were down in the mud again. Two things seemed pretty apparent to me. One was that in order to be a pilot a man had got to learn more than any one man ought to be allowed to know, and the other was that he must learn it all over again in a different way every twenty-four hours.

That night we had the watch until twelve. Now it was an ancient river custom for the two pilots to chat a bit when the watch changed. While the relieving pilot put on his gloves and lit his cigar, his partner, the retiring pilot, would say something like this:

"I judge the upper bar is making down a little at Hale's point; had quarter twain with the lower lead and mark twain with the other."

"Yes, I thought it was making down a little, last trip. Meet any boats?"

"Met one abreast the head of 21 but she was away over hugging the bar, and I couldn't make her out entirely. I took her for the *Sunny South*—hadn't any skylights forward of the chimneys."

And so on. And as the relieving pilot took the wheel his partner would mention that we were in such-and-such a bend, and say we were abreast of such-and-such a man's wood-yard or plantation. This was courtesy; I supposed it was *necessity*. But Mr. W. came on watch full twelve minutes late on this particular night, a tremendous breach of ettiquette; in fact, it is the unpardonable sin among pilots. So Mr. Bixby gave him no greeting whatever but simply surrendered the wheel and marched out of the pilot-house without a word. I was appalled; it was a villainous night for blackness, we were in a particularly wide and blind part of the river where there was no shape or substance to anything, and it seemed incredible that Mr. Bixby should have left that poor fellow to kill the boat, trying to find out where he was. But I resolved that I would stand by him anyway. He should find that he was not wholly friendless. So I stood around and waited to be asked where we were. But Mr. W. plunged on serenely through the solid firmament of black cats that stood for an atmosphere, and never opened his mouth. "Here is a proud devil!" thought I, "here is a limb of Satan that would rather send us all to destruction than put himself under obligations to me, because I am not yet one of the salt of the earth and privileged to snub captains and lord it over everything dead and alive in a steamboat." I presently climbed up on the bench; I did not think it was safe to go to sleep while this lunatic was on watch.

However, I must have gone to sleep in the course of time, because the next thing I was aware of was the fact that day was breaking, Mr. W. gone, and Mr. Bixby at the wheel again. So it was four o'clock and all well—but me; I felt like a skinful of dry bones, and all of them trying to ache at once.

Mr. Bixby asked me what I had stayed up there for. I confessed that it was to do Mr. W. a benevolence—tell him where he was. It took five minutes for the entire preposterousness of the thing to filter into Mr. Bixby's system, and then I judge it filled him nearly up to the chin; because he paid me a compliment, and not much of a one either. He said:

"Well, taking you by and large, you do seem to be more different kinds of an ass than any creature I ever saw before. What did you suppose he wanted to know for?"

I said I thought it might be a convenience to him.

"Convenience! D———nation! Didn't I tell you that a man's got to know the river in the night the same as he'd know his own front hall?"

"Well, I can follow the front hall in the dark, if I know it *is* the front hall, but suppose you set me down in the middle of it in the dark and not tell me which hall it is, how am *I* to know?"

"Well, you've *got* to, on the river!"

"All right. Then I'm glad I never said anything to Mr. W."

"I should say so! Why he'd have slammed you through the window and utterly ruined a hundred dollars' worth of window-sash and stuff."

I was glad this damage had been saved, for it would have made me unpopular with the owners. They always hated anybody who had the name of being careless and injuring things.

I went to work now to learn the shape of the river, and of all the eluding and ungraspable objects that ever I tried to get mind or hands on, that was the chief. I would fasten my eyes upon a sharp, wooded point that projected far into the river some miles ahead of me and go to laboriously photographing its shape upon my brain, and just as I was beginning to succeed to my satisfaction, we would draw up toward it and the exasperating thing would begin to melt away and fold back into the bank! If there had been a conspicuous dead tree standing upon the very point of the cape, I would find that tree inconspicuously merged into the general forest and occupying the middle of a straight shore, when I got abreast of it! No prominent hill would stick to its shape long enough for me to make up my mind what its form really was, but it was as dissolving and changeful as if it had been a mountain of butter in the hottest corner of the tropics. Nothing ever had the same shape when I was coming down-stream that it had borne when I went up. I mentioned these little difficulties to Mr. Bixby. He said:

"That's the very main virtue of the thing. If the shapes didn't change every three seconds they wouldn't be of any use. Take this place where we are now, for instance. As long as that hill over yonder is only one hill, I can boom right along the way I'm going, but the moment it splits at the top and forms a V, I know I've got to scratch to starboard in a hurry or I'll bang this boat's brains out against a rock, and then the moment one of the prongs of the V swings behind the other, I've got to waltz to larboard again or I'll have a misunderstanding with a snag that would scratch the keelson out of this steamboat as neatly as if it were a sliver in your hand. If that hill didn't change its shape on bad nights there would be an awful steamboat graveyard around here inside of a year."

It was plain that I had got to learn the shape of the river in all the different ways that could be thought of—upside down, wrong end first, inside out, fore-and-aft, and "thort-ships"—and then know what to do on gray nights when it hadn't any shape at all. So I set about it. In the course of time I began to get the best of this knotty lesson and my self-complacency moved to the front once more. Mr. Bixby was all fixed and ready to start it to the rear again. He opened on me after this fashion:

"How much water did we have in the middle crossing at Hole-in-the-Wall, trip before last?"

I considered this an outrage. I said:

"Every trip, down and up, the leadsmen are singing through that tangled place for three-quarters of an hour on a stretch. How do you reckon I can remember such a mess as that?"

"My boy, you've got to remember it. You've got to remember the exact spot and the exact marks the boat lay in when we had the shoalest water, in every one of the five hundred shoal places between St. Louis and New Orleans, and you mustn't get the shoal soundings and marks of one trip mixed up with the shoal soundings and marks of another, either, for they're not often twice alike. You must keep them separate."

"When I get so that I can do that, I'll be able to raise the dead, and then I won't have to pilot a steamboat to make a living. I want to retire from this business. I want a slush-bucket and a brush, I'm only fit for a roustabout. I haven't got brains enough to be a pilot, and if I had I wouldn't have strength enough to carry them around, unless I went on crutches."

"Now drop that! When I say I'll learn a man the river, I mean it. And you can depend on it, I'll learn him or kill him."

There was no use in arguing with a person like this. I promptly put such a strain on my memory that by and by even the shoal water and the countless crossing-marks began to stay with me. But the result was just the same. I never could more than get one knotty thing learned before another presented itself. Now I had often seen pilots gazing at the water and pretending to read it as if it were a book, but it was a book that told me nothing. A time came at last, however, when Mr. Bixby seemed to think me far enough advanced to bear a lesson on water-reading. So he began:

"Do you see that long, slanting line on the face of the water? Now, that's a reef. Moreover, it's a bluff reef. There is a solid sand-bar under it that is nearly as straight up and down as the side of a house. There is plenty of water close up to it, but mighty little on top of it. If you were to hit it you would knock the boat's brains out. Do you see where the line fringes out at the upper end and begins to fade away?"

"Yes, sir."

"Well, that is a low place; that is the head of the reef. You can climb over there and not hurt anything. Cross over, now, and follow along close under the reef—easy water there—not much current."

I followed the reef along till I approached the fringed end. Then Mr. Bixby said:

"Now get ready. Wait till I give the word. She won't want to mount the reef; a boat hates shoal water. Stand by—wait—*wait*—keep her well in hand. *Now* cramp her down! Snatch her! snatch her!"

He seized the other side of the wheel and helped to spin it around until it was hard down, and then we held it so. The boat resisted and refused to answer for a while, and next she came surging to starboard, mounted the reef, and sent a long angry ridge of water foaming away from her bows.

"Now watch her, watch her like a cat, or she'll get away from you. When she fights strong and the tiller slips a little, in a jerky, greasy sort of way, let up on her a trifle; it is the way she tells you at night that the water is too shoal; but keep edging her up, little by little, toward the point. You are well up on the bar now; there is a bar under every point, because the water that comes down around it forms an eddy and allows the sediment to sink. Do you see those fine lines on the face of the water that branch out like the ribs of a fan? Well, those are little reefs; you want to just miss the ends of them but run them pretty close. Now look out—look out! Don't you crowd that slick, greasy-looking place, there ain't nine feet there, she won't stand it. She begins to smell it; look sharp, I tell you! Oh, blazes, there you go! Stop the starboard wheel! Quick! Ship up to back! Set her back!"

The engine bells jingled and the engines answered promptly, shooting white columns of steam far aloft out of the 'scape-pipes, but it was too late. The boat had "smelt" the bar in good earnest; the foamy ridges that radiated from her bows suddenly disappeared, a great dead swell came rolling forward, and swept ahead of her, she careened far over to larboard and went tearing away toward the shore as if she were about scared to death. We were a good mile from where we ought to have been when we finally got the upper hand of her again.

During the afternoon watch the next day, Mr. Bixby asked me if I knew how to run the next few miles. I said:

"Go inside the first snag above the point, outside the next one, start out from the lower end of Higgins's wood-yard, make a square crossing and—"

"That's all right. I'll be back before you close up on the next point."

But he wasn't. He was still below when I rounded it and entered upon a piece of the river which I had some misgivings about. I did not know that he was hiding behind a chimney to see how I would perform. I went gaily along, getting prouder and prouder, for he had never left the boat in my sole charge such a length of time before. I even got to "setting" her and letting the wheel go entirely, while I vaingloriously turned my back and inspected the stern marks and hummed a tune, a sort of easy indifference which I had prodigiously admired in Bixby and other great pilots. Once I inspected rather long, and when I faced to the front again my heart flew into my mouth so suddenly that if I hadn't clapped my teeth together I should have lost it. One of those frightful bluff reefs was stretching its deadly length right across our bows! My head was gone in a moment; I did not know which end I stood on; I gasped and could not get my breath; I spun the wheel down with such rapidity that it wove itself together like a spider's web; the boat answered and turned square away from the reef, but the reef followed her! I fled but still it kept—right across my bows! I never looked to see where I was going, I only fled. The awful crash was imminent. Why didn't that villain come? If I committed the crime of ringing a bell I might get thrown overboard. But better that than kill the boat. So in blind desperation, I started such a rattling "shivaree" down below as never had astounded an engineer in this world before, I fancy. Amidst the frenzy of the bells the engines began to back and fill in a curious way and my reason forsook its throne—we were about to crash into the woods on the other side of the river. Just then Mr. Bixby stepped calmly into view on the hurricane-deck. My soul went out to him in gratitude. My distress vanished; I would have felt safe on the brink of Niagara with Mr. Bixby on the hurricane-deck. He blandly and sweetly took his toothpick out of his mouth between his fingers, as if it were a cigar—we were just in the act of climbing an overhanging big tree and the passengers were scudding astern like rats—and lifted up these commands to me ever so gently:

"Stop the larboard! Come ahead on it! Stop the starboard! Come ahead on it! Point her for the bar!"

I sailed away as serenely as a summer's morning. Mr. Bixby came in and said with mock simplicity:

"When you have a hail, my boy, you ought to tap the big bell three times before you land, so that the engineers can get ready."

I blushed under the sarcasm and said I hadn't had any hail.

"Ah! Then it was for wood, I suppose. The officer of the watch will tell you when he wants to wood up."

I went on consuming and said I wasn't after wood.

"Indeed? Why, what could you want over here in the bend, then? Did you ever know of a boat following a bend up-stream at this stage of the river?"

."No, sir—and *I* wasn't trying to follow it. I was getting away from a bluff reef."

"No, it wasn't a bluff reef; there isn't one within three miles of where you were."

"But I saw it. It was as bluff as that one yonder."

"Just about. Run over it!"

"Do you give it as an order?"

"Yes. Run over it!"

"If I don't, I wish I may die."

"All right; I am taking the responsibility."

I was just as anxious to kill the boat, now, as I had been to save it before. I impressed my orders upon my memory, to be used at the inquest, and made a straight break for the reef. As it disappeared under our bows I held my breath, but we slid over it like oil.

"Now, don't you see the difference? It wasn't anything but a *wind* reef. The wind does that."

"So I see. But it is exactly like a bluff reef. How am I ever going to tell them apart?"

"I can't tell you. It is an instinct. By and by you will just naturally *know* one from the other, but you never will be able to explain why or how you know them apart."

from

OLD GLORY

The river had settled into a smooth, loping stride. Just south of Caruthersville, Missouri dissolved into Arkansas somewhere behind the levee on my right. Around the wide curve of Barfield Bend I saw two tow fleets coming upstream in convoy. There was plenty of room for all of us; the Mississippi was more than a mile across here, and although the channel stuck close in to the Arkansas shore, there was a broad reach of open water on the Tennessee side. I had wanted to stop and look at Tomato, Arkansas; the first town in my eighth state was named so enjoyably that I thought it couldn't help holding other pleasures too. Seeing the tows push up toward Tomato Landing, I decided to skip it and cut away to the far side of the river.

It was easy water. I could fill a pipe and let the boat take care of itself, idling along a few hundred yards out from the edge of the forest. I had gone a mile or so when I saw a line of long, crookbacked breakers with an edge of white peeling from their tops. For a tow's wake they seemed to have traveled an unusual distance across the river, but then, both tow fleets were big, and perhaps their wakes had married. Running the engine as fast as it would go, I turned the boat around and headed upstream toward the shore.

At least, that was what I had meant to do. I couldn't work out what was wrong. I seemed to be going faster than I'd ever been before, with the entire surface of the river pouring by in a glassy race of logs, twigs, cola cans and orange crates. The whole world was going past, a stream of pure motion. Yet I was making no wake at all. The river behind me was as unruffled as the river in front, although I could feel the propellor churning hard against the torrential movement of the water. I had quite lost my sense of place and dimension. I looked across to the trees on the bank. They were moving too: wavering slightly, then slipping back, as if they were being tugged up against the grain of the current. So if I was moving at all, I must be going backward downstream, when it felt as if I were traveling up it at an improbable speed.

There was no question of running in to the shore. The forest grew right out into the river, and the trees were knee-deep in water, with no space to slip a boat between them. I tried to get my bearings by switching my eyes from the boat to the streaming current, to the willows and to the sky. We were all out of sync with each other: all in motion, but in different directions and at different speeds. The line of breakers was now only a hundred yards behind me. I spun the boat around and went with the flow of things. For a few minutes, there was a lot of jolting and splashing, and then the long calm of the main channel again.

It was as near as I had come to meeting the river face to face. The Mississippi had behaved perfectly in character. It had been a neat and nasty confidence trick. That invitingly placid water must have been racing at fourteen or fifteen miles an hour over a shallow ledge of sand. Its speed had made it look deep when in reality there was probably only three or four feet between the surface and the bottom. I was still enough of a greenhorn to have been completely gulled.

Yet there was a queer scary elation in feeling myself poised so fragilely on that sweep of river, watching the forest and sky tremble and start to run. I had touched the deep stillness of the Mississippi; it was as if the world moved around the river and not the river through the world.

Considerations

1. Both of these episodes deal with education, the subject matter being one of the world's great rivers. For Raban, the lesson left "a queer, scary elation in feeling myself poised so fragilely on that sweep of river...." How would you describe Twain's probable response to *his* harrowing lesson? Consider Bixby's teaching technique. Is it cruel, wise, harsh but effective, all of the above, or what?

2. What does the cub pilot really learn, beyond discovering what a "wind reef" is? Is it anything like what Raban learns? Explain. What did you as a reader learn, if anything?

Exercises

1. In your own education there have been times when meaning came through unconventional experiences, whether they were terrifying, humorous, or whatever. Write about one of these times. You needn't confine yourself to your formal education; we never stop being students from birth to death, and certainly the larger part of our education comes from outside the classroom. Keep in mind how powerful the *story* element is in each piece.

2. Or write about your relationship with and understanding of some natural element, whether it's a river, pond, mountain, patch of woods, or whatever comes to mind. (You might find it useful to read Loren Eiseley's "The Flow of the River" in Part IV in connection with this assignment.)

15. TWO VIEWS OF THE RIVER

These selections are also from Mark Twain's works. The first is from his best-known novel, *The Adventures of Huckleberry Finn*, the second, another passage from *Life on the Mississippi*. It has been said by more than one critic that this novel is the embodiment of the American myth—that here is the big, wild beauty of our country, its power, its innocence; and that in Huckleberry himself is the personification of our questing spirit. From your reading of this brief excerpt, do you sense any mythic connections, any stirrings of personal association with Huck Finn, any sense of Yes, this is how it is, or should be? Explain.

Although the same hand penned both books, *Life on the Mississippi* gives us a somewhat different view of the river. Which one do you find yourself more sympathetic with, trusting of? Be sure to use annotations and your double-entry notebook in connection with your reading.

from

THE ADVENTURES OF HUCKLEBERRY FINN

Two or three days and nights went by; I reckon I might say they swum by, they slid along so quiet and smooth and lovely. Here is the way we put in the time. It was a monstrous big river down there—sometimes a mile and a half wide; we run nights, and laid up and hid day-times; soon as night was most gone, we stopped navigating and tied up—nearly always in the dead water under a tow-head; and then cut young cottonwoods and willows and hid the raft with them. Then we set out the lines. Next we slid into the river and had a swim, so as to freshen up and cool off; then we set down on the sandy bottom where the water was about knee deep, and watched the daylight come. Not a sound, anywheres—perfectly still—just like the whole world was asleep, only sometimes the bull-frogs a-cluttering, maybe. The first thing to see, looking away over the water, was a kind of dull line—that was the woods on t'other side—you couldn't make nothing else out; then a pale place in

·the sky; then more paleness, spreading around; then the river softened up, away off, and warn't black any more, but gray; you could see little dark spots drifting along, ever so far away—trading scows, and such things; and long black streaks—rafts; sometimes you could hear a sweep screaking; or jumbled up voices, it was so still, and sounds come so far; and by and by you could see a streak on the water which you know by the look of the streak that there's a snag there in a swift current which breaks on it and makes that streak look that way; and you see the mist curl up off of the water, and the east reddens up, and the river, and you make out a log cabin in the edge of the woods, away on the bank on t'other side of the river, being a wood-yard, likely, and piled by them cheats so you can throw a dog through it anywheres; then the nice breeze springs up, and comes fanning you from over there, so cool and fresh, and sweet to smell, on account of the woods and the flowers; but sometimes not that way, because they've left dead fish laying around, gars, and such, and they do get pretty rank; and next you've got the full day, and everything smiling in the sun, and the song-birds just going it!

A little smoke couldn't be noticed now, so we would take some fish off of the lines, and cook up a hot breakfast. And afterwards we would watch the lonesomeness of the river, and kind of lazy along, and by-and-by lazy off to sleep. Wake up, by-and-by, and look to see what done it, and maybe see a steamboat coughing along up stream, so far off towards the other side you couldn't tell nothing about her only whether she was stern-wheel or side-wheel; then for about an hour there wouldn't be nothing to hear nor nothing to see—just solid lonesomeness. Next you'd see a raft sliding by, away off yonder, and maybe a galoot on it chopping, because they're almost always doing it on a raft; you'd see the ax flash, and come down—you don't hear nothing; you see that ax go up again, and by the time it's above the man's head, then you hear the *k'chunk!*—it had took all that time to come over the water. So we would put in the day, lazying around, listening to the stillness. Once there was a thick fog, and the rafts and things that went by was beating tin pans so the steamboats wouldn't run over them. A scow or a raft went by so close we could hear them talking and cussing and laughing—heard them plain; but we couldn't see no sign of them; it made you feel crawly, it was like spirits carrying on that way in the air. Jim said he believed it was spirits; but I says:

"No, spirits wouldn't say, 'dern the dern fog.'"

Soon as it was night, out we shoved; when we got her out to about the middle, we let her alone, and let her float wherever the current wanted her to; then we lit the pipes, and dangled our legs in the water and talked about all kinds of things—we was always naked, day and night, whenever the mosquitoes would let us—the new clothes Buck's folks made for me was too good to be comfortable, and besides I didn't much go on clothes, nohow.

Sometimes we'd have that whole river all to ourselves for the longest time. Yonder was the banks and the islands, across the water; and maybe a spark—which was a candle in a cabin window—and sometimes on the water you could see a spark or two—on a raft or a scow, you know; and maybe you could hear a fiddle or a song coming over from one of them crafts. It's lovely to live on a raft. We had the sky, up there, all speckled with stars, and we used to lay on our backs and look up at them, and discuss about whether they was made, or only just happened—Jim he allowed they was made, but I allowed they happened; I judged it would have took too long to *make* so many. Jim said the moon could a *laid* them; well, that looked kind of reasonable, so I didn't say nothing against it, because I've seen a frog lay most as many, so of course it could be done. We used to watch the stars that fell, too, and see them streak down. Jim allowed they'd got spoiled and was hove out of the nest.

Once or twice of a night we would see a steamboat slipping along in the dark, and now and then she would belch a whole world of sparks up out of her chimbleys, and they would rain down in the river and look awful pretty; then she would turn a corner and her lights would wink out and her pow-wow shut off and leave the river still again; and by-and-by her waves would get to us, a long time after she was gone, and joggle the raft a bit, and after that you wouldn't hear nothing for you couldn't tell how long, except maybe frogs or something.

from
LIFE ON THE MISSISSIPPI

It turned out to be true. The face of the water in time became a wonderful book—a book that was a dead language to the uneducated passenger but which told its mind to me without reserve, delivering its most cherished secrets as clearly as if it uttered them with a voice. And it was not a book to be read once and thrown aside, for it had a new story to tell every day. Throughout the long twelve hundred miles there was never a page that was void of interest, never one that you could leave unread without loss, never one that you would want to skip, thinking you could find higher enjoyment in some other thing. There never was so wonderful a book written by man, never one whose interest was so absorbing, so unflagging, so sparklingly renewed with every reperusal. The passenger who could not read it was charmed with a peculiar sort of faint dimple on its surface (on the rare occasions when he did not overlook it altogether) but to the pilot, that was an italicized passage; indeed it was more than that, it was a legend of the largest capitals with a string of shouting exclamation-points at the end of it, for it meant that a wreck or a rock was buried there that could tear the life out of the strongest vessel that ever floated. It is the faintest and simplest expression the water ever makes, and the most hideous to a pilot's eye. In truth, the passenger who could not read this book saw nothing but all manner of pretty pictures in it, painted by the sun and shaded by the clouds, whereas to the trained eye these were not pictures at all, but the grimmest and most dead-earnest of reading matter.

Now when I had mastered the language of this water and had come to know every trifling feature that bordered the great river as familiarly as I knew the letters of the alphabet, I had made a valuable acquisition. But I had lost something, too. I had lost something which could never be restored to me while I lived. All the grace, the beauty, the poetry, had gone out of the majestic river! I still kept in mind a certain wonderful sunset which I witnessed when steamboating was new to me. A broad expanse of the river was turned to blood; in the middle distance the red hue brightened into gold, through which a solitary log came floating, black and conspicuous; in one place a long, slanting mark was broken by boiling, tumbling rings, that were as many-tinted as an opal; where the ruddy flush was faintest, was a smooth spot that was covered with graceful circles and radiating lines, ever so delicately traced; the shore on our left was densely wooded and the somber shadow that fell from this forest was broken in one place by a long, ruffled trail that shone like silver; and high above the forest wall a clean-stemmed dead tree waved a single leafy bough that glowed like a flame in the unobstructed splendor that was flowing from the sun. There were graceful curves, reflected images, woody heights, soft distances, and over the whole scene, far and near, the dissolving lights drifted steadily, enriching it every passing moment with new marvels of coloring.

I stood like one bewitched. I drank it in, in a speechless rapture. The world was new to me and I had never seen anything like this at home. But as I have said, a day came when I began to cease from noting the glories and the charms which the moon and the sun and the twilight wrought upon the river's face; another day came when I ceased altogether to note them. Then, if that sunset scene had been repeated, I should have looked upon it without rapture, and should have commented upon it inwardly after this fashion: "This sun means that we are going to have wind to-morrow; that floating log means that the river is rising, small thanks to it; that slanting mark on the water refers to a bluff reef which is going to kill somebody's steamboat one of these nights, if it keeps on stretching out like that; those tumbling 'boils' show a dissolving bar and a changing channel there; the lines and circles in the slick water over yonder are a warning that that troublesome place is shoaling up dangerously; that silver streak in the shadow of the forest is the 'break' from a new snag and he has located himself in the very place he could have found to fish for steamboats; that tall dead tree, with a single living branch, is not going to last long, and then how is a body ever going to get through this blind place at night without the friendly old landmark?

No, the romance and beauty were all gone from the river. All the value any feature of it had for me now was the amount of usefulness it could furnish toward compassing the safe piloting of a steamboat. Since those days, I have pitied doctors from my heart. What does the lovely flush in a beauty's cheek mean to a doctor but a "break" that ripples above some deadly disease? Are not all her visible charms sown thick with what are to him the signs and symbols of hidden decay? Does he ever see her beauty at all, or doesn't he simply view her professionally and comment upon her unwholesome condition all to himself? And doesn't he sometimes wonder whether he has gained most or lost most by learning his trade?

Considerations

1. Consider again Blake's implied definitions of innocence and experience. Is it possible to find in these two responses to the same river a "song of innocence" and a "song of experience"? If so, how are these two (never entirely separable) states different from Blake's? Cite lines in support of your answer. ("The world was new to me" is a good place to start, a comparison of concluding paragraphs is a good place to finish.)

2. In Huck we are meant to hear the voice of an uneducated adolescent, who lacks any skill with language. But compare his imagery with that of the other narrator. Can it be argued that Huck is as eloquent? Which lines seem most evocative to you? Where do you find him commenting on matters most like those examined in the second paragraph of *Life on . . .* ? What figures of speech most move or amuse you?

16. THE FISH: SCUDDER/SHALER

Louis Agassiz (1807–1873), a Harvard professor of paleontology, educated his graduate students by requiring them to look at specimens of plant and animal life with scrupulous attention to detail and with minds flexible and open enough to see what they did not expect to see. These accounts of his teaching were written by two of his students. Although you'll gain a specific sense of Agassiz from these pieces, they should also point you toward deeper understandings about seeing and learning—about learning how to see and seeing how to learn.

REMEMBERING AGASSIZ
Samuel Scudder

It was more than fifteen years ago that I entered the laboratory of Professor Agassiz, and told him I had enrolled my name in the Scientific School as a student of natural history. He asked me a few questions about my object in coming, my antecedents generally, the mode in which I afterwards proposed to use the knowledge I might acquire, and finally, whether I wished to study any special branch. To the latter I replied that, while I wished to be well grounded in all departments of zoology, I purposed to devote myself specially to insects.

"When do you wish to begin?" he asked.

"Now," I replied.

This seemed to please him, and with an energetic "Very well!" he reached from a shelf a huge jar of specimens in yellow alcohol. "Take this fish," he said, "and look at it; we call it a haemulon; by and by I will ask what you have seen."

With that he left me, but in a moment returned with explicit instructions as to the care of the object entrusted to me.

"No man is fit to be a naturalist," said he, "who does not know how to take care of specimens."

I was to keep the fish before me in a tin tray, and occasionally moisten the surface with alcohol from the jar, always taking care to replace the stopper tightly. Those were not the days of ground-glass stoppers and elegantly shaped exhibition jars; all the old students will recall the huge neckless glass bottles with their leaky, wax besmeared corks, half eaten by insects, and begrimed with cellar dust. Entomology was a cleaner science than ichthyology, but the example of the Professor, who had unhesitatingly plunged to the bottom of the jar to produce the fish, was infectious; and though this alcohol had a "very ancient and fishlike smell," I really dared not show any aversion within these sacred precincts, and treated the alcohol as though it were pure water. Still I was conscious of a passing feeling of disappointment, for gazing at a fish did not commend itself to an ardent entomologist. My friends at home, too, were annoyed when they discovered that no amount of eau-de-Cologne would drown the perfume which haunted me like a shadow.

In ten minutes I had seen all that could be seen in that fish, and started in search of the Professor—who had, however, left the Museum; and when I returned, after lingering over some of the odd animals stored in the upper apartment, my specimen was dry all over. I dashed the fluid over the fish as if to resuscitate the beast from a fainting fit, and looked with anxiety for a return of the normal sloppy appearance. This little excitement over, nothing was to be done but to return to a steadfast gaze at my mute companion. Half an hour passed—an hour—another hour; the fish began to look loathsome. I turned it over and around; looked it in the face—ghastly; from behind, beneath, above, sideways, at a three-quarters' view—just as ghastly. I was in despair; at an early hour I concluded that lunch was necessary; so, with infinite relief, the fish was carefully replaced in the jar, and for an hour I was free.

On my return, I learned that Professor Agassiz had been at the Museum, but had gone, and would not return for several hours. My fellow-students were too busy to be disturbed by continued conversation. Slowly I drew forth that hideous fish, and with a feeling of desperation again looked at it. I might not use a magnifying-glass; instruments of all kinds were interdicted. My two hands, my two eyes, and the fish: it seemed a most limited field. I pushed my finger down its throat to feel how sharp the teeth were. I began to count the scales in the different rows, until I was convinced that was nonsense. At last a happy thought struck me—I would draw the fish; and now with surprise I began to discover new features in the creature. Just then the Professor returned.

"That is right," said he; "a pencil is one of the best of eyes. I am glad to notice, too, that you keep your specimen wet, and your bottle corked."

With these encouraging words, he added:

"Well, what is it like?"

He listened attentively to my brief rehearsal of the structure of parts whose names were still unknown to me: the fringed gill-arches and moveable operculum; the pores of the head, fleshy lips and lidless eyes; the lateral line, the spinous fins and forked tail; the compressed and arched body. When I finished, he waited as if expecting more, and then, with an air of disappointment:

"You have not looked very carefully; why," he continued more earnestly, "you haven't even seen one of the most conspicuous features of the animal, which is plainly before your eyes as the fish itself; look again, look again!" and he left me to my misery.

I was piqued; I was mortified. Still more of that wretched fish! But now I set myself to my task with a will, and discovered one new thing after another, until I saw how just the Professor's criticism had been. The afternoon passed quickly; and when, towards its close, the Professor inquired:

"Do you see it yet?"

"No," I replied, "I am certain I do not, but I see how little I saw before."

"That is next best," said he, earnestly, "but I won't hear you now; put away your fish and go home; perhaps you will be ready with a better answer in the morning. I will examine you before you look at the fish."

This was disconcerting. Not only must I think of my fish all night, studying, without the object before me, what this unknown but most visible feature might be; but also, without reviewing my discoveries, I must give an exact account of them the next day. I had a bad memory; so I walked home by Charles River in a distracted state, with my two perplexities.

The cordial greeting from the Professor the next morning was reassuring; here was a man who seemed to be quite as anxious as I that I should see for myself what he saw.

"Do you perhaps mean," I asked, "that the fish has symmetrical sides with aspired organs?"

His thoroughly pleased "of course! of course!" repaid the wakeful hours of the previous night. After he had discoursed most happily and enthusiastically—as he always did—upon the importance of this point, I ventured to ask what I should do next.

"Oh, look at your fish!" he said, and left me again to my own devices. In a little more than an hour he returned, and heard my new catalogue.

"That is good, that is good!" he repeated; "but that is not all; go on"; and so for three long days he placed that fish before my eyes, forbidding me to look at anything else, or to use any artificial aid. "Look, look, look," was his repeated injunction.

This was the best entomological lesson I ever had—a lesson whose influence has extended to the details of every subsequent study; a legacy the Professor had left to me, as he has left it to so many others, of inestimable value, which we could not buy, with which we cannot part.

A year afterward, some of us were amusing ourselves with chalking outlandish beasts on the Museum blackboard. We drew prancing starfishes; frogs in mortal combat; hydra-headed worms; stately crawfishes, standing on their tails, bearing aloft umbrellas; and grotesque fishes with gaping mouths and staring eyes. The Professor came in shortly after, and was as amused as any at our experiments. He looked at the fishes.

"Haemulons, every one of them," he said; "Mr. ―― drew them."

True; and to this day, if I attempt a fish, I can draw nothing but haemulons.

The fourth day, a second fish of the same group was placed beside the first, and I was bidden to point out the resemblances and differences between the two; another and another followed, until the entire family lay before me, and a whole legion of jars covered the table and surrounding shelves; the odor had become a pleasant perfume; and even now, the sight of an old, six-inch, worm-eaten cork brings fragrant memories.

The whole group of haemulons was thus brought in review; and, whether engaged upon the dissection of the internal organs, the preparation and examination of the bony framework, or the description of the various parts, Agassiz's training in the method of observing facts and their orderly arrangement was ever accompanied by the urgent exhortation not to be content with them.

"Facts are stupid things," he would say, "until brought into connection with some general law."

At the end of eight months, it was almost with reluctance that I left these friends and turned to insects; but what I had gained by this outside experience has been of greater value than years of later investigation in my favorite groups.

Considerations

1. Agassiz's remark that "facts are stupid things until brought into connection with some general law" is worth examining. What is "stupid" about a fact? What term(s) would you substitute to clarify his observation? What is the difference between a fact and a "general law"? Is Agassiz's statement applicable only to the exact sciences, or does it have broader implications? Give and explain examples, preferably based on your own experience.

2. Agassiz dealt with graduate students, well along in their areas of specilization. How would his teaching techniques work with undergrads or

high school students? Discuss (but seriously) the possible outcomes of your English instructor's handing you a difficult poem with no more guidance than the injunction to "Look, look, look." How considerable a part of our education, both formal and informal, involves *looking*? Explain.

3. How might lateral thinking have aided Scudder in seeing the fish the way Agassiz determined he should? And what does Agassiz mean by the observation that "a pencil is one of the best of eyes"?

from
THE AUTOBIOGRAPHY OF NATHANIEL SHALER

When I sat me down before my tin pan, Agassiz brought me a small fish, placing it before me with the rather stern requirement that I should study it, but should on no account talk to any one concerning it, nor read anything relating to fishes, until I had his permission so to do. To my inquiry, "What shall I do?" he said in effect: "Find out what you can without damaging the specimen; when I think that you have done the work I will question you." In the course of an hour I thought I had compassed that fish; it was rather an unsavory object, giving forth the stench of old alcohol, then loathsome to me, though in time I came to like it. Many of the scales were loosened so that they fell off. It appeared to me to be a case for a summary report, which I was anxious to make and get on to the next stage of the business. But Agassiz, though always within call, concerned himself no further with me that day, nor the next, nor for a week. At first, this neglect was distressing; but I saw that it was a game, for he was, as I discerned rather than saw, covertly watching me. So I set my wits to work upon the thing, and in the course of a hundred hours or so thought I had done much—a hundred times as much as seemed possible at the start. I got interested in finding out how the scales went in series, their shape, the form and placement of the teeth, etc. Finally, I felt full of the subject, and probably expressed it in my bearing; as for words about it then, there were none from my master except his cheery "Good morning." At length, on the seventh day, came the question, "Well?" and my disgorge of learning to him as he sat on the edge of my table puffing his cigar. At the end of the hour's telling, he swung off and away, saying: "That is not right." Here I began to think that, after all, perhaps the rules for scanning Latin verse were not the worst infliction in the world. Moreover, it was clear that he was playing a game with me to find if I were capable of doing hard, continuous work without the support of a teacher, and this stimulated me to labor. I went at the task anew, discarded my first notes, and in another week of ten hours a day labor I had results which astonished myself and satisfied him. Still there was no trace of praise in words or manner. He signified that it would do by placing before me about a half a peck of bones, telling me to see what I could make of them, with no further directions to guide me. I soon found that they were the skeletons of half a dozen fishes of different species; the jaws told me so much at a first inspection. The task evidently was to fit the separate bones together in their proper order. Two months or more went to this task with no other help than an occasional looking over my grouping with the stereotyped remark: "That is not right." Finally, the task was done, and I was again set upon alcoholic specimens—this time a remarkable lot of specimens representing, perhaps, twenty species of the side-swimmers or Pleuronectidae.

I shall never forget the sense of power in dealing with things which I felt in beginning the more extended work on a group of animals. I had learned the art of comparing objects, which is the basis of the naturalist's work. At this stage I was allowed to read, and to discuss my work with others about me. I did both eagerly, and acquired a considerable knowledge of the literature of ichthyology, becoming especially interested in the system of classification, then most imperfect. I tried to follow Agassiz's scheme of division into the order of ctenoids and ganoids, with the result that I found one of my species of side-swimmers had cycloid scales on one side and ctenoid on the other. This not only shocked my sense of the value of classification in a way that permitted no full recovery of my original respect for the process, but for a time shook my confidence in my master's knowledge. At the same time I had a malicious pleasure in exhibiting my "find" to him expecting to repay in part the humiliation which he had evidently tried to inflict on my conceit. To my question as to how the nondescript should be classified he said: "My boy, there are now two of us who know that."

Considerations

1. The paired readings in this section of *Connections* are based on, to quote Shaler, "the art of comparing objects, which is the basis of the naturalist's work." In comparing Scudder's account with Shaler's, and in comparing other readings, have you found this method helpful? If yes, in what particular ways? If no, explain why it doesn't work for you.

2. Toward the end of his remarks, Shaler describes his shock at discovering that one of his specimens wouldn't fit neatly into either of the two groups he had "available" for it. Why should such a discovery shock him? What lasting value might such an experience hold for a young scientist? For you? For anyone? Have you ever experienced a similar jolt when you encountered something that didn't fit into your previous way of categorizing things? Detail the experience, including what you did about it.

17. OWNING LAND

In the two selections that follow, Henry David Thoreau and Ralph Waldo Emerson prompt us to question what it means for man to "own" or "possess" property. They do it in different ways, with differing degrees of seriousness, but they get to a remarkably similar point. Here's Thoreau:

BUYING A FARM

At a certain season of our life we are accustomed to consider every spot as the possible site of a house. I have thus surveyed the country on every side within a dozen miles of where I live. In imagination I have bought all the farms in succession, for all were to be bought and I knew their price. I walked over each farmer's premises, tasted his wild apples, discoursed on husbandry with him, took his farm at his price, at any price, mortgaging it to him in my mind; even put a higher price on it,—took every thing but a deed of it,—took his word for his deed, for I dearly love to talk,—cultivated it, and him too to some extent, I trust, and withdrew when I had enjoyed it long enough, leaving him to carry it on. This experience entitled me to be regarded as a sort of real-estate broker by my friends. Wherever I sat, there I might live, and the landscape radiated from me accordingly. What is a house but a *sedes*, a seat?—better if a country seat. I discovered many a site for a house not likely to be soon improved, which some might have thought too far from the village, but to my eyes the village was too far from it. Well, there I might live, I said; and there I did live, for an hour, a summer and a winter life; saw how I could let the years run off, buffet the winter through, and see the spring come in. The future inhabitants of this region, wherever they may place their houses, may be sure that they have been anticipated. An afternoon sufficed to lay out the land into orchard woodlot and pasture, and to decide what fine oaks or pines should be left to stand before the door, and whence each blasted tree could be seen to the best advantage; and then I let it lie, fallow perchance, for a man is rich in proportion to the number of things which he can afford to let alone.

My imagination carried me so far that I even had the refusal of several farms,—the refusal was all I wanted,—but I never got my fingers burned by actual possession. The nearest that I came to actual possession was when I bought the Hollowell Place, and had begun to sort my seeds, and collected materials with which to make a wheelbarrow to carry it on or off with; but before the owner gave me a deed of it, his wife—every man has such a wife—changed her mind and wished to keep it, and he offered me ten dollars to release him. Now, to speak the truth, I had but ten cents in the world, and it surpassed my arithmetic to tell, if I was that man who had ten cents, or who had a farm, or ten dollars, or all together. However, I let him keep the ten dollars and the farm too, for I had carried it far enough; or rather, to be generous, I sold him the farm for just what I gave for it, and, as he was not a rich man, made him a present of ten dollars, and still had my ten cents, and seeds, and materials for a wheelbarrow left. I found thus that I had been a rich man without any damage to my poverty. But I retained the landscape, and I have since annually carried off what it yielded without a wheelbarrow. With respect to landscapes,—

> "I am monarch of all I *survey*,
> My right there is none to dispute."

I have frequently seen a poet withdraw, having enjoyed the most valuable part of a farm, while the crusty farmer supposed that he had got a few wild apples only. Why, the owner does not know it for many years when a poet has put his farm in rhyme, the most admirable kind of invisible fence, has fairly impounded it, milked it, skimmed it, and got all the cream, and left the farmer only the skimmed milk.

The real attractions of the Hollowell farm, to me, were; its complete retirement, being about two miles from the village, half a mile from the nearest neighbor, and separated from the highway by a broad field; its bounding on the river, which the owner said protected it by its fogs from frosts in the spring, though that was nothing to me; the gray color and ruinous state of the house and barn, and the dilapidated fences, which put such an interval between me and the last occupant; the hollow and lichen-covered apple trees, gnawed by rabbits, showing what kind of neighbors I should have; but above all, the recollection I had of it from my earliest voyages up the river, when the house was concealed behind a dense grove of red maples, through which I heard the house-dog bark. I was in haste to buy it, before the proprietor finished getting out some rocks, cutting down the hollow apple trees, and grubbing up some young birches which had sprung up in the pasture, or, in short, had made any more of his improvements. To enjoy these advantages I was ready to carry it on; like Atlas, to take the world on my shoulders,—I never heard what compensation he received for that,—and do all those things which had no other motive or excuse but that I might pay for it and be unmolested in my possession of it; for I knew all the while that it would yield the most abundant crop of the kind I wanted if I could only afford to let it alone. But it turned out as I have said.

All that I could say, then, with respect to farming on a large scale, (I have always cultivated a garden,) was, that I had had my seeds ready. Many think that seeds improve with age. I have no doubt that time discriminates between the good and the bad; and when at last I shall plant, I shall be less likely to be disappointed. But I would say to my fellows, once for all, As long as possible live free and uncommitted. It makes but little difference whether you are committed to a farm or the county jail.

Old Cato, whose "De Re Rusticâ" is my "Cultivator," says, and the only translation I have seen makes sheer nonsense of the passage, "When you think of getting a farm, turn it thus in your mind, not to buy greedily; nor spare your pains to look at it, and do not think it enough to go round it once. The oftener you go there the more it will please you, if it is good." I think I shall not buy greedily, but go round and round it as long as I live and be buried in it first, that it may please me the more at last.

Considerations

1. Thoreau's response to his failed purchase of the Hollowell farm is amusingly complicated. Explain the logic (or illogic) of his claim that he had been a rich man "without any damage to my poverty." What does he mean by "every man has such a wife"? Could such a remark fairly be labeled "sexist"? Why or why not?

2. Do you find yourself agreeing with Thoreau that there is far more joy and satisfaction in imagining yourself the owner of something you desire deeply than in actually acquiring it? That ownership in fact is burdensome, while ownership in fancy is pleasurable? That, as Thoreau observes, "It makes little difference whether you are committed to a farm or the county jail"? Comment on the basis of your own experiences.

3. There is much light-hearted punning in this piece, especially toward the beginning. Find examples (the punning on "seat," "cultivate," for instance) and comment on (a) how they contribute to tone, and (b) what influence they have on how you perceive the author as a person.

HAMATREYA

    Minott, Lee, Willard, Hosmer, Meriam, Flint
    Possessed the land which rendered to their toil
    Hay, corn, roots, hemp, flax, apples, wool, and wood.
    Each of these landlords walked amidst his farm,
5 Saying, ''Tis mine, my children's, and my name's:
    How sweet the west wind sounds in my own trees!
    How graceful climb those shadows on my hill!
    I fancy these pure waters and the flags
    Know me, as does my dog: we sympathize;
10 And, I affirm, my actions smack of the soil.'
    Where are these men? Asleep beneath their grounds;
    And strangers, fond as they, their furrows plough.

    Earth laughs in flowers, to see her boastful boys
    Earth-proud, proud of the earth which is not theirs;
15 Who steer the plough, but cannot steer their feet
    Clear of the grave.
    They added ridge to valley, brook to pond,
    And sighed for all that bounded their domain.
    'This suits me for a pasture; that's my park;
20 We must have clay, lime, gravel, granite-ledge,
    And misty lowland, where to go for peat.
    The land is well,—lies fairly to the south.
    'Tis good, when you have crossed the sea and back,
    To find the sitfast acres where you left them.'
25 Ah! the hot owner sees not Death, who adds
    Him to his land, a lump of mould the more.
    Hear what the Earth says:—

EARTH-SONG

    'Mine and yours;
    Mine, not yours.
30 Earth endures;
    Stars abide—
    Shine down in the old sea;
    Old are the shores;
    But where are old men?
35 I who have seen much,
    Such have I never seen.

    'The lawyer's deed
    Ran sure,
    In tail,
40 To them, and to their heirs
    Who shall succeed,
    Without fail,
    Forevermore.

    'Here is the land,
45 Shaggy with wood,
    With its old valley,
    Mound and flood.
    But the heritors?
    Fled like the flood's foam,—
50 The lawyer, and the laws,
    And the kingdom,
    Clean swept herefrom.

    They called me theirs,
    Who so controlled me;
55 Yet every one
    Wished to stay, and is gone.
    How am I theirs,
    If they cannot hold me,
    But I hold them?'

60 When I heard the Earth-song,
    I was no longer brave;
    My avarice cooled
    Like lust in the chill of the grave.

Considerations

1. There are three voices in this poem. To whom does each belong? Who is the "I" in line 8 of the first part? The "I" in the thirty-fifth line? The "I" in the final stanza?

2. Thoreau and Emerson come at a common theme from quite different directions. How and where do their points of view converge?

Exercises

1. Put in your own words, either poetry or prose, what you take to be the meaning of the fourth stanza of "Earth-Song," and if in the process you discover that your thinking and writing are pulling you in surprising directions, go with them.

2. Develop a dialogue between Emerson and Thoreau on the subject of ownership or some closely related topic; or between you and Thoreau, or you and Emerson, or even among the three of you.

18. THREE READINGS ON READING

The three following selections examine the act of reading, a skill we tend to make little of once we've mastered it. Here, though, reading is seen as something more than simply one of the three R's. In "The House Was Quiet and the World Was Calm," consider what Wallace Stevens makes of it.

THE HOUSE WAS QUIET AND THE WORLD WAS CALM

The house was quiet and the world was calm.
The reader became the book; and summer night

Was like the conscious being of the book.
The house was quiet and the world was calm.

5 The words were spoken as if there was no book,
Except that the reader leaned above the page,

Wanted to lean, wanted much most to be
The scholar to whom his book is true, to whom

The summer night is like a perfection of thought.
10 The house was quiet because it had to be.

The quiet was part of the meaning, part of the mind:
The access of perfection to the page.

And the world was calm. The truth in a calm world,
In which there is no other meaning, itself

15 Is calm, itself is summer and night, itself
Is the reader leaning late and reading there.

"Continuity of Parks" by Julio Cortázar also deals with a quiet house and the reader within it. Beyond these elements, poem and short-short story have nothing in common. Or do they? In reading and reflecting on the following selection, do you find any connections with the poem's central meaning? With what Stevens might have meant by "The access of perfection to the page"?

CONTINUITY OF PARKS

He had begun to read the novel a few days before. He had put it down because of some urgent business conferences, opened it again on his way back to the estate by train; he permitted himself a slowly growing interest in the plot, in the characterizations. That afternoon, after writing a letter giving his power of attorney and discussing a matter of joint ownership with the manager of his estate, he returned to the book in the tranquillity of his study which looked out upon the park with its oaks. Sprawled in his favorite armchair, its back toward the door—even the possibility of an intrusion would have irritated him, had he thought of it—he let his left hand caress repeatedly the green velvet upholstery and set to reading the final chapters. He remembered effortlessly the names and his mental image of the characters; the novel spread its glamour over him almost at once. He tasted the almost perverse pleasure of disengaging himself line by line from the things around him, and at the same time feeling his head rest comfortably on the green velvet of the chair with its high back, sensing that the cigarettes rested within reach of his hand, that beyond the great windows the air of afternoon danced under the oak trees in the park. Word by word, licked up by the sordid dilemma of the hero and heroine, letting himself be absorbed to the point where the images settled down and took on color and movement, he was witness to the final encounter in the mountain cabin. The woman arrived first, apprehensive; now the lover came in, his face cut by the backlash of a branch. Admirably, she stanched the blood with her kisses, but he rebuffed her caresses, he had not come to perform again the ceremonies of a secret passion, protected by a world of dry leaves and furtive paths through the forest. The dagger warmed itself against his chest, and underneath liberty pounded, hidden close. A lustful, panting dialogue raced down the pages like a rivulet of snakes, and one felt it had been decided from eternity. Even to those caresses which writhed about the lover's body, as though wishing to keep him there, to dissuade him from it; they sketched abominably the frame of that other body it was necessary to destroy. Nothing had been forgotten: alibis, unforeseen hazards, possible mistakes. From this hour on, each instant had its use minutely assigned. The cold-blooded, twice-gone-over reexamination of the details was barely broken off so that a hand could caress a cheek. It was beginning to get dark.

Not looking at one another now, rigidly fixed upon the task which awaited them, they separated at the cabin door. She was to follow the trail that led north. On the path leading in the opposite direction, he turned for a moment to watch her running, her hair loosened and flying. He ran in turn, crouching among the trees and hedges until, in the yellowish fog of dusk, he could distinguish the avenue of trees which led up to the house. The dogs were not supposed to bark, they did not bark. The estate manager would not be there at this hour, and he was not there. He went up the three porch steps and entered. The woman's words reached him over the thudding of blood in his ears: first a blue chamber, then a hall, then a carpeted stairway. At the top, two doors. No one in the first room, no one in the second. The door of the salon, and then, the knife in hand, the light from the great windows, the high back of an armchair covered in green velvet, the head of the man in the chair reading a novel.

In this next poem, Philip Larkin talks about two kinds of escape, only one of them provided by reading. The central question posed in this piece may be whether or not to believe the speaker. What do you think?

A STUDY OF READING HABITS

When getting my nose in a book
Cured most things short of school,
It was worth ruining my eyes
To know I could still keep cool,
5 And deal out the old right hook
To dirty dogs twice my size.

Later, with inch-thick specs,
Evil was just my lark:
Me and my cloak and fangs
10 Had ripping times in the dark.
The women I clubbed with sex!
I broke them up like meringues.

Don't read much now: the dude
Who lets the girl down before
15 The hero arrives, the chap
Who's yellow and keeps the store,
Seem far too familiar. Get stewed:
Books are a load of crap.

Considerations

1. One of the more difficult qualities of a poem to understand in the abstract is how, beyond its literal meaning, a poem's form can resemble or echo its subject. I'm not referring to the typographic shape of a work such as Hollander's or Herbert's, but to sound, meter, rhyme being so appropriate to what the poem *says* that meaning and form seem inseparable. How is the Stevens poem "quiet," "calm"? How (if you agree) does it manage to sound like a "summer night"? Note the number of words in the poem that have the same vowel sound as "calm." In line 7 does the repetition of "wanted" have a quieting effect for you? Stevens begins 9 of the poem's 16 lines with "The." Do you think that this was a conscious device meant to produce a specific response in the reader (if so, how and what kind?), or is it more likely that

this most common of words simply fell into place? What is the effect of repeating the first line in line 4? Consider the poet's use of 2-line stanzas: What is the possible function of space between them? (If you eliminated the spaces, would the poem's total effect be changed or lessened for you? Why or why not?)

2. What is the poem's meaning so far as you are concerned? Stevens is rarely easy, but neither is he impossible. Ideally, can quiet become "part of the meaning" of reading, the truth of it calm the world outside, the reader become the book? If so, how? Have you ever sensed while reading that there is no book, just you and the meaning working in an intimate relationship? An earlier note on Stevens' "Peter Quince . . ." described a poem as an invitation rather than a locked door. How is "The House . . ." inviting? What do *you* bring to it that another would not? What of its meaning is probably your own?

3. "Continuity of Parks" is the kind of story we'd expect to see on a *Twilight Zone* rerun: a reader becomes engrossed in a novel, until his and the writer's imaginations meet and somehow, impossibly, a murderer is loosed from the pages to stalk the reader "sprawled in his favorite armchair." Absurd, but nevertheless compelling, oddly believable. Consider *how* you believe—what about the tale saves it (if you agree) from being *only* absurd, what urges on you "a willing suspension of disbelief." Which is easier to "believe," this or the Stevens poem? Consider the latter's "The reader became the book." Compare the poem's "The house was quiet because it had to be" with the story's "The dogs were not supposed to bark; they did not bark." Consider and explain which work more represents "The access of perfection to the page."

4. In "A Study of Reading Habits" who is the speaker belting with "the old right hook?" Who are "The women I clubbed with sex"? And why is it that he doesn't "read much now"? Does the fall from innocence theme possibly apply here? Explain. Consider too whether "getting my nose in a book" and its outcomes as Larkin puts them is (or isn't) pretty much the same as what happens in the Stevens and Cortázar selections. Are we meant to believe the speaker when he observes that "Books are a load of crap"? Why or why not?

Exercises

1. Respond to the following comments on reading by Donald Hall. Support, modify, or refute Hall's views in a few thoughtful paragraphs.

> "People surround the idea of reading with piety, and do not take into account the purpose of reading or the value of what is being read. Teachers and parents praise the child who reads, and praise themselves, whether the text be *The Reader's Digest* or *Moby Dick*. The advent of TV has increased the false values ascribed to reading, since TV provides a vulgar alternative. But this piety is silly; and most reading is no more cultural nor intellectual nor imaginative than shooting pool or watching *What's My Line*."

2. Write a response to the following statements about reading by Henry David Thoreau:

- a) "To read well, that is, to read books in a true spirit, is a noble exercise, and one that will task the reader more than any exercise which the customs of the day esteem."
- b) "Reading requires a training such as the athletes underwent, the steady intention almost of the whole life to this object."
- c) "Books must be read as deliberately and reservedly as they were written."
- d) "Books are the treasured wealth of the world and the fit inheritance of generations and nations . . . Their authors are a natural and irresistible aristocracy in every society, and, more than kings or emperors, exert an influence on mankind."
- e) "How many a man has dated a new era in his life from the reading of a book!"

3. Set Thoreau's comments over against Hall's. Write a piece that reacts to both Hall and Thoreau and one that plays off their ideas against yours, against each other's, perhaps against the ideas implied in the selections by Larkin, Cortázar, and Stevens.

19. FIVE SHORT POEMS: STEPHEN CRANE

As an exercise in making connections, read and comment on the poems below. Briefly annotate each, but let the connections accumulate as you move from poem to poem. Having done that, you should have developed sufficient insight into Crane's overriding point of view to carry out the final aspect of this assignment: write a sixth poem.

I STOOD

I stood upon a high place,
And saw, below, many devils
Running, leaping,
And carousing in sin.
One looked up, grinning,
And said: "Comrade! Brother!"

MANY RED DEVILS

Many red devils ran from my heart
And out upon the page.
They were so tiny
The pen could mash them.
And many struggled in the ink.
It was strange
To write in this red muck
Of things from my heart.

YOU SAY YOU ARE HOLY

You say you are holy,
And that
Because I have not seen you sin.
Ay, but there are those
Who see you sin, my friend.

A MAN FEARED

A man feared that he might find an assassin;
Another that he might find a victim.
One was more wise than the other.

THE SAGE LECTURED

The sage lectured brilliantly.
Before him, two images:
"Now this one is a devil,
And this one is me."
He turned away.
Then a cunning pupil
Changed the positions.
Turned the sage again:
"Now this one is a devil,
And this one is me."
The pupils sat, grinning,
And rejoiced in the game.
But the sage was a sage.

20. POE ON POE

"The Black Cat" is one of Edgar Allan Poe's most famous and horrifying stories. "The Imp of the Perverse", not nearly as well-known, seems to comment on "The Black Cat." Read "The Imp" with an eye to how it helps you interpret "The Black Cat."

THE BLACK CAT

For the most wild yet most homely narrative which I am about to pen, I neither expect nor solicit belief. Mad indeed would I be to expect it, in a case where my very senses reject their own evidence. Yet, mad am I not—and very surely do I not dream. But to-morrow I die, and to-day I would unburden my soul. My immediate purpose is to place before the world, plainly, succinctly, and without comment, a series of mere household events. In their consequences, these events have terrified—have tortured—have destroyed me. Yet I will not attempt to expound them. To me, they have presented little but horror—to many they will seem less terrible than *baroques*. Hereafter, perhaps, some intellect may be found which will reduce my phantasm to the commonplace—some intellect more calm, more logical, and far less excitable than my own, which will perceive, in the circumstances I detail with awe, nothing more than an ordinary succession of very natural causes and effects.

From my infancy I was noted for the docility and humanity of my disposition. My tenderness of heart was even so conspicuous as to make me the jest of my companions. I was especially fond of animals, and was indulged by my parents with a great variety of pets. With these I spent most of my time, and never was so happy as when feeding and caressing them. This peculiarity of character grew with my growth, and, in my manhood, I derived from it one of my principal sources of pleasure. To those who have cherished an affection for a faithful and sagacious dog, I need hardly be at the trouble of explaining the nature or the intensity of the gratification thus derivable. There is something in the unselfish and self-sacrificing love of a brute, which goes directly to the heart of him who has had frequent occasion to test the paltry friendship and gossamer fidelity of mere *Man*.

I married early, and was happy to find in my wife a disposition not uncongenial with my own. Observing my partiality for domestic pets, she lost no opportunity of procuring those of the most agreeable kind. We had birds, gold-fish, a fine dog, rabbits, a small monkey, and a *cat*.

This latter was a remarkably large and beautiful animal, entirely black, and sagacious to an astonishing degree. In speaking of his intelligence, my wife, who at heart was not a little tinctured with superstition, made frequent allusion to the ancient popular notion, which regarded all black cats as witches in disguise. Not that she was ever *serious* upon this point—and I mention the matter at all for no better reason than that it happens, just now, to be remembered.

Pluto—this was the cat's name—was my favorite pet and playmate. I alone fed him, and he attended me wherever I went about the house. It was even with difficulty that I could prevent him from following me through the streets.

Our friendship lasted, in this manner, for several years, during which my general temperament and character—through the instrumentality of the Fiend Intemperance—had (I blush to confess it) experienced a radical alteration for the worse. I grew, day by day, more moody, more irritable, more regardless of the feelings of others. I suffered myself to use intemperate language to my wife. At length, I even offered her personal violence. My pets, of course, were made to feel the change in my disposition. I not only neglected, but ill-used them. For Pluto, however, I still retained sufficient regard to restrain me from maltreating him, as I made no scruple of maltreating the rabbits, the monkey, or even the dog, when, by accident, or through affection, they came in my way. But my disease grew upon me—for what disease is like Alcohol!—and at length even Pluto, who was now becoming old, and consequently somewhat peevish—even Pluto began to experience the effects of my ill temper.

One night, returning home, much intoxicated, from one of my haunts about town, I fancied that the cat avoided my presence. I seized him; when, in his fright at my violence, he inflicted a slight wound upon my hand with his teeth. The fury of a demon instantly possessed me. I knew myself no longer. My original soul seemed, at once, to take its flight from my body; and a more than fiendish malevolence, gin-nurtured, thrilled every fibre of my frame. I took from my waistcoat-pocket a penknife, opened it, grasped the poor beast by the throat, and deliberately cut one of its eyes from the socket! I blush, I burn, I shudder, while I pen the damnable atrocity.

When reason returned with the morning—when I had slept off the fumes of the night's debauch—I experienced a sentiment half of horror, half of remorse, for the crime of which I had been guilty; but it was, at best, a feeble and equivocal feeling, and the soul remained untouched. I again plunged into excess, and soon drowned in wine all memory of the deed.

In the meantime the cat slowly recovered. The socket of the lost eye presented, it is true, a frightful appearance, but he no longer appeared to suffer any pain. He went about the house as usual, but, as might be expected, fled in extreme terror at my approach. I had so much of my old heart left, as to be at first grieved by this evident dislike on the part of a creature which had once so loved me. But this feeling soon gave place to irritation. And then came, as if to my final and irrevocable overthrow, the spirit of PERVERSENESS. Of this spirit philosophy takes no account. Yet I am not more sure that my soul lives, than I am that perverseness is one of the primitive impulses of the human heart—one of the indivisible primary faculties, or sentiments, which give direction to the character of Man. Who has not, a hundred times, found himself committing a vile or stupid action, for no other reason than because he knows he should *not*? Have we not a perpetual inclination, in the teeth of our best judgment, to violate that which is *Law,* merely because we understand it to be such? This spirit of perverseness, I say, came to my final overthrow. It was this unfathomable longing of the soul *to vex itself*—to offer violence to its own nature—to do wrong for the wrong's sake only—that urged me to continue and finally to consummate the injury I had inflicted upon the unoffending brute. One morning, in cold blood, I slipped a noose about its neck and hung it to the limb of a tree;—hung it with the tears streaming from my eyes, and with the bitterest remorse at my heart;—hung it *because* I knew that it had loved me, and *because* I felt it had given me no reason of offence;—hung it *because* I knew that in so doing I was committing a sin—a deadly sin that would so jeopardize my immortal soul as to place it—if such a thing were possible—even beyond the reach of the infinite mercy of the Most Merciful and Most Terrible God.

On the night of the day on which this most cruel deed was done, I was aroused from sleep by the cry of fire. The curtains of my bed were in flames. The whole house was blazing. It was with great difficulty that my wife, a servant, and myself, made our escape from the conflagration. The destruction was complete. My entire worldly wealth was swallowed up, and I resigned myself thenceforward to despair.

I am above the weakness of seeking to establish a sequence of cause and effect, between the disaster and the atrocity. But I am detailing a chain of facts—and wish not to leave even a possible link imperfect. On the day succeeding the fire, I visited the ruins. The walls, with one exception, had fallen in. This exception was found in a compartment wall, not very thick, which stood about the middle of the house, and against which had rested the head of my bed. The plastering had here, in great measure, resisted the action of the fire—a fact which I attributed to its having been recently spread. About this wall a dense crowd were collected, and many persons seemed to be examining a particular portion of it with very minute and eager attention. The words "strange!" "singular!" and other similar expressions, excited my curiosity. I approached and saw, as if graven in *bas-relief* upon the white surface, the figure of a gigantic *cat*. The impression was given with an accuracy truly marvellous. There was a rope about the animal's neck.

When I first beheld this apparition—for I could scarcely regard it as less—my wonder and my terror were extreme. But at length reflection came to my aid. The cat, I remembered, had been hung in a garden adjacent to the house. Upon the alarm of fire, this garden had been immediately filled by the crowd—by some one of whom the animal must have been cut from the tree and thrown, through an open window, into my chamber. This had probably been done with the view of arousing me from sleep. The falling of other walls had compressed the victim of my cruelty into the substance of the freshly-spread plaster, the lime of which, with the flames, and the *ammonia* from the carcass, had then accomplished the portraiture as I saw it.

Although I thus readily accounted to my reason, if not altogether to my conscience, for the startling fact just detailed, it did not the less fail to make a deep impression upon my fancy. For months I could not rid myself of the phantasm of the cat; and, during this period, there came back into my spirit a half-sentiment that seemed, but was not, remorse. I went so far as to regret the loss of the animal, and to look about me, among the vile haunts which I now habitually frequented, for another pet of the same species, and of somewhat similar appearance, with which to supply its place.

One night as I sat, half stupefied, in a den of more than infamy, my attention was suddenly drawn to some black object, reposing upon the head of one of the immense hogsheads of gin, or of rum, which constituted the chief furniture of the apartment. I had been looking steadily at the top of this hogshead for some minutes, and what now caused me surprise was the fact that I had not sooner perceived the object thereupon. I approached it, and touched it with my hand. It was a black cat—a very large one—fully as large as Pluto, and closely resembling him in every respect but one. Pluto had not a white hair upon any portion of his body; but this cat had a large, although indefinite splotch of white, covering nearly the whole region of the breast.

Upon my touching him, he immediately arose, purred loudly, rubbed against my hand, and appeared delighted with my notice. This, then, was the very creature of which I was in search. I at once offered to purchase it of the landlord; but this person made no claim to it—knew nothing of it—had never seen it before.

I continued my caresses, and when I prepared to go home, the animal evinced a disposition to accompany me. I permitted it to do so; occasionally stooping and patting it as I proceeded. When it reached the house it domesticated itself at once, and became immediately a great favorite with my wife.

For my own part, I soon found a dislike to it arising within me. This was just the reverse of what I had anticipated; but—I know not how or why it was—its evident fondness for myself rather disgusted and annoyed me. By slow degrees these feelings of disgust and annoyance rose into the bitterness of hatred. I avoided the creature; a certain sense of shame, and the remembrance of my former deed of cruelty, preventing me from physically abusing it. I did not, for some weeks, strike, or otherwise violently ill use it; but gradually—very gradually—I came to look upon it with unutterable loathing, and to flee silently from its odious presence, as from the breath of a pestilence.

What added, no doubt, to my hatred of the beast, was the discovery on the morning after I brought it home, that, like Pluto, it also had been deprived of one of its eyes. This circumstance, however, only endeared it to my wife, who, as I have already said, possessed, in a high degree, that humanity of feeling which had once been my distinguishing trait, and the source of many of my simplest and purest pleasures.

With my aversion to this cat, however, its partiality for myself seemed to increase. It followed my footsteps with a pertinacity which it would be difficult to make the reader comprehend. Whenever I sat, it would crouch beneath my chair, or spring upon my knees, covering me with its loathsome caresses. If I arose to walk it would get between my feet and thus nearly throw me down, or, fastening its long and sharp claws in my dress, clamber, in this manner, to my breast. At such times, although I longed to destroy it with a blow, I was yet withheld from so doing, partly by a memory of my former crime, but chiefly—let me confess it at once—by absolute dread of the beast.

This dread was not exactly a dread of physical evil—and yet I should be at a loss how otherwise to define it. I am almost ashamed to own—yes, even in this felon's cell, I am almost ashamed to own—that the terror and horror with which the animal inspired me, had been heightened by one of the merest chimeras it would be possible to conceive. My wife had called my attention, more than once, to the character of the mark of white hair, of which I have spoken, and which constituted the sole visible difference between the strange beast and the one I had destroyed. The reader will remember that this mark, although large, had been originally very indefinite; but, by slow degrees—degrees nearly imperceptible, and which for a long time my reason struggled to reject as fanciful —it had, at length, assumed a rigorous distinctness of outline. It was now the representation of an object that I shudder to name—and for this, above all, I loathed, and dreaded, and would have rid myself of the monster *had I dared*—it was now, I say, the image of a hideous—of a ghastly thing—of the GALLOWS!—oh, mournful and terrible engine of Horror and of Crime—of Agony and of Death!

And now was I indeed wretched beyond the wretchedness of mere Humanity. And *a brute beast*—whose fellow I had contemptuously destroyed—*a brute beast* to work out for *me*—for me, a man fashioned in the image of the High God—so much of insufferable woe! Alas! neither by day nor by night knew I the blessing of rest any more! During the former the creature left me no moment alone, and in the latter I started hourly from dreams of unutterable fear to find the hot breath of *the thing* upon my face, and its vast weight—an incarnate nightmare that I had not power to shake off—incumbent eternally upon my *heart!*

Beneath the pressure of torments such as these the feeble remnant of the good within me succumbed. Evil thoughts became my sole intimates—the darkest and most evil of thoughts. The moodiness of my usual temper increased to hatred of all things and of all mankind; while from the sudden, frequent, and ungovernable outbursts of a fury to which I now blindly abandoned myself, my uncomplaining wife, alas, was the most usual and the most patient of sufferers.

One day she accompanied me, upon some household errand, into the cellar of the old building which our poverty compelled us to inhabit. The cat followed me down the steep stairs, and, nearly throwing me headlong, exasperated me to madness. Uplifting an axe, and forgetting in my wrath the childish dread which had hitherto stayed my hand, I aimed a blow at the animal, which, of course, would have proved instantly fatal had it descended as I wished. But this blow was arrested by the hand of my wife. Goaded by the interference into a rage more than demoniacal, I withdrew my arm from her grasp and buried the axe in her brain. She fell dead upon the spot without a groan.

This hideous murder accomplished, I set myself forthwith, and with entire deliberation, to the task of concealing the body. I knew that I could not remove it from the house, either by day or by night, without the risk of being observed by the neighbors. Many projects entered my mind. At one period I thought of cutting the corpse into minute fragments, and destroying them by fire. At another, I resolved to dig a grave for it in the floor of the cellar. Again, I deliberated about casting it in the well in the yard—about packing it in a box, as if merchandise, with the usual arrangements, and so getting a porter to take it from the house. Finally I hit upon what I considered a far better expedient than either of these. I determined to wall it up in the cellar, as the monks of the Middle Ages are recorded to have walled up their victims.

For a purpose such as this the cellar was well adapted. Its walls were loosely constructed, and had lately been plastered throughout with a rough plaster, which the dampness of the atmosphere had prevented from hardening. Moreover, in one of the walls was a projection, caused by a false chimney, or fireplace, that had been filled up and made to resemble the rest of the cellar. I made no doubt that I could readily displace the bricks at this point, insert the corpse, and wall the whole up as before, so that no eye could detect anything suspicious.

And in this calculation I was not deceived. By means of a crowbar I easily dislodged the bricks, and, having carefully deposited the body against the inner wall, I propped it in that position, while with little trouble I relaid the whole structure as it originally stood. Having procured mortar, sand, and hair, with every possible precaution, I prepared a plaster which could not be distinguished from the old, and with this, I very carefully went over the new brick-work. When I had finished, I felt satisfied that all was right. The wall did not present the slightest appearance of having been disturbed. The rubbish on the floor was picked up with the minutest care. I looked around triumphantly, and said to myself: "Here at least, then, my labor has not been in vain."

My next step was to look for the beast which had been the cause of so much wretchedness; for I had, at length, firmly resolved to put it to death. Had I been able to meet with it at the moment, there could have been no doubt of its fate; but it appeared that the crafty animal had been alarmed at the violence of my previous anger, and forbore to present itself in my present mood. It is impossible to describe or to imagine the deep, blissful sense of relief which the absence of the detested creature occasioned in my bosom. It did not make its appearance during the night; and thus for one night, at least, since its introduction into the house, I soundly and tranquilly slept; aye, slept even with the burden of murder upon my soul.

The second and the third day passed, and still my tormentor came not. Once again I breathed as a freeman. The monster, in terror, had fled the premises for ever! I should behold it no more! My happiness was supreme! The guilt of my dark deed disturbed me but little. Some few inquiries had been made, but these had been readily answered. Even a search had been instituted—but of course nothing was to be discovered. I looked upon my future felicity as secured.

Upon the fourth day of the assassination, a party of the police came, very unexpectedly, into the house, and proceeded again to make a rigorous investigation of the premises. Secure, however, in the inscrutability of my place of concealment, I felt no embarrassment whatever. The officers bade me accompany them in their search. They left no nook or corner unexplored. At length, for the third or fourth time, they descended into the cellar. I quivered not in a muscle. My heart beat calmly as that of one who slumbers in innocence. I walked the cellar from end to end. I folded my arms upon my bosom, and roamed easily to and fro. The police were thoroughly satisfied and prepared to depart. The glee at my heart was too strong to be restrained. I burned to say if but one word, by way of triumph, and to render doubly sure their assurance of my guiltlessness.

"Gentlemen," I said at last, as the party ascended the steps, "I delight to have allayed your suspicions. I wish you all health and a little more courtesy. By the bye, gentlemen, this—this is a very well-constructed house," (in the rabid desire to say something easily, I scarcely knew what I uttered at all),—"I may say an excellently well-constructed house. These walls—are you going, gentlemen?—these walls are solidly put together"; and here, through the mere frenzy of bravado, I rapped heavily with a cane which I held in my hand, upon that very portion of the brick-work behind which stood the corpse of the wife of my bosom.

But may God shield and deliver me from the fangs of the Arch-Fiend! No sooner had the reverberation of my blows sunk into silence, than I was answered by a voice from within the tomb!—by a cry, at first muffled and broken, like the sobbing of a child, and then quickly swelling into one long, loud, and continuous scream, utterly anomalous and inhuman—a howl—a wailing shriek, half of horror and half of triumph, such as might have arisen only out of hell, conjointly from the throats of the damned in their agony and of the demons that exult in the damnation.

Of my own thoughts it is folly to speak. Swooning, I staggered to the opposite wall. For one instant the party on the stairs remained motionless, through extremity of terror and awe. In the next a dozen stout arms were toiling at the wall. It fell bodily. The corpse, already greatly decayed and clotted with gore, stood erect before the eyes of the spectators. Upon its head, with red extended mouth and solitary eye of fire, sat the hideous beast whose craft had seduced me into murder, and whose informing voice had consigned me to the hangman. I had walled the monster up within the tomb.

Considerations

1. It's interesting to speculate about what a modern psychiatrist would make of the narrator of many of Poe's stories. "Mad am I not," he asserts in the first paragraph. What contrary evidences does he provide here and in the following paragraph?

2. How would you classify the man's mental state, using the psychiatric jargon we're all more or less familiar with? What, for example, is the modern term for what the narrator calls "perverseness," the "longing of the soul to vex itself—to offer violence to its own nature—to do wrong for the wrong's sake only"?

3. Debate whether or not the narrator would in today's courts be successful in pleading innocence on the basis of insanity. Consider the narrow

legal definition of "insanity," the character and mental state of the man as it is revealed in his narration, and the actual circumstances of the crime(s).

from
THE IMP OF THE PERVERSE

... We have a task before us which must be speedily performed. We know that it will be ruinous to make delay. The most important crisis of our life calls, trumpet-tongued, for immediate energy and action. We glow, we are consumed with eagerness to commence the work, with the anticipation of whose glorious result our whole souls are on fire. It must, it shall be undertaken to-day, and yet we put it off until to-morrow; and why? There is no answer, except that we feel *perverse*, using the word with no comprehension of the principle. To-morrow arrives, and with it a more impatient anxiety to do our duty, but with this very increase of anxiety arrives, also, a nameless, a positively fearful, because unfathomable, craving for delay. This craving gathers strength as the moments fly. The last hour for action is at hand. We tremble with the violence of the conflict within us,—of the definite with the indefinite—of the substance with the shadow. But, if the contest have proceeded thus far, it is the shadow which prevails,—we struggle in vain. The clock strikes, and is the knell of our welfare. At the same time, it is the chanticleer-note to the ghost that has so long overawed us. It flies—it disappears—we are free. The old energy returns. We will labor *now*. Alas, it is *too late!*

We stand upon the brink of a precipice. We peer into the abyss—we grow sick and dizzy. Our first impulse is to shrink from the danger. Unaccountably we remain. By slow degrees our sickness, and dizziness, and horror, become merged in a cloud of unnameable feeling. By gradations, still more imperceptible, this cloud assumes shapes as did the vapor from the bottle out of which arose the genius in the Arabian Nights. But out of this *our* cloud upon the precipice's edge, there grows into palpability, a shape, far more terrible than any genius, or any demon of a tale, and yet it is but a thought, although a fearful one, and one which chills the very marrow of our bones with the fierceness of the delight of its horror. It is merely the idea of what would be our sensations during the sweeping precipitancy of a fall from such a height. And this fall—this rushing annihilation—for the very reason that it involves that one most ghastly and loathsome of all the most ghastly and loathsome images of death and suffering which have ever presented themselves to our imagination—for this very cause do we now the most vividly desire it. And because our reason violently deters us from the brink, *therefore,* do we the most impetuously approach it. There is no passion in nature so demoniacally impatient, as that of him who shuddering upon the edge of a precipice, thus meditates a plunge. To indulge for a moment, in any attempt at *thought,* is to be inevitably lost; for reflection but urges us to forbear, and *therefore* it is, I say, that we *cannot*. If there be no friendly arm to check us, or if we fail in a sudden effort to prostrate ourselves backward from the abyss, we plunge, and are destroyed.

Examine these and similar actions as we will, we shall find them resulting solely from the spirit of the *Perverse*. We perpetrate them merely because we feel that we should *not*. Beyond or behind this, there is no intelligible principle; and we might, indeed, deem this perverseness a direct instigation of the arch-fiend, were it not occasionally known to operate in furtherance of good.

I have said thus much, that in some measure I may answer your question—that I may explain to you why I am here—that I may assign to you something that shall have at least the faint aspect of a cause for my wearing these fetters, and for my tenanting this cell of the condemned. Had I not been thus prolix, you might either have misunderstood me altogether, or, with the rabble, have fancied me mad. As it is, you will easily perceive that I am one of the many uncounted victims of the Imp of the Perverse.

It is impossible that any deed could have been wrought with a more thorough deliberation. For weeks, for months, I pondered upon the means of the murder. I rejected a thousand schemes, because their accomplishment involved a *chance* of detection. At length, in reading some French memoirs, I found an account of a nearly fatal illness that occurred to Madame Pilau, through the agency of a candle accidentally poisoned. The idea struck my fancy at once. I knew my victim's habit of reading in bed. I knew, too, that his apartment was narrow and ill-ventilated. But I need not vex you with impertinent details. I need not describe the easy artifices by which I substituted, in his bed-room candle-stand, a wax-light of my own making, for the one which I found. The next morning he was discovered dead in his bed, and the coroner's verdict was,—"Death by the visitation of God."

Having inherited his estate, all went well with me for years. The idea of detection never once entered my brain. Of the remains of the fatal taper, I had myself carefully disposed. I had left no shadow of a clue by which it would be possible to convict, or even to suspect me of the crime. It is inconceivable how rich a sentiment of satisfaction arose in my bosom as I reflected upon my absolute security. For a very long period of time, I was accustomed to revel in this sentiment. It afforded me more real delight than all the mere worldly advantages accruing from my sin. But there arrived at length an epoch, from which the pleasurable feeling grew, by scarcely perceptible gradations, into a haunting and harassing thought. It harassed because it haunted. I could scarcely get rid of it for an instant. It is quite a common thing to be thus annoyed with the ringing in our ears, or rather in our memories, of the burthen of some ordinary song, or some unimpressive snatches from an opera. Nor will we be the less tormented if the song in itself be good, or the opera air meritorious. In this manner, at last, I would perpetually catch myself pondering upon my security, and repeating, in a low under-tone, the phrase, "I am safe."

One day, whilst sauntering along the streets, I arrested myself in the act of murmuring, half aloud, these customary syllables. In a fit of petulance, I re-modelled them thus:—"I am safe—I am safe—yes—if I be not fool enough to make open confession!"

No sooner had I spoken these words, than I felt an icy chill creep to my heart. I had had some experience in these fits of perversity (whose nature I have been at some trouble to explain) and I remembered well that in no instance, I had successfully resisted their attacks. And now my own casual self-suggestion, that I might possibly be fool enough to confess the murder of which I had been guilty, confronted me, as if the very ghost of him whom I had murdered—and beckoned me on to death.

At first, I made an effort to shake off this nightmare of the soul. I walked vigorously—faster—still faster—at length I ran. I felt a maddening desire to shriek aloud. Every succeeding wave of thought overwhelmed me with new terror, for alas! I well, too well, understood that to *think,* in my situation, was to be lost. I still quickened my pace. I bounded like a madman through the crowded thoroughfares. At length, the populace took the alarm, and pursued me. I felt *then* the consummation of my fate. Could I have torn out my tongue, I would have done it—but a rough voice resounded in my ears—a rougher grasp seized me by the shoulder. I turned—I gasped for breath. For a moment, I experienced all the pangs of suffocation; I became blind, and deaf, and giddy; and then, some invisible fiend, I thought, struck me with his broad palm upon the back. The long-imprisoned secret burst forth from my soul.

They say that I spoke with a distinct enunciation, but with marked emphasis and passionate hurry, as if in dread of interruption before concluding the brief but pregnant sentences that consigned me to the hangman and to hell.

Having related all that was necessary for the fullest judicial conviction, I fell prostrate in a swoon.

But why shall I say more? Today I wear these chains, and am *here!* Tomorrow I shall be fetterless!—*but where?*

Considerations

1. Specifically how does this story (or is it more an essay?) help you to make sense of "The Black Cat"? Or does it? Account for your response.

2. Read either "The Tell-tale Heart" or "The Cask of Amontillado," and detail the connections you find between that story and one or both of the two reprinted here.

21. MADAME BOVARY REVISITED

In his comic short story, "The Kugelmass Episode," Woody Allen has made use of a classic nineteenth-century French novel, Gustave Flaubert's *Madame Bovary*. Excerpted is one chapter from Flaubert's novel. It should give you enough of a sense of the book's emphasis and tone to see how Allen adapts it to his own comic purposes.

from

MADAME BOVARY
Part II, Chapter 9

Six weeks passed. Rodolphe did not come again. At last one evening he appeared.

The day after the fair he told himself:

"Let's not go back too soon; that would be a mistake."

And at the end of a week he had gone off hunting. After the hunting he first feared that too much time had passed, and then he reasoned thus:

"If she loved me from the first day, impatience must make her love me even more. Let's persist!"

And he knew that his calculation had been right when, on entering the room, he saw Emma turn pale.

She was alone. Night was falling. The small muslin curtain along the windows deepened the twilight, and the gilding of the barometer, on which the rays of the sun fell, shone in the looking-glass between the meshes of the coral.

Rodolphe remained standing, and Emma hardly answered his first conventional phrases.

"I have been busy," he said, "I have been ill."

"Nothing serious?" she cried.

"Well," said Rodolphe, sitting down at her side on a footstool, "no . . . It was because I did not want to come back."

"Why?"

"Can't you guess?"

He looked at her again, but so hard that she lowered her head, blushing. He pursued:

"Emma . . ."

"Monsieur!" she exclaimed, drawing back a little.

"Ah! you see," he replied in a melancholy voice, "that I was right not to come back; for this name, this name that fills my whole soul, and that escaped me, you forbid me its use! Madame Bovary! . . . why, the whole world calls you thus! Moreover, it is not your name; it is the name of another!"

He repeated,

"Of another!"

And he hid his face in his hands.

"Yes, I think of you constantly! . . . The thought of you drives me to despair. Ah! forgive me! . . . I'll go . . . Adieu . . . I'll go far away, so far that you will never hear of me again; yet . . . today . . . I don't know what force made me come here. For one does not struggle against Heaven; it is impossible to resist the smile of angels; one is carried away by the beautiful, the lovely, the adorable."

It was the first time that Emma had heard such words addressed to her, and her pride unfolded languidly in the warmth of this language, like someone stretching in a hot bath.

"But if I didn't come," he continued, "if I couldn't see you, at least I have gazed long on all that surrounds you. At night, every night, I arose; I came here; I watched your house, the roof glimmering in the moon, the trees in the garden swaying before your window, and the little lamp, a gleam shining through the window-panes in the darkness. Ah! you never knew that there, so near you, so far from you, was a poor wretch . . ."

She turned towards him with a sob.

"Oh, you are kind!" she said.

"No, I love you, that is all! You do not doubt that! Tell me; one word, one single word!"

And Rodolphe imperceptibly glided from the footstool to the ground; but a sound of wooden shoes was heard in the kitchen, and he noticed that the door of the room was not closed.

"You would do an act of charity," he went on, rising, "if you accepted to gratify a whim!" It was to visit her home, he wished to see it, and since Madame Bovary could see no objection to this, they both rose just when Charles came in.

"Good morning, doctor," Rodolphe said to him.

Flattered by this unexpected title, Charles launched into elaborate displays of politeness. Of this the other took advantage to pull himself together.

"Madame was speaking to me," he then said, "about her health."

Charles interrupted; she was indeed giving him thousands of worries; her palpitations were beginning again. Then Rodolphe asked if riding would not be helpful.

"Certainly! excellent, just the thing! What a good idea! You ought to try it."

And as she objected that she had no horse, Monsieur Rodolphe offered one. She refused his offer; he did not insist. Then to explain his visit he said that his ploughman, the man of the blood-letting, still suffered from dizziness.

"I'll drop by," said Bovary.

"No, no! I'll send him to you; we'll come; that will be more convenient for you."

"Ah! very good! I thank you."

And as soon as they were alone, "Why don't you accept Monsieur Boulanger's offer? It was so gracious of him."

She seemed to pout, invented a thousand excuses, and finally declared that perhaps it would look odd.

"That's the least of my worries!" said Charles, turning on his heel. "Health first! You are making a mistake."

"Could I go riding without proper clothes?"

"You must order a riding outfit," he answered.

The riding-habit decided her.

When it was ready, Charles wrote to Monsieur Boulanger that his wife was able to accept his invitation and thanked him in advance for his kindness.

The next day at noon Rodolphe appeared at Charles's door with two saddle-horses. One had pink rosettes at his ears and a deerskin side-saddle.

Rodolphe had put on high soft boots, assuming that she had never seen the likes of them. In fact Emma was charmed with his appearance as he stood on the landing in his great velvet coat and white corduroy breeches. She was ready; she was waiting for him.

Justin escaped from the store to watch her depart, and the pharmacist himself also came out. He was giving Monsieur Boulanger some good advice.

"An accident happens so easily. Be careful! Your horses may be skittish!"

She heard a noise above her; it was Félicité drumming on the window-pane to amuse little Berthe. The child blew her a kiss; her mother answered with a wave of her whip.

"Have a pleasant ride!" cried Monsieur Homais. "Be careful! above all, be careful!"

And he flourished his newspaper as he saw them disappear.

As soon as he felt the ground, Emma's horse set off at a gallop. Rodolphe galloped by her side. Now and then they exchanged a word. With slightly bent head, her hand well up, and her right arm stretched out, she gave herself up to the cadence of the movement that rocked her in her saddle.

At the bottom of the hill Rodolphe gave his horse its head; they set off together at a bound, then at the top suddenly the horses stopped, and her large blue veil fell about her.

It was early in October. There was fog over the land. Hazy clouds hovered on the horizon between the outlines of the hills; others, rent asunder, floated up and disappeared. Sometimes through a rift in the clouds, beneath a ray of sunshine, gleamed from afar the roofs of Yonville, with the gardens at the water's edge, the yards, the walls and the church steeple. Emma half closed her eyes to pick out her house, and never had this poor village where she lived appeared so small. From the height on which they were the whole valley seemed an immense pale lake sending off its vapour into the air. Clumps of trees here and there stood out like black rocks, and the tall lines of the poplars that rose above the mist were like a beach stirred by the wind.

By the side, on the grass between the pines, a brown light shimmered in the warm atmosphere. The earth, ruddy like the powder of tobacco, deadened the noise of their steps, and as they walked, the horses kicked up fallen pine cones before them.

Rodolphe and Emma thus skirted the woods. She turned away from time to time to avoid his look, and then she saw only the line of pine trunks, whose monotonous succession made her a little giddy. The horses were panting; the leather of the saddles creaked.

Just as they were entering the forest the sun came out.

"God is with us!" said Rodolphe.

"Do you think so?" she said.

"Forward! forward!" he continued.

He clucked with his tongue. The horses set off at a trot.

Long ferns by the roadside caught in Emma's stirrup. Rodolphe leant forward and removed them as they rode along. At other times, to turn aside the branches, he passed close to her, and Emma felt his knee brushing against her leg. The sky was blue now. The leaves no longer stirred. There were spaces full of heather in flower, and patches of purple alternated with the confused tangle of the trees, grey, fawn, or golden colored, according to the nature of their leaves. Often in the thicket one could hear the fluttering of wings, or else the hoarse, soft cry of the ravens flying off amidst the oaks.

They dismounted. Rodolphe fastened up the horses. She walked on in front on the moss between the paths.

But her long dress got in her way, although she held it by by the skirt; and Rodolphe, walking behind her, saw between the black cloth and the black shoe the delicacy of her white stocking, that seemed to him as if it were a part of her nakedness.

She stopped.

"I am tired," she said.

"Come, try some more," he went on. "Courage!"

Some hundred paces further on she stopped again, and through her veil, that fell sideways from her man's hat over her hips, her face appeared in a bluish transparency as if she were floating under azure waves.

"But where are we going?"

He did not answer. She was breathing irregularly. Rodolphe looked round him biting his moustache.

They came to a larger space which had been cleared of undergrowth. They sat down on the trunk of a fallen tree, and Rodolphe began speaking to her of his love.

He did not frighten her at first with compliments. He was calm, serious, melancholy.

Emma listened to him with bowed head, and stirred the bits of wood on the ground with the tip of her foot.

But at the words, "Are not our destinies now forever united?"

"Oh, no!" she replied. "You know they aren't. It is impossible!"

She rose to go. He seized her by the wrist. She stopped. Then, having gazed at him for a few moments with an amorous and moist look, she said hurriedly:

"Well let's not speak of it again! Where are the horses? Let's go back."

He made a gesture of anger and annoyance. She repeated:

"Where are the horses? Where are the horses?"

Then smiling a strange smile, looking straight at her, his teeth set, he advanced with outstretched arms. She recoiled trembling. She stammered:

"Oh, you frighten me! You hurt me! Take me back!"

"If it must be," he went on, his face changing; and he again became respectful, caressing, timid. She gave him her arm. They went back. He said:

"What was the matter with you? Why? I do not understand. You were mistaken, no doubt. In my soul you are as a Madonna on a pedestal, in a place lofty, secure, immaculate. But I cannot live without you! I need your eyes, your voice, your thought! Be my friend, my sister, my angel!"

And he stretched out his arm and caught her by the waist. Gently she tried to disengage herself. He supported her thus as they walked along.

They heard the two horses browsing on the leaves.

"Not quite yet!" said Rodolphe. "Stay a minute longer! Please stay!"

He drew her farther on to a small pool where duckweeds made a greenness on the water. Faded waterlilies lay motionless between the reeds. At the noise of their steps in the grass, frogs jumped away to hide themselves.

"I shouldn't, I shouldn't!" she said. "I am out of my mind listening to you!"

"Why? . . . Emma! Emma!"

"Oh, Rodolphe! . . ." she said slowly and she pressed against his shoulder.

The cloth of her dress clung to the velvet of his coat. She threw back her white neck which swelled in a sigh, and, faltering, weeping, and hiding her face in her hands, with one long shudder, she abandoned herself to him.

The shades of night were falling; the horizontal sun passing between the branches dazzled the eyes. Here and there around her, in the leaves or on the ground, trembled luminous patches, as if humming-birds flying about had scattered their feathers. Silence was everywhere; something sweet seemed to come forth from the trees. She felt her heartbeat return, and the blood coursing through her flesh like a river of milk. Then far away, beyond the wood, on the other hills, she heard a vague prolonged cry, a voice which lingered, and in silence she heard it mingling like music with the last pulsations of her throbbing nerves. Rodolphe, a cigar between his lips, was mending with his penknife one of the two broken bridles.

They returned to Yonville by the same road. On the mud they saw again the traces of their horses side by side, the same thickets, the same stones in the grass; nothing around them seemed changed; and yet for her something had happened more stupendous than if the mountains had moved in their places. Rodolphe now and again bent forward and took her hand to kiss it.

She was charming on horseback—upright, with her slender waist, her knee bent on the mane of her horse, her face somewhat flushed by the fresh air in the red of the evening.

On entering Yonville she made her horse prance in the road.

People looked at her from the windows.

At dinner her husband thought she looked well, but she pretended not to hear him when he inquired about her ride, and she remained sitting there with her elbow at the side of her plate between the two lighted candles.

"Emma!" he said.

"What?"

"Well, I spent the afternoon at Monsieur Alexandre's. He has an old filly, still very fine, just a little broken in the knees, and that could be bought, I am sure, for a hundred crowns." He added, "And thinking it might please you, I have reserved her . . . I bought her . . . Have I done right? Do tell me!"

She nodded her head in assent; then a quarter of an hour later:

"Are you going out tonight?" she asked.

"Yes. Why?"

"Oh, nothing, nothing, dear!"

And as soon as she had got rid of Charles she went and shut herself up in her room.

At first she felt stunned; she saw the trees, the paths, the ditches, Rodolphe, and she again felt the pressure of his arms, while the leaves rustled and the reeds whistled.

But when she saw herself in the mirror she wondered at her face. Never had her eyes been so large, so black, nor so deep. Something subtle about her being transfigured her.

She repeated: "I have a lover! a lover!" delighting at the idea as if a second puberty had come to her. So at last she was to know those joys of love, that fever of happiness of which she had despaired! She was entering upon a marvelous world where all would be passion, ecstasy, delirium. She felt herself surrounded by an endless rapture. A blue space surrounded her and ordinary existence appeared only intermittently between these heights, dark and far away beneath her.

Then she recalled the heroines of the books that she had read, and the lyric legion of these adulterous women began to sing in her memory with the voice of sisters that charmed her. She became herself, as it were, an actual part of these lyrical imaginings; at long last, as she saw herself among those lovers she had so envied, she fulfilled the love-dream of her youth. Besides, Emma felt a satisfaction of revenge. How she had suffered! But she had won out at last, and the love so long pent up erupted in joyous outbursts. She tasted it without remorse, without anxiety, without concern.

The next day brought a new-discovered sweetness. They exchanged vows: She told him of her sorrows. Rodolphe interrupted her with kisses; and she, looking at him thought half-closed eyes, asked him to call her again by her name and to say that he loved her. They were in the forest, as yesterday, this time in the hut of some *sabot* makers. The walls were of straw, and the roof so low they had to stoop. They were seated side by side on a bed of dry leaves.

From that day on they wrote to one another regularly every evening. Emma placed her letter at the end of the garden, by the river, in a crack of the wall. Rodolphe came to fetch it, and put another in its place that she always accused of being too short.

One morning, when Charles had gone out before daybreak, she felt the urge to see Rodolphe at once. She would go quickly to La Huchette, stay there an hour, and be back again at Yonville while every one was still asleep. The idea made her breathless with desire, and she soon found herself in the middle of the field, walking with rapid steps, without looking behind her.

Day was just breaking. Emma recognised her lover's house from a distance. Its two dove-tailed weathercocks stood out black against the pale dawn.

Beyond the farmyard there was a separate building that she assumed must be the chateau. She entered it as if the doors at her approach had opened wide of their own accord. A large straight staircase led up to the corridor. Emma raised the latch of a door, and suddenly at the end of the room she saw a man sleeping. It was Rodolphe. She uttered a cry.

"You here? You here?" he repeated. "How did you manage to come? Ah! your dress is wet."

"I love you!" she answered, winding her arm around his neck.

This first bold attempt having been successful, now every time Charles went out early Emma dressed quickly and slipped on tiptoe down the steps that led to the waterside.

But when the cow plank was taken up, she had to follow the walls alongside the river; the bank was slippery; to keep from falling, she had to catch hold of the tufts of faded wall-flowers. Then she went across ploughed fields, stumbling, her thin shoes sinking in the heavy mud. Her scarf, knotted round her head, fluttered to the wind in the meadows. She was afraid of the oxen; she began to run; she arrived out of breath, with rosy cheeks, and breathing out from her whole person a fresh perfume of sap, of verdure, of the open air. At this hour Rodolphe was still asleep. It was like a spring morning bursting into his room.

The golden curtains along the windows let a heavy, whitish light filter into the room. Emma would find her way gropingly, with blinking eyes, the drops of dew hanging from her hair, making a topaz halo around her face. Rodolphe, laughing, would draw her to him and press her to his breast.

Then she inspected the room, opened the drawers of the tables, combed her hair with his comb, and looked at herself in his shaving mirror. Often she put between her teeth the big pipe that lay on the bedtable, amongst lemons and pieces of sugar near the water bottle.

It took them a good quarter of an hour to say good-bye. Then Emma cried: she would have wished never to leave Rodolphe. Something stronger than herself drew her to him; until, one day, when she arrived unexpectedly, he frowned as one put out.

"What is wrong?" she said. "Are you ill? tell me!"

He ended up declaring earnestly that her visits were too dangerous and that she was compromising herself.

THE KUGELMASS EPISODE
Woody Allen

Kugelmass, a professor of humanities at City College, was unhappily married for the second time. Daphne Kugelmass was an oaf. He also had two dull sons by his first wife, Flo, and was up to his neck in alimony and child support.

"Did I know it would turn out so badly?" Kugelmass whined to his analyst one day. "Daphne had promise. Who suspected she'd let herself go and swell up like a beach ball? Plus she had a few bucks, which is not in itself a healthy reason to marry a person, but it doesn't hurt, with the kind of operating nut I have. You see my point?"

Kugelmass was bald and as hairy as a bear, but he had soul.

"I need to meet a new woman," he went on, "I need to have an affair. I may not look the part, but I'm a man who needs romance. I need softness, I need flirtation. I'm not getting younger, so before it's too late I want to make love in Venice, trade quips at '21' and exchange coy glances over red wine and candlelight. You see what I'm saying?"

Dr. Mandel shifted in his chair and said, "An affair will solve nothing. You're so unrealistic. Your problems run much deeper."

"And also this affair must be discreet," Kugelmass continued. "I can't afford a second divorce. Daphne would really sock it to me."

"Mr. Kugelmass—"

"But it can't be anyone at City College, because Daphne also works there. Not that anyone on the faculty of C.C.N.Y. is any great shakes, but some of those co-eds . . ."

"Mr. Kugelmass—"

"Help me. I had a dream last night. I was skipping through a meadow holding a picnic basket and the basket was marked 'Options.' And then I saw there was a hole in the basket."

"Mr. Kugelmass, the worst thing you could do is act out. You must simply express your feelings here, and together we'll analyze them. You have been in treatment long enough to know there is no overnight cure. After all, I'm an analyst, not a magician."

"Then perhaps what I need is a magician," Kugelmass said, rising from his chair. And with that he terminated his therapy.

A couple of weeks later, while Kugelmass and Daphne were moping around in their apartment one night like two pieces of old furniture, the phone rang.

"I'll get it," Kugelmass said. "Hello."

"Kugelmass?" a voice said. "Kugelmass, this is Persky."

"Who?"

"Persky. Or should I say The Great Persky?"

"Pardon me?"

"I hear you're looking all over town for a magician to bring a little exotica into your life? Yes or no?"

"Sh-h-h," Kugelmass whispered. "Don't hang up. Where are you calling from, Persky?"

Early the following afternoon, Kugelmass climbed three flights of stairs in a broken-down apartment house in the Bushwick section of Brooklyn. Peering through the darkness of the hall, he found the door he was looking for and pressed the bell. I'm going to regret this, he thought to himself.

Seconds later, he was greeted by a short, thin, waxy-looking man.

"*You're* Perksy the Great?" Kugelmass said.

"The Great Persky. You want a tea?"

"No, I want romance. I want music. I want love and beauty."

"But not tea, eh? Amazing. O.K., sit down."

Persky went to the back room, and Kugelmass heard the sounds of boxes and furniture being moved around. Persky reappeared, pushing before him a large object on squeaky roller-skate wheels. He removed some old silk handkerchiefs that were lying on its top and blew away a bit of dust. It was a cheap-looking Chinese cabinet, badly lacquered.

"Persky," Kugelmass said, "what's your scam?"

"Pay attention," Persky said. "This is some beautiful effect. I developed it for a Knights of Pythias date last year, but the booking fell through. Get into the cabinet."

"Why, so you can stick it full of swords or something?"

"You see any swords?"

Kugelmass made a face and, grunting, climbed into the cabinet. He couldn't help noticing a couple of ugly rhinestones glued onto the raw plywood just in front of his face. "If this is a joke," he said.

"Some joke. Now, here's the point. If I throw any novel into this cabinet with you, shut the doors, and tap it three times, you will find yourself projected into that book."

"It's the emess," Persky said. "My hand to God. Not just a novel, either. A short story, a play, a poem. You can meet any of the women created by the world's best writers. Whoever you dreamed of. You could carry on all you like with a real winner. Then when you've had enough you give a yell, and I'll see you're back here in a split second."

"Persky, are you some kind of outpatient?"

"I'm telling you it's on the level," Persky said.

Kugelmass remained skeptical. "What are you telling me—that this cheesy homemade box can take me on a ride like you're describing?"

"For a double sawbuck."

Kugelmass reached for his wallet. "I'll believe this when I see it," he said.

Persky tucked the bills in his pants pocket and turned toward his bookcase. "So who do you want to meet? Sister Carrie? Hester Prynne? Ophelia? Maybe someone by Saul Bellow? Hey, what about Temple Drake? Although for a man your age she'd be a workout."

"French. I want to have an affair with a French lover."

"Nana?"

"I don't want to have to pay for it."

"What about Natasha in *War and Peace*?"

"I said French. I know! What about Emma Bovary? That sounds to me perfect."

"You got it, Kugelmass. Give me a holler when you've had enough." Persky tossed in a paperback copy of Flaubert's novel.

"You sure this is safe?" Kugelmass asked as Persky began shutting the cabinet doors.

"Safe. Is anything safe in this crazy world?" Persky rapped three times on the cabinet and then flung open the doors.

Kugelmass was gone. At the same moment, he appeared in the bedroom of Charles and Emma Bovary's house at Yonville. Before him was a beautiful woman, standing alone with her back turned to him as she folded some linen. I can't believe this, thought Kugelmass, staring at the doctor's ravishing wife. This is uncanny. I'm here. It's her.

Emma turned in surprise. "Goodness, you startled me," she said. "Who are you?" She spoke in the same fine English translation as the paperback.

It's simply devastating, he thought. Then, realizing that it was he whom she had addressed, he said, "Excuse me. I'm Sidney Kugelmass. I'm from City College. A professor of humanities. C.C.N.Y.? Uptown. I—oh, boy!"

Emma Bovary smiled flirtatiously and said, "Would you like a drink? A glass of wine, perhaps?"

She is beautiful, Kugelmass thought. What a contrast with the troglodyte who shared his bed! He felt a sudden impulse to take this vision into his arms and tell her she was the kind of woman he had dreamed of all his life.

"Yes, some wine," he said hoarsely. "White. No, red. No, white. Make it white."

"Charles is out for the day," Emma said, her voice full of playful implication.

After the wine, they went for a stroll in the lovely French countryside. "I've always dreamed that some mysterious stranger would appear and rescue me from the monotony of this crass rural existence," Emma said, clasping his hand. They passed a small church. "I love what you have on," she murmured. "I've never seen anything like it around here. It's so . . . so modern."

"It's called a leisure suit," he said romantically. "It was marked down." Suddenly he kissed her. For the next hour they reclined under a tree and whispered together and told each other deeply meaningful things with their eyes. Then Kugelmass sat up. He had just remembered he had to meet Daphne at Bloomingdale's. "I must go," he told her. "But don't worry, I'll be back."

"I hope so," Emma said.

He embraced her passionately, and the two walked back to the house. He held Emma's face cupped in his palms, kissed her again, and yelled, "O.K., Persky! I got to be at Bloomingdale's by three-thirty."

There was an audible pop, and Kugelmass was back in Brooklyn.

"So? Did I lie?" Persky asked triumphantly.

"Look, Persky, I'm right now late to meet the ball and chain at Lexington Avenue, but when can I go again? Tomorrow?"

"My pleasure. Just bring a twenty. And don't mention this to anybody."

"Yeah. I'm going to call Rupert Murdoch."

Kugelmass hailed a cab and sped off to the city. His heart danced on point. I am in love, he thought, I am the possessor of a wonderful secret. What he didn't realize was that at this very moment students in various classrooms across the country were saying to their teachers, "Who is this character on page 100? A bald Jew is kissing Madame Bovary?" A teacher in Sioux Falls, South Dakota, sighed and thought, Jesus, these kids with their pot and acid. What goes through their minds!

Daphne Kugelmass was in the bathroom-accessories department at Bloomingdale's when Kugelmass arrived breathlessly. "Where've you been?" she snapped. "It's four-thirty."

"I got held up in traffic," Kugelmass said.

□   □   □

Kugelmass visited Persky the next day, and in a few minutes was again passed magically to Yonville. Emma couldn't hide her excitement at seeing him. The two spent hours together, laughing and talking about their different backgrounds. Before Kugelmass left, they made love.

"My God, I'm doing it with Madame Bovary!" Kugelmass whispered to himself. "Me, who failed freshman English."

As the months passed, Kugelmass saw Persky many times and developed a close and passionate relationship with Emma Bovary. "Make sure and always get me into the book before page 120," Kugelmass said to the magician one day. "I always have to meet her before she hooks up with this Rodolphe character."

"Why?" Persky asked. "You can't beat his time?"

"Beat his time. He's landed gentry. Those guys have nothing better to do than flirt and ride horses. To me, he's one of those faces you see in the pages of *Women's Wear Daily*. With the Helmut Berger hairdo. But to her he's hot stuff."

"And her husband suspects nothing?"

"He's out of his depth. He's a lacklustre little paramedic who's thrown in his lot with a jitterbug. He's ready to go to sleep by ten, and she's putting on her dancing shoes. Oh, well . . . See you later."

And once again Kugelmass entered the cabinet and passed instantly to the Bovary estate at Yonville. "How you doing, cupcake?" he said to Emma.

"Oh, Kugelmass," Emma sighed. "What I have to put up with. Last night at dinner, Mr. Personality dropped off to sleep in the middle of the dessert course. I'm pouring out my heart about Maxim's and the ballet, and out of the blue I hear snoring."

"It's O.K., darling. I'm here now," Kugelmass said, embracing her. I've earned this, he thought, smelling Emma's French perfume and burying his nose in her hair. I've suffered enough. I've paid enough analysts. I've searched till I'm weary. She's young and nubile, and I'm here a few pages after Leon and just before Rodolphe. By showing up during the correct chapters, I've got the situation knocked.

Emma, to be sure, was just as happy as Kugelmass. She had been starved for excitement, and his tales of Broadway night life, of fast cars and Hollywood and TV stars enthralled the young French beauty.

"Tell me again about O. J. Simpson," she implored that evening, as she and Kugelmass strolled past Abbé Bournisien's church.

"What can I say? The man is great. He sets all kinds of rushing records. Such moves. They can't touch him."

"And the Academy Awards?" Emma said wistfully. "I'd give anything to win one."

"First you've got to be nominated."

"I know. You explained it. But I'm convinced I can act. Of course, I'd want to take a class or two. With Strasberg maybe. Then, if I had the right agent—"

"We'll see, we'll see. I'll speak to Persky."

That night, safely returned to Persky's flat, Kugelmass brought up the idea of having Emma visit him in the big city.

"Let me think about it," Persky said. "Maybe I could work it. Stranger things have happened." Of course, neither of them could think of one.

"Where the hell do you go all the time?" Daphne Kugelmass barked at her husband as he returned home late that evening. "You got a chippie stashed somewhere?"

"Yeah, sure, I'm just the type," Kugelmass said wearily. "I was with Leonard Popkin. We were discussing Socialist agriculture in Poland. You know Popkin. He's a freak on the subject."

"Well, you've been very odd lately," Daphne said. "Distant. Just don't forget about my father's birthday. On Saturday?"

"Oh, sure, sure," Kugelmass said, heading for the bathroom.

"My whole family will be there. We can see the twins. And Cousin Hamish. You should be more polite to Cousin Hamish—he likes you."

"Right, the twins," Kugelmass said, closing the bathroom door and shutting out the sound of his wife's voice. He leaned against it and took a deep breath. In a few hours, he told himself, he would be back in Yonville again, back with his beloved. And this time, if all went well, he would bring Emma back with him.

At three-fifteen the following afternoon, Persky worked his wizardry again. Kugelmass appeared before Emma, smiling and eager. The two spent a few hours at Yonville with Binet and then remounted the Bovary carriage. Following Persky's instructions, they held each other tightly, closed their eyes, and counted to ten. When they opened them, the carriage was just drawing up at the side door of the Plaza Hotel, where Kugelmass had optimistically reserved a suite earlier in the day.

"I love it! It's everything I dreamed it would be," Emma said as she swirled joyously around the bedroom, surveying the city from their window. "There's F.A.O. Schwarz. And there's Central Park, and the Sherry is which one? Oh, there—I see. It's too divine."

On the bed there were boxes from Halston and Saint Laurent. Emma unwrapped a package and held up a pair of black velvet pants against her perfect body.

"The slacks suit is by Ralph Lauren," Kugelmass said. "You'll look like a million bucks in it. Come on, sugar, give us a kiss."

"I've never been so happy!" Emma squealed as she stood before the mirror. "Let's go out on the town. I want to see *Chorus Line* and the Guggenheim and this Jack Nicholson character you always talk about. Are any of his flicks showing?"

"I cannot get my mind around this," a Stanford professor said. "First a strange character named Kugelmass, and now she's gone from the book. Well, I guess the mark of a classic is that you can reread it a thousand times and always find something new."

☐ ☐ ☐

The lovers passed a blissful weekend. Kugelmass had told Daphne he would be away at a symposium in Boston and would return Monday. Savoring each moment, he and Emma went to the movies, had dinner in Chinatown, passed two hours at a discotheque, and went to bed with a TV movie. They slept till noon on Sunday, visited SoHo, and ogled celebrities at Elaine's. They had caviar and champagne in their suite on Sunday night and talked until dawn. That morning, in the cab taking them to Persky's apartment, Kugelmass thought, It was hectic but worth it. I can't bring her here too often, but now and then it will be a charming contrast with Yonville.

At Persky's, Emma climbed into the cabinet, arranged her new boxes of clothes neatly around her, and kissed Kugelmass fondly. "My place next time," she said with a wink. Persky rapped three times on the cabinet. Nothing happened.

"Hmm," Persky said, scratching his head. He rapped again, but still no magic. "Something must be wrong," he mumbled.

"Persky, you're joking!" Kugelmass cried. "How can it not work?"

"Relax, relax. Are you still in the box, Emma?"

"Yes."

Persky rapped again—harder this time.

"I'm still here, Persky."

"I know, darling. Sit tight."

"Persky, we *have* to get her back," Kugelmass whispered. "I'm a married man, and I have a class in three hours. I'm not prepared for anything more than a cautious affair at this point."

"I can't understand it," Persky muttered. "It's such a reliable little trick."

But he could do nothing. "It's going to take a little while," he said to Kugelmass. "I'm going to have to strip it down. I'll call you later."

Kugelmass bundled Emma into a cab and took her back to the Plaza. He barely made it to his class on time. He was on the phone all day, to Persky and to his mistress. The magician told him it might be several days before he got to the bottom of the trouble.

"How was the symposium?" Daphne asked him that night.

"Fine, fine," he said, lighting the filter end of a cigarette.

"What's wrong? You're as tense as a cat."

"Me? Ha, that's a laugh. I'm as calm as a summer night. I'm just going to take a walk." He eased out the door, hailed a cab, and flew to the Plaza.

"This is no good," Emma said. "Charles will miss me."

"Bear with me, sugar," Kugelmass said. He was pale and sweaty. He kissed her again, raced to the elevators, yelled at Persky over a pay phone in the Plaza lobby, and just made it home before midnight.

"According to Popkin, barley prices in Krakow have not been this stable since 1971," he said to Daphne, and smiled wanly as he climbed into bed.

▫ ▫ ▫

The whole week went by like that.

On Friday night, Kugelmass told Daphne there was another symposium he had to catch, this one in Syracuse. He hurried back to the Plaza, but the second weekend there was nothing like the first. "Get me back into the novel or marry me," Emma told Kugelmass. "Meanwhile, I want to get a job or go to class, because watching TV all day is the pits."

"Fine. We can use the money," Kugelmass said. "You consume twice your weight in room service."

"I met an Off Broadway producer in Central Park yesterday, and he said I might be right for a project he's doing," Emma said.

"Who is this clown?" Kugelmass asked.

"He's not a clown. He's sensitive and kind and cute. His name's Jeff Something-or-Other, and he's up for a Tony."

Later that afternoon, Kugelmass showed up at Persky's drunk.

"Relax," Persky told him. "You'll get a coronary."

"Relax. The man says relax. I've got a fictional character stashed in a hotel room, and I think my wife is having me tailed by a private shamus."

"O.K., O.K. We know there's a problem." Persky crawled under the cabinet and started banging on something with a large wrench.

"I'm like a wild animal," Kugelmass went on. "I'm sneaking around town, and Emma and I have had it up to here with each other. Not to mention a hotel tab that reads like the defense budget."

"So what should I do? This is the world of magic," Persky said. "It's all nuance."

"Nuance, my foot. I'm pouring Dom Pérignon and black eggs into this little mouse, plus her wardrobe, plus she's enrolled at the Neighborhood Playhouse and suddenly needs professional photos. Also, Persky, Professor Fivish Kopkind, who teaches Comp Lit and who has always been jealous of me, has identified me as the sporadically appearing character in the Flaubert book. He's threatened to go to Daphne. I see ruin and alimony; jail. For adultery with Madame Bovary, my wife will reduce me to beggary."

"What do you want me to say? I'm working on it night and day. As far as your personal anxiety goes, that I can't help you with. I'm a magician, not an analyst."

By Sunday afternoon, Emma had locked herself in the bathroom and refused to respond to Kugelmass's entreaties. Kugelmass stared out the window at the Wollman Rink and contemplated suicide. Too bad this is a low floor, he thought, or I'd do it right now. Maybe if I ran away to Europe and started life over . . . Maybe I could sell the *International Herald Tribune*, like those young girls used to.

The phone rang. Kugelmass lifted it to his ear mechanically.

"Bring her over," Persky said. "I think I got the bugs out of it."

Kugelmass's heart leaped. "You're serious?" he said. "You got it licked?"

"It was something in the transmission. Go figure."

"Persky, you're a genius. We'll be there in a minute. Less than a minute."

Again the lovers hurried to the magician's apartment, and again Emma Bovary climbed into the cabinet with her boxes. This time there was no kiss. Persky shut the doors, took a deep breath, and tapped the box three times. There was the reassuring popping noise, and when Persky peered inside, the box was empty. Madame Bovary was back in her novel. Kugelmass heaved a great sigh of relief and pumped the magician's hand.

"It's over," he said. "I learned my lesson. I'll never cheat again, I swear it." He pumped Persky's hand again and made a mental note to send him a necktie.

Three weeks later, at the end of a beautiful spring afternoon, Persky answered his doorbell. It was Kugelmass, with a sheepish expression on his face.

"O.K., Kugelmass," the magician said. "Where to this time?"

"It's just this once," Kugelmass said. "The weather is so lovely, and I'm not getting any younger. Listen, you've read *Portnoy's Complaint?* Remember The Monkey?"

"The price is now twenty-five dollars, because the cost of living is up, but I'll start you off with one freebie, due to all the trouble I caused you."

"You're good people," Kugelmass said, combing his few remaining hairs as he climbed into the cabinet again. "This'll work all right?"

"I hope. But I haven't tried it much since all that unpleasantness."

"Sex and romance," Kugelmass said from inside the box. "What we go through for a pretty face."

Persky tossed in a copy of *Portnoy's Complaint* and rapped three times on the box. This time, instead of a popping noise there was a dull explosion, followed by a series of crackling noises and a shower of sparks. Persky leaped back, was seized by a heart attack, and dropped dead. The cabinet burst into flames, and eventually the entire house burned down.

Kugelmass, unaware of this catastrophe, had his own problems. He had not been thrust into *Portnoy's Complaint,* or into any other novel, for that matter. He had been projected into an old textbook, *Remedial Spanish,* and was running for his life over a barren, rocky terrain as the word *tener* ("to have")—a large and hairy irregular verb—raced after him on its spindly legs.

22. OEDIPUS AND JOCASTA

This last pair of selections combines an ancient classical Greek tragedy, *Oedipus Rex,* by Sophocles, with a contemporary poem, "Jocasta," by Ruth Eisenberg. "Jocasta" is a retelling of the Oedipus story from Jocasta's point of view. Following the poem is a brief set of questions, then excerpts from early drafts of the poem. Rounding out the discussion is a statement by Eisenberg about its genesis and development.

OEDIPUS REX

CHARACTERS

OEDIPUS, *King of Thebes, supposed son of Polybos and Merope, King and Queen of Corinth*
IOKASTE, *wife of Oedipus and widow of the late King Laios*
KREON, *brother of Iokaste, a prince of Thebes*
TEIRESIAS, *a blind seer who serves Apollo*
PRIEST
MESSENGER, *from Corinth*
SHEPHERD, *former servant of Laios*
SECOND MESSENGER, *from the palace*
CHORUS OF THEBAN ELDERS
CHORAGOS, *leader of the Chorus*
ANTIGONE *and* ISMENE, *young daughters of Oedipus and Iokaste. They appear in the Exodus but do not speak.*
SUPPLIANTS, GUARDS, SERVANTS

THE SCENE. *Before the palace of* OEDIPUS, *King of Thebes. A central door and two lateral doors open onto a platform which runs the length of the facade. On the platform, right and left, are altars; and three steps lead down into the orchestra, or chorus-ground. At the beginning of the action these steps are crowded by suppliants who have brought branches and chaplets of olive leaves and who sit in various attitudes of despair.* OEDIPUS *enters.*

PROLOGUE

OEDIPUS. My children, generations of the living
    In the line of Kadmos,[1] nursed at his ancient hearth:
    Why have you strewn yourselves before these altars
    In supplication, with your boughs and garlands?
    The breath of incense rises from the city   5
    With a sound of prayer and lamentation.
                                            Children,
    I would not have you speak through messengers,
    And therefore I have come myself to hear you—
    I, Oedipus, who bear the famous name.
    (*To a* PRIEST) You, there, since you are eldest in the company,   10
    Speak for them all, tell me what preys upon you,
    Whether you come in dread, or crave some blessing:

---

[1] Legendary founder of Thebes.

        Tell me, and never doubt that I will help you
        In every way I can; I should be heartless
        Were I not moved to find you suppliant here.
PRIEST. Great Oedipus, O powerful king of Thebes!
        You see how all the ages of our people
        Cling to your altar steps: here are boys
        Who can barely stand alone, and here are priests
        By weight of age, as I am a priest of God,
        And young men chosen from those yet unmarried;
        As for the others, all that multitude,
        They wait with olive chaplets in the squares,
        At the two shrines of Pallas,[2] and where Apollo[3]
        Speaks in the glowing embers.
                                    Your own eyes
        Must tell you: Thebes is tossed on a murdering sea
        And can not lift her head from the death surge.
        A rust consumes the buds and fruits of the earth;
        The herds are sick; children die unborn,
        And labor is vain. The god of plague and pyre
        Raids like detestable lightning through the city,
        And all the house of Kadmos is laid waste,
        All emptied, and all darkened: Death alone
        Battens upon the misery of Thebes.

        You are not one of the immortal gods, we know;
        Yet we have come to you to make our prayer
        As to the man surest in mortal ways
        And wisest in the ways of God. You saved us
        From the Sphinx,[4] that flinty singer, and the tribute
        We paid to her so long; yet you were never
        Better informed than we, nor could we teach you:
        A god's touch, it seems, enabled you to help us.

        Therefore, O mighty power, we turn to you:
        Find us our safety, find us a remedy,
        Whether by counsel of the gods or of men.
        A king of wisdom tested in the past
        Can act in a time of troubles, and act well.
        Noblest of men, restore
        Life to your city! Think how all men call you
        Liberator for your boldness long ago;
        Ah, when your years of kingship are remembered,
        Let them not say *We rose, but later fell*—

---

[2] Athena, goddess of wisdom, patroness of Athens.
[3] God of the sun, music, and medicine.
[4] A winged monster, with the body of a lion and the breasts and head of a woman.

Keep the State from going down in the storm!
Once, years ago, with happy augury,
You brought us fortune; be the same again!   55
No man questions your power to rule the land:
But rule over men, not over a dead city!
Ships are only hulls, high walls are nothing,
When no life moves in the empty passageways.

OEDIPUS. Poor children! You may be sure I know   60
All that you longed for in your coming here.
I know that you are deathly sick; and yet,
Sick as you are, not one is as sick as I.
Each of you suffers in himself alone
His anguish, not another's; but my spirit   65
Groans for the city, for myself, for you.

I was not sleeping, you are not waking me.
No, I have been in tears for a long while
And in my restless thought walked many ways.
In all my search I found one remedy,   70
And I have adopted it: I have sent Kreon,
Son of Menoikeus, brother of the queen,
To Delphi, Apollo's place of revelation,
To learn there, if he can,
What act or pledge of mine may save the city.   75
I have counted the days, and now, this very day,
I am troubled, for he has overstayed his time.
What is he doing? He has been gone too long.
Yet whenever he comes back, I should do ill
Not to take any action the god orders.   80

PRIEST. It is a timely promise. At this instant
They tell me Kreon is here.

OEDIPUS.   O Lord Apollo!
May his news be fair as his face is radiant!

PRIEST. Good news, I gather! he is crowned with bay,
The chaplet is thick with berries.

OEDIPUS.   We shall soon know;   85
He is near enough to hear us now.

(*Enter* KREON.)

                    O prince:
Brother: son of Menoikeus:
What answer do you bring us from the god?

KREON. A strong one. I can tell you, great afflictions
Will turn out well, if they are taken well.   90

OEDIPUS. What was the oracle? These vague words
Leave me still hanging between hope and fear.

KREON. Is it your pleasure to hear me with all these
    Gathered around us? I am prepared to speak,
    But should we not go in?
OEDIPUS.   Speak to them all, 95
    It is for them I suffer, more than for myself.
KREON. Then I will tell you what I heard at Delphi.
    In plain words
    The god commands us to expel from the land of Thebes
    An old defilement we are sheltering. 100
    It is a deathly thing, beyond cure;
    We must not let it feed upon us longer.
OEDIPUS. What defilement? How shall we rid ourselves of it?
KREON. By exile or death, blood for blood. It was
    Murder that brought the plague-wind on the city. 105
OEDIPUS. Murder of whom? Surely the god has named him?
KREON. My lord: Laios once ruled this land,
    Before you came to govern us.
OEDIPUS.   I know;
    I learned of him from others; I never saw him.
KREON. He was murdered; and Apollo commands us now 110
    To take revenge upon whoever killed him.
OEDIPUS. Upon whom? Where are they? Where shall we find a clue
    To solve that crime, after so many years?
KREON. Here in this land, he said. Search reveals
    Things that escape an inattentive man. 115
OEDIPUS. Tell me: Was Laios murdered in his house,
    Or in the fields, or in some foreign country?
KREON. He said he planned to make a pilgrimage.
    He did not come home again.
OEDIPUS.   And was there no one,
    No witness, no companion, to tell what happened? 120
KREON. They were all killed but one, and he got away
    So frightened that he could remember one thing only.
OEDIPUS. What was that one thing? One may be the key
    To everything, if we resolve to use it.
KREON. He said that a band of highwaymen attacked them, 125
    Outnumbered them, and overwhelmed the king.
OEDIPUS. Strange, that a highwayman should be so daring—
    Unless some faction here bribed him to do it.
KREON. We thought of that. But after Laios' death
    New troubles arose and we had no avenger. 130
OEDIPUS. What troubles could prevent your hunting down the killers?
KREON. The riddling Sphinx's song
    Made us deaf to all mysteries but her own.
OEDIPUS. Then once more I must bring what is dark to light.
    It is most fitting that Apollo shows, 135

As you do, this compunction for the dead.
You shall see how I stand by you, as I should,
Avenging this country and the god as well,
And not as though it were for some distant friend,
But for my own sake, to be rid of evil. 140
Whoever killed King Laios might—who knows?—
Lay violent hands even on me—and soon.
I act for the murdered king in my own interest.

Come, then, my children: leave the altar steps,
Lift up your olive boughs!
                       One of you go 145
And summon the people of Kadmos to gather here.
I will do all that I can; you may tell them that.

(*Exit a* PAGE.)

So, with the help of God,
We shall be saved—or else indeed we are lost.
PRIEST. Let us rise, children. It was for this we came, 150
And now the king has promised it.
Phoibus[5] has sent us an oracle; may he descend
Himself to save us and drive out the plague.

(*Exeunt* OEDIPUS *and* KREON *into the palace by the central door. The* PRIEST *and the* SUPPLIANTS *disperse right and left. After a short pause the* CHORUS *enters the orchestra.*)

PARADOS[6]

STROPHE 1

CHORUS. What is God singing in his profound
    Delphi of gold and shadow? 155
    What oracle for Thebes, the sunwhipped city?
    Fear unjoints me, the roots of my heart tremble.
    Now I remember, O Healer, your power, and wonder:
    Will you send doom like a sudden cloud, or weave it
    Like nightfall of the past? 160
    Speak to me, tell me, O
    Child of golden Hope, immortal Voice.

ANTISTROPHE 1

    Let me pray to Athene, the immortal daughter of Zeus,
    And to Artemis her sister

---

[5] Phoebus Apollo, god of the sun, whose oracle was at Delphi.
[6] The Parados is the poetic song of the entering Chorus.

Who keeps her famous throne in the market ring, 165
And to Apollo, archer from distant heaven—
O gods, descend! Like three streams leap against
The fires of our grief, the fires of darkness;
Be swift to bring us rest!
As in the old time from the brilliant house 170
Of air you stepped to save us, come again!

STROPHE 2

Now our afflictions have no end,
Now all our stricken host lies down
And no man fights off death with his mind;
The noble plowland bears no grain, 175
And groaning mothers can not bear—
See, how our lives like birds take wing,
Like sparks that fly when a fire soars,
To the shore of the god of evening.

ANTISTROPHE 2

The plague burns on, it is pitiless, 180
Though pallid children laden with death
Lie unwept in the stony ways,
And old gray women by every path
Flock to the strand about the altars
There to strike their breasts and cry 185
Worship of Phoibus in wailing prayers:
Be kind, God's golden child!

STROPHE 3

There are no swords in this attack by fire,
No shields, but we are ringed with cries.
Send the beseiger plunging from our homes 190
Into the vast sea-room of the Atlantic
Or into the waves that foam eastward of Thrace—
For the day ravages what the night spares—
Destroy our enemy, lord of the thunder!
Let him be riven by lightning from heaven! 195

ANTISTROPHE 3

Phoibus Apollo, stretch the sun's bowstring,
That golden cord, until it sing for us,
Flashing arrows in heaven!
                           Artemis, Huntress,
Race with flaring lights upon our mountains!

O scarlet god, O golden-banded brow,
O Theban Bacchos in a storm of Maenads,[7]

(*Enter* OEDIPUS, *center.*)

Whirl upon Death, that all the Undying hate!
Come with blinding torches, come in joy!

SCENE I

OEDIPUS.   Is this your prayer? It may be answered. Come,
Listen to me, act as the crisis demands,
And you shall have relief from all these evils.

Until now I was a stranger to this tale,
As I had been a stranger to the crime.
Could I track down the murderer without a clue?
But now, friends,
As one who became a citizen after the murder,
I make this proclamation to all Thebans:
If any man knows by whose hand Laios, son of Labdakos,
Met his death, I direct that man to tell me everything,
No matter what he fears for having so long withheld it.
Let it stand as promised that no further trouble
Will come to him, but he may leave the land in safety.
Moreover: If anyone knows the murderer to be foreign,
Let him not keep silent: he shall have his reward from me.
However, if he does conceal it; if any man
Fearing for his friend or for himself disobeys this edict,
Hear what I propose to do:

I solemnly forbid the people of this country,
Where power and throne are mine, ever to receive that man
Or speak to him, no matter who he is, or let him
Join in sacrifice, lustration,[8] or in prayer.
I decree that he be driven from every house,
Being, as he is, corruption itself to us: the Delphic
Voice of Apollo has pronounced this revelation.
Thus I associate myself with the oracle
And take the side of the murdered king.

As for the criminal, I pray to God—
Whether it be a lurking thief, or one of a number—
I pray that that man's life be consumed in evil and wretchedness.
And as for me, this curse applies no less
If it should turn out that the culprit is my guest here,

---

[7] Bacchos: the god of wine and revelry. Maenads were female attendants of the god.
[8] lustration: ritual purification.

Sharing my hearth.
                    You have heard the penalty.
I lay it on you now to attend to this
For my sake, for Apollo's, for the sick
Sterile city that heaven has abandoned.
Suppose the oracle had given you no command:
Should this defilement go uncleansed for ever?
You should have found the murderer: your king,
A noble king, had been destroyed!
                                    Now I,
Having the power that he held before me,
Having his bed, begetting children there
Upon his wife, as he would have, had he lived—
Their son would have been my children's brother,
If Laios had had luck in fatherhood!
(And now his bad fortune has struck him down)—
I say I take the son's part, just as though
I were his son, to press the fight for him
And see it won! I'll find the hand that brought
Death to Labdakos' and Polydoros' child,
Heir of Kadmos' and Agenor's line.[9]
And as for those who fail me,
May the gods deny them the fruit of the earth,
Fruit of the womb, and may they rot utterly!
Let them be wretched as we are wretched, and worse!

For you, for loyal Thebans, and for all
Who find my actions right, I pray the favor
Of justice, and of all the immortal gods.
CHORAGOS.[10] Since I am under oath, my lord, I swear
    I did not do the murder, I can not name
    The murderer. Phoibos ordained the search:
    Why did he not say who the culprit was?
OEDIPUS. An honest question. But no man in the world
    Can make the gods do more than the gods will.
CHORAGOS. There is an alternative, I think—
OEDIPUS.   Tell me.
    Any or all, you must not fail to tell me.
CHORAGOS. A lord clairvoyant to the lord Apollo,
    As we all know, is the skilled Teiresias.
    One might learn much about this from him, Oedipus.
OEDIPUS. I am not wasting time:
    Kreon spoke of this, and I have sent for him—
    Twice, in fact; it is strange that he is not here.

---

[9] The royal line of descent: Kadmos=Polydoros=Labdakos = Laios=Oedipus.
[10] The Choragos is the leader of the Chorus.

CHORAGOS. The other matter—the old report—seems useless.
OEDIPUS. What was that? I am interested in all reports.
CHORAGOS. The king was said to have been killed by highwaymen.
OEDIPUS. I know. But we have no witnesses to that.
CHORAGOS. If the killer can feel a particle of dread,
    Your curse will bring him out of hiding!
OEDIPUS.   No.
    The man who dared that act will fear no curse.

(Enter the blind seer TEIRESIAS, *led by a* PAGE.)

CHORAGOS. But there is one man who may detect the criminal.
    This is Teiresias, this is the holy prophet
    In whom, alone of all men, truth was born.
OEDIPUS. Teiresias: seer: student of mysteries,
    Of all that's taught and all that no man tells,
    Secrets of Heaven and secrets of the earth:
    Blind though you are, you know the city lies
    Sick with plague; and from this plague, my lord,
    We find that you alone can guard or save us.

    Possibly you did not hear the messengers?
    Apollo, when we sent to him,
    Sent us back word that this great pestilence
    Would lift, but only if we established clearly
    The identity of those who murdered Laios.
    They must be killed or exiled.
                            Can you use
    Birdflight[11] or any art of divination
    To purify yourself, and Thebes, and me
    From this contagion? We are in your hands.
    There is no fairer duty
    Than that of helping others in distress.
TEIRESIAS. How dreadful knowledge of the truth can be
    When there's no help in truth! I knew this well,
    But did not act on it: else I should not have come.
OEDIPUS. What is troubling you? Why are your eyes so cold?
TEIRESIAS. Let me go home. Bear your own fate, and I'll
    Bear mine. It is better so: trust what I say.
OEDIPUS. What you say is ungracious and unhelpful
    To your native country. Do not refuse to speak.
TEIRESIAS. When it comes to speech, your own is neither temperate
    Nor opportune. I wish to be more prudent.
OEDIPUS. In God's name, we all beg you—

---

[11] The flight patterns of birds were used to foretell the future.

TEIRESIAS.   You are all ignorant.
   No; I will never tell you what I know.
   Now it is my misery; then, it would be yours.
OEDIPUS. What! You do know something, and will not tell us?
   You would betray us all and wreck the State?
TEIRESIAS. I do not intend to torture myself, or you.
   Why persist in asking? You will not persuade me.
OEDIPUS. What a wicked old man you are! You'd try a stone's
   Patience! Out with it! Have you no feeling at all?
TEIRESIAS. You call me unfeeling. If you could only see
   The nature of your own feelings . . .
OEDIPUS.   Why,
   Who would not feel as I do? Who could endure
   Your arrogance toward the city?
TEIRESIAS.   What does it matter?
   Whether I speak or not, it is bound to come.
OEDIPUS. Then, if "it" is bound to come, you are bound to tell me.
TEIRESIAS. No, I will not go on. Rage as you please.
OEDIPUS. Rage? Why not!
                              And I'll tell you what I think:
   You planned it, you had it done, you all but
   Killed him with your own hands: if you had eyes,
   I'd say the crime was yours, and yours alone.
TEIRESIAS. So? I charge you, then,
   Abide by the proclamation you have made:
   From this day forth
   Never speak again to these men or to me;
   You yourself are the pollution of this country.
OEDIPUS. You dare say that! Can you possibly think you have
   Some way of going free, after such insolence?
TEIRESIAS. I have gone free. It is the truth sustains me.
OEDIPUS. Who taught you shamelessness? It was not your craft.
TEIRESIAS. You did. You made me speak. I did not want to.
OEDIPUS. Speak what? Let me hear it again more clearly.
TEIRESIAS. Was it not clear before? Are you tempting me?
OEDIPUS. I did not understand it. Say it again.
TEIRESIAS. I say that you are the murderer whom you seek.
OEDIPUS. Now twice you have spat out infamy. You'll pay for it!
TEIRESIAS. Would you care for more? Do you wish to be really angry?
OEDIPUS. Say what you will. Whatever you say is worthless.
TEIRESIAS. I say you live in hideous shame with those
   Most dear to you. You can not see the evil.
OEDIPUS. Can you go on babbling like this for ever?
TEIRESIAS. I can, if there is power in truth.
OEDIPUS.   There is:
   But not for you, not for you,
   You sightless, witless, senseless, mad old man!

TEIRESIAS. You are the madman. There is no one here
   Who will not curse you soon, as you curse me.
OEDIPUS. You child of total night! I would not touch you;
   Neither would any man who sees the sun. 360
TEIRESIAS. True: it is not from you my fate will come.
   That lies within Apollo's competence,
   As it is his concern.
OEDIPUS.   Tell me, who made
   These fine discoveries? Kreon? or someone else?
TEIRESIAS. Kreon is no threat. You weave your own doom. 365
OEDIPUS. Wealth, power, craft of statemanship!
   Kingly position, everywhere admired!
   What savage envy is stored up against these,
   If Kreon, whom I trusted, Kreon my friend,
   For this great office which the city once 370
   Put in my hands unsought—if for this power
   Kreon desires in secret to destroy me!

   He has brought this decrepit fortune-teller, this
   Collector of dirty pennies, this prophet fraud—
   Why, he is no more clairvoyant than I am!
                              Tell us: 375
   Has your mystic mummery every approached the truth?
   When that hellcat the Sphinx was performing here,
   What help were you to these people?
   Her magic was not for the first man who came along:
   It demanded a real exorcist. Your birds— 380
   What good were they? or the gods, for the matter of that?
   But I came by,
   Oedipus, the simple man, who knows nothing—
   I thought it out for myself, no birds helped me!
   And this is the man you think you can destroy, 385
   That you may be close to Kreon when he's king!
   Well, you and your friend Kreon, it seems to me,
   Will suffer most. If you were not an old man,
   You would have paid already for your plot.
CHORAGOS. We can not see that his words or yours 390
   Have been spoken except in anger, Oedipus,
   And of anger we have no need. How to accomplish
   The god's will best: that is what most concerns us.
TEIRESIAS. You are a king. But where argument's concerned
   I am your man, as much a king as you. 395
   I am not your servant, but Apollo's.
   I have no need of Kreon or Kreon's name.

   Listen to me. You mock my blindness, do you?
   But I say that you, with both your eyes, are blind:

You can not see the wretchedness of your life,
Nor in whose house you live, no, nor with whom.
Who are your father and mother? Can you tell me?
You do not even know the blind wrongs
That you have done them, on earth and in the world below.
But the double lash of your parents' curse will whip you
Out of this land some day, with only night
Upon your precious eyes.
Your cries then—where will they not be heard?
What fastness of Kithairon[12] will not echo them?
And that bridal-descant of yours—you'll know it then,
The song they sang when you came here to Thebes
And found your misguided berthing.
All this, and more, that you can not guess at now,
Will bring you to yourself among your children.

Be angry, then. Curse Kreon. Curse my words.
I tell you, no man that walks upon the earth
Shall be rooted out more horribly than you.
OEDIPUS. Am I to bear this from him?—Damnation
 Take you! Out of this place! Out of my sight!
TEIRESIAS. I would not have come at all if you had not asked me.
OEDIPUS. Could I have told that you'd talk nonsense, that
 You'd come here to make a fool of yourself, and of me?
TEIRESIAS. A fool? Your parents thought me sane enough.
OEDIPUS. My parents again!—Wait: who were my parents?
TEIRESIAS. This day will give you a father, and break your heart.
OEDIPUS. Your infantile riddles! Your damned abracadabra!
TEIRESIAS. You were a great man once at solving riddles.
OEDIPUS. Mock me with that if you like; you will find it true.
TEIRESIAS. It was true enough. It brought about your ruin.
OEDIPUS. But if it saved this town?
TEIRESIAS (*to the* PAGE.)   Boy, give me your hand.
OEDIPUS. Yes, boy; lead him away.
                         —While you are here
 We can do nothing. Go; leave us in peace.
TEIRESIAS. I will go when I have said what I have to say.
 How can you hurt me? And I tell you again:
 The man you have been looking for all this time,
 The damned man, the murderer of Laios,
 That man is in Thebes. To your mind he is foreign-born,
 But it will soon be shown that he is a Theban,
 A revelation that will fail to please.
                         A blind man,

---

[12] A mountain range near Thebes where the infant Oedipus was left to die.

Who has his eyes now; a penniless man, who is rich now; 440
And he will go tapping the strange earth with his staff.
To the children with whom he lives now he will be
Brother and father—the very same; to her
Who bore him, son and husband—the very same
Who came to his father's bed, wet with his father's blood. 445

Enough. Go think that over.
If later you find error in what I have said,
You may say that I have no skill in prophecy.

(*Exit* TEIRESIAS, *led by his* PAGE. OEDIPUS *goes into the palace.*)

ODE I

STROPHE 1

CHORUS.   The Delphic stone of prophecies
    Remembers ancient regicide 450
    And a still bloody hand.
    That killer's hour of flight has come.
    He must be stronger than riderless
    Coursers of untiring wind,
    For the son of Zeus[13] armed with his father's thunder 455
    Leaps in lightning after him;
    And the Furies hold his track, the sad Furies.[14]

ANTISTROPHE 1

    Holy Parnassos' peak of snow
    Flashes and blinds that secret man,
    That all shall hunt him down: 460
    Though he may roam the forest shade
    Like a bull gone wild from pasture
    To rage through glooms of stone.
    Doom comes down on him; flight will not avail him;
    For the world's heart calls him desolate, 465
    And the immortal voices follow, for ever follow.

STROPHE 2

    But now a wilder thing is heard
    From the old man skilled at hearing Fate in the wing-beat of a bird.
    Bewildered as a blown bird, my soul hovers and can not find
    Foothold in this debate, or any reason or rest of mind. 470

---

[13] Apollo.
[14] Avenging goddesses.

But no man ever brought—none can bring
Proof of strife between Thebes' royal house,
Labdakos' line, and the son of Polybos;[15]
And never until now has any man brought word
Of Laios' dark death staining Oedipus the King.

ANTISTROPHE 2

Divine Zeus and Apollo hold
Perfect intelligence alone of all tales ever told;
And well though this diviner works, he works in his own night;
No man can judge that rough unknown or trust in second sight,
For wisdom changes hands among the wise.
Shall I believe my great lord criminal
At a raging word that a blind old man let fall?
I saw him, when the carrion woman faced him of old,
Prove his heroic mind. These evil words are lies.

SCENE II

KREON. Men of Thebes:
    I am told that heavy accusations
    Have been brought against me by King Oedipus.

    I am not the kind of man to bear this tamely.

    If in these present difficulties
    He holds me accountable for any harm to him
    Through anything I have said or done—why, then,
    I do not value life in this dishonor.
    It is not as though this rumor touched upon
    Some private indiscretion. The matter is grave.
    The fact is that I am being called disloyal
    To the State, to my fellow citizens, to my friends.
CHORAGOS. He may have spoken in anger, not from his mind.
KREON. But did you not hear him say I was the one
    Who seduced the old prophet into lying?
CHORAGOS. The thing was said; I do not know how seriously.
KREON. But you were watching him! Were his eyes steady?
    Did he look like a man in his right mind?
CHORAGOS.   I do not know.
    I can not judge the behavior of great men.
    But here is the king himself.

    (*Enter* OEDIPUS.)

---

[15] Oedipus is mistakenly assumed to be Polybos's son.

OEDIPUS.   So you dared come back.
    Why? How brazen of you to come to my house, 505
    You murderer!
                    Do you think I do not know
    That you plotted to kill me, plotted to steal my throne?
    Tell me, in God's name: am I coward, a fool,
    That you should dream you could accomplish this?
    A fool who could not see your slippery game? 510
    A coward, not to fight back when I saw it?
    You are the fool, Kreon, are you not? hoping
    Without support or friends to get a throne?
    Thrones may be won or bought: you could do neither.
KREON. Now listen to me. You have talked; let me talk, too. 515
    You can not judge unless you know the facts.
OEDIPUS. You speak well: there is one fact; but I find it hard
    To learn from the deadliest enemy I have.
KREON. That above all I must dispute with you.
OEDIPUS. That above all I will not hear you deny. 520
KREON. If you think there is anything good in being stubborn
    Against all reason, then I say you are wrong.
OEDIPUS. If you think a man can sin against his own kind
    And not be punished for it, I say you are mad.
KREON. I agree. But tell me: what have I done to you? 525
OEDIPUS. You advised me to send for that wizard, did you not?
KREON. I did. I should do it again.
OEDIPUS.   Very well. Now tell me:
    How long has it been since Laios—
KREON.   What of Laios?
OEDIPUS. Since he vanished in that onset by the road?
KREON. It was long ago, a long time.
OEDIPUS.   And this prophet, 530
    Was he practicing here then?
KREON.   He was; and with honor, as now.
OEDIPUS. Did he speak of me at that time?
KREON.   He never did,
    At least, not when I was present.
OEDIPUS.   But . . . the enquiry?
    I suppose you held one?
KREON.   We did, but we learned nothing.
OEDIPUS. Why did the prophet not speak against me then? 535
KREON. I do not know; and I am the kind of man
    Who holds his tongue when he has no facts to go on.
OEDIPUS. There's one fact that you know, and you could tell it.
KREON. What fact is that? If I know it, you shall have it.
OEDIPUS. If he were not involved with you, he could not say 540
    That it was I who murdered Laios.

KREON. If he says that, you are the one that knows it!—
  But now it is my turn to question you.
OEDIPUS. Put your questions. I am no murderer.
KREON. First, then: You married my sister?
OEDIPUS.   I married your sister.   545
KREON. And you rule the kingdom equally with her?
OEDIPUS. Everything that she wants she has from me.
KREON. And I am the third, equal to both of you?
OEDIPUS. That is why I call you a bad friend.
KREON. No. Reason it out, as I have done.   550
  Think of this first: Would any sane man prefer
  Power, with all a king's anxieties,
  To that same power and the grace of sleep?
  Certainly not I.
  I have never longed for the king's power—only his rights.   555
  Would any wise man differ from me in this?
  As matters stand, I have my way in everything
  With your consent, and no responsibilities.
  If I were king, I should be a slave to policy.
  How could I desire a scepter more   560
  Than what is now mine—untroubled influence?
  No, I have not gone mad; I need no honors,
  Except those with the perquisites I have now.
  I am welcome everywhere; every man salutes me,
  And those who want your favor seek my ear,   565
  Since I know how to manage what they ask.
  Should I exchange this ease for that anxiety?
  Besides, no sober mind is treasonable.
  I hate anarchy
  And never would deal with any man who likes it.   570

  Test what I have said. Go to the priestess
  At Delphi, ask if I quoted her correctly.
  And as for this other thing: if I am found
  Guilty of treason with Teiresias,
  Then sentence me to death. You have my word   575
  It is a sentence I should cast my vote for—
  But not without evidence!
                  You do wrong
  When you take good men for bad, bad men for good.
  A true friend thrown aside—why, life itself
  Is not more precious!
                  In time you will know this well: 580
  For time, and time alone, will show the just man,
  Though scoundrels are discovered in a day.
CHORAGOS. This is well said, and a prudent man would ponder it.
  Judgments too quickly formed are dangerous.

OEDIPUS. But is he not quick in his duplicity? 585
And shall I not be quick to parry him?
Would you have me stand still, hold my peace, and let
This man win everything, through my inaction?
KREON. And you want—what is it, then? To banish me?
OEDIPUS. No, not exile. It is your death I want, 590
So that all the world may see what treason means.
KREON. You will persist, then? You will not believe me?
OEDIPUS. How can I believe you?
KREON.   Then you are a fool.
OEDIPUS. To save myself?
KREON.   In justice, think of me.
OEDIPUS. You are evil incarnate.
KREON.   But suppose you are wrong? 595
OEDIPUS. Still I must rule.
KREON.   But not if you rule badly.
OEDIPUS. O city, city!
KREON.   It is my city, too!
CHORAGOS. Now, my lords, be still. I see the queen,
Iokaste, coming from her palace chambers;
And it is time she came, for the sake of you both. 600
This dreadful quarrel can be resolved through her.

(*Enter* IOKASTE.)

IOKASTE. Poor foolish men, what wicked din is this?
With Thebes sick to death, is it not shameful
That you should rake some private quarrel up?
(*To* OEDIPUS.) Come into the house.
                             —And you, Kreon, go now: 605
Let us have no more of this tumult over nothing.
KREON. Nothing? No, sister: what your husband plans for me
Is one of two great evils: exile or death.
OEDIPUS. He is right.
                Why, woman I have caught him squarely
Plotting against my life.
KREON.   No! Let me die 610
Accurst if ever I have wished you harm!
IOKASTE. Ah, believe it, Oedipus!
In the name of the gods, respect this oath of his
For my sake, for the sake of these people here!

STROPHE 1

CHORAGOS. Open your mind to her, my lord. Be ruled by her, I
    beg you! 615
OEDIPUS. What would you have me do?

CHORAGOS.   Respect Kreon's word. He has never spoken like a fool,
    And now he has sworn an oath.
OEDIPUS.   You know what you ask?
CHORAGOS.   I do.
OEDIPUS.   Speak on, then.
CHORAGOS.   A friend so sworn should not be baited so,
    In blind malice, and without final proof.   620
OEDIPUS.   You are aware, I hope, that what you say
    Means death for me, or exile at the least.

STROPHE 2

CHORAGOS.   No, I swear by Helios, first in heaven!
        May I die friendless and accurst,
            The worst of deaths, if ever I meant that!   625
            It is the withering fields
                That hurt my sick heart:
            Must we bear all these ills,
                And now your bad blood as well?
OEDIPUS.   Then let him go. And let me die, if I must,   630
    Or be driven by him in shame from the land of Thebes.
    It is your unhappiness, and not his talk,
    That touches me.
            As for him—
    Wherever he goes, hatred will follow him.
KREON.   Ugly in yielding, as you were ugly in rage!   635
    Natures like yours chiefly torment themselves.
OEDIPUS.   Can you not go? Can you not leave me?
KREON.   I can.
    You do not know me; but the city knows me,
    And in its eyes I am just, if not in yours. (*Exit* KREON.)

ANTISTROPHE 1

CHORAGOS.   Lady Iokaste, did you not ask the King to go to his
        chambers?   640
IOKASTE.   First tell me what has happened.
CHORAGOS.   There was suspicion without evidence; yet it rankled
    As even false charges will.
IOKASTE.   On both sides?
CHORAGOS.   On both.
IOKASTE.   But what was said?
CHORAGOS.   Oh let it rest, let it be done with!
    Have we not suffered enough?   645
OEDIPUS.   You see to what your decency has brought you:
    You have made difficulties where my heart saw none.

ANTISTROPHE 2

CHORAGOS. Oedipus, it is not once only I have told you—
 You must know I should count myself unwise
  To the point of madness, should I now forsake you— 650
 You, under whose hand,
  In the storm of another time,
   Our dear land sailed out free.
    But now stand fast at the helm!
IOKASTE. In God's name, Oedipus, inform your wife as well: 655
 Why are you so set in this hard anger?
OEDIPUS. I will tell you, for none of these men deserves
 My confidence as you do. It is Kreon's work,
 His treachery, his plotting against me.
IOKASTE. Go on, if you can make this clear to me. 660
OEDIPUS. He charges me with the murder of Laios.
IOKASTE. Has he some knowledge? Or does he speak from hearsay?
OEDIPUS. He would not commit himself to such a charge,
 But he has brought in that damnable soothsayer
 To tell his story.
IOKASTE.   Set your mind at rest. 665
 If it is a question of soothsayers, I tell you
 That you will find no man whose craft gives knowledge
 Of the unknowable.
       Here is my proof:
 An oracle was reported to Laios once
 (I will not say from Phoibos himself, but from 670
 His appointed ministers, at any rate)
 That his doom would be death at the hands of his own son—
 His son, born of his flesh and of mine!

 Now, you remember the story: Laios was killed
 By marauding strangers where three highways meet; 675
 But his child had not been three days in this world
 Before the king had pierced the baby's ankles
 And left him to die on a lonely mountainside.

 Thus, Apollo never caused that child
 To kill his father, and it was not for Laios' fate 680
 To die at the hands of his son, as he had feared.
 This is what prophets and prophecies are worth!
 Have no dread of them.
          It is God himself
 Who can show us what he wills, in his own way.
OEDIPUS. How strange a shadowy memory crossed my mind. 685
 Just now while you were speaking; it chilled my heart.
IOKASTE. What do you mean? What memory do you speak of?

OEDIPUS. If I understand you, Laios was killed
   At a place where three roads meet.
IOKASTE.   So it was said;
   We have no later story.
OEDIPUS.   Where did it happen?
IOKASTE. Phokis, it is called: at a place where the Theban Way
   Divides into the roads toward Delphi and Daulia.
OEDIPUS. When?
IOKASTE.   We had the news not long before you came
   And proved the right to your succession here.
OEDIPUS. Ah, what net has God been weaving for me?
IOKASTE. Oedipus! Why does this trouble you?
OEDIPUS.   Do not ask me yet.
   First, tell me how Laios looked, and tell me
   How old he was.
IOKASTE.   He was tall, his hair just touched
   With white; his form was not unlike your own.
OEDIPUS. I think that I myself may be accurst
   By my own ignorant edict.
IOKASTE.   You speak strangely.
   It makes me tremble to look at you, my king.
OEDIPUS. I am not sure that the blind man can not see.
   But I should know better if you were to tell me—
IOKASTE. Anything—though I dread to hear you ask it.
OEDIPUS. Was the king lightly escorted, or did he ride
   With a large company, as a ruler should?
IOKASTE. There were five men with him in all: one was a herald;
   And a single chariot, which he was driving.
OEDIPUS. Alas, that makes it plain enough!
                                   But who—
   Who told you how it happened?
IOKASTE.   A household servant,
   The only one to escape.
OEDIPUS.   And is he still
   A servant of ours?
IOKASTE.   No; for when he came back at last
   And found you enthroned in the place of the dead king,
   He came to me, touched my hand with his, and begged
   That I would send him away to the frontier district
   Where only the shepherds go—
   As far away from the city as I could send him.
   I granted his prayer; for although the man was a slave,
   He had earned more than this favor at my hands.
OEDIPUS. Can he be called back quickly?
IOKASTE.   Easily.
   But why?

OEDIPUS.   I have taken too much upon myself
    Without enquiry; therefore I wish to consult him.
IOKASTE.   Then he shall come.
                        But am I not one also
    To whom you might confide these fears of yours?   725
OEDIPUS.   That is your right; it will not be denied you,
    Now least of all; for I have reached a pitch
    Of wild foreboding. Is there anyone
    To whom I should sooner speak?

    Polybos of Corinth is my father.   730
    My mother is a Dorian: Merope.
    I grew up chief among the men of Corinth
    Until a strange thing happened—
    Not worth my passion, it may be, but strange.
    At a feast, a drunken man maundering in his cups   735
    Cries out that I am not my father's son!

    I contained myself that night, though I felt anger
    And a sinking heart. The next day I visited
    My father and mother, and questioned them. They stormed,
    Calling it all the slanderous rant of a fool;   740
    And this relieved me. Yet the suspicion
    Remained always aching in my mind;
    I knew there was talk; I could not rest;
    And finally, saying nothing to my parents,
    I went to the shrine at Delphi.   745

    The god dismissed my question without reply;
    He spoke of other things.
                        Some were clear,
    Full of wretchedness, dreadful, unbearable:
    As, that I should lie with my own mother, breed
    Children from whom all men would turn their eyes;   750
    And that I should be my father's murderer.

    I heard all this, and fled. And from that day
    Corinth to me was only in the stars
    Descending in that quarter of the sky,
    As I wandered farther and farther on my way   755
    To a land where I should never see the evil
    Sung by the oracle. And I came to this country
    Where, so you say, King Laios was killed.

    I will tell you all that happened there, my lady.

    There were three highways   760
    Coming together at a place I passed;
    And there a herald came towards me, and a chariot

             Drawn by horses, with a man such as you describe
             Seated in it. The groom leading the horses
             Forced me off the road at his lord's command;
             But as this charioteer lurched over towards me
             I struck him in my rage. The old man saw me
             And brought his double goad down upon my head
             As I came abreast.
                              He was paid back, and more!
             Swinging my club in this right hand I knocked him
             Out of his car, and he rolled on the ground.
                                              I killed him.

             I killed them all.
             Now if that stranger and Laios were—kin,
             Where is a man more miserable than I?
             More hated by the gods? Citizen and alien alike
             Must never shelter me or speak to me—
             I must be shunned by all.
                                    And I myself
             Pronounced this malediction upon myself!

             Think of it: I have touched you with these hands,
             These hands that killed your husband. What defilement!

             Am I all evil, then? It must be so,
             Since I must flee from Thebes, yet never again
             See my own countrymen, my own country,
             For fear of joining my mother in marriage
             And killing Polybos, my father.
                                           Ah,
             If I was created so, born to this fate,
             Who would deny the savagery of God?

             O holy majesty of heavenly powers!
             May I never see that day! Never!
             Rather let me vanish from the race of men
             Than know the abomination destined me!
CHORAGOS.   We too, my lord, have felt dismay at this.
             But there is hope: you have yet to hear the shepherd.
OEDIPUS.   Indeed, I fear no other hope is left me.
IOKASTE.   What do you hope from him when he comes?
OEDIPUS.   This much:
             If his account of the murder tallies with yours,
             Then I am cleared.
IOKASTE.   What was it that I said
             Of such importance?
OEDIPUS.   Why, "marauders," you said,

>   Killed the king, according to this man's story.
>   If he maintains that still, if there were several, 800
>   Clearly the guilt is not mine: I was alone.
>   But if he says one man, singlehanded, did it,
>   Then the evidence all points to me.
> IOKASTE. You may be sure that he said there were several;
>   And can he call back that story now? He can not. 805
>   The whole city heard it as plainly as I.
>   But suppose he alters some detail of it:
>   He can not ever show that Laios' death
>   Fulfilled the oracle: for Apollo said
>   My child was doomed to kill him; and my child— 810
>   Poor baby!—it was my child that died first.
>
>   No. From now on, where oracles are concerned,
>   I would not waste a second thought on any.
> OEDIPUS. You may be right.
>   But come: let someone go
>   For the shepherd at once. This matter must be settled. 815
> IOKASTE. I will send for him.
>   I would not wish to cross you in anything,
>   And surely not in this.—Let us go in.
>
> (*Exeunt into the palace.*)

ODE II

STROPHE 1

> CHORUS. Let me be reverent in the ways of right,
>   Lowly the paths I journey on; 820
>   Let all my words and actions keep
>   The laws of the pure universe
>   From highest Heaven handed down.
>   For Heaven is their bright nurse,
>   Those generations of the realms of light; 825
>   Ah, never of mortal kind were they begot,
>   Nor are they slaves of memory, lost in sleep:
>   Their Father is greater than Time, and ages not.

ANTISTROPHE 1

> The tyrant is a child of Pride
> Who drinks from his great sickening cup 830
> Recklessness and vanity,
> Until from his high crest headlong
> He plummets to the dust of hope.

>   That strong man is not strong.
>   But let no fair ambition be denied;
>   May God protect the wrestler for the State
>   In government, in comely policy,
>   Who will fear God, and on His ordinance wait.

STROPHE 2

>   Haughtiness and the high hand of disdain
>   Tempt and outrage God's holy law;
>   And any mortal who dares hold
>   No immortal Power in awe
>   Will be caught up in a net of pain:
>   The price for which his levity is sold.
>   Let each man take due earnings, then,
>   And keep his hands from holy things,
>   And from blasphemy stand apart—
>   Else the crackling blast of heaven
>   Blows on his head, and on his desperate heart.
>   Though fools will honor impious men,
>   In their cities no tragic poet sings.

ANTISTROPHE 2

>   Shall we lose faith in Delphi's obscurities,
>   We who have heard the world's core
>   Discredited, and the sacred wood
>   Of Zeus at Elis praised no more?
>   The deeds and the strange prophecies
>   Must make a pattern yet to be understood.
>   Zeus, if indeed you are lord of all,
>   Throned in light over night and day,
>   Mirror this in your endless mind:
>   Our masters call the oracle
>   Words on the wind, and the Delphic vision blind!
>   Their hearts no longer know Apollo,
>   And reverence for the gods has died away.

SCENE III

Enter IOKASTE.

IOKASTE.   Princes of Thebes, it has occurred to me
           To visit the altars of the gods, bearing
           These branches as a suppliant, and this incense.
           Our king is not himself: his noble soul
           Is overwrought with fantasies of dread,
           Else he would consider

The new prophecies in the light of the old.
He will listen to any voice that speaks disaster,
And my advice goes for nothing.

(*She approaches the altar, right.*)

                                        To you, then, Apollo,
Lycean lord, since you are nearest, I turn in prayer.
Receive these offerings, and grant us deliverance   875
From defilement. Our hearts are heavy with fear
When we see our leader distracted, as helpless sailors
Are terrified by the confusion of their helmsman.

(*Enter* MESSENGER.)

MESSENGER. Friends, no doubt you can direct me:
    Where shall I find the house of Oedipus,   880
    Or, better still, where is the king himself?
CHORAGOS. It is this very place, stranger; he is inside.
    This is his wife and mother of his children.
MESSENGER. I wish her happiness in a happy house,
    Blest in all the fulfillment of her marriage.   885
IOKASTE. I wish as much for you: your courtesy
    Deserves a like good fortune. But now, tell me:
    Why have you come? What have you to say to us?
MESSENGER. Good news, my lady, for your house and your husband.
IOKASTE. What news? Who sent you here?
MESSENGER.   I am from Corinth.   890
    The news I bring ought to mean joy for you,
    Though it may be you will find some grief in it.
IOKASTE. What is it? How can it touch us in both ways?
MESSENGER. The word is that the people of the Isthmus
    Intend to call Oedipus to be their king.   895
IOKASTE. But old King Polybos—is he not reigning still?
MESSENGER. No. Death holds him in his sepulchre.
IOKASTE. What are you saying? Polybos is dead?
MESSENGER. If I am not telling the truth, may I die myself.
IOKASTE (*to a* MAIDSERVANT). Go in, go quickly; tell this to
    your master.   900
    O riddlers of God's will, where are you now!
    This was the man whom Oedipus, long ago,
    Feared so, fled so, in dread of destroying him—
    But it was another fate by which he died.

(*Enter* OEDIPUS, *center.*)

OEDIPUS. Dearest Iokaste, why have you sent for me?   905
IOKASTE. Listen to what this man says, and then tell me
    What has become of the solemn prophecies.

OEDIPUS.   Who is this man? What is his news for me?
IOKASTE.   He has come from Corinth to announce your father's death!
OEDIPUS.   Is it true, stranger? Tell me in your own words.   910
MESSENGER.   I can not say it more clearly: the king is dead.
OEDIPUS.   Was it by treason? Or by an attack of illness?
MESSENGER.   A little thing brings old men to their rest.
OEDIPUS.   It was sickness, then?
MESSENGER   Yes, and his many years.   915
OEDIPUS.   Ah!
    Why should a man respect the Pythian hearth, or
    Give heed to the birds that jangle above his head?
    They prophesied that I should kill Polybos,
    Kill my own father; but he is dead and buried,
    And I am here—I never touched him, never,   920
    Unless he died of grief for my departure,
    And thus, in a sense, through me. No. Polybos
    Has packed the oracles off with him underground.
    They are empty words.
IOKASTE.   Had I not told you so?
OEDIPUS.   You had; it was my faint heart that betrayed me.   925
IOKASTE.   From now on never think of those things again.
OEDIPUS.   And yet—must I not fear my mother's bed?
IOKASTE.   Why should anyone in this world be afraid,
    Since Fate rules us and nothing can be foreseen?
    A man should live only for the present day.   930

    Have no more fear of sleeping with your mother:
    How many men, in dreams, have lain with their mothers!
    No reasonable man is troubled by such things.
OEDIPUS.   That is true; only—
    If only my mother were not still alive!   935
    But she is alive. I can not help my dread.
IOKASTE.   Yet this news of your father's death is wonderful.
OEDIPUS.   Wonderful. But I fear the living woman.
MESSENGER.   Tell me, who is this woman that you fear?
OEDIPUS.   It is Merope, man; the wife of King Polybos.   940
MESSENGER.   Merope? Why should you be afraid of her?
OEDIPUS.   An oracle of the gods, a dreadful saying.
MESSENGER.   Can you tell me about it or are you sworn to silence?
OEDIPUS.   I can tell you, and I will.
    Apollo said through his prophet that I was the man   945
    Who should marry his own mother, shed his father's blood
    With his own hands. And so, for all these years
    I have kept clear of Corinth, and no harm has come—
    Though it would have been sweet to see my parents again.
MESSENGER.   And this is the fear that drove you out of Corinth?   950
OEDIPUS.   Would you have me kill my father?

MESSENGER.   As for that
   You must be reassured by tne news I gave you.
OEDIPUS. If you could reassure me, I would reward you.
MESSENGER. I had that in mind, I will confess: I thought
   I could count on you when you returned to Corinth.   955
OEDIPUS. No: I will never go near my parents again.
MESSENGER. Ah, son, you still do not know what you are doing—
OEDIPUS. What do you mean? In the name of God tell me!
MESSENGER. —If these are your reasons for not going home.
OEDIPUS. I tell you, I fear the oracle may come true.   960
MESSENGER. And guilt may come upon you through your parents?
OEDIPUS. That is the dread that is always in my heart.
MESSENGER. Can you not see that all your fears are groundless?
OEDIPUS. Groundless? Am I not my parents' son?
MESSENGER. Polybos was not your father.
OEDIPUS.   Not my father?   965
MESSENGER. No more your father than the man speaking to you.
OEDIPUS. But you are nothing to me!
MESSENGER.   Neither was he.
OEDIPUS. Then why did he call me son?
MESSENGER.   I will tell you:
   Long ago he had you from my hands, as a gift.
OEDIPUS. Then how could he love me so, if I was not his?   970
MESSENGER. He had no children, and his heart turned to you.
OEDIPUS. What of you? Did you buy me? Did you find me by chance?
MESSENGER. I came upon you in the woody vales of Kithairon.
OEDIPUS. And what were you doing there?
MESSENGER.   Tending my flocks.
OEDIPUS. A wandering shepherd?
MESSENGER.   But your savior, son, that day.   975
OEDIPUS. From what did you save me?
MESSENGER.   Your ankles should tell you that.
OEDIPUS. Ah, stranger, why do you speak of that childhood pain?
MESSENGER. I pulled the skewer that pinned your feet together.
OEDIPUS. I have had the mark as long as I can remember.
MESSENGER. That was why you were given the name you bear.   980
OEDIPUS. God! Was it my father or my mother who did it?
   Tell me!
MESSENGER. I do not know. The man who gave you to me
   Can tell you better than I.
OEDIPUS. It was not you that found me, but another?
MESSENGER. It was another shepherd gave you to me.   985
OEDIPUS. Who was he? Can you tell me who he was?
MESSENGER. I think he was said to be one of Laios' people.
OEDIPUS. You mean the Laios who was king here years ago?
MESSENGER. Yes; King Laios; and the man was one of his herdsmen.

OEDIPUS. Is he still alive? Can I see him?
MESSENGER.   These men here   990
    Know best about such things.
OEDIPUS.   Does anyone here
    Know this shepherd that he is talking about?
    Have you seen him in the fields, or in the town?
    If you have, tell me. It is time things were made plain.
CHORAGOS. I think the man he means is that same shepherd   995
    You have already asked to see. Iokaste perhaps
    Could tell you something.
OEDIPUS.   Do you know anything
    About him, Lady? Is he the man we have summoned?
    Is that the man this shepherd means?
IOKASTE.   Why think of him?
    Forget this herdsman. Forget it all.   1000
    This talk is a waste of time.
OEDIPUS.   How can you say that,
    When the clues to my true birth are in my hands?
IOKASTE. For God's love, let us have no more questioning!
    Is your life nothing to you?
    My own is pain enough for me to bear.   1005
OEDIPUS. You need not worry. Suppose my mother a slave,
    And born of slaves: no baseness can touch you.
IOKASTE. Listen to me, I beg you: do not do this thing!
OEDIPUS. I will not listen; the truth must be made known.
IOKASTE. Everything that I say is for your own good!
OEDIPUS.   My own good   1010
    Snaps my patience, then; I want none of it.
IOKASTE. You are fatally wrong! May you never learn who you are!
OEDIPUS. Go, one of you, and bring the shepherd here.
    Let us leave this woman to brag of her royal name.
IOKASTE. Ah, miserable!   1015
    That is the only word I have for you now.
    That is the only word I can ever have. (*Exit into the palace.*)
CHORAGOS. Why has she left us, Oedipus? Why has she gone
    In such a passion of sorrow? I fear this silence:
    Something dreadful may come of it.
OEDIPUS.   Let it come!   1020
    However base my birth, I must know about it.
    The Queen, like a woman, is perhaps ashamed
    To think of my low origin. But I
    Am a child of Luck; I can not be dishonored.
    Luck is my mother; the passing months, my brothers,   1025
    Have seen me rich and poor.
                        If this is so,
    How could I wish that I were someone else?
    How could I not be glad to know my birth?

ODE III

STROPHE

CHORAGOS. If ever the coming time were known
    To my heart's pondering,   1030
    Kithairon, now by Heaven I see the torches
    At the festival of the next full moon,
    And see the dance, and hear the choir sing
    A grace to your gentle shade:
    Mountain where Oedipus was found,   1035
    O mountain guard of a noble race!
    May the god who heals us lend his aid,
    And let that glory come to pass
    For our king's cradling-ground.

ANTISTROPHE

    Of the nymphs that flower beyond the years,   1040
    Who bore you, royal child,
    To Pan of the hills or the timberline Apollo,
    Cold in delight where the upland clears,
    Or Hermes for whom Kyllene's heights are piled?
    Or flushed as evening cloud,   1045
    Great Dionysos, roamer of mountains,
    He—was it he who found you there,
    And caught you up in his own proud
    Arms from the sweet god-ravisher
    Who laughed by the Muses' fountains?   1050

SCENE IV

OEDIPUS. Sirs: though I do not know the man,
    I think I see him coming, this shepherd we want:
    He is old, like our friend here, and the men
    Bringing him seem to be servants of my house.
    But you can tell, if you have ever seen him.   1055

(*Enter* SHEPHERD *escorted by* SERVANTS.)

CHORAGOS. I know him, he was Laios' man. You can trust him.
OEDIPUS. Tell me first, you from Corinth: is this the shepherd
    We were discussing?
MESSENGER.   This is the very man.
OEDIPUS. (*to* SHEPHERD). Come here. No, look at me. You must answer
    Everything I ask.—You belonged to Laios?   1060
SHEPHERD. Yes: born his slave, brought up in his house.
OEDIPUS. Tell me: what kind of work did you do for him?

SHEPHERD. I was a shepherd of his, most of my life.
OEDIPUS. Where mainly did you go for pasturage?
SHEPHERD. Sometimes Kithairon, sometimes the hills near-by. 1065
OEDIPUS. Do you remember ever seeing this man out there?
SHEPHERD. What would he be doing there? This man?
OEDIPUS. This man standing here. Have you ever seen him before?
SHEPHERD. No. At least, not to my recollection.
MESSENGER. And that is not strange, my lord. But I'll refresh 1070
    His memory: he must remember when we two
    Spent three whole seasons together, March to September,
    On Kithairon or thereabouts. He had two flocks;
    I had one. Each autumn I'd drive mine home
    And he would go back with his to Laios' sheepfold.— 1075
    Is this not true, just as I have described it?
SHEPHERD. True, yes; but it was all so long ago.
MESSENGER. Well, then: do you remember, back in those days,
    That you gave me a baby boy to bring up as my own?
SHEPHERD. What if I did? What are you trying to say? 1080
MESSENGER. King Oedipus was once that little child.
SHEPHERD. Damn you, hold your tongue!
OEDIPUS.   No more of that!
    It is your tongue needs watching, not this man's.
SHEPHERD. My king, my master, what is it I have done wrong?
OEDIPUS. You have not answered his question about the boy. 1085
SHEPHERD. He does not know . . . He is only making trouble . . .
OEDIPUS. Come, speak plainly, or it will go hard with you.
SHEPHERD. In God's name, do not torture an old man!
OEDIPUS. Come here, one of you; bind his arms behind him.
SHEPHERD. Unhappy king! What more do you wish to learn? 1090
OEDIPUS. Did you give this man the child he speaks of?
SHEPHERD.   I did.
    And I would to God I had died that very day.
OEDIPUS. You will die now unless you speak the truth.
SHEPHERD. Yet if I speak the truth, I am worse than dead.
OEDIPUS (*to* ATTENDANT). He intends to draw it out, apparently— 1095
SHEPHERD. No! I have told you already that I gave him the boy.
OEDIPUS. Where did you get him? From your house? From somewhere
    else?
SHEPHERD. Not from mine, no. A man gave him to me.
OEDIPUS. Is that man here? Whose house did he belong to?
SHEPHERD. For God's love, my king, do not ask me any more! 1100
OEDIPUS. You are a dead man if I have to ask you again.
SHEPHERD. Then . . . Then the child was from the palace of Laios.
OEDIPUS. A slave child? or a child of his own line?
SHEPHERD. Ah, I am on the brink of dreadful speech!
OEDIPUS. And I of dreadful hearing. Yet I must hear. 1105

SHEPHERD. If you must be told, then . . .
                              They said it was Laios' child;
    But it is your wife who can tell you about that.
OEDIPUS. My wife!—Did she give it to you?
SHEPHERD.   My lord, she did.
OEDIPUS. Do you know why?
SHEPHERD.   I was told to get rid of it.
OEDIPUS. Oh heartless mother!
SHEPHERD.   But in dread of prophecies . . .   1110
OEDIPUS. Tell me.
SHEPHERD.   It was said that the boy would kill his own father.
OEDIPUS. Then why did you give him over to this old man?
SHEPHERD. I pitied the baby, my king,
    And I thought that this man would take him far away
        To his own country.
                        He saved him—but for what a fate!   1115
    For if you are what this man says you are,
    No man living is more wretched than Oedipus.
OEDIPUS. Ah God!
    It was true!
            All the prophecies!
                            —Now,
    O Light, may I look on you for the last time!   1120
    I, Oedipus,
    Oedipus, damned in his birth, in his marriage damned,
    Damned in the blood he shed with his own hand! (*He rushes into the
        palace.*)

ODE IV

STROPHE 1

CHORUS. Alas for the seed of men.
    What measure shall I give these generations   1125
    That breathe on the void and are void
    And exist and do not exist?
    Who bears more weight of joy
    Than mass of sunlight shifting in images,
    Or who shall make his thought stay on   1130
    That down time drifts away?
    Your splendor is all fallen.
    O naked brow of wrath and tears,
    O change of Oedipus!
    I who saw your days call no man blest—   1135
    Your great days like ghosts gone.

ANTISTROPHE 1

    That mind was a strong bow.
    Deep, how deep you drew it then, hard archer,
    At a dim fearful range,
    And brought dear glory down!   1140
    You overcame the stranger—
    The virgin with her hooking lion claws—
    And though death sang, stood like a tower
    To make pale Thebes take heart.
    Fortress against our sorrow!   1145
    True king, giver of laws,
    Majestic Oedipus!
    No prince in Thebes had ever such renown,
    No prince won such grace of power.

STROPHE 2

    And now of all men ever known   1150
    Most pitiful is this man's story:
    His fortunes are most changed, his state
    Fallen to a low slave's
    Ground under bitter fate.
    O Oedipus, most royal one!   1155
    The great door that expelled you to the light
    Gave at night—ah, gave night to your glory:
    As to the father, to the fathering son.
    All understood too late.
    How could that queen whom Laios won,   1160
    The garden that he harrowed at his height,
    Be silent when that act was done?

ANTISTROPHE 2

    But all eyes fail before time's eye,
    All actions come to justice there.
    Though never willed, though far down the deep past,   1165
    Your bed, your dread sirings,
    Are brought to book at last.
    Child by Laios doomed to die,
    Then doomed to lose that fortunate little death,
    Would God you never took breath in this air   1170
    That with my wailing lips I take to cry:
    For I weep the world's outcast.
    I was blind, and now I can tell why:
    Asleep, for you had given ease of breath
    To Thebes, while the false years went by.   1175

EXODOS

Enter, from the palace, SECOND MESSENGER.

SECOND MESSENGER.   Elders of Thebes, most honored in this land,
    What horrors are yours to see and hear, what weight
    Of sorrow to be endured, if, true to your birth,
    You venerate the line of Labdakos!
    I think neither Istros nor Phasis, those great rivers,
    Could purify this place of all the evil
    It shelters now, or soon must bring to light—
    Evil not done unconsciously, but willed.

    The greatest griefs are those we cause ourselves.
CHORAGOS.   Surely, friend, we have grief enough already;
    What new sorrow do you mean?
SECOND MESSENGER.   The queen is dead.
CHORAGOS.   O miserable queen! But at whose hand?
SECOND MESSENGER.   Her own.
    The full horror of what happened you can not know,
    For you did not see it; but I, who did, will tell you
    As clearly as I can how she met her death.

    When she had left us,
    In passionate silence, passing through the court,
    She ran to her apartment in the house,
    Her hair clutched by the fingers of both hands.
    She closed the doors behind her; then, by that bed
    Where long ago the fatal son was conceived—
    That son who should bring about his father's death—
    We heard her call upon Laios, dead so many years,
    And heard her wail for the double fruit of her marriage,
    A husband by her husband, children by her child.

    Exactly how she died I do not know:
    For Oedipus burst in moaning and would not let us
    Keep vigil to the end: it was by him
    As he stormed about the room that our eyes were caught.
    From one to another of us he went, begging a sword,
    Hunting the wife who was not his wife, the mother
    Whose womb had carried his own children and himself.
    I do not know: it was none of us aided him,
    But surely one of the gods was in control!
    For with a dreadful cry
    He hurled his weight, as though wrenched out of himself,
    At the twin doors: the bolts gave, and he rushed in.
    And there we saw her hanging, her body swaying
    From the cruel cord she had noosed about her neck.

A great sob broke from him, heartbreaking to hear, 1215
As he loosed the rope and lowered her to the ground.

I would blot out from my mind what happened next!
For the king ripped from her gown the golden brooches
That were her ornament, and raised them, and plunged them down
Straight into his own eyeballs, crying, "No more, 1220
No more shall you look on the misery about me,
The horrors of my own doing! Too long you have known
The faces of those whom I should never have seen,
Too long been blind to those for whom I was searching!
From this hour, go in darkness!" And as he spoke, 1225
He struck at his eyes—not once, but many times;
And the blood spattered his beard,
Bursting from his ruined sockets like red hail.

So from the unhappiness of two this evil has sprung,
A curse on the man and woman alike. The old 1230
Happiness of the house of Labdakos
Was happiness enough: where is it today?
It is all wailing and ruin, disgrace, death—all
The misery of mankind that has a name—
And it is wholly and for ever theirs. 1235

CHORAGOS. Is he in agony still? Is there no rest for him?
SECOND MESSENGER. He is calling for someone to open the doors wide
    So that all the children of Kadmos may look upon
    His father's murderer, his mother's—no,
    I can not say it!
                    And then he will leave Thebes, 1240
    Self-exiled, in order that the curse
    Which he himself pronounced may depart from the house.
    He is weak, and there is none to lead him,
    So terrible is his suffering.
                    But you will see:
    Look, the doors are opening; in a moment 1245
    You will see a thing that would crush a heart of stone.

(*The central door is opened;* OEDIPUS, *blinded, is led in.*)

CHORAGOS. Dreadful indeed for men to see.
    Never have my own eyes
    Looked on a sight so full of fear.

    Oedipus! 1250
    What madness came upon you, what daemon
    Leaped on your life with heavier
    Punishment than a mortal man can bear?
    No: I can not even

     Look at you, poor ruined one.
     And I would speak, question, ponder,
     If I were able. No.
     You make me shudder.
OEDIPUS. God. God.
     Is there a sorrow greater?
     Where shall I find harbor in this world?
     My voice is hurled far on a dark wind.
     What has God done to me?
CHORAGOS. Too terrible to think of, or to see.

STROPHE 1

OEDIPUS. O cloud of night,
     Never to be turned away: night coming on,
     I can not tell how: night like a shroud!
     My fair winds brought me here.
                              O God. Again
     The pain of the spikes where I had sight,
     The flooding pain
     Of memory, never to be gouged out.
CHORAGOS. This is not strange.
     You suffer it all twice over, remorse in pain,
     Pain in remorse.

ANTISTROPHE 1

OEDIPUS. Ah dear friend
     Are you faithful even yet, you alone?
     Are you still standing near me, will you stay here,
     Patient, to care for the blind?
                              The blind man!
     Yet even blind I know who it is attends me,
     By the voice's tone—
     Though my new darkness hide the comforter.
CHORAGOS. Oh fearful act!
     What god was it drove you to rake black
     Night across your eyes?

STROPHE 2

OEDIPUS. Apollo. Apollo. Dear
     Children, the god was Apollo.
     He brought my sick, sick fate upon me.
     But the blinding hand was my own!
     How could I bear to see
     When all my sight was horror everywhere?

CHORAGOS. Everywhere; that is true.
OEDIPUS. And now what is left?
　　Images? Love? A greeting even,
　　Sweet to the senses? Is there anything?
　　Ah, no, friends: lead me away.
　　Lead me away from Thebes.
　　　　　　　　　　Lead the great wreck
　　And hell of Oedipus, whom the gods hate.
CHORAGOS. Your misery, you are not blind to that.
　　Would God you had never found it out!

ANTISTROPHE 2

OEDIPUS. Death take the man who unbound
　　My feet on that hillside
　　And delivered me from death to life! What life?
　　If only I had died,
　　This weight of monstrous doom
　　Could not have dragged me and my darlings down.
CHORAGOS. I would have wished the same.
OEDIPUS. Oh never to have come here
　　With my father's blood upon me! Never
　　To have been the man they call his mother's husband!
　　Oh accurst! Oh child of evil,
　　To have entered that wretched bed—
　　　　　　　　　　the selfsame one!
　　More primal than sin itself, this fell to me.
CHORAGOS. I do not know what words to offer you.
　　You were better dead than alive and blind.
OEDIPUS. Do not counsel me any more. This punishment
　　That I have laid upon myself is just.
　　If I had eyes,
　　I do not know how I could bear the sight
　　Of my father, when I came to the house of Death,
　　Or my mother: for I have sinned against them both
　　So vilely that I could not make my peace
　　By strangling my own life.
　　　　　　　　Or do you think my children,
　　Born as they were born, would be sweet to my eyes?
　　Ah never, never! Nor this town with its high walls,
　　Nor the holy images of the gods.
　　　　　　　　For I,
　　Thrice miserable! Oedipus, noblest of all the line
　　Of Kadmos, have condemned myself to enjoy
　　These things no more, by my own malediction
　　Expelling that man whom the gods declared

> To be a defilement in the house of Laios.
> After exposing the rankness of my own guilt,
> How could I look men frankly in the eyes?
> No, I swear it,
> If I could have stifled my hearing at its source,
> I would have done it and made all this body
> A tight cell of misery, blank to light and sound:
> So I should have been safe in my dark mind
> Beyond external evil.
>   Ah Kithairon!
> Why did you shelter me? When I was cast upon you,
> Why did I not die? Then I should never
> Have shown the world my execrable birth.
>
> Ah Polybos! Corinth, city that I believed
> The ancient seat of my ancestors: how fair
> I seemed, your child! And all the while this evil
> Was cancerous within me!
>   For I am sick
> In my own being, sick in my origin.
>
> O three roads, dark ravine, woodland and way
> Where three roads met: you, drinking my father's blood,
> My own blood, spilled by my own hand: can you remember
> The unspeakable things I did there, and the things
> I went on from there to do?
>   O marriage, marriage!
> The act that engendered me, and again the act
> Performed by the son in the same bed—
>   Ah, the net
> Of incest, mingling fathers, brothers, sons,
> With brides, wives, mothers: the last evil
> That can be known by men: no tongue can say
> How evil!
>   No. For the love of God, conceal me
> Somewhere far from Thebes; or kill me; or hurl me
> Into the sea, away from men's eyes for ever.
>
> Come, lead me. You need not fear to touch me.
> Of all men, I alone can bear this guilt.

(*Enter* KREON.)

CHORAGOS. Kreon is here now. As to what you ask,
> He may decide the course to take. He only
> Is left to protect the city in your place.

OEDIPUS. Alas, how can I speak to him? What right have I
> To beg his courtesy whom I have deeply wronged?

KREON. I have not come to mock you, Oedipus,
   Or to reproach you, either.
      (*To* ATTENDANTS)   —You, standing there:
   If you have lost all respect for man's dignity,
   At least respect the flame of Lord Helios: 1370
   Do not allow this pollution to show itself
   Openly here, an affront to the earth
   And Heaven's rain and the light of day. No, take him
   Into the house as quickly as you can.
   For it is proper   1375
   That only the close kindred see his grief.
OEDIPUS. I pray you in God's name, since your courtesy
   Ignores my dark expectations, visiting
   With mercy this man of all men most execrable:
   Give me what I ask—for your good, not for mine.   1380
KREON. And what is it that you turn to me begging for?
OEDIPUS. Drive me out of this country as quickly as may be
   To a place where no human voice can ever greet me.
KREON. I should have done that before now—only,
   God's will had not been wholly revealed to me.   1385
OEDIPUS. But his command is plain: the parricide
   Must be destroyed. I am that evil man.
KREON. That is the sense of it, yes; but as things are,
   We had best discover clearly what is to be done.
OEDIPUS. You would learn more about a man like me?   1390
KREON. You are ready now to listen to the god.
OEDIPUS. I will listen. But it is to you
   That I must turn for help. I beg you, hear me.

   The woman in there—
   Give her whatever funeral you think proper: 1395
   She is your sister.
           —But let me go, Kreon!
   Let me purge my father's Thebes of the pollution
   Of my living here, and go out to the wild hills,
   To Kithairon, that has won such fame with me,
   The tomb my mother and father appointed for me,   1400
   And let me die there, as they willed I should.
   And yet I know
   Death will not ever come to me through sickness
   Or in any natural way: I have been preserved
   For some unthinkable fate. But let that be.   1405

   As for my sons, you need not care for them.
   They are men, they will find some way to live.
   But my poor daughters, who have shared my table,

Who never before have been parted from their father—
Take care of them, Kreon; do this for me.

And will you let me touch them with my hands
A last time, and let us weep together?
Be kind, my lord,
Great prince, be kind!
     Could I but touch them,
They would be mine again, as when I had my eyes.

(*Enter* ANTIGONE *and* ISMENE, *attended.*)

Ah, God!
Is it my dearest children I hear weeping?
Has Kreon pitied me and sent my daughters?
KREON. Yes, Oedipus: I knew that they were dear to you
 In the old days, and know you must love them still.
OEDIPUS. May God bless you for this—and be a friendlier
 Guardian to you than he has been to me!

Children, where are you?
Come quickly to my hands: they are your brother's—
Hands that have brought your father's once clear eyes
To this way of seeing—
    Ah dearest ones,
I had neither sight nor knowledge then, your father
By the woman who was the source of his own life!
And I weep for you—having no strength to see you—,
I weep for you when I think of the bitterness
That men will visit upon you all your lives.
What homes, what festivals can you attend
Without being forced to depart again in tears?
And when you come to marriageable age,
Where is the man, my daughters, who would dare
Risk the bane that lies on all my children?
Is there any evil wanting? Your father killed
His father; sowed the womb of her who bore him;
Engendered you at the fount of his own existence!
That is what they will say of you.
      Then, whom
Can you ever marry? There are no bridegrooms for you,
And your lives must wither away in sterile dreaming.

O Kreon, son of Menoikeus!
You are the only father my daughters have,
Since we, their parents, are both of us gone for ever.
They are your own blood: you will not let them

Fall into beggary and loneliness;
You will keep them from the miseries that are mine!
Take pity on them; see, they are only children,
Friendless except for you. Promise me this, 1450
Great prince, and give me your hand in token of it.

(KREON *clasps his right hand.*)

Children:
I could say much, if you could understand me,
But as it is, I have only this prayer for you:
Live where you can, be as happy as you can— 1455
Happier, please God, than God has made your father.
KREON. Enough. You have wept enough. Now go within.
OEDIPUS. I must; but it is hard.
KREON. Time eases all things.
OEDIPUS. You know my mind, then?
KREON. Say what you desire.
OEDIPUS. Send me from Thebes!
KREON. God grant that I may! 1460
OEDIPUS. But since God hates me . . .
KREON. No, he will grant your wish.
OEDIPUS. You promise?
KREON. I can not speak beyond my knowledge.
OEDIPUS. Then lead me in.
KREON. Come now, and leave your children.
OEDIPUS. No! Do not take them from me!
KREON. Think no longer
That you are in command here, but rather think 1465
How, when you were, you served your own destruction.

(*Exeunt into the house all but the* CHORUS; *the* CHORAGOS *chants directly to the audience.*)

CHORAGOS. Men of Thebes: look upon Oedipus.

This is the king who solved the famous riddle
And towered up, most powerful of men.
No mortal eyes but looked on him with envy, 1470
Yet in the end ruin swept over him.

Let every man in mankind's frailty
Consider his last day; and let none
Presume on his good fortune until he find
Life, at his death, a memory without pain. 1475

JOCASTA
Ruth F. Eisenberg

I

When she learned the king's power,
Jocasta lost delight in being queen.
Laius was a cold, dry man. Looking at him
brought the image of her baby, his feet
pierced and bound, her baby left to die
on the mountain slope. They would
have no other children.

> I remember Laius drunk that night, crying
> for Chrysippus, the source of his curse.
> Wanting his boy, he took me instead
> and threw me on my back to have his way.
> I am fifteen and afraid to resist
> and tell myself it is my husband's right;
> the gods decree a wife obey her spouse.

> Sober, Laius recalls Apollo's threat:
> our son will kill him, beget upon me.
> Nine months drag like oxen ploughing.
> With icy eyes Laius watches me swell.
> I fear the gods and beg Hera, for a girl,
> but as foretold, I give birth to a son.
> Laius takes the child to bind its feet.
> The baby cries, and Laius turns away.
> He summons a servant and orders me to hand
> my baby over, threatening me when I cry.
> The king will keep his own hands clean.

At the public altar, Laius
offered bulls and lambs in ritual
slaughter. The everburning fire raged
so the offerings charred, and Jocasta
trembled at the gods' displeasure.

> Upon the gates this dawn, a strange creature
> appeared and woke all Thebes. In raucous voice
> she cried, "A riddle. Who'll solve my riddle?"
> At first our people came to gawk, then marvel.
> Some trembled, children hid their heads and cried.
> I've heard old tales the minstrels sing of her,
> but never did expect to really see
> a Sphinx—part woman, bird, and lion too . . .
> And what she asks is strange as well: four legs,
> then two, then three. What can it be? No one
> knows the answer. No one.

  The Sphinx brought pestilence and
drought. Rivers and streams ran dry, vines
shriveled. But until her riddle was solved,
the creature would not leave. On the gates
she stayed, her destructive song echoing
from empty wells.

    My life is a toad. All day and all night
    the Sphinx. We cannot escape her song.
    Song! More like wail or whine or scream.
    Laius is useless as always. Deceitful
    man, I hate him, hate his touch.

    The land is parched; flocks die. Our people
    haggard, starving, plead to ease their distress.
    What can we do? Mortals cannot make the rain.
    I suggest Laius seek Apollo's help.
    To get away, he welcomes the idea to go
    to Delphi and proclaims a pilgrimmage.

  On the sunswept road to Delphi,
Laius was killed. The servant reporting
the death begged Jocasta to let him tend
flocks in the hills. Sending him on his way,
she shut herself in the palace.

    The prophesy was false. How can that be
    if gods control all things? For surely chance
    does not . . . No, no. Yet Laius killed our son
    and not the other way. That sin diseased
    his soul. I bless the gods that I,
    at last, am free.

    I dream of my baby night after night.
    He is dancing for the gods with bound feet.
    I do not understand how he can dance so.
    When he jumps, he trips, falling in a heap.
    The gods just laugh and turn away to drink.
    I sit ravelling knots. The knots become rope.
    I wake shaking and muffle my tears in the sheets.

II

  "Man" answered the young stranger
whose red hair caught the sun's rays,
and the riddle was solved. True to her
promise, the Sphinx dashed herself to
death. Thebes was free.

           Hailing their hero, the people
    elected Oedipus king. Gratefully,
    he accepted the rule and with it the hand
    of Thebes' queen, Jocasta.   85

               I see young Oedipus in radiant
           sunlight, Apollo blinding me to all
           but young and vital strength. Deep in myself
           I feel a pulsebeat, something asleep
           begins to wake, as though a dormant seed   90
           sends up a shoot, opens a leaf. That's how
           Aphrodite touches me. I love this youth.
           My sun, I rise to him and rise with him.

       From a land of rock and misery, Thebes
    became a bower. Brilliant poppies   95
    dotted the land. The wells filled, crops
    flourished, and the flocks grew fat again.

        Before the people's eyes, Jocasta
    became young. Her dark hair gleamed, her
    eye was bright and her laughter cheered   100
    the halls of the palace.

               Oedipus has become my Apollo warming
           my days and nights. I am eighteen again
           with poppies in my hair. I am the poppies,
           bright little blooms with milk in them.   105
           Like them, I seem to spring from rocky ground.
           Like their color and his hair, our love flames.

               Sweet Aphrodite, you rush through me, a stream
           until you burst like foam that crests the sea.
           Your blessing washes what was once a barren   110
           ground. I walk among the roses, feel
           your blush upon my cheeks. Oh lovely goddess,
           I send you swans and doves.

        Thebes prospered these years:
    the gnarled olive bent lower with fruit.   115
    Lambs frisked in the fields and pipers'
    songs rang through the hills. Jocasta had
    four children. Psalms of joy were sung
    and danced for the gods.

               With four children, the hours run away.   120
           Their hunger, games and tears take all my time.
           In bed, with Oedipus, I sleep in peace.
           He was at first my headstrong bull, but now
           he is what a man, a king, should be.

> I like to see him walking in the yard,
> his funny stiff gait, his hair burnished
> by Apollo's brilliant rays.
>
> Mine turns gray but he doesn't seem to mind.
> Our love has brought to me the joy I missed
> when I was young and thought I'd never know.
>
> At last, I lay to rest my little boy,
> his shadow vanished now from all my dreams.

III

Years of plenty at an end, Thebes
was inflicted with drought. The earth
burned as crops withered, cattle and
sheep sickened.

> While days were once too short, now each one drags
> a slow furrow, the earth heavy with heat,
> lament and prayer. When I go the fields
> the women clutch my gown and plead my help.
> Too many children sicken. The healthy droop.
> At home, the girls sit listless, my sons tangle
> while Oedipus complains his ankles twinge.
> He limps and growls just like a wounded pup.

Jocasta, very gray now, walked
with a more measured step. More than
a loving wife, she was also counsellor
to Oedipus.

> Blaming himself because the land is parched,
> Oedipus frets alarmed he's failed the gods
> in some unknown way, searching within himself.
> In turn, I pray, lighting fire after fire,
> but none burn true. I call on Aphrodite
> and offer her doves, but they flap their wings
> and peck each others' eyes. When I ask Apollo
> to dim his eye, his answer scalds.

No relief at hand, Oedipus sought
aid from Delphi. The report came back
a confusing riddle about Laius' death.
Suspecting treason, Oedipus feared
conspiracy against his own throne.

> Oedipus needs someone to blame. He calls
> Creon traitor, Tiresias false seer.
> I take him in my arms and stroke his hair.
> He tells me what Tiresias has foreseen.

>   I laugh and tell him I too once believed
>   that prophesy controlled our lives, that seers
>   had magic vision the rest of us did not.
>   I tell the story of Laius, how it
>   was foretold he would die at his son's hand   170
>   and how that baby died when one week old.
>
>   As I speak I feel so strange, as though my tale
>   came from another life about someone else.
>
>   My words do not comfort, they flame new fears.
>   He relates what drove him from home, tales that he   175
>   would kill his father and bring rank fruit
>   from his mother's womb. He fears he has
>   been cursed. Dear gods, how can I comfort him?

IV

From Corinth, a messenger
brought news of Polybus' death,   180
the king whom Oedipus called father.

>   You say that Polybus is dead. Dare I
>   greet death with joy? Can that be blasphemy?
>   My heart flies into song: His father's dead—
>   my Oedipus lives safe. His prophesy   185
>   is false. Is false as Laius' was. Oh bless
>   your fate, dear love, you need no longer fear.

Corinth wished Oedipus to return
and rule. Fearing he would sleep with
his mother, Oedipus refused. Nothing   190
to fear, the messenger assured. Merope
was a barren woman.

>   Jocasta began to tremble. Her hands
> rose to cover her mouth.
>
>   What's this? What's this? What words do I hear?   195
>   How can I shut his silly mouth, tell him
>   Go. Leave. We will not heed your words.
>   My tongue stops, rooted in my mouth.
>   I look at Oedipus. He does not see
>   me watching him. His face is strained, his eyes   200
>   are glaring blue. I try to stop the questions.
>   "Oedipus, I beg you, do not hear this out."

When Oedipus insisted, the
messenger told the story of the king's
infancy—how he, a shepherd then,   205

had helped to save the king's life
when a baby, a baby with bound feet.

> Oh God. Oh cold, gold God. Apollo,
> you chill me. My mind is ice, and I hear
> my mouth say freezing words to Oedipus.
> To my husband. My son. "God keep you from
> the knowledge of who you are. Unhappy,
> Oedipus, my poor, damned Oedipus,
> that is all I can call you, and the last thing
> I shall ever call you."

V

Her face ashen, Jocasta rushed
into the palace, her hands showing her
the way to her own quarters. She
ordered the guards to let no one in.
Ignoring all offers of help, she commanded
her women to leave her alone.

> I can't believe. I can't believe. Oh God.
> He is my son. I've loved my son but not
> as mothers should, but in my bed, in me.
> All that I loved the most, his youth that made
> our love the summer sun, wrong, all wrong.
> Vile. He caressed me here and here. And I
> returned his touch. Odious hands. My flesh
> crawls with worms.

> My God, we've had four children.

In her chamber, she looked at her
bed, sat on it, then jumped up as though
stung. Covering her eyes with her hands,
she shook her head back and forth, again
and again, her body rocking.

> Oh, Oedipus, what good was our love if
> it comes only to shame? To children whom
> all Thebes can curse? Such children, even ours,
> are rightly damned.

> Although we could not know who we were
> and loved in innocence, still we are monsters
> in the eyes of god and man. Our names will mean
> disgrace and guilt forever.

Walking to her dressing table,
she stood before it picking up small
objects: combs, a gold box, a pair of

brooches. Noticing a bracelet given her
by her father when she was a bride,
she let forth a dreadful groan.

    Oh Laius, Laius, you brought this on me.
My fate was sealed my wedding day. Chrysippus
was innocent as I; for you this curse
was uttered, a curse that falls on me. Oh,
that I must bear the shame, that I must be
destroyed by your corruption. And our son,
because you sinned, is ruined, damned.

    My marriage day . . . what choices did I have?
As many as the night you came to me.
The only choice a woman has is that she wed
accepting what the gods and men decree.
It is not just. It never can be right.

Moving decisively, she walked to the
doors and bolted them, straining against
their heavy weight. The women on the other
side called to her, but again she bade them
go away.

    Falling on her knees, she pummeled
her stomach as though to punish her
womb. As she did, she called her children's names, one name, Oedipus, again
and again.

    I thought him buried, forgotten. But no,
for countless days and nights these many years
he's thrust himself on me instead. My bed
once stained with birthing blood is now forever
stained; what once was love become a rank
corruption.

Rising painfully, sore, she turned
to the small altar in her chamber.
Smashing a jar which held incense, she
began in a voice of char to call on
Apollo and Aphrodite.

    As she raised her eyes, she raised
her fist and shook it against
the silent air.

    Apollo, you blinded me to his scars,
his age, any resemblance to Laius.
And you, Aphrodite, cruel sister of the sun,

> set my woman's body afire, matching my
> ripe years and hungers with his youth and strength. 290
> Paralyzing my mind, you inflamed my heart.
>
> The years I prayed to you and praised you
> were all charade. You so enjoyed my dance.
> We are your fools to trifle with, your joke.
>
> We tremble to question what the future holds. 295
> As though it matters, we think asking will spoil
> our luck, but your injustice mocks all hope.
>
> I hear a chant pounding inside my head.
> Five babies. Five abominations.
> As though a chorus raises call to prayer. 300
> Five babies. Five abominations.
>
> No call to prayer. It is a call to curse
> the gods. No longer will I be their fool.

From her robe, she removed her
braided belt. As she looped its strands, 305
she heard, from the courtyard, a man's
voice scream in anguish. Undeflected, she
tied the necessary knots, slipping the loop
back and forth. Satisfied, she settled
the noose around her neck. 310

> Five babies cursed by heavenly whim,
> cursed in their lives without chance or hope.
> Mothers ought not love their children so.

Gathering her skirts, she climbed
up on the stool. 315

> And wives be more than merely bedside pawns.
> Those who cannot shape their lives are better
> dead.

She stepped onto the air.

Considerations

1. These paired works, like some of the preceding ones, offer two ways of seeing a story. Sexton, Stevens and Eisenberg have used poetry to reexamine a classical fairy tale, Bible story, and tragic drama. In relative and general terms, comment on who of the three has taken the greatest degree of liberty in departing from the original work, and how. Again, generally, which of the modern versions works best for you? Why?

2. Is "Jocasta" closer to an answer to Oedipus or a retelling of the story? Is it reasonably possible to retell without reseeing and to some degree

producing an answer rather than a reiteration? Explain your response. But think a bit first; this isn't an easy question.

3. Is the Jocasta we hear in Eisenberg's poem essentially the same woman we come to know in the play? If not, how do they differ? For which of the two do you feel the greater sympathy, and why? What central ironies are common to play and poem? Discuss the varied ways they're viewed, presented.

4. Title the five sections of "Jocasta," and explain why you labeled them as you did.

5. "Jocasta" didn't spring full-blown from the author's head; it is the result of many drafts. Below are a couple of earlier versions of Part I. Although we can't determine from them what prompted the poet to revise them—exactly what went on in her thinking—we can look at the differences and do some intelligent guessing: What seem to have been Eisenberg's motives for revision? What significant changes are you able to detect from draft to draft?

6. Now read the poet's essay about how she came to write "Jocasta" and then revise it and revise it again. In what ways do her comments reflect your own current sense of what revision is? How do they vary from that sense? Is there a right or wrong way to revise? How is revision different from what Eisenberg labels "a final tidying up"? Or is it? Finally (but not rhetorically), why bother with revision in the first place? Discuss . . . then discuss some more.

DRAFT #1
JOCASTA PART I

Laius was never any good after that.
She'd lie with him and imagine that baby
Tied and immobile
Cold on the mountain
5   Stony Cithaeron,
Her husband's arm a bent dry stick.

Privately she blamed him.
She knew the prophesy but
Laius, not Apollo, had come to her
10   Seeded in
That baby.
Once she felt used,
His cold root no longer filled her.

Nothing could warm them.
15   Together they prayed,
Built fires, burned incense;
The fires roared,
Their offerings charred,
Husband and wife remained cold
20   And Thebes barren.

At Laius's death
Jocasta grieved but
was angry too.
Doubt assailed her.
25 Was her baby killed for false prophesy?
Confusion reigned.

DRAFT #2
PART I

Laius was never any good after that
She'd lie with him remembering
her baby cold on the mountain
tied, immobile
Her husband's arm a bent dry stick   5
his root could not fill her

    That fateful night, he comes in drunk, crying
    For Chryssipus, the source of his curse.
    Wanting his boy, he takes me instead
    Pouring his libation into my womb.   10
    Sober, he remembers Apollo's threat:
    Our son will kill him, beget upon me.
    My pregnancy is no joy. With eyes of ice
    Laius watches me swell. I fear the gods and pray
    For a daughter. In good time, I birth our son.   15
    Even as I weep on my still bloody bed,
    Laius takes the baby, and binds his feet,
    He calls a servant to carry him away
    To Kithaeron, to die on the mountain's slopes.

    Publicly, they prayed   20
burned incense, sacrificed lambs.
Fires charred their offerings and
husband and wife trembled
Why were the gods displeased?
In barren Thebes   25
the land thrust rocks
Soon the Sphinx's song
echoed from empty wells
On the sun-swept road to Delphi
Laius died   30
killed by bandits, they said
Hearing the news, Jocasta shuttered herself in
Let Creon rule

    The prophecy was false. He killed my child
    To save his cursed life. I can not grieve.   35
    He killed my boy for his own corrupt hide.

> My son was never given any chance.
> I dream of my baby night after night.
> He is dancing for the gods with bound feet.
> He dances, turns, trips, and falls. The gods laugh.
> I am raveling knots. The knots become rope.   40
> Feeling entangled, I wake with raw throat.

WRITING "JOCASTA"
Ruth F. Eisenberg

I don't know when the idea first took hold of me that Jocasta had a story to tell. I'd taught *Oedipus* so many times, I don't know when or why the realization first broke through. At any rate, I do remember voicing the thought at a poetry workshop. "Some day," I mused out loud, "someone ought to write a poem about Jocasta." Quick as a match, Natale Safir, our workshop leader, struck, "Why don't you?" I answered with a truly modest, who me? and dismissed the idea. I didn't know enough, I wasn't skilled enough. Heck, I'd only been writing poetry seriously for about nine months.

Well, some kids run before they can walk properly, and six weeks later, I began. The poem started in the middle of the night (most of my poems begin unexpectedly and inconveniently). I had to flick the lamp on and off through the early morning hours as bunches of lines came to me. By the time I'd finished that first handwritten draft it ran to six and a half pages. That was December, 1978. In the course of the next three and a half years, the poem would almost triple in length and change from free verse and one voice into the more complex structure involving two voices. Many subtle shifts in point of view and imagery also came into being as my commitment to my character became deeper.

For that first version, I had done no research, relying on what I had learned from my many classroom preparations of *Oedipus*. But I had a clear formulation of Jocasta's relationships with Oedipus and Laius, which came from thinking of them as real people and considering their ages at the time of the critical events. I figured that if Oedipus was seventeen to nineteen when he came to Thebes, that would make Jocasta thirty-three to thirty-five. She couldn't be any older and still have four children with him. These ages put them both at their sexual prime—which is important. Looking back, I realized Jocasta would have been about sixteen when she gave birth, fifteen or so at marriage. That was reasonable for that time and place. Therefore, if Jocasta and Oedipus were loving partners (which we are led to believe from Sophocles' play), by way of contrast Jocasta and Laius would not be. So I made him cold, essentially impotent.

The images that dominated were of hot and cold. This was natural because Apollo, after all, is the dominant god of both the play and the poem. In the first version, the opening stanza had the baby "cold on the mountain" and Laius cold as a lover. Besides references to the sun god, there was lots of fire. I just kept working those images through—working them to death I might add. Much, much later I would introduce the paradoxical idea of a chilling Apollo.

In structure, the poem emerged as a narrative. I simply retold the story from Jocasta's point of view. In all the early versions, the poem opened with Laius: "Laius was never any good after that"; it closed with the focus on Oedipus: "When Oedipus bulled his way into her chamber/Her swaying body had already grown cold." This happened in the writing unconsciously; later when I realized it, I thought it made an interesting commentary of its own: as men shaped her life, they framed its retelling. Later, I would change that.

The first version on paper, I went to the library to research. But I didn't find much about Jocasta other than alternate spellings of her name and some family background. Many indexes didn't list her at all, although they always listed Oedipus and sometimes Laius. So I checked out Laius. Not only did that confirm my feeling that he was much older than she, but it also gave me fuller information on the source of the curse (which I may have once known but forgot). Laius' homoerotic relationship with Chrysippus supported handily my decision to make him a lousy husband and lover.

The research also revealed conflicting stories about the night of Oedipus' conception. One version said they were both drunk, but all the others had only Laius drunk, so of course I went with the majority. Jocasta was not just Laius' wife, she was his victim, caught in his curse, and ultimately destroyed through no fault of her own.

If the research gave me no other information, it uncovered an injustice: whether the source was myth, anthropology, or psychology, the emphasis was on the men. Jocasta, as full a player in this tragedy as the others, was ignored. Looking back now, I think this awareness fired me to do the many revisions. Consciously, I was trying to make a better poem. Unconsciously, I was righting a wrong, doing what I could to give equal importance to the female figure in this most significant of western myths.

The most significant change—the one that transformed the poem—was the decision to split it into two voices. Natale felt, rightly, that the poem was too much a narrative. Jocasta needed to speak for herself. This meant more than a change in form and structure. It meant that if I was going to deal with Jocasta's feelings, I was going to have to go deep inside myself. This was no easy task, for several reasons, one of which was an anachronism. I am a 20th-century American woman strongly influenced by existential thinking, and I was writing about a primitive Greek. While I see Jocasta as a representative figure, someone who speaks for all women of any time, I didn't want her to be out of her time. I had to think of an agricultural society but keep in mind universal feelings.

I used my own experiences as a woman in love to generate the feelings in the love passages (still among my favorite lines). I am a mother who has known what it's like to have time melt away because of household tasks and children's demands. I had to use my imagination for the fright and disgust of the rape and the horror she feels when she confronts her incest. But Jocasta is speaking for me directly in her closing lines because it is the feminist and existentialist in me that created her feelings about her dominated, if not fated, life.

As my involvement with her life grew deeper, my imagery grew richer. Hot and cold would no longer do; images of poppies would express her love, her pregnancy would drag "like oxen ploughing"; when she was depressed, her life was "a toad." Thus nature and farm images entered into the poem.

One of the more difficult tasks was in finding a verse form for Jocasta. I tried rhyme, even rhymed couplets, but they were awful. Finally, I chose blank verse, which seemed right. It's a controlled form and it has dignity. Dominated now by iambic pentameter, I sat at the typewriter counting syllables and beats. There were times that, struggling with a line, I regretted the decision, but all in all, I think it was the correct one.

The narrative voice provided other problems. At first I continued the free verse. My lines became barer and more linear as I tried to keep from telling too much. It began to have a staccato beat. I had wanted the narrative voice to be a Chorus character; not just to tell the story, but to indicate commentary as well. Casting it in prose finally gave me that freedom. I could retain a slightly ironic tone; I had room enough now for description with the narration. The prose was in the past tense, a contrast to Jocasta's voice in the present tense.

The divisions of the poem almost formed themselves. The easiest for me to write was II; the most challenging V. Later I would realize the hardest ones were III and IV because I was scared to death of Sophocles. However, dividing the poem into sections turned out to be helpful. It made revision easier; I could treat each section as an entity as well as a part of a whole concept.

Somewhat more than two years had now passed since that December night. Of course, I didn't work on the poem steadily, but in fits and starts. Sometimes I'd quit just because I couldn't stand putting the same page through the typewriter one more time (I'm a rotten typist). The poem sat waiting, and I'd come back.

About this time, I saw a dramatization of the play. The audience watched Oedipus, I watched the actress who played Jocasta. She gave me new ideas about action: Jocasta would stroke his hair, hold Oedipus in her arms, would pick up and drop her jewelry, and pummel her stomach. Some of the ideas I copied from the actress; the rest I invented.

My focus on her had deepened. Now the poem opened with "When Jocasta learned the king's power, she lost delight . . ." and ended with "She stepped onto the air." For the last line, I owe a small debt to

Housman ("And dead on air will stand"). My line, I think, extends the meaning of her death. Jocasta steps into eternity and our consciousness.

By this time, I had also discovered some things about the poem. For instance, in its structure, without conscious plan, I had placed the gods in each section, thus giving the poem some of its unity. All the settings, I realized, are indoor or near the palace. When we were working on the videotape of the poem, I became more conscious that it opens and closes in the bedroom, reflecting the domestic and circumscribed life she led.

And Jocasta speaks for me often. Any moral urgency in the poem is mine. As I said earlier, her final injunctions, her final defiance of tradition and values for their own and the gods' sake is inevitably mine. The viewpoint was there from the beginning, only to be modified for diction or rhythm, not for the thought.

I needed to hear the poem. For me poetry is a spoken art, and as I write I always say the lines out loud. But to hear the poem in a voice other than mine, to hear the responses of others to the lines, would be, I knew, a great help. When it happened, interestingly enough, three women read the poem. My imaginative director friend, Joan Thorne, saw Jocasta as three women in one: the innocent, the queen, and the wife-mother. She also saw the five sections in two different ways: first as musical themes, and secondly as a progressive movement towards a woman's interior life.

The reading revealed weaknesses in Sections III and IV. They were the least dramatically alive: the most narrative, most derivative, and the least felt. At this revelation I became aware of how intimidated I was by the play. How dare I to have trespassed on sacred ground? For me Oedipus Rex is the greatest play ever written. How could I challenge Sophocles on his own turf?

Then I realized I wasn't challenging him, that my turf and his were different. He was concerned with Oedipus. Jocasta's lines were for his reaction; she was his foil, and in her recognition scene, his antagonist. Sophocles didn't even give her many lines in that scene. Therefore, anything I had added didn't challenge him; rather, I had accepted an opportunity to fill in the blanks. I added new verses in her voice. Jocasta goes through an absolute roller coaster of feeling when she hears the words of the messenger from Corinth, from a sense of false reassurance to horror. She tries to protect Oedipus from the knowledge (he, if you recall, turns on her and mistakes her motive) and stands not just awed but appalled at the work of the gods.

Readying "Jocasta" for this book meant a final tidying up. All along I was confronted with pronoun reference problems, sentence balance and variety, punctuation, working a balanced statement out from the demands of the meter. Now I had to prepare my "fair copy." However, I am reasonably sure that even when the proofs come back, the process will continue of trying to make a poem worthy of its tragic protagonist.

PART III

Playing with Language
Words, Sentences, and Punctuation

> When we encounter a natural style we are always surprised and delighted, for we thought to see an author and found a person.
> *Blaise Pascal*

> The pervasive stylistic traits of a writer, his recurrent words and images, his special cadence and tone, are as personal to him as his face or his way of walking. His style is his own way of living in the world given a verbal form.
> *J. Hillis Miller*

> The proper force of words lies not in the words themselves, but in their application. A word may be a fine-sounding word . . . and yet in the connection in which it is introduced may be quite pointless and irrelevant. It is not pomp or presentation, but the adaptation of the expression to the idea that clenches a writer's meaning.
> *William Hazlitt*

When you string together three or four statements, whether they're written or spoken, you reveal not only what you may know or feel about a subject, but also something about who you are. Together, the words you choose (diction), the order you put them in (syntax), the images you use (imagery), and the forms you select amount to your *style,* your way of putting it.

This, at least, is one way to look at it. But it can also be observed that we don't so much *have* a style as *use* a number of them (somewhat the way you choose a mode of dress), depending on the circumstances. From this point of view, we're linguistic chameleons of sorts, without a central *persona*.

It probably doesn't matter to you, though, where or how your style(s) originates, so long as it works—gets you listened to and accepted and liked—and just as importantly, so long as you find yourself able to say pretty much what you want to say and can shape it to sound close to how you want it to sound.

This section of *Connections* involves you in some conscious considerations of stylistic elements that we're always choosing among as we seek the right sounds and shapes. Unless you're aware of the choosing—unless you're aware of the range of possibilities implicit in even the simplest utterance—it isn't likely that you'll ever acquire a fully developed sense of what style is, whether it's yours or someone else's.

WORDS

In addition to literal meanings, words also possess identities. Each has a distinctive shade of meaning, a singular set of implications, a peculiar texture, shape, and sound. The following exercises are meant to illustrate some of these facets.

Exercises

1. For each of the following words or phrases, write a few words indicating what you think of when you see or hear it. You're not being asked to *define*, but simply to react to each. You can write one word or more—or nothing. (Use a dictionary only as a last resource.)

> vacation
> dictator
> home
> skeleton
> hydrogen sulphate (H_2SO_4)
> prunes
> metaphalanges
> childlike
>
> Pythagorean theorem
> black
> myocardial infarction
> silk
> temptation
> eagle
> red

Where did your responses to these words come from, if not the dictionary? For which words was your response intense? For which was it minimal? Divide the list of words into two categories. Label each and explain the basis of your division. Compare your responses and categories with those of other students. You'll probably discover that different people respond differently to some words and similarly to others. How do you account for this?

If you haven't already made a distinction between two kinds of "meaning," denotative and connotative, this is the time to do it. Denotation is a word's dictionary meaning; connotation is its emotional resonance, its power to stimulate imagination, memory, and feeling. Denotative meaning is public, shared, conventional meaning. Connotative meaning is sometimes private, sometimes public; in both instances, connotative meaning refers to feelings and attitudes, not just to information or facts.

Some words are essentially denotative, possessing little if any connotative reverberation; others are heavily connotative, rich in implication and suggestion. To some words you'll react with strong emotion; to others you'll hardly respond at all, in either feeling or thought. If you're not aware of this already, look back over the list of words from this perspective.

2. For the following groups of words, jot down a brief explanation of how the words differ in connotation. Then fill in the blanks with other words appropriate to the group.

1. dog   mutt   pooch   _____   _____
2. mother   mom   ma   mama   _____
3. male   man   fellow   guy   _____
4. female   woman   gal   _____   _____
5. eat   dine   _____   _____
6. house   home   _____   _____
7. work   job   _____   _____
8. thin   trim   _____   _____
9. smart   bright   _____   _____
10. drunk   inebriated   _____   _____

3. In working with the last exercise you began to discriminate between words close in meaning. You also began to see and hear differences in levels of formality, in the degree and range of connotation. To gain an even better feeling for some of these features, you'll need to write at least a few sentences using these words.

1. Write sentences for each of the words in three different groups.

2. For another group, write a few sentences explaining the similarities and differences between one word and another.

An example of how the connotations of a word carry a heavy burden of judgment is provided in the following essay. Written by a student, the piece explores the differences in connotation among different terms used to denote the men in blue, the guardians of civil order, in short, the police.

POLICE! POLICE!
Lisa Bogdonoff

It is the middle of the night. You peer out of your second story window in an attempt to find out what is causing the scratching noise that woke you from sleep. Frozen with fear, you realize that two shadowed amorphous forms on the ground below are breaking into your home. Groping for the phone, you call the police. Just as the cops arrive, you hear a voice rasp, "Here come the Fuzz," and you barely see two potential burglars escaping under the cover of darkness.

Very often we refer to the conservators of public peace as "police," "cops," "fuzz," even "pigs." Although each of these words refers to members of the peacekeeping force, the implications connoted by each are quite different. Describing the scene of an accident, a news reporter would employ the more respectable term "police," whereas the man on the street would be inclined to give equal time to the substantive "cops." "Fuzz," an appellation which became popular in the 1930's and 40's, is a deprecating term not often used by the upper classes. More a slang term than a colloquial expression, "fuzz" has not yet achieved social respectability. Possibly derived from "fuss," one who is overly particular and difficult to please, "fuzz" originally referred to a prison warden or detective. The demeaning "pig" emerged in the riotous 1960's and blatantly expressed a disgust with the nation's police force. "Pig," also a nickname for a prison guard, resulted from a transformation of the Middle English "pigge," slang for a wanton woman. Like the slang "fuzz," "pig" tends to predominate among the young as a disrespectful and rebellious term for what they take to be an oppressive authority.

Not surprisingly, members of the force would preferably be called policemen and policewomen, and on occasion may even refer to themselves as "cops." Coined in 1530, "police" has its roots in the Greek "polis" or city, and branches its way up to the Lower Latin "politia" or governmental administration and to the French "poli" (*Oxford English Dictionary*). By 1829, "policemen" and "policewomen" were known as those of the police force paid to keep order. During the same year, Sir Robert Peel organized London's police force: from Sir Robert (Bobby) came the term for London's police—"bobbies" (*World Book Encyclopedia*).

In America the copper star-shaped badges that adorned the law enforcers' uniforms may have led to the nickname "cop." Another theory is that "cop" stood for "Constables on Patrol." More likely is the *Oxford English Dictionary's* explanation that "cop" is a variation on cap or capture, derived from the Old French "capere." Certain dialects of Black English also define "cop" as a prison (*Dictionary of Afro-American Slang*). Under most circumstances, the average American will interchange cop and police, with "police" the preferred usage.

Daily use and disuse of such words dictate their life spans. And thus, it is likely that "fuzz" and "pigs" will follow "Peelers" and "beaks" into oblivion. While "cop" and "police" still predominate, new words with different connotations such as the C.B. term "smokies" will emerge. Curiously, the fate of these appellations in the language is in the mouths of people.

Exercise

Even though you're aware of the differences in the meanings of words, connotative and denotative both, you may still run into problems. Words can be slippery and elusive, hard to get hold of and hang on to. In this exercise you're presented with some word pairs. For each pair decide which word carries a positive and which a negative association. You may find both words in a given number "positive" or "negative" partly because the words appear outside of any context that would direct and limit their meanings, and partly also because of your own experience, which may vary greatly from the experience of others.

1. adventurous — reckless
2. independent — stubborn
3. stubborn — firm
4. shy — reserved
5. sensitive — touchy
6. playboy — elegible bachelor
7. athlete — jock
8. frugal — parsimonious
9. average — mediocre
10. plodding — methodical
11. individualist — eccentric
12. clever — conniving

Perhaps it was easy for you to decide which word connoted what, perhaps not. What matters more than the relative ease or difficulty with which you decided, though, is an awareness that someone else chose differently. It's even more important that you see how, quite frequently, words carry built-in judgments, and how often when you think you're stating or reading "facts" you're actually making or reading judgments. In the following exercise you'll see how complicated (and persuasive) judgmental language can be. First, a few words of introduction.

You may have heard about the famous case of Kitty Genovese, who was murdered as she returned home from work one night. About 3:00 a.m., Miss Genovese had parked her car and headed toward her apartment when a man assaulted her. She screamed for help, and some neighbors in the apartment building adjacent to the parking lot turned on their lights. A few came to their windows to see what was going on. One yelled out "Let that girl alone!" Some, thinking it was a lovers' quarrel, returned to bed. Frightened by the commotion, Miss Genovese's attacker ran off, but not until he had repeatedly stabbed her. And when the neighbors turned off their lights and went back to bed, he returned and stabbed her again, just how many times remains uncertain. For the second time she cried out for help. Again lights went on. And again the attacker ran off. Bleeding, Miss Genovese made her way into the vestibule of a neighboring apartment. There the attacker found her and continued his assault. Finally, one neighbor convinced another to call the police. This was about 3:25. The police arrived at 3:30, but Kitty Genovese was dead.

The incident sparked considerable public interest. It received extensive press coverage, with newspaper and magazine articles appearing for weeks and months afterward. More than a year later a book was written about the incident. The main question in the minds of most who hear about the circumstances of Miss Genovese's death is: "Why didn't somebody help her? Why didn't somebody at least call the police right away?"

If you're interested in finding out more about what happened, or if you want to follow the responses to the incident in the press, you can begin with the New York newspapers for March 14, 1964, and then with the article by Martin Gansberg, published in *The New York Times* on March 27, 1964. For now, however, we'll look at the headlines from three papers—*The New York Times*, *The New York Herald Tribune*, and *The New York Daily News*.

Times: Queens Woman Stabbed to Death in Front of Home
Tribune: Help Cry Ignored, Girl Dies of Knifing

What do you immediately notice about these two headlines? Which relies more heavily on connotative words? Why in each case do you think those words were chosen? (How, for example, do the connotations of "Girl" differ from those of "Woman"? Do you think the difference is even greater today than in 1964, when Kitty Genovese was killed?) Consider, finally, how each headline makes you feel about the victim. Here's the third headline from the *Daily News*:

Queens Barmaid Stabbed, Dies

What does the word "Barmaid" suggest? Has it altered your response to the *Times* and *Tribune* headlines? How? What is implied in the *News* headline about Kitty Genovese? In the *Times* and *Tribune* headlines? Which of these three headlines seems the most objective, the most neutral in what it states? Can we say that the other two headlines share an interest in eliciting an emotional response from their readers? Or is something else evoked as well?

Exercises

1. Write one or two more headlines for the fictitious *New York Star* and *New York Inquirer*. Use words other than "woman," "girl," or "barmaid" to refer to Kitty Genovese.

2. Examine the following opening lines from each of the three news accounts whose headlines you read above. Explain how they reinforce or depart from the implications of the headlines.

Times: A 28-year-old Queens woman was stabbed to death early yesterday morning outside her apartment house in Kew Gardens.

Tribune: The neighbors had grandstand seats for the slaying of Kitty Genovese. And yet, when the pretty, diminutive 28-year-old brunette called for help, she called in vain.

(Why, by the way, is she described as "pretty"? And why is her hair color given? Have you ever read an account of a man's murder which included information about his hair color or physical attractiveness? What's implied by the inclusion of these details?)

News: An attractive 28-year-old brunette who had given up a more prosaic life for a career as a barmaid and residence in a tiny Bohemian section of Queens was stabbed to death early yesterday.

Considerations

1. How would you characterize the tone and purpose of each opening?
2. Explain the implications of the following words: "diminutive," "grandstand seats," "slaying," "prosaic," "career," and "Bohemian."
3. What does each of these lines suggest about the paper that printed it: their editorial policy, the audience they each address?

Exercise

Look over the following list of details. Then flesh the list out by inventing more specific circumstances. You might explain what the man is doing, where he's going, what he's carrying, what kind of hat or gloves he's wearing. And you can add other details. But in embellishing, choose your words to suggest either a positive or negative view of the man.

a man
wearing a coat, hat, and gloves
moves along a street
at night
with a dog close by
the man is six feet tall
weighs 200 pounds
is bald
bearded
appears young
is carrying a parcel

In playful ways, the following two poems consider the connotative dimension of language. Enjoy the play of mind and sound. Then think about the connotations of the following words from "Jabberwocky": "jabberwock" (jabber? wock?) "brillig," "slithy," "Jubjub," "Bandersnatch," "frumious," "Tumtum," "uffish," "whiffling," "burbled," and "galumphing." (For "Adam's Task" see the questions following the poem.)

How do the sounds and connotations of the words that describe the monster affect your response to it? How do the words that describe the hero's action serve to characterize him?

JABBERWOCKY
Lewis Carroll

'Twas brillig, and the slithy toves
   Did gyre and gimble in the wabe;
All mimsy were the borogoves,
   And the mome raths outgrabe.

>   "Beware the Jabberwock, my son!
>   The jaws that bite, the claws that catch!
>   Beware the Jubjub bird, and shun
>   The frumious Bandersnatch!"
>
> He took his vorpal sword in hand;
>   Long time the manxome foe he sought—
> So rested he by the Tumtum tree,
>   And stood awhile in thought.
>
> And, as in uffish thought he stood,
>   The Jabberwock, with eyes of flame,
> Came whiffling through the tulgey wood,
>   And burbled as it came!
>
> One, two! One, two! And through and through
>   The vorpal blade went snicker-snack!
> He left it dead, and with its head
>   He went galumphing back.
>
> "And hast thou slain the Jabberwock?
>   Come to my arms, my beamish boy!
> O frabjous day! Callooh! Callay!"
>   He chortled in his joy.
>
> 'Twas brillig, and the slithy toves
>   Did gyre and gimble in the wabe;
> All mimsy were the borogoves,
>   And the mome raths outgrabe.

ADAM'S TASK
John Hollander

> *"And Adam gave names to all cattle, and
> to the fowl of the air, and to every beast
> of the field. . ."*—Gen. 2:20

> Thou, paw-paw; thou, glurd; thou, spotted
>   Glurd; thou, whitestap, lurching through
> The high-grown brush; thou, pliant-footed,
>   Implex; thou, awagabu.
>
> Every burrower, each flier
>   Came for the name he had to give;
> Gay, first work, ever to be prior,
>   Not yet sunk to primitive.
>
> Thou, verdle; thou, McFleery's pomma;
>   Thou; thou; thou—three types of grawl;
> Thou, flisket; thou, kabash; thou, comma-
>   Eared mashawk; thou, all; thou, all.

>   Were, in a fire of becoming,
>   Laboring to be burned away,
> 15 Then work, half-measuring, half-humming,
>   Would be as serious as play.
>
>   Thou, pambler; thou, rivarn; thou, greater
>   Wherret, and thou, lesser one;
>   Thou, sproal; thou, zant; thou, lily-eater.
> 20   Naming's over. Day is done.

Considerations

1. Hollander plays on the sounds of words to stir up associations we have with other similar sounding words with which we are familiar. A "grawl," for example, though we've never heard of it before, certainly *sounds* like an animal that crawls, and probably crawls slowly. It doesn't make "sound-sense" that such a beast would fly or swim. How about a "flisket"? How do you think that gets around? It would be a good idea to pronounce aloud the names of all the animals in the poem, particularly those in stanza two. Which of these do you suppose are "burrowers" and which "fliers"? Why?

2. How many different kinds of names does Hollander use for his animals? Why, for example, is "McFleery's pomma" not simply "pomma"? How about the "greater" and "lesser" wherrets of stanza five? And what about the "lily-eater"? Can you think of any real animals that are named in the manner illustrated in "Adam's Task"?

3. Explain the difference between "prior" and "primitive" (stanza 2). How is Hollander playing on the meaning of "first"?

Exercises

1. Make up your own names for the following classes of animals: fliers, crawlers, swimmers, runners, leapers, jumpers.

2. Make a list of words from one area of human experience such as love, war, sports, technology. Analyze the words on your list for their connotations.

ETYMOLOGY

Etymology refers to the ancestry of a word, its derivation and history. In his book-length essay, *Nature*, Ralph Waldo Emerson has noted that "every word which is used to express a moral or intellectual fact, if traced to its root, is found to be borrowed from some material appearance. *Right* means straight; *wrong* means twisted." Emerson's purpose is to show that words, abstract as they may be, once had a physical basis in reality. A writer whose prose repeatedly makes us aware of the concrete reality of words, of the original meanings behind the abstraction of language, is Emerson's friend and disciple, Henry David Thoreau. Here are a couple of examples from Thoreau's *Walden*:

"I was more independent than any farmer in Concord, for I was not anchored to a house or a farm, but could follow the bent of my genius, which is a very crooked one, every moment."

"I fear chiefly lest my expression may not be extra-vagant enough, may not wander far enough beyond the narrow limits of my daily experience, so as to be adequate to the truth of which I have been convinced. *Extra-vagance!* . . . I desire to speak somewhere *without* bounds."

Exercises

1. Explain how Thoreau makes us aware of the concrete realities of and the original meanings behind the words *bent* and *extravagance*.

2. Look up the following words in *The Oxford English Dictionary* or a standard desk dictionary if the O.E.D. is not handy. Then use each in a sentence that makes the word's etymology apparent.

right
supercilious
spirit
deliberate (as both verb and adjective)
scale (as both noun and verb)
transgression
wrong

METAPHOR

The word *metaphor* means to transfer or carry across. *Meta* is Greek for across; *phor* is Greek for bear or carry. The word *transfer* can be broken down in the same way: *trans* is Latin for across (think of the words *translation, transit, transpose, transcribe*); *fer* is Latin for carry or bear (think of what a ferry does or think of the name for a cone-bearing tree—conifer).

Metaphor involves a transfer of meaning, a carrying across from one area of meaning to another. The heart of metaphor is resemblance, stating how one thing is like another, seeing one thing in terms of another. Metaphors make connections, often of a kind and with a power otherwise impossible to achieve. When the metaphorical connection is made with the words *like, as* or *as though,* the comparison is technically a *simile,* as in these examples: "O my love is like a red, red rose"; "I wandered lonely as a cloud."

Exercises

1. Explain the connections and resemblances that lie at the heart of similes and metaphors in the following examples. Consider, that is, how their authors sharpen your perception of one thing by likening it to another or by proposing that one thing *is* another.

1. And yonder all before us lie
   Deserts of vast eternity.   *Andrew Marvell*

2. The strongest oaths are straw
   To the fire i' the blood.   *William Shakespeare*

3. What happens to a dream deferred?
   Does it dry up like a raisin in the sun?   *Langston Hughes*

4. Somewhere in the dead of the Southern night my life had switched onto the wrong track and the locomotive of my heart was rushing down a dangerously steep slope, heading for a collision.   *Richard Wright*

5. I was spending money I didn't have on people I didn't care about; I was hooked on them, like a junky, loathing them and the need for them, yet needing more and more of them all the time.   *Sammy Davis, Jr.*

6. Mind in its purest play is like some bat
   That beats about in caverns all alone.   *Richard Wilbur*

7. How dull it is to pause, to make an end,
   To rust unburnished, not to shine in use.   *Alfred, Lord Tennyson*

8. 'Tis with our judgment, as our watches, none
   Go just alike, yet each believes his own.   *Alexander Pope*

9. Taylor, as is his wont, played just one number, but it lasted forty minutes. It was full of his usual devices—the slamming chords, the agitated staccato passages, the breathtaking arpeggios, the blizzard density—but it had two new qualities: lyricism and gentleness. Again and again, after Taylor had launched one of his tidal waves, his hands going up and down like driving rods, he slipped into clear lagoons where shadows of melody glided just below the surface.   *Whitney Balliett*

10. The music of the eighteenth century is all dance music. A dance is a symmetrical pattern of steps that are pleasant to move to; and its music is a symmetrical pattern of sound that is pleasant to listen to even when you are not dancing to it. Consequently, the sound patterns, though they begin by being as simple as chessboards, get lengthened and elaborated and enriched with harmonies until they are more like Persian carpets; and the composers who design these patterns no longer expect people to dance to them. Only a whirling Dervish could dance to a Mozart symphony.   *George Bernard Shaw*

In thinking about the examples above, try to explain how the metaphorical connection helps you understand what's being said. Here's some guidance for one of the examples. In number four, Richard Wright has set up a series of metaphorical equivalences. On the literal level we are given a locomotive, a track, a slope, and a collision. What does each represent? When you consider them together, what point do they add up to?

2. The following passage is packed tightly with metaphors. Try to unpack the lines, laying out the implications of each metaphor. What, for ex-

ample, are we to make of the candle? What, in a word, is the "tale," and why, given the circumstances, is the comparison not only reasonable but moving? Before you begin, you'll need to know the context of the passage. It comes from Shakespeare's *Macbeth.* The lines are spoken by Macbeth, the man who, goaded by Lady Macbeth, has risen to power by murderous means. The passage comes at the point where Macbeth has just discovered that his wife has killed herself, and in that moment he comes to know fully the enormity of their actions.

> Out, out, brief candle!
> Life's but a walking shadow, a poor player
> That struts and frets his hour upon the stage
> And then is heard no more. It is a tale
> Told by an idiot, full of sound and fury,
> Signifying nothing.

When we need a way to explain the intensity of our feelings or a particular state of mind, we reach almost instinctively for metaphor. We do it regularly (though we're often unaware of it) as, for example, when we say things like, "I was so embarrassed (or angry or upset or . . .) I could have . . ." Admittedly, the kinds of comparisons we often make off the cuff are not as thoughtprovoking, as interesting, or as creative as those we're capable of when we make meanings more deliberately. But the important thing is to realize the value of metaphor for discovering ideas and expressing feelings.

To see how prevalent metaphorical expression is in our lives and how persistently we use metaphor to think, consider the following examples of how we talk about love. They have been adapted from *Metaphors We Live By,* by George Lakoff and Mark Johnson.

Love is a physical force:

> I could feel the *electricity* between us.
> The atmosphere around them is *charged.*
> There is incredible *energy* in their relationship.
> They *gravitated* toward one another.
> He felt irresistibly *attracted* toward her.

Love is a patient:

> This is a *sick* relationship.
> He was deeply *wounded* by his divorce.
> They have a *strong, healthy* marriage.
>   Or: They have an *ailing* marriage.
> Their relationship is *dead.*
> We've been *getting back on our feet.*

Exercises

1. Here are three additional ways we talk about love. For each you've been provided with one example of a specific statement exemplifying that

metaphor. Provide additional examples of these metaphorical ways of talking and thinking about love.

A. Love is war:
  1. She *fled* from his advances
  2.
  3.
  4.

B. Love is magic:
  1. I was *enchanted* by her. She was absolutely *charming*.
  2.
  3.
  4.

C. Love is madness:
  1. George is *crazy* about Ingrid.
  2.
  3.
  4.

2. Make up sentences that illustrate some of the following metaphors we live by:
a. Ideas are food.
b. Ideas are commodities.
c. Ideas are plants.
d. Ideas are fashions.
e. Ideas are money.
f. Time is money.
g. Time is a commodity.
h. Time is . . . .

3. The following poem is a list of metaphors. Each metaphor suggests something of how Stephen Crane thinks or feels about his subject. What is his subject?

A _____ is a collection of half-injustices
Which, bawled by boys from mile to mile,
Spreads its curious opinion
To a million merciful and sneering men,
While families cuddle the joys of the fireside
When spurred by a tale of dire lone agony.

A _____ is a court
Where every one is kindly and unfairly tried
By a squalor of honest men.

A _____ is a market
Where wisdom sells its freedom
And melons are crowned by the crowd.

A_____ is a game
Where his error scores the player victory
While another's skill wins death.

> A _____ is a symbol;
> It is feckless life's chronicle,
> A collection of loud tales
> Concentrating eternal stupidities
> That in remote ages lived unhaltered,
> Roaming through a fenceless world.

Try your own metaphor poem in the manner of Crane's. Simply make a list of metaphors about your subject. They might be a set of metaphors that have a common idea, attitude or feeling. Or they might not. See what develops. Here are some possible subjects: man, woman, child; doctor, lawyer, teacher, athlete, executive, laborer, etc.; a house, a school, a prison, a street, a neighborhood, etc.; a gun, a sword, a pen, a computer, a car, a boat, etc.

CLICHÉ

In your first conscious attempts at metaphor you may lean toward comparisons you've heard before, perhaps too many times before. If so, you'll almost invariably use clichés. A cliché is trite and usually predictable, so much so that as reader or listener you can almost always finish the one someone else has begun. You've heard these, haven't you? "Easier said than . . . ;" "Slow but . . . ;" "Better late than . . . ;" "Haste makes . . . ;" "Last but not . . . ;" "Truer words were . . . ."

What's wrong with these and other clichés? These things at least: they're boring, bland, mindless, and terribly contagious. And they're far too easily available; nobody gets through life without resorting to them. Perhaps worst of all, they can oversimplify and misrepresent the way things are. To raise your consciousness about clichés, complete the following set of exercises. And enjoy yourself; they're meant to be fun.

Exercises

1. Write a paragraph of 8–10 sentences using as many clichés as you can. Work like a horse; go for broke. (You might like to team up with someone on this one.)

2. Take three or four of the following common expressions and write comic variations. You can change a word, a phrase, or the entire expression. But your changed wording should reveal a buried cliché. Your object, simply, is to revitalize the clichéd expression, to bring it back to life. The American humorist, James Thurber, for example, changes "Woman's place is in the home," to "Woman's place is in the wrong." S. J. Perelman refers to a visit to the dentist as "cuspid's last stand." And, once again, Thoreau: "In any weather at any hour of the day or night, I have been anxious to improve the nick of time, and notch it on my stick too; to stand on the meeting of two eternities, the past and future, which is precisely the present moment; to toe that line." (Thoreau here reanimates two clichés. What are they?) Here are some you might tinker with:

1. steady as a rock
2. as plain as day
3. like taking candy from a baby
4. like a bolt out of the blue
5. sadder but wiser
6. last but not least
7. quick as a flash
8. as easy as pie
9. hit below the belt
10. all the world's a stage
11. time flies when you're having fun
12. absence makes the heart grow fonder
13. stubborn as a mule
14. a man's home is his castle
15. sharp as a tack
16. apple of my eye
17. thrown off the track
18. in the twinkling of an eye
19. tried and true
20. the style to which I have become accustomed
21. the not too distant future

3. Go through one of your papers—a paper written for any of your classes. For every cliché, substitute another word or phrase, something you devise yourself.

4. Find an article in a popular magazine or the daily paper and copy out all the clichés. Substitute fresh language for the clichés.

5. Watch a TV segment of news, sports, a string of commercials, a sitcom, or a talk show. Keep a pad and pencil handy to collect clichés. Then write up a brief account of your observations about the clichés you collected.

6. Identify the clichés in the following poem:

THE MISTER QUEENS COLLEGE CONTEST
Anthony Litwinko

What we want's a winner with sensual lips
and expressive eyes, who's got the lead out
and knows how to dress to kill.
A man out of the ordinary, built like a brick
5   outhouse, Johnny-on-the-spot, two-fisted son of a gun.
What we want is a mover in all his glory,
A top-notch, knock-down, drag-
out specimen of humanity,
the guy who makes a real effort
10 to give you the shirt off his back,
true-blue, cool as a cucumber, slick
as a whistle, strong as a bull, good ol' boy
who plays it fast and loose and runs true to form.
I mean what we want are bulging muscles and great lines,
15 belly flat as a board and a good head
on his shoulders, you know, the boy next door.
If we don't get him we're in a jam,
I mean like we shot our wad
plastering the walls with signs,
20 we've gone out of our way

to spread the news.
We've done everything under the sun.

Now get out there and bring me
a cock of the walk
25 with his head held high.
We need an Adonis
with a poker face,
engaging smile,
and firm chin,
30 a mean, clean
top banana with arms of steel,
broad back, and rosy cheeks, or maybe tan.
You know there's a dude can make the grade.
Get me a Mister Queens College MAN!

Write a poem along similar lines; that is, a cliché-filled piece with a central focus and subject. (You might want to collaborate on this exercise.)

7. In this brief poem, Emily Dickinson has reanimated a cliché. Find the buried cliché, then explain how the poem is built around it and how Dickinson revitalizes it.

The Bustle in a House
The Morning after Death
Is solemnest of industries
Enacted upon Earth—

The Sweeping up the Heart
And putting Love away
We shall not want to use again
Until Eternity.

JARGON

When you come away from a reading or listening experience muttering to yourself, "Why can't they say it in plain English?" the chances are that you're complaining about someone's use of *jargon,* that infuriatingly wordy, high-sounding, technical gobbledegook that seems increasingly to be cluttering up and uglifying "plain English." The truth is, though, that we Americans have a love-hate relationship with jargon. We may despise it when the other guy is using it, but we also find it satisfying to use the kinds of jargon that mark us as members of a trade, profession, or interest group, or simply as being very up on things technical. For example, the average car owner (or salesperson) doesn't have a clear understanding of terms like *turbocharger, rack and pinion steering,* or *drag coefficient,* but that so many of us delight in hearing and using such language isn't lost on auto manufacturers, who tend to load their ads with it. Not that the practice is limited to the automotive industry. What other industries or interest groups trade on this tendency of ours? (Seen an ad for a tennis racket lately?)

Here are a few examples of jargon:

1. Maximum utilization of the components of the oral cavity is of paramount importance for the development of gustatory discrimination.
2. The assumption of stationarity upon which many models are based limits their applicability to successive iterations of the initial configuration.
3. The learning environment situation is interdependent upon professionals with the inclination and preparation to enhance the intellectual capacities of potential learners and on the development of adequate pedagogical matrixes which are necessary instruments for repairing the cognitive deficiencies of the nontutored.
4. The group consisted almost exclusively of non-professional people with a mean high school educational experience, a diversificatory range of interest areas and patterns of low interest orientation involvement in self-realization activities.

Exercises

1. From what disciplines did each of these statements probably come? Who specifically might have made each? (The answer "an idiot" won't do.) Translate at least one of these into "plain old English," unless you think they're too far gone to be saved.

2. Find some examples of jargon in a textbook or periodical or news broadcast. (Listen especially to politicians and military spokespeople; they are rich mines of jargon.) Bring them in for discussion. Be fair, though; technical language isn't necessarily jargon. The test for jargon is whether or not the same information could be conveyed more simply, directly, attractively without a loss of accuracy, or, simply, whether the technical terminology is appropriate to the intended audience or is meant to baffle and impress them.

3. Rewrite two of the following sentences using as much jargon and as many words as you can.

1. Food satisfies hunger.
2. Eating satisfies hunger.
3. Dogs make good pets.
4. Cars are status symbols.
5. Children say the darndest things.
6. Haste makes waste.

4. Look through one of your essays or term papers for examples of high-sounding phrases, for vague and abstract language. Revise for clarity and economy.

SOUND AND SENSE

We've been attending to the meanings of words, to their connotations and denotations, to their metaphorical potentialities. In Hollander's "Adam's Task," and Carroll's "Jabberwocky," however, you discovered that the sound of a word is an important aid to its meaning. Still, we ought to say a few things more about how writers use sound to solidify and substantiate meaning. Poets especially use sound to echo sense, as Alexander Pope does in these famous lines from "An Essay on Criticism":

> True ease in writing comes from art, not chance,
> As those move easiest who have learned to dance.
> 'Tis not enough no harshness gives offense,
> The sound must seem an echo to the sense:
> Soft is the strain when Zephyr gently blows,
> And the smooth stream in smoother numbers flows;
> But when loud surges lash the sounding shore,
> The hoarse, rough verse should like the torrent roar;
> When Ajax strives some rock's vast weight to throw,
> The line too labors, and the words move slow;
> Not so, when swift Camilla scours the plain,
> Flies o'er the unbending corn, and skims along the main.

Lines 1–4 make two points: 1) good writing doesn't occur accidentally; it involves skill; 2) the sound of a sentence, a line, a phrase should support its sense, should, if possible, imitate its sense. Notice that each of these ideas is accented with rhyme: chance-dance; offense-sense. Each statement is further emphasized by its internal structure: lines 1–2 form an analogy; lines 3–4 a contrast. In lines 5–8, however, Pope illustrates how sound can echo or imitate sense. The smooth, flowing sounds of lines 5–6 contrast the harsher, rougher sounds of lines 7–8. Lines 5–6 imitate the west wind (Zephyr) blowing gently; lines 7–8 mimic the roar of the surf pounding the shore. This congruence of sound and sense is continued through the next four lines as well. Lines 9–10 describe Ajax, a Greek warrior, as he attempts to lift and hurl a large rock. Pope emphasizes the laboriousness of Ajax's labor by clustering consonants together, which makes the lines a struggle to pronounce, and which slows the speed at which we read them. By contrast, Pope moves lines 11–12 more swiftly; they are easier to pronounce. Such fluidity and speed is appropriate to their subject: Camilla, a fleet-footed legendary queen quickly passing over field and ocean.

Prose writers also exploit sound in the service of meaning, using the sounds of words and the rhythms of phrasing to enhance tone and meaning. Here are brief examples from two modern fiction writers, James Joyce and William Faulkner. As you read the opening paragraph of Joyce's "Two Gallants," underline all repeated words, phrases, and sounds. Do the same for the Faulkner passage, taken from the end of his story, "A Rose for Emily." See if you can sense what the control of sound and rhythm contributes to each passage.

> The grey warm evening of August had descended upon the city and a mild warm air, a memory of summer, circulated in the streets. The streets, shuttered for the repose of Sunday, swarmed with a gaily colored crowd. Like illumined pearls the lamps shone from the summits

of their tall poles upon the living texture below which, changing shape and hue unceasingly, sent up into the warm grey evening air an unchanging unceasing murmur.

Why are there no commas separating *grey* and *warm* in the phrase "grey warm evening"? In "mild warm air"? In "warm grey evening air"? How would they differ with commas separating the adjectives? Also, what is the effect of repeating, with slight variations, the words *changing* and *unceasingly* in the final sentence? In addition, notice how Joyce picks up the "s" sound from the end of the first sentence and continues it through the second and third sentences. Read the passage aloud, slowly. Then read the following revised version. Account for whatever differences you see and hear.

The grey, warm evening of August had descended upon the city, and a mild, warm air, a memory of summer, circulated in the streets, which, shuttered for the quiet of Sunday, swarmed with a gaily dressed crowd of people. The lamps shone from the summits of their tall poles upon the crowd below. Changing shape and hue unceasingly, the living texture below sent an unchanging, continuing murmur up into the warm, grey evening air.

Read aloud the following passage from William Faulkner's "A Rose for Emily." Note the effects of sound Faulkner establishes in the selection. Explain how sound contributes to the tone and meaning of the passage.

The violence of breaking down the door seemed to fill this room with pervading dust. A thin, acrid pall as of the tomb seemed to lie everywhere upon this room decked and furnished as for a bridal: upon the valance curtains of faded rose color, upon the rose-shaded lights, upon the dressing table, upon the delicate array of crystal and the man's toilet things backed with tarnished silver, silver so tarnished that the monogram was obscured. Among them lay a collar and tie, as if they had just been removed, which, lifted, left upon the surface a pale crescent in the dust. Upon a chair hung the suit, carefully folded; beneath it the two mute shoes and the discarded socks.

The man himself lay in the bed.

For a long time we just stood there, looking down at the profound and fleshless grin. The body had apparently once lain in the attitude of an embrace, but now the long sleep that outlasts love, that conquers even the grimace of love, had cuckolded him. What was left of him, rotted beneath what was left of the nightshirt, had become inextricable from the bed in which he lay; and upon him and upon the pillow beside him lay that even coating of the patient and biding dust.

You may have noticed that the word *dust* occurs three times, each time at the end of a sentence (first, third, and last). Consider that its placement was not accidental, and that furthermore in each instance it is preceded by a word beginning with *p* and containing the same long vowel sound, *a*. Discuss

Faulkner's possible intent. What are the effects on eye and ear of "pervading dust," "pale . . . dust," "patient . . . dust"?

Developing an ear for words won't assure that you'll write like Joyce or Faulkner. But it will enable you to better estimate the nature of their achievement. Equally important, it will alert you to the way your sentences strike the ears of your readers. By listening to writing as well as looking at it, by hearing it as well as seeing it, you'll develop a surer sense of how sound affects meaning.

Rhyme, Alliteration, Simulation (Onomatopeia)

Words rhyme when their vowel sounds chime—as in this sentence. Sometimes the chime of rhyme works well in a sentence; sometimes it doesn't. The same holds true for alliteration, the repetition of similar consonant sounds, usually at the beginning of words. A famous humorous example is "Peter Piper picked a peck of pickled peppers." Simulation or onomatopeia is the technique of imitating actions with words that are meant to sound like the things they describe. Some examples of sound-simulating words are: *clank, clink, zip, rip, (or r-r-r-rip), crunch, squash, crack, snap, cackle, rumble.*

In each of the following sentences, insert a word whose sound blends in with at least one other word in the sentence. For each sentence try to provide at least two different sound connections: rhyme and alliteration or rhyme and onomatopeia; or alliteration and onomatopeia.

1. The wheels _____ as the truck _____ to a stop.
                   verb   verb
2. As he _____ through the woods, the branch of a sapling _____ him across the cheek.
         verb   verb
3. The eagle is a(n) _____ bird; it _____ down on its prey with _____.
                         adjective   verb
4. The _____ clattered over the _____ with a noise like _____.
           noun   noun
5. The _____ slithered along the ground, _____ing _____.
           noun   verbal
6. The fire _____ed, _____ing and _____ing through the woods.
                verb   verbal   verbal
7. Ives loved Thoreau. He loved him for his _____ and for his _____.
                                                         noun
   noun
8. The breeze blew through the _____, bending the _____.
                                            noun   noun
9. Hemingway is known for his _____, Faulkner for his _____.
10. Silently, the surfer _____ over the waves.
                                    verb

Assonance, Consonance, and Dissonance

Some other sound effects you might play with are assonance, consonance, and dissonance. Assonance is the repetition of identical or related vowel sounds. Samuel Taylor Coleridge's poem "Kubla Khan" provides an example:

> In Xanadu did Kubla Khan
> A stately pleasure dome decree.

Consonance is the repetition of a pattern of consonants with differences in the vowels. W. H. Auden's poem " 'O Where are you going?' said *reader* to *rider*," is one example. Another is the sentence: *He'll never leave alive; she'll never live alone.* Dissonance occurs when the sounds of a sentence jar and grate clamorously, as in these examples from Wilfred Owen's "Dulce et Decorum Est":

> Bent double, like old beggars under sacks,
> Knock-kneed, coughing like hags, we cursed through sludge . . . .
>
> If you could hear, at every jolt, the blood
> Come gargling from the froth-corrupted lungs . . . .

Playing with sound won't make you a poet. Nor will it make you a better writer overnight. But it will raise your consciousness about the sound-sense of language. It will help you hear what the sound of your language expresses. The following exercise leads you further in that direction.

Exercise

Read the following passages both silently and aloud. Note the authors' use of repeated sounds, words, and phrases. Discuss, passage by passage, the particulars of sound as they intensify or otherwise enhance meaning. Then choose one passage and write an imitation, using similar techniques but different word choices and subject matter. (Example: An imitation of the first Baldwin sentence might read "It is impossible to put up with a parrot that stutters.")

1. James Baldwin, from "Notes of a Native Son":

> It was necessary to hold on to the things that mattered. The dead man mattered, the new life mattered; blackness and whiteness did not matter; to believe that they did was to acquiesce in one's own destruction. Hatred, which could destroy so much, never failed to destroy the man who hated . . . .

2. Henry David Thoreau, from *Walden*:

> The mass of men lead lives of quiet desperation. What is called resignation is confirmed desperation. From the desperate city you go into the desperate country . . . . A stereotyped but unconscious despair is concealed even under what are called the games and amusements of mankind. There is no play in them, for this comes after work. But it is characteristic of wisdom not to do desperate things.

3. E. B. White, from "The Ring of Time":

For me the circus is at its best before it has been put together. It is at its best at certain moments when it comes to a point, as through a burning glass, in the activity and destiny of a single performer out of so many. One ring is always bigger than three. One rider, one aerialist, is always greater than six.

4. John Donne, from *Devotions Upon Emergent Occasions*:

Variable and therefore miserable condition of man! this minute I was well, and am ill this minute. I am surprised with a sudden change and alteration to worse, and can impute it to no cause, nor call it by any name. We study health, and we deliberate upon our meats and drink and air and exercises, and we hew and we polish every stone that goes to that building; and so our health is a long and regular work. But in a minute a cannon batters all, overthrows all, demolishes all; a sickness unprevented for all our diligence, unsuspected for all our curiosity, nay undeserved, if we consider only disorder, summons us, seizes us, possesses us, destroys us in an instant. O miserable condition of man!

5. Mark Twain, from "In Defense of Harriet Shelley":

It takes some little time to find out that phrases which seem intended to guide the reader aright are there to mislead him; that phrases which seem intended to throw light are there to throw darkness; that phrases which seem intended to interpret a fact are there to misinterpret it; that phrases which seem intended to forestall prejudice are there to create it; that phrases which seem antidotes are poisons in disguise.

SENTENCES

There are books filled with rules about how to make English sentences, lots of books, lots of rules. The chances are quite good, though, that if you're a native speaker of English, you already know the rules and that you didn't learn them from books but from growing up in an English-speaking land. You've known how to make sentences—some sentences, anyway—from the time you were still in diapers. As you grew older, you learned how to form more kinds of sentences. This doesn't mean that there are sentence types you don't learn until you are nine or ten, and still others that only people over eighteen are capable of handling. Some kinds of sentences are more complicated than others, but no form that's recognized as an English sentence is too much for native users of our language, even quite young ones.

What follows, then, isn't aimed at teaching you new forms or offering a crash course in sentence-making so you can begin talking and writing like a real live college student. Instead, these next pages classify and provide labels for some sentence forms, examine some of the elements that make them what they are, and ask that you do some writing within the same forms.

The Cumulative Sentence

The cumulative sentence adds details as it goes along; it accumulates specific details after the primary subject and verb of the sentence appear. Here's an example:

> *We caught two bass,*
>   hauling them in briskly as though they were mackerel,
>   pulling them in over the side of the boat in a
>   businesslike manner without any landing net,
>   and stunning them with a blow on the back of the head.
>
> E. B. White

White's sentence and the example that follows have been set up to highlight their parallelism. The parallel forms of each sentence have been "stacked" to help you see their structures. White, for example, strings three "ing" verbs (present participles) together as the focal points of the accumulation. In a structurally similar way, Baldwin lists a series of four parallel nouns accompanied by modifying words and phrases. Notice too the way he repeats words, especially in the last part of the sentence.

> *The wide windows looked out on Harlem's invincible and indescribable squalor:*
>   the Park Avenue railroad tracks around which, about forty years ago,
>   the present dark community began;
>   the unrehabilitated houses, bowed down, it would seem, under the
>   great weight of frustration and bitterness they contain;
>   the dark, the ominous schoolhouses from which the child may emerge
>   maimed,
>   blinded,
>   hooked
>   or enraged for life;
> and the churches, churches, block upon block of churches,
>   niched in the walls like cannon in the walls of a fortress.
>
> James Baldwin

The Periodic Sentence

A periodic sentence reverses the order of details in a cumulative sentence. Instead of making a statement and then adding specifying, amplifying detail as in the cumulative sentence, a periodic sentence begins with details, saving its statement for the end. A periodic sentence becomes grammatically complete only at the end, unlike a cumulative sentence which achieves grammatical completeness near the beginning. Here's a short example:

> Like habitations depopulated by plague, even with their lights on, *the houses looked abandoned.*
>
> John Gardner

And a longer, more elaborate one:

If we had only a single center in our brains, capable of responding only when a correct decision was to be made, instead of the jumble of different, credulous, easily conned clusters of neurons that provide for being flung off into blind alleys,
>
> up trees,
> down dead ends,
> out into blue sky,
> along wrong turnings,
> around bends,
>
> *we could only stay the way we are today, stuck fast.*
>
> Lewis Thomas

While you might be surprised and impressed with yourself to discover it, you have many times combined the cumulative and periodic sentence. Here are two examples which, despite the many syllabled label *cumulative-periodic sentence,* are comfortably familiar in sound and shape. (The main clauses are italicized.):

> During the entire celebration, *revelers consistently lost consciousness,* sometimes injuring themselves in the process.

> With the advent of the personal computer, *home entertainment patterns have been changing,* with time for video game playing now eating into that previously given over to watching television or listening to music.

The Parallel and Antithetical Sentence

Both periodic and cumulative sentences include balanced parts, whether balances of words, phrases, or clauses. Such balances are visible in the "stacked" examples above. The repetition of similarly formed sentence elements is useful for tightening your prose, and for alerting your readers to the structure of your thought. In addition, balanced phrasing will enhance the rhythm of your writing and make it more emphatic as well. Here are three brief sentences that employ balanced phrasing; all are from Francis Bacon's "Of Studies."

> Crafty men condemn studies,
> simple men admire them,
> and wise men use them.

> Some books are to be tasted,
> others   to be swallowed,
> and some few   to be chewed and digested.

> Read not to contradict and confute;
>   nor to believe and take for granted;
>   nor to find talk and discourse;
>   but to weigh and consider.

In these examples, the parallel sections are similar in grammatical form: noun is balanced against noun, verb against verb, adjective against adjective, negative against negative. The last of the examples is parallel through the third line, but turns on a contrastive point in the last—with "but to weigh and consider." Parallel sentences needn't be elaborate. We could rewrite Bacon's sentence as a simple contrastive or antithetical sentence. It might look like this:

> Read not to contradict and confute,
> > but to weigh and consider.

or like this:

> Read not to believe and take for granted,
> > but to weigh and consider.

In the following sentences the oppositions gain emphasis from their balanced parallel form:

> Buddies bonded, but friends loved.
>
> Buddies seek approval, but friends seek acceptance.
> > > > *Ellen Goodman*

And for a more elaborate contrast:

> I would not live over my hours past,
> > or begin again the thread of my days,
> > > not because I have lived them well,
> > > > but for fear I should live them worse.
> > > > > *Sir Thomas Browne*

An additional possibility with parallel antithetical sentences is to underscore the antithesis with sound effects:

> The valve permits influx
> > but   prevents outflow.
>
> It is not necessary to desire things
> > in order to acquire them.
> > > *E. B. White*

Notice how White highlights his parallel phrasing by employing the sound play of *permits-prevents, influx-outflow,* and *desire-acquire.* And finally a virtuoso balancing act, not with exact parallel or antithetical phrasing, but with a set of balances with variations.

> The idea, here, seemed to be,
> > that a man should have the ability to go up in a hurtling piece of
> > > > > > machinery,
> > > > put his life on the line,
> > and then have the moxie,
> > > the reflexes,
> > > the experience,

                              the coolness to pull it back in the last yawning
                                                                       moment,
                         to go up again
         and then the next day,
         and   the next day,
         and every   next day, even if the series should prove infinite—
    and ultimately, in its best expression,
                              do so in a cause that
                         means something to thousands,
                                        to a people,
                                        a nation,
                                        to humanity,
                                        to God.
                                                         Tom Wolfe

The Questioning Sentence

We don't always ask questions in search of answers. When a driver rolls down his window and bellows at the motorist who's trying to nose into his lane, "Who do you think you are?" it isn't because he's even slightly interested in the other's identity. And when we on occasion gaze Heavenward and ask, "What did I do to deserve this?" we'd be pretty rattled to get a response. Neither is properly a question, or, more accurately, they're both rather extreme examples of the *rhetorical question,* statements with question marks at their ends but otherwise a different species from the answer-seeking interrogative sentence, such as "What time is it?"

Writers use both kinds of question to vary the shape and tone of their writing. Like any other stylistic device, the so-called questioning sentence (a) can be overused; and (b) shouldn't be stuck into a piece of writing simply and only for the sake of variety. Trust your ear and eye; if it sounds and looks pleasing, use it. If not, don't.

Here are some examples of questions that work well in context.

> No matter how sensibly their needs have been anticipated, however, I wind up pitying wild animals and want them released. But where released? They are pushed face to face with us wherever they survive. Even in the effort to help them survive there are absurd misplays. Recently an entrepreneur somehow gathered together two hundred specimens of a South American sidenecked turtle which is on the list of endangered species and flew them to California, where he hoped to capitalize on their rarity. Instead they were identified and seized by federal officials. So the federal men confiscated the shipment of turtles to teach him a lesson. What did they do then—fly them back? No, killed them.
>
> Edward Hoagland

Notice how Hoagland answers his questions right after he asks them. Notice also how the two questions and accompanying answers advance his argument. In the second example, you'll find unanswered questions. In writing about the poverty of Marrakech, George Orwell asks questions whose answers are implied rather than directly stated. Such rhetorical questions are really observations of a sort, with their own implied answers. What *are* the implied answers?

> When you walk through a town like this—two hundred thousand inhabitants, of whom at least twenty thousand own literally nothing except the rags they stand up in—when you see how the people live, and still more how easily they die, it is always difficult to believe that you are walking among human beings. All colonial empires are in reality founded upon that fact. The people have brown faces—besides there are so many of them! Are they really the same flesh as yourself? Do they even have names? Or are they merely a kind of undifferentiated brown stuff, about as individual as bees or coral insects?
>
> *George Orwell*

Notice, by the way, how Orwell varies the length of his sentences: one long sentence, then two short ones, followed by three questions, two of which are short and one moderately long. And don't miss the periodic character of the first sentence. Orwell's paragraph continues with statements rather than questions. Here's the rest of it:

> They rise out of the earth, they sweat and starve for a few years, and then they sink back into the nameless mounds of the graveyard and nobody notices that they are gone. And even the graves themselves soon fade back into the soil. Sometimes, out for a walk, as you break your way through the prickly pear, you notice that it is rather bumpy underfoot, and only a certain regularity in the bumps tells you that you are walking over skeletons.

Again, in this last part of the paragraph, Orwell mixes the lengths and forms of his sentences, concluding with a periodic sentence, the full sense of which is delayed to the end for impact.

The Fragmentary Sentence

You've probably been told at one time or another that sentence fragments are not acceptable in serious writing. Not so. A fragment is a special kind of truncated sentence, which, when carefully used, can give your writing the movement and emphasis of the speaking voice. Like this. Nothing more, nothing less. The reason fragments have a bad name is that, when carelessly used, they cause confusion. Or perhaps call attention to themselves unintentionally. As a sign the writer is unsure of herself. They distract the reader. Because the writer is not using them in ways the reader can readily understand. (As in the examples from the middle to the end of this paragraph.)

But there's an enormous difference between the unconscious use of fragments and an exploitation of the capabilities of the sentence fragment as a rhetorical instrument. The fragment judiciously used indicates a confident writer who isn't afraid to violate grammatical convention to say what he or she has to say in the most natural way.

Exercise

Fragments make sense, of course, only in the context of a dialogue or a written discourse. Read through the following passages, noticing the fragments. Rewrite them as grammatically complete sentences. What is gained or lost in such an alteration?

> When the friends get to the burying ground they hack an oblong hole a foot or two deep, dump the body in it and fling over it a little of the dried-up, lumpy earth, which is like broken brick. No gravestone, no name, no identifying mark of any kind . . . .
>
> As they went past, a tall, very young Negro turned and caught my eye. But the look he gave me was not in the least the kind of look you might expect. Not hostile, not contemptuous, not sullen, not even inquisitive.
>
> George Orwell

> It's a health spa. The place you come to when you want to get in shape. Of course, no one defines what "in shape" means. It's assumed. Inherent in the culture. Western societies of the 1980's define "in shape" to mean lean, trim, taut. And the ability to breathe normally after a six-mile run. A steady pitch heard across America: "Take care of your body, it's a precious commodity." Tiny Tim knew it when he said, "You are what you eat." And out came a generation of tofu-eating, beansprout-picking, exercise addicted people striving for bodily perfection. No longer do we need Socrates to explain the absolutes of beauty and truth—we have Arnold Schwarzennager. And health spas.
>
> Mary Fitzgerald

The Inverted Sentence

Inversion serves two purposes: variation from the normal pattern of subject-verb-object, and emphasis. To vary the pattern of the standard English sentence, reverse the position of subject and object, as in this sentence about the circus:

> And buried in the familiar boasts of its advance agents lies the modesty of most of its people.
>
> E. B. White

This sentence, by the way, is also periodic since the subject and predicate come close to the end. In this example it works to create anticipation, even a faint sense of suspense.

Here's another sentence by White, this one in three parts, with each part an inversion of the normal S-V-O order.

> Out of its wild disorder comes order;
> from its rank smell rises the good aroma of courage and daring;
> out of its preliminary shabbiness comes its final splendor.

We could rewrite this triply inverted sentence in normal order this way:

> Order comes out of its wild disorder;
> the good aroma of courage and daring rises from its rank smell;
> its final splendor comes out of its preliminary shabbiness.

Although the three parts of this revised sentence are balanced, the emphasis falls on all the wrong things: the disorder, the rank smell, and the shabbiness. In White's sentence, the emphasis falls on order, courage and daring, and splendor. In addition, the rhythm of White's sentence is more graceful and natural. Read both aloud to hear the difference.

The Interrupted Sentence

Sentences that contain breaks in the march from subject to verb to object can be called *interrupted sentences*. The interrupting words and phrases change the pace of the sentence; they alter the rhythm of the writing. They also increase emphasis at the ends of sentences. Notice what happens to the following when it is stripped of its interrupting words and phrases.

First, the original sentences as James Baldwin wrote them in the opening paragraph of his essay, "Notes of a Native Son" (The interrupters are in italics.):

> On the 29th of July, *in 1943,* my father died. On the same day, *a few hours later,* his last child was born. Over a month before this, *while all our energies were concentrated in waiting for these events,* there had been, *in Detroit,* one of the bloodiest race riots of the century. A few hours after my father's funeral, *while he lay in state in the undertaker's chapel,* a race riot broke out in Harlem. On the morning of the 3rd of August, we drove my father to the graveyard through a wilderness of smashed plate glass.

> My father died on July 29th, 1943. His last child was born a few hours later on the same day. While all our energies had been concentrated in waiting for these events, one of the bloodiest race riots of the century had broken out in Detroit over a month before. A few hours after my father's funeral, a race riot broke out in Harlem while he lay in state in the undertaker's chapel. We drove my father to the graveyard through a wilderness of smashed plate glass on the morning of the 3rd of August.

The words of this second version are, with a few minor exceptions, the same as those of the original. But their order has been changed. Gone is the dignified tone and stately rhythm created by the interrupting phrases of Baldwin's writing; gone also is the emphasis at the ends of his sentences.

Sentence Length

To say that varying the length of your sentence will result in better writing is woefully simplistic; no amount of purely mechanical tinkering will have a very powerful effect on the quality of your writing. It won't hurt, though, to heighten your awareness that here too there's room for choice—that a string of sentences uniform in length and shape may inspire a numbing monotony in the reader; is, indeed, a sign that the author herself is suffering a numbness of spirit and has no heart for the work.

Exercise

Examine the following passages for sentence length and for variety of sentence forms. (Reading them aloud, slowly and deliberately, will help.) Write imitations of the passages using your own subject and ideas, but following as closely as you can the pattern and length of each writer's sentences.

> There is something uneasy in the Los Angeles air this afternoon, some unnatural stillness, some tension. What it means is that tonight a Santa Ana will begin to blow, a hot wind from the northeast whining down through the Cajon and San Gorgonio passes, blowing up sandstorms out along Route 66, drying the hills and the nerves to the flash point. For a few days now we will see smoke back in the canyons, and hear sirens in the night. I have neither heard nor read that a Santa Ana is due, but I know it, and almost everyone I have seen today knows it too. We know it because we feel it. The baby frets. The maid sulks. I rekindle a waning argument with the telephone company, then cut my losses and lie down, given over to whatever it is in the air.
>
> *Joan Didion*

> I learned this, at least, by my experiment: that if one advances confidently in the direction of his dreams, and endeavors to live the life which he has imagined, he will meet with a success unexpected in common hours. He will put some things behind, will pass an invisible boundary; new, universal, and more liberal laws will begin to establish themselves around and within him; or the old laws be expanded, and interpreted in his favor in a more liberal sense, and he will live with the license of a higher order of beings. In proportion as he simplifies his life, the laws of the universe will appear less complex, and solitude will not be solitude, nor poverty poverty, nor weakness weakness. If you have built castles in the air, your work need not be lost; that is where they should be. Now put the foundations under them.
>
> *Henry David Thoreau*

> Call me Ishmael. Some years ago—never mind how long precisely—having little or no money in my purse, and nothing particular to interest me on shore, I thought I would sail about a little and see the watery part of the world. It is a way I have of driving off the spleen, and regulating the circulation. Whenever I find myself growing grim about the

mouth; whenever it is a damp, drizzly November in my soul; whenever I find myself involuntarily pausing before coffin warehouses, and bringing up the rear of every funeral I meet; and especially whenever my hypos get such an upper hand of me, that it requires a strong moral principle to prevent me from deliberately stepping into the street, and methodically knocking people's hats off—then, I account it high time to get to sea as soon as I can. This is my substitute for pistol and ball. With a philosophical flourish Cato throws himself upon his sword; I quietly take to the ship. There is nothing surprising in this. If they but knew it, almost all men in their degree, some time or other, cherish very nearly the same feelings toward the ocean with me.

Herman Melville

PUNCTUATION

When you think of punctuation, you probably think of lists of rules to follow, especially about commas. But a more useful way to think of it is as an aid to constructing sentences when you write and to construing them when you read. Try to think of punctuation less as a system of rules and more as an aid to expressing and clarifying ideas.

You should realize, too, that rules of punctuation are not moral imperatives; they're not set in stone, never to be altered. Rather, they are conventions, generally agreed upon ways of doing things. But as with most elements of writing, there are exceptions to most of the rules and occasional changes in standard practice. To find out what standards prevail at a given time, you can consult any substantial dictionary or a style manual such as *The Chicago Manual of Style*. What follows is a short review of the major punctuation conventions.

Colon

Let's begin with the colon (:). The colon is a sign pointing to something that will follow. Here's a simple example:

> She wanted two things before she was through: to achieve fame and to establish financial security.

You're familiar, most likely, with the colon's frequent use as an introduction to a list such as this one:

> These are the requirements for the course: faithful attendance, intelligent participation in class, and completion of all written assignments.

In this case, when you see the colon, you know there's something specific coming, something that will clarify the part of the sentence that came before. Sometimes this clarification or specification may be a single word; on other occasions it may be a complete statement, something that could stand alone as a sentence. Here are a few examples illustrating the possibilities:

> He wanted only one thing from her: money.

> He wanted only one thing before he died: the gift of his son's forgiveness.

In these two examples the colon is followed by a fragment. Perfectly all right. In the next example it's followed by a grammatically complete sentence. Notice that there's a full statement on both sides of the colon.

> She was sure that her mother was going to win the contest: she had dreamed about it for five successive nights.

In this sentence the part following the colon serves to explain or clarify what precedes the colon. Suppose, however, that the statements had been punctuated like this:

> She was sure that her mother was going to win the contest. She had dreamed about it for five successive nights.

Is anything lost in this version? How does the colon help you to construe and understand the idea?

Exercise

Note how colons are used in the following passages. Explain how the parts to the right of the colon relate to the parts on the left.

> A home is like a reservoir equipped with a check valve: the valve permits influx but prevents outflow.
>
> E. B. White

> Bad ions in the air, bad stars, or bad luck: call it what you will—a run of bad luck, in fact.
>
> Edward Hoagland

> The sight held awesome wonders: power and beauty, grace tangled in a rapture with violence.
>
> Annie Dillard

Dash

The dash (indicated in typing by a double hyphen --) can add variety to your writing. Less formal than the colon, it's frequently used for comic and satiric purposes:

> He was shy, modest, simply dressed—and obsessed with success.

> Each person is born to one possession which outlasts all others—his last breath.
>
> Mark Twain

This use of the dash, however, doesn't suggest that dashes are funnier than colons. They're not. Like colons, dashes create emphasis:

> Her remark sparkled with wit—a wit that was wisdom.

> He had spent several weeks preparing his report—a report that would, he hoped, gain him the promotion he desired.

You can also use the dash to explain or amplify a statement:

> He loved everything about his room—the quiet space it afforded him, the way light filtered through the tiny paned windows, the posters and memorabilia that adorned his walls and bureau.

And you can use it to indicate a sudden break in thought or an interruption in a dialogue:

> I always wanted to own land—no, not always, just the last five or six years.
> "I want to build my own house."
> "But you don't even know how to—"
> "You'd be surprised what I can do when I am determined."

And finally, you can use the dash after a series of details:

> Honesty, decency, courage, integrity—these are the ideals Thoreau valued and tried to live by.
>
> Broken appointments, interminable meetings, multitudinous complaints—such were the elements of his everyday routine.

Notice, by the way, that if you reverse the parts of these last two examples, you get sentences that could be punctuated with colons:

> The qualities Thoreau valued and tried to live by are these: honesty, decency, courage, and integrity.
>
> The elements of his everyday routine were these: broken appointments, interminable meetings, multitudinous complaints.

A last note: the dash should not be used as a substitute for a period. It's not a terminal or end punctuation mark.

Exercise

Write imitations of at least four of the dash-model sentences above and below.

> My attendance at meals may be a little spotty—for a twelvemonth I shall not adjust my steps to a souffle.
>
> E. B. White

> I thought of two friends in the city who had recently suffered crises—heart attacks at forty.
>
> Edward Hoagland

> He knew the arguments for the war, and against the war—finally they bored him.
>
> Norman Mailer

They would put a strap around your head, clamp some sort of instrument over your eyes—and then stick a hose into your ear and pump cold water into your ear canal.

Tom Wolfe

What did you expect to see—angels?

Annie Dillard

Double Dash and Parentheses

Besides the single dash as used in the sentences above, you can also use the double dash, which frequently accompanies words and phrases interpolated in a sentence. That is, the interpolated elements are not essential to the meaning of the sentence, and the sentence can be read or written omitting them. Consider the following examples:

He was among the majority—some 60%—who default on their alimony payments.

Ellen Goodman

The individual parts played by other instrumentalists—crickets or earthworms, for instance—may not have the sound of music by themselves.

Lewis Thomas

Parentheses, like commas and dashes, may be used to set off explanatory or digressive words and phrases. You have a good deal of leeway in whether to punctuate with commas, double dashes or parentheses. Generally you can use parentheses for digressive detail and dashes for slightly more emphatic information, reserving commas for parenthetical elements that retain a close logical connection to the rest of the sentence. Consider these examples:

The Reagan proposal was, not surprisingly, extremely favorable to business.

The author's first novel (written on a summer fishing trip in Vermont) was extremely self-indulgent and highly autobiographical.

Exercise

Punctuate the sentences with dashes, commas, or parentheses.

He had long suspected that the three candidates Smith, Wesson, and Colt would outdo each other in making fools of themselves.

The Woodstock concert it had already been interrupted twice by rain was postponed indefinitely.

He believes in the efficacy of free writing a kind of informal, exploratory writing as a way to discover what he thinks and feels.

Hyphen

Don't confuse the dash with the hyphen. Dashes are used to separate sentence elements—that is, they are used between words or groups of words. Hyphens are used within words; they're used both to separate elements of compound words and to join them. Here are a few examples:

The year-end festival is only a month away.

A well-run meeting is a rare delight.

You can also use the hyphen in the following ways:

— To indicate that a word continues beyond the end of a line. Remember to hyphenate (hy-phen-ate) only between syllables, where syllables normally break the word into parts. Check your dictionary if you're uncertain about the syllabication of a word you need to hyphenate.

— To join the elements of compound numbers from twenty-one to ninety-nine, and to connect the terms or parts of fractions: thirty-two dollars; three-fourths of the class.

Learning to use the hyphen is a matter of learning the rules. Learning to use the dash is a matter of rhetoric—of writing sentences that capitalize on its expressive potential.

Exercises

1. Consult several standard dictionaries to determine if the following terms are hyphenated: upside-down, upsidedown, or upside down? topsy-turvy or topsy turvy? Do the dictionaries agree?

2. Explain the difference between recovering and re-covering, between recreation and re-creation.

Semicolon

The semicolon often functions as a fulcrum, a balance point in a sentence. Thus: Light purse; heavy heart. Or: The Yankees have strong hitting and weak pitching; the Dodgers have strong pitching and weak hitting. The semicolon, as you can see from these examples, is useful for statements in parallel form, especially statements that express a contrasting idea.

Generally you can follow these guidelines in using the semicolon:

1. Use the semicolon to join two statements that could normally stand by themselves as grammatically complete sentences if the two statements are closely related in thought or if they are parallel in form. Consider these examples:

    a. I refused the prize; the rules of the contest were unfair, I thought, to some contestants.

    b. Hemingway's prose is lean, spare, taut; Faulkner's is full, rich, sonorous.

2. Use a semicolon to link word groups in sentences that contain heavy use of commas. An example:

Some college graduate would enter Navy aviation through the Reserves, simply as an alternative to the Army draft, fully intending to return to civilian life, to some waiting profession or family business; would become involved in the obsessive business of ascending the ziggurat pyramid of flying; and, at the end of his enlistment, would astound everyone back home and very likely himself as well by signing up for another one.

Tom Wolfe

3. Use a semicolon before words and phrases that summarize or explain the first part of the sentence. Thus:

Student writers should not be afraid to take chances; for example, they should experiment with different sentence patterns, try out extravagant metaphors, and generally plunge in before knowing for sure what will come of it all.

A final note on semicolons. It's conventional to use a semicolon before conjunctive adverbs such as "however," "therefore," "moreover," and "furthermore."

I went to the meeting expecting to be bored and narcotized; however, I found it enlivening.

I'm entitled to a large refund; moreover, I'm entitled to it without delay.

There are occasions, however, when these words appear between two commas, as in this sentence and the following example:

I am entitled to it, moreover, without delay.

Comma

Unlike periods, colons, and semicolons, which all stop discourse sharply, commas only slow it down. You can simplify your life with commas if you master these four basic uses: to separate, to co-ordinate, to interrupt, and to link.

1. Use a comma to separate an introductory word or phrase from the main idea of your sentence.

After an uneventful opening scene, the movie began to interest me.

In a quick shift of attitude, he argued for the plan, not against it.

2. Use a comma to co-ordinate two statements—two subjects with two verbs.

He encouraged her, and his encouragement helped.

He wanted to attend the party, but a stiff neck immobilized him.

It wasn't the best of times, but neither was it the worst.

3. Use commas to bracket words, phrases, or clauses, which, if omitted, will not destroy the sense of grammatical completeness of the sentence.

Hemingway, on the other hand, is a modern writer.

Consider, however, a different approach.

The earliest manuscript version, which is now in the Cornell University Library, has been badly damaged.

Everything depends on how relentlessly one forces from this experience the last drop, sweet or bitter, it can possibly give.

James Baldwin

The small tribe of Iks, formerly nomadic hunters and gatherers in the mountain valleys of northern Uganda, have become celebrities.

Lewis Thomas

4. Use a comma to link or to append ideas or information. The most common way is to join items in a series.

fish, flesh, or fowl

to read, to write, to think

He struggled, he became frustrated, yet he didn't quit.

Or to join contrastive elements:

He wanted the bread, not the butter.

Or to add details to a general statement:

I shall miss them all, the old and the young, the rich and the poor.

Exercise

The following paragraphs have been stripped of their punctuation. Punctuate each, then compare your versions with those of other students.

As a stutterer I learned not to write notes you put yourself at someone's mercy more when you write him a note than if you just stand there like a rhinoceros and snort I could write a Stutterer's Guide to Europe too the titters in old Vienna the knowing English remembering their King the raw scorching baitings I met with in Greece surrounded sometimes like a muzzled bear the fourth means of effecting a cure I heard about was based on the fact that stutterers are able to sing without stuttering hence the victim should swing one of his arms like a big pendulum and talk in time to this which again was obviously a worse fate than the impediment though I didn't try it I was sent to a lady voice teacher who laid my hand on her conspicuous chest so that I could feel her breathe for just that moment the lessons worked wonderfully if I wasn't speechless I spoke in a rush.

modified version of a paragraph from
Edward Hoagland's "The Threshhold and the Jolt of Pain"

My friend stayed outside the restaurant long enough to misdirect my pursuers and the police who arrived he told me at once I do not know what I said to him when he came to my room that night I could not have said much I felt in the oddest most awful way that I had somehow betrayed him I lived it over and over and over again the way one relives an automobile accident after it has happened and one finds oneself alone and safe I could not get over two facts both equally difficult for the imagination to grasp and one was that I could have been murdered but the other was that I had been ready to commit murder I saw nothing very clearly but I did see this that my life my real life was in danger and not from anything other people might do but from the hatred I carried in my own heart.

modified version of a paragraph from
James Baldwin's "Notes of a Native Son"

PART IV

Making Connections
The Discovery of Relationships

In writing, as in life, the connections of all sorts of relationships and kinds lie in wait of discovery, and give out their signals to the Geiger counter of the charged imagination.

Eudora Welty

Perception sees analogies—the relationship between things and ideas; it is observation plus comment, and as much the comment of the emotions as of the mind.

Holbrook Jackson

Really, universally, relations stop nowhere.

Henry James

Only connect.

E. M. Forster

A few hundred pages back, I noted that all learning involves making connections, which was, I admit, a bland-sounding, textbookish observation. Maybe by now, however, it has taken on a sharper and more useful meaning. I hope so, because there's really something to all this connection-making business beyond the obvious. This *is* the way we learn. More pointedly, it's the way organized academic learning should happen, the way to make new information—new and strange subjects—yield to us.

What follows is a *potpourri* (a French term meaning a medley or miscellany, a stew) of readings. Responding to them through annotating, discussing, writing—and reviewing, rethinking, rewriting—should leave you with a confidence, even an enthusiasm, about finding and making useful links between yourself and the widely various kinds of reading and writing demands you have here and now and in the future. As reader and writer and thinker you'll find yourself coming at such stuff *aggressively,* with an eye to the work's wildest possibilities—connections—rather than its tamer probability. Wherever else this book may have brought you, let it be to that point where you're convinced that learning doesn't amount to a narrow quest for the "right" response—that, in fact, there isn't any "right" response that lives in the material, that pre-exists or pre-empts your involvement with it.

From the Book of Jonah to the three contemporary essays that close this section and the book you're invited to make the material your own—to put it to the test of your experiences, your insights, your perspectives; to shape it to fit you; to let it deepen your understanding of who you are and what you've been through. You'll find editorial comments in headnotes and afternotes (*Considerations*) and occasional questions about style, intention, possible interpretations. You're invited to respond to, enlarge on, take issue with the comments and questions, but above all you're invited to make the material your own in ways that are satisfying to you.

THE BOOK OF JONAH

The chances are that you first heard the fascinating Jonah story when you were quite young. Along with David and Goliath, Noah and the Ark, and Samson and Delilah, this tale is not only a Sunday School favorite, but has also been popularized in cartoons, songs, and children's books. Indeed, the trouble is that we often consider these grand old tales as being strictly for kids and leave them behind us, along with fairy tales and fables.

The Jonah story *is* for kids—there's something wrong with any youngster who isn't fascinated by a tale about a fellow getting swallowed by a fish—but it's also a quite complex story about the nature of the Old Testament God, the philosophical concepts of free will, right and wrong, sin and repentance. Finally, it's a story about Jonah himself, and he is one of the most interesting people in the Bible.

As you read about Jonah and his misadventures, consider to what extent your response may be colored by the *associations* this story has for you—how much, for example, the story's Biblical context is coloring your reading, and why. Fill up the margins with comments, and comments on the comments.

1   Now the word of the Lord came unto Jonah the son of Amittai,
2 saying, Arise, go to Nineveh, that great city, and cry against it; for their
3 wickedness is come up before me. But Jonah rose up to flee unto Tarshish from the presence of the Lord, and went down to Joppa; and he found a ship going to Tarshish: so he paid the fare thereof, and went down into it, to go with them unto Tarshish from the presence of the Lord.

4   But the Lord sent out a great wind into the sea, and there was a
5   mighty tempest in the sea, so that the ship was like to be broken. Then the mariners were afraid, and cried every man unto his god, and cast forth the wares that were in the ship into the sea, to lighten it of them. But Jonah was gone down into the sides of the ship; and he lay, and was
6   fast asleep. So the shipmaster came to him, and said unto him, What meanest thou, O sleeper? arise, call upon thy God, if so be that God will think upon us, that we perish not.
7   And they said every one to his fellow, Come, and let us cast lots, that we may know for whose cause this evil is upon us. So they cast lots, and
8   the lot fell upon Jonah. Then said they unto him, Tell us, we pray thee, for whose cause this evil is upon us; What is thine occupation? and whence comest thou? what is thy country? and of what people art
9   thou? And he said unto them, I am a Hebrew; and I fear the Lord, the
10 God of heaven, which hath made the sea and the dry land. Then were the men exceedingly afraid, and said unto him, Why hast thou done this? For the men knew that he fled from the presence of the Lord, because he had told them.
11 Then said they unto him, What shall we do unto thee, that the sea
12 may be calm unto us? for the sea wrought, and was tempestuous. And he said unto them, Take me up, and cast me forth into the sea; so shall the sea be calm unto you: for I know that for my sake this great tempest
13 is upon you. Nevertheless the men rowed hard to bring it to the land; but they could not: for the sea wrought and was tempestuous against
14 them. Wherefore they cried unto the Lord, and said, We beseech thee, O Lord, we beseech thee, let us not perish for this man's life, and lay not upon us innocent blood: for thou, O Lord, hast done as it pleased
15 thee. So they took up Jonah, and cast him forth into the sea: and the
16 sea ceased from her raging. Then the men feared the Lord exceedingly, and offered a sacrifice unto the Lord, and made vows.
17 Now the Lord had prepared a great fish to swallow up Jonah. And
2   Jonah was in the belly of the fish three days and three nights. Then
2   Jonah prayed unto the Lord his God out of the fish's belly, And said,

> I cried by reason of mine affliction unto the Lord,
>   and he heard me;
> out of the belly of hell cried I,
>   and thou heardest my voice.

3   For thou hadst cast me into the deep, in the midst of the seas;
      and the floods compassed me about:
    all thy billows and thy waves passed over me.

5   The waters compassed me about, even to the soul:
      the depth closed me round about,
      the weeds were wrapped about my head.

7   When my soul fainted within me I remembered the Lord:
      and my prayer came in unto thee, into thine holy temple.

8   They that observe lying vanities forsake their own mercy.
9   But I will sacrifice unto thee with the voice of thanksgiving;
             I will pay that that I have vowed.
        Salvation is of the Lord.

10   And the Lord spake unto the fish, and it vomited out Jonah upon the dry land.

3:1,2   And the word of the Lord came unto Jonah the second time, saying, Arise, go unto Nineveh, that great city, and preach unto it the preaching 3 that I bid thee. So Jonah arose, and went unto Nineveh, according to the word of the Lord. Now Nineveh was an exceeding great city of three 4 days' journey. And Jonah began to enter into the city a day's journey, and he cried, and said, Yet forty days, and Nineveh shall be overthrown.

5   So the people of Nineveh believed God, and proclaimed a fast, and put on sackcloth, from the greatest of them even to the least of them. 6 For word came unto the king of Nineveh, and he arose from his throne, and he laid his robe from him, and covered him with sackcloth, and sat 7 in ashes. And he caused it to be proclaimed and published through Nineveh by the decree of the king and his nobles, saying, Let neither man nor beast, herd nor flock, taste any thing: let them not feed, nor 8 drink water: But let man and beast be covered with sackcloth, and cry mightily unto God: yea, let them turn every one from his evil way, and 9 from the violence that is in their hands. Who can tell if God will turn and repent, and turn away from his fierce anger, that we perish not?

10   And God saw their works, that they turned from their evil way; and God repented of the evil, that he had said that he would do unto them; and he did it not.

4:1,2   But it displeased Jonah exceedingly, and he was very angry. And he prayed unto the Lord, and said, I pray thee, O Lord, was not this my saying, when I was yet in my country? Therefore I fled before unto Tarshish: for I knew that thou art a gracious God, and merciful, slow to anger, and of great kindness, and repentest thee of the evil. Therefore 3 now, O Lord, take, I beseech thee, my life from me; for it is better for me to die than to live.

4,5   Then said the Lord, Doest thou well to be angry? So Jonah went out of the city, and sat on the east side of the city, and there made him a booth, and sat under it in the shadow, till he might see what would become of the city.

6   And the Lord God prepared a gourd, and made it to come up over Jonah, that it might be a shadow over his head, to deliver him from his 7 grief. So Jonah was exceedingly glad of the gourd. But God prepared a worm when the morning rose the next day, and it smote the gourd 8 that it withered. And it came to pass, when the sun did arise, that God prepared a vehement east wind; and the sun beat upon the head of Jonah, that he fainted, and wished in himself to die, and said, It is better for me to die than to live.

9   And God said to Jonah, Doest thou well to be angry for the gourd? And he said, I do well to be angry, even unto death.
10 Then said the Lord, Thou hast had pity on the gourd, for the which thou hast not labored, neither madest it grow; which came up in a single
11 night, and perished in a night: And should not I spare Nineveh, that great city, wherein are more than sixscore thousand persons that cannot discern between their right hand and their left hand; and also much cattle?

Considerations

1. Jonah isn't the only character you know of who is swallowed by a fish. Generally the same thing occurs in many mythical tales. It's thought to be a metaphorical way to represent the acquisition of wisdom bestowed on the few whom the spirits favor; or the passage from life through death to a higher plane of existence. Which seems better to fit Jonah's experience? If neither, then what is the literal equivalent of being swallowed by a great fish? (If you have ever been swallowed by one, you may skip this question.)

2. There's something quite touching about the shipboard scene. Among other things, it seems an observation that to be human is ever to be out of sight of land, menaced by terrifying forces we don't understand, and yet to make the best of it—to maintain a charity and decency in the midst of the tempest. Consider what goes on between Jonah, a stranger of a different tribe, and the crew. That they don't simply toss him overboard to save their skins is at least remarkable. Consider Jonah's courage, too. He's not one of those tin-plated heroes without fear; he's scared silly. Yet he tells the crew to throw him over the side. (Why didn't he throw himself over? Would you have?) Look past the ageless archetype itself. Where have you heard this story before? Where have you seen it worked out with other characters in other times and places? Is there a little Jonah in all of us? What do we call this quality? How is the Jonah story possibly a metaphorical way to comment on the relative value placed on individual life?

3. It's quite possible to find humor in the Jonah tale, although the chances are you haven't approached it that way. Most of us have been brought up to believe that there's not even a crumb of humor between the Bible's covers, that religion and smiles simply don't mix. It stands to reason, though, that a people wise enough to frame such a great work were also wise enough to know humor as a blessing. Try reexamining Jonah in this light. What, for you, is a potentially funny scene? (There are at least four possibilities.) Don't stop with Jonah, however. What other Old Testament tales offer potentially funny possibilities in whole or part? You might have fun scripting a comic dialogue between a couple of Biblical characters, or writing out a familiar episode seen from another perspective.

4. What serious concerns in your life do you sometimes (or most of the time) treat with humor, yet with reverence? How is doing so different from treating serious matters with humor that is essentially cynical or mocking?

MEDITATION XVII
John Donne

Meditation XVII isn't being paired with Jonah. That is, it wasn't assigned this place in the text because it has significantly similar textual elements as the Biblical story. What's interesting, however, is that it seems so irresistibly to connect with the Jonah tale. When Donne, the early 17th-century preacher and poet, meditates on the significance of the individual—sees him as a chapter in the book of humankind—we understand him somewhat the way we can understand the Jonah story: we count for something, each of us; any death diminishes us. The two pieces seem to address one another: Jonah pities the gourd, although it (like us, metaphorically) "came up in a night, and perished in a night." Doesn't that connect with Donne's "If a clod be washed away by the sea, Europe is the less"? Jonah is furious because God chooses to spare the sixscore thousand people in Nineveh. Donne responds by observing that not only is all life significant, but so is *any* life.

So what? We can read Donne without reading Jonah or vice versa; little is lost. The faint dialogue between the two pieces is not that important. But something about such connections *is* important, profoundly so. Had I not made a minor issue of the Jonah-Donne possibilities, you would have ignored them. This doesn't mean you wouldn't have sensed the connections, just that you would probably have dismissed them as being oddly your own and therefore of no consequence. Both these pieces are powerfully *humane*—concerned with the human condition, assumptive of our divine origins, our tendency to the good act over the evil one, to loving over hating. These are, in fact, the deepest convictions we harbor, even if they seem occasionally preposterous. And we need them reiterated—we need to see and hear them voiced again and again. We actually *need* the kind of connection that can be found in Donne and the Biblical Jonah, because it verifies what we've heard all our lives and what can otherwise be terribly difficult to believe.

> Perchance he for whom this bell tolls may be so ill, as that he knows not it tolls for him; and perchance I may think myself so much better than I am, as that they who are about me, and see my state, may have caused it to toll for me, and I know not that. The church is Catholic, universal, so are all her actions; all that she does belongs to all. When she baptizes a child, that action concerns me; for that child is thereby connected to that body which is my head too, and ingrafted into that body whereof I am a member. And when she buries a man, that action concerns me: all mankind is of one author, and is one volume; when one man dies, one chapter is not torn out of the book, but translated into a better language; and every chapter must be so translated; God employs several translators; some pieces are translated by age, some by sickness, some by war, some by justice; but God's hand is in every translation, and his hand shall bind up all our scattered leaves again for that library where every book shall lie open to one another. As therefore the

bell that rings to a sermon calls not upon the preacher only, but upon the congregation to come, so this bell calls us all; but how much more me, who am brought so near the door by this sickness. There was a contention as far as a suit (in which both piety and dignity, religion and estimation, were mingled), which of the religious orders should ring to prayers first in the morning; and it was determined, that they should ring first that rose earliest. If we understand aright the dignity of this bell that tolls for our evening prayer, we would be glad to make it ours by rising early, in that application, that it might be ours as well as his, whose indeed it is. The bell doth toll for him that thinks it doth; and though it intermit again, yet from that minute that that occasion wrought upon him, he is united to God. Who casts not up his eye to the sun when it rises? but who takes off his eye from a comet when that breaks out? Who bends not his ear to any bell which upon any occasion rings? but who can remove it from that bell which is passing a piece of himself out of this world? No man is an island, entire of itself; every man is a piece of the continent, a part of the main. If a clod be washed away by the sea, Europe is the less, as well as if a promontory were, as well as if a manor of thy friend's or of thine own were: any man's death diminishes me, because I am involved in mankind, and therefore never send to know for whom the bell tolls; it tolls for thee. Neither can we call this a begging of misery, or a borrowing of misery, as though we were not miserable enough of ourselves, but must fetch in more from the next house, in taking upon us the misery of our neighbors. Truly it were an excusable covetousness if we did, for affliction is a treasure, and scarce any man hath enough of it. No man hath affliction enough that is not matured and ripened by it, and made fit for God by that affliction. If a man carry treasure in bullion, or in a wedge of gold, and have none coined into current money, his treasure will not defray him as he travels. Tribulation is treasure in the nature of it, but it is not current money in the use of it, except we get nearer and nearer our home, heaven, by it. Another man may be sick too, and sick to death, and this affliction may lie in his bowels, as gold in a mine, and be of no use to him; but this bell, that tells me of his affliction, digs out and applies that gold to me: if by this consideration of another's danger I take mine own into contemplation, and so secure myself, by making my recourse to my God, who is our only security.

Considerations

1. Throughout this selection, Donne develops a number of extended metaphors. What is the symbolic equivalent of each of these terms: *volume, author, chapter, translation, better language, scattered leaves*?

2. Donne's punctuation was probably somewhat irksome for you. What's different about it? confusing? annoying? What other mechanical aspects of *Meditation XVII* are at all bothersome? Discuss to what possible degree such externals as punctuation, capitalization, etc. work to color your

view, even in extreme cases blind you to the underlying promise of the piece. Consider and discuss how much you may be alienated by antiquated forms (*thou* for *you, doth* for *does,* etc.).

3. Discuss any predispositions that you may have harbored about this work based on its author, title, the headnote that introduced it, whatever. Would you possibly have responded differently to this piece (or any other that comes sharply to mind) if it were modern? If you'd come across it in other than a textbook? Why or why not?

4. Ernest Hemingway used a phrase from *Meditation XVII* as the title for one of his best-known novels. Find a "title" of your own somewhere in the piece, a phrase that holds a particular attraction for you and that in your opinion has a title-like ring to it. Next, explain what your novel (or movie or play or whatever) will deal with, and what the connection is between title and text.

Exercise

Find a poem in Donne. Use his phrasing but your imaginative reseeing of his meditation. Single out lines and phrases that appeal to you and move them around in relation to one another until they form a new statement. Don't worry about rhyme or meter; be satisfied to have shaped something that pleases you and may inform and please another. Make your poem at least ten lines. There are countless possibilities in this short work. Here's a beginning simply to show you how this kind of "writing" works:

> I am involved in mankind,
> A begging of misery,
> A borrowing of misery.
> I am a chapter torn from a book,
> Washed away by the sea, etc.

OF REVENGE
Francis Bacon

"... a man that studieth revenge keeps his own wounds green." So writes Francis Bacon, 17th-century essayist-moralist-philosopher. What he means is clear enough: for as long as you itch to get back at someone, you keep fresh ("green") the pain you want to avenge. Better to forget it, or at least to look at it in a wiser way. The trouble with such aphoristic advice is that when you most need it, you're usually too riled up to call it to mind. As you read and annotate "Of Revenge," keep in mind another observation on the subject, this one an old Spanish saying: "Revenge is a dish best served cold." Taking all of Bacon's argument into account and not just the quote above, judge for yourself which advice is more workable for you.

> Revenge is a kind of wild justice, which the more man's nature runs to, the more ought law to weed it out. For as for the first wrong, it doth but offend the law, but the revenge of that wrong putteth the law out

of office. Certainly in taking revenge, a man is but even with his enemy, but in passing it over, he is superior, for it is a prince's part to pardon. And Solomon, I am sure, saith, "It is the glory of a man to pass by an offense." That which is past is gone and irrevocable, and wise men have enough to do with things present and to come; therefore they do but trifle with themselves that labor in past matters. There is no man doth a wrong for the wrong's sake, but thereby to purchase himself profit, or pleasure, or honor, or the like. Therefore why should I be angry with a man for loving himself better than me? And if any man should do wrong merely out of ill nature, why, yet it is but like the thorn or briar, which prick and scratch because they can do no other. The most tolerable sort of revenge is for those wrongs which there is no law to remedy, but then let a man take heed the revenge be such as there is no law to punish; else a man's enemy is still beforehand, and it is two for one. Some, when they take revenge, are desirous the party should know whence it cometh. This the more generous. For the delight seemeth to not be so much in doing the hurt as in making the party repent. But base and crafty cowards are like the arrow that flieth in the dark. Cosmus, duke of Florence, had a desperate saying against perfidious or neglecting friends, as if those wrongs were unpardonable: "You shall read," saith he, "that we are commanded to forgive our enemies; but you never read that we are commanded to forgive our friends." But yet the spirit of Job was in better tune: "Shall we," saith he, "take good at God's hands, and not be content to take evil also?" And so of friends in a proportion. This is certain, that a man that studieth revenge keeps his own wounds green, which otherwise would heal and do well. Public revenges are for the most part fortunate, as that for the death of Caesar, for the death of Pertinax, for the death of Henry the Third of France, and many more. But in private revenges it is not so. Nay rather, vindictive persons live the life of witches, who, as they are mischievous, so end they unfortunate.

Considerations

1. Why, according to Bacon, do men do wrong? Do you agree with Bacon's explanations, or hasn't he gone far enough? (What about the statement, "no man doth a wrong for the wrong's sake"? Comment.)

2. Bacon makes a careful distinction between his attitude about open and concealed revenge. Does this distinction work today? Why or why not?

3. Bacon cites Job's observation that we have to expect to take the bitter with the sweet as being "in a better tune" than Cosmus's. What was Cosmus's "tune"? Which do you find yourself siding with?

4. "Of Revenge" is one paragraph. How does this possibly influence your understanding of the piece, your reaction to it? Would dividing it into smaller paragraphs alter its effects? Why or why not? (Try it.)

Exercise

Use either of the quotes in the headnote, or any especially quotable line from the text, as the moral for a fable or the theme of a parable.

TWO LETTERS TO TWO SONS

One institution that refuses to go out of style is the offering of "fatherly advice." Giving it is one of the compensations of aging; receiving it is one of the penalities of being young. Here, in letter form, are two letters written within a few years of each other, both of them from a father to a son. Because these *are* letters—private, even intimate; meant for an audience of one—it's nearly impossible to put aside the person of the writer and heed only the message. There's an almost physical presence in both of these letters, a nearly audible voice. And so singularly directed is the advice that we can without difficulty know something about the sons too, as well as what their relationship was with their fathers.

LORD CHESTERFIELD TO HIS SON

LONDON, *March* 27, O.S. 1747.

DEAR BOY,

Pleasure is the rock which most people split upon; they launch out with crowded sails in quest of it, but without a compass to direct their course, or reason sufficient to steer the vessel; for want of which, pain and shame, instead of Pleasure, are the returns of their voyage. Do not think that I mean to snarl at Pleasure, like a Stoic, or to preach against it, like a parson; no, I mean to point it out, and recommend it to you, like an Epicurean: I wish you a great deal; and my only view is to hinder you from mistaking it.

The character which most young men first aim at is, that of a Man of Pleasure; but they generally take it upon trust; and, instead of consulting their own taste and inclinations, they blindly adopt whatever those, with whom they chiefly converse, are pleased to call by the name of Pleasure; and a *Man of Pleasure*, in the vulgar acceptation of that phrase, means only a beastly drunkard, an abandoned ..., and a profligate swearer and curser. As it may be of use to you, I am not unwilling, though at the same time ashamed, to own, that the vices of my youth proceeded much more from my silly resolution of being what I heard called a Man of Pleasure, than from my own inclinations. I always naturally hated drinking; and yet I have often drunk, with disgust at the time, attended by great sickness the next day, only because I then considered drinking as a necessary qualification for a fine gentleman, and a Man of Pleasure.

The same as to gaming. I did not want money, and consequently had no occasion to play for it; but I thought Play another necessary ingredient in the composition of a Man of Pleasure, and accordingly I plunged into it without desire, at first; sacrificed a thousand real pleasures to it; and made myself solidly uneasy by it, for thirty of the best years of my life.

I was even absurd enough, for a little while, to swear, by way of adorning and completing the shining character which I affected; but this folly I soon laid aside, upon finding both the guilt and the indecency of it.

Thus seduced by fashion, and blindly adopting nominal pleasures, I lost real ones; and my fortune impaired, and my constitution shattered, are, I must confess, the just punishment of my errors.

Take warning then by them; choose your pleasures for yourself, and do not let them be imposed upon you. Follow nature, and not fashion: weigh the present enjoyment of your pleasures against the necessary consequences of them, and then let your own common sense determine your choice.

ALEXANDER BOSWELL TO HIS SON

If you'll at all reflect, you must be sensible what I suffer by your means. Is it not hard that after all the tenderness I have shown you and the expense and labour I have bestowed upon you, you should not only neglect your own reputation, but do what you can to bring me to shame on your account? The offices I hold entitle me to some respect, and I get it beyond my merit from all that know me except from you, who by the laws of God, nature, gratitude, and interest are bound to do what you can to make me happy, in place of striving, as it were, to find out the things will be most galling to me and making these your pursuit. What I have said will account for my not having wrote you these three months. Indeed, finding that I could be of no use to you, I had determined to abandon you, to free myself as much as possible from sharing your ignominy, and to take the strongest and most public steps for declaring to the world that I was come to this resolution. But I have been so much importuned by your excellent mother, the partaker of my distresses and shame on your account, again to write to you, and your last letter, which I received at Ayr when on the Circuit, is wrote in a strain that is becoming and speaks out that you are satisfied of some of your errors; therefore it is that you receive this from me in answer to those you sent me since the Session rose.

As in yours you desire me to give you my advice with freedom, you cannot be dissatisfied with the introduction to this letter. Every wise man would rather be informed for what things he is censured, that he may correct them, than be flattered when he don't deserve it; and he alone is a true friend who informs us of our faults. It is true such a friend is rarely to be met with, but you have had such friend in me.

You are under a mistake in your last when you write I have been struggling for authority over you. I have a right to it, indeed, but it is a thing I never wished or desired. And every step in my conduct has shown that to be the case. I always used you with lenity and tenderness; and though you were behaving in a way highly disrespectful to me, settled an annuity upon you for life and so put you in a state of independency. You say that you was struggling for independency. What you mean by becoming independent I am at a loss to conceive, for it would seem to be something very different from what anybody else would aim at. Your notion of independency seems to consist in contemning your relations and your native country, where and from whom you have a natural right to receive regard and friendship, and to live in dependence upon strangers in another country, where you have no title to notice, and from whom you have nothing to expect but fair words. They have their relations to provide, their political connections to keep up, and must look on one who comes from Scotland as an idle person to have no right to share of their bounty; in the same way that we here would never think of bestowing anything upon a vaguing Englishman except a dinner or a supper. When you left this, I told you that you would find this to be true on trial. You would not then believe it, but now you candidly own you have found the thing turn out according as I said it would do.

You desire my advice as to your after schemes in life. As to this, I have already told you I have no authority; and the mention I have made of sundry things in your conduct that vex and distress me and every friend and acquaintance of yours who has common sense, is not from authority but from friendship. I am bound by the ties of nature to love you; and though it is disagreeable still to be finding fault, I should be wanting in my duty not to tell you my mind. If you'll call to remembrance sundry of your past schemes which I advised you against and were happily disappointed, you must be sensible how dangerous it is for a young man to propose to give himself up to be governed by whims. You have escaped from a variety of ruinous snares that you were quite bent upon, and now are convinced were such as behoved to have brought you to misery. This should make you cautious in time coming. The poet says, "Felix quem faciunt aliena pericula cautum," but he must be unhappy indeed who won't learn from his own past dangers. To come more close to the point in your letter wherein you ask my advice as to what scheme of life you should follow, I shall convince you that I do not insist on authority, for though you tell me you will return to Scotland if I tell you your absence from it makes me unhappy, I will not insist either on one thing or another, but fairly and candidly lay matters before you. All that ever I insisted upon was that you should behave as the young gentlemen of your station do and act with prudence and discretion. If you set up in the character of my eldest son, you may expect regard and respect, but in the style of a vagrant must meet with the reverse. Be assured of this; for even I, who am your father and who, while you trod the paths of virtue and discretion was bound up in you and carried on all my projects with a view to you in whom I flattered myself to find a representative worthy of this respectable family—I say, even I by your strange conduct had come to the resolution of selling all off, from the principle that it is better to snuff a candle out than leave it to stink in a socket. And this purpose, though interrupted at present by your last letters being wrote in a strain that gives hopes of amendment, upon my being disappointed in that hope, I should certainly carry into execution.

As for your manner of life, I never declared positively against any kind of life except that of dissipation and vice, and as a consequence against your going into the Guards. But I told you if you chose to be a soldier and make that your business in good earnest, though I did not like the business, I should procure you a commission in a marching regiment, and had one pressed upon me by my good friend General Sinclair, now no more. But you signified your unwillingness to serve in a marching regiment, so that scheme went over and you fell to the study of the law; and I can say with truth, showed as much genius for it when you applied as any ever I knew. Be assured that your following the study of the law, whether as a lawyer or as a gentleman, to fit you to be useful in the world, is what to me is most agreeable, and what I verily think is the only thing will make you go through life agreeably; for as you well observe, without some pursuit that is rational, one of your turn can never be happy. In the plan I propose you have for your objects being respected, being useful with your advice, getting into Parliament, and having the power of conferring places, instead of going about begging one. And to these I may add, you have the satisfaction of making your parents happy and adding more lustre to the family you have the honour to be come of. And if you were truly fixed on this plan, I would make no difficulty, when you were a little settled from your reelings, to let you go abroad for a while. But if you are bent on the Army, as you say you have the offer of an ensigncy in a marching regiment, though I am far from liking the thing, if better cannot be, take it, and hold by that as your business for life. But be more on your guard for the future against mimicry, journals, and publications, still acting with prudence and discretion, which is as necessary for a soldier as for a man of any other employment. I would further recommend to you to endeavor to find out some person of worth who may be a friend, not one who will say as you say when with you and when he is away will make a jest of you as much as of any other.

Your mother is in her ordinary, so is Johnny. Both remember you with affection.

Farewell. It is in your power to make us all happy and yourself too. May God dispose you to the best.

Considerations

1. The Scots have a reputation for being dour—stern and humorless, that is. Although it amounts to just one more ethnic stereotype, it *is* tempting to apply to Boswell. Is he, though, entirely without humor or affection? Look deeply, and support your answers with specific citations.

2. What do we know of Chesterfield? About his relationship with his son? What is he really counseling here (maybe without knowing it himself)? Does Chesterfield see himself as others probably see him? As his son sees him?

3. Both letter-writers give us insights into how they see their sons. What is each father especially worried about? Under what label(s) would you group their concerns today? What, in your experience, is the chief theme of parental advice today?

Which of the two men are you more drawn to? How do you know? Which letter reveals more about its recipient? Lastly, from what these writers reveal of themselves, which would you prefer as a father, and why?

4. Reconstrue Bacon's essay as a letter of similar intent. If the essay had begun with a salutation and an introductory sentence along the lines of "I write to you in order that you may know my feelings about your latest action . . . ," and had it ended with a complimentary close, would it take on the appearance of a letter somewhat like the other two? If so, a letter to the writer's own offspring? What is/isn't letter-like about the Bacon piece?

HINTS TOWARD AN ESSAY ON CONVERSATION
Jonathan Swift

The way Swift begins this essay, you can be led to believe that it will shape itself to resemble Franklin's "Arriving at Perfection," that here is another formula for self-improvement. In fact, the author takes pains to establish that "without any great genius or study" the reader can expect to master the art of conversation. "Nature," Swift observes, "has left every man a capacity of being agreeable," and what should follow from this, we feel, is a lesson on how to make the most of this natural talent for being nice. But it doesn't take long for Swift the satirist to surface, and for the alert reader to discover that "Hints Toward an Essay on Conversation" bristles with annoyance at boorish conversationalists; is not meant to improve anybody but instead to let off steam, as if Swift had just stalked out of a drawingroom filled with dreadful types and had to get his feelings down on paper. Not only that, however; there's the richness of Swift's wit to take into account, and past that the names that come to mind for you and me as the author marches us from one type of fool to the next. Perhaps if we could roll the Franklin and D. H. Lawrence pieces into one essay, the result would be approximately the same as Swift's.

> I have observed few obvious subjects to have been so seldom or at least so slightly, handled as this; and indeed I know few so difficult to be treated as it ought, not yet upon which there seems so much to be said.
> Most things pursued by men for the happiness of public or private life, our wit or folly have so refined, that they seldom subsist but in idea; a true friend, a good marriage, a perfect form of government, with some others, require so many ingredients, so good in their several kinds, and so much niceness in mixing them, that for some thousands of years

men have despaired of reducing their schemes to perfection: but in conversation it is, or might be, otherwise; for here we are only to avoid a multitude of errors, which, although a matter of some difficulty, may be in every man's power, for want of which it remains as mere an idea as the other. Therefore it seems to me, that the truest way to understand conversation, is to know the faults and errors to which it is subject, and from thence every man to form maxims to himself whereby it may be regulated, because it requires few talents to which most men are not born, or at least may not acquire, without any great genius or study. For nature has left every man a capacity of being agreeable, though not of shining in company; and there are a hundred men sufficiently qualified for both, who, by a very few faults that they might correct in half an hour, are not so much as tolerable.

I was prompted to write my thoughts upon this subject by mere indignation, to reflect that so useful and innocent a pleasure, so fitted for every period and condition of life, and so much in all men's power, should be so much neglected and abused.

And in this discourse it will be necessary to note those errors that are obvious, as well as others which are seldomer observed, since there are few so obvious, or acknowledged, into which most men, some time or other, are not apt to run.

For instance: nothing is more generally exploded than the folly of talking too much; yet I rarely remember to have seen five people together, where some one among them has not been predominant in that kind, to the great constraint and disgust of all the rest. But among such as deal in multitudes of words, none are comparable to the sober deliberate talker, who proceeds with much thought and caution, makes his preface, branches out into several digressions, finds a hint that puts him in mind of another story, which he promises to tell you when this is done; comes back regularly to his subject, cannot readily call to mind some person's name, holding his head, complains of his memory; the whole company all this while in suspense; at length says, it is no matter, and so goes on. And, to crown the business, it perhaps proves at last a story the company has heard fifty times before; or, at best, some insipid adventure of the relater.

Another general fault in conversation is that of those who affect to talk of themselves: some, without any ceremony, will run over the history of their lives; will relate the annals of their diseases, with the several symptoms and circumstances of them; will enumerate the hardships and injustice they have suffered in court, in parliament, in love, or in law. Others are more dexterous, and with great art will lie on the watch to hook in their own praise: they will call a witness to remember they always foretold what would happen in such a case, but none would believe them; they advised such a man from the beginning, and told him the consequences, just as they happened; but he would have his own way. Others make a vanity of telling their faults; they are the strangest men in the world; they cannot dissemble; they own it is a folly; they have lost abundance of advantages by it; but if you would give them the world, they cannot help it; there is something in their nature that abhors insincerity and constraint; with many other insufferable topics of the same altitude.

Of such mighty importance every man is to himself, and ready to think he is so to others; without once making this easy and obvious reflection, that his affairs can have no more weight with other men, than theirs have with him; and how little that is he is sensible enough.

Where a company has met, I often have observed two persons discover, by some accident, that they were bred together at the same school or university; after which the rest are condemned to silence, and to listen while these two are refreshing each other's memory, with the arch tricks and passages of themselves and their comrades.

I know a great officer of the army who will sit for some time with a supercilious and impatient silence, full of anger and contempt for those who are talking; at length, of a sudden, demanding audience, decide the matter in a short dogmatical way; then withdraw within himself again, and vouchsafe to talk no more, until his spirits circulate again to the same point.

There are some faults in conversation which none are so subject to as the men of wit, nor ever so much as when they are with each other. If they have opened their mouths without endeavoring to say a witty thing, they think it is so many words lost: it is a torment to the hearers, as much as to themselves, to see them upon the rack for invention, and in perpetual constraint, with so little success. They must do something extraordinary in order to acquit themselves, and answer their character, else the standers-by may be disappointed, and be apt to think them only like the rest of mortals. I have known two men of wit industriously brought together in order to entertain the company, where they have made a very ridiculous figure, and provided all the mirth at their own expense.

I know a man of wit who is never easy but where he can be allowed to dictate and preside; he neither expects to be informed or entertained, but to display his own talents. His business is to be good company, and not good conversation; and therefore he chooses to frequent those who are content to listen, and profess themselves his admirers. And indeed the worst conversation I ever remember to have heard in my life was that at Will's coffee-house, where the wits (as they were called) used formerly to assemble; that is to say, five or six men who had writ plays, or at least prologues, or had share in a miscellany, came thither, and entertained one another with their trifling composures, in so important an air as if they had been the noblest efforts of human nature, or that the fate of kingdoms depended on them; and they were usually attended with an humble audience of young students from the inns of court, or the universities; who, at due distance, listened to these oracles, and returned home with great contempt for their law and philosophy, their heads filled with trash, under the name of politeness, criticism, and belles lettres.

By these means the poets, for many years past, were all overrun with pedantry. For, as I take it, the word is not properly used; because pedantry is the too frequent or unseasonable obtruding of our own knowledge in common discourse, and placing too great a value upon it; by which definition, men of the court, or the army, may be as guilty of pedantry as a philosopher or a divine; and it is the same vice in women, when they are over copious upon the subject of their petticoats, or their fans, or their china. For which reason, although it be a piece of prudence, as well as good manners, to put men upon talking on subjects they are best versed in, yet that is a liberty a wise man could hardly take; because, beside the imputation of pedantry, it is what he would never improve by.

The great town is usually provided with some player, or mimic, or buffoon, who has a general reception at the good tables; familiar and domestic with persons of the first quality, and usually sent for at every meeting to divert the company; against which I have no objection. You go there as to a farce or a puppetshow; your business is only to laugh in season, either out of inclination or civility, while this merry companion is acting his part. It is a business he has undertaken, and we are to suppose he is paid for his day's work. I only quarrel, when, in select and private meetings, where men of wit and learning are invited to pass an evening, this jester should be admitted to run over his circle of tricks, and make the whole company unfit for any other conversation, beside the indignity of confounding men's talents at so shameful a rate.

Raillery is the finest part of conversation; but, as it is our usual custom to counterfeit and adulterate whatever is too clear for us, so we have done with this, and turned it all into what is generally called repartee, or being smart; just as when an expensive fashion comes up, those who are not able to reach it, content themselves with some paltry imitation. It now passes for raillery to run a man down in discourse, to put him out of countenance, and make him ridiculous; sometimes to expose the defects of his person or understanding; on all occasions, he is obliged not to be angry, to avoid the imputation of not being able to take a jest. It is admirable to observe one who is dexterous at this art, singling out a weak adversary, getting the laugh on his side, and then carrying all before him. The French, from whence we borrow the word, have a quite different idea of the thing, and so had we in the politer age of our fathers. Raillery was to say something that at first appeared a reproach or reflection, but, by some turn of wit, unexpected and surprising, ended always in a compliment, and to the advantage of the person it was addressed to. And surely one of the best rules in conversation is, never to say a thing which any of the company can reasonably wish we had rather left unsaid: nor can there anything be well more contrary to the ends for which people meet together, than to part unsatisfied with each other or themselves.

There are two faults in conversation, which appear very different, yet arise from the same root, and are equally blameable; I mean an impatience to interrupt others; and the uneasiness of being interrupted ourselves. The two chief ends of conversation are to entertain and improve those we are among, or to receive those benefits ourselves; which whoever will consider, cannot easily run into either of these two errors; because, when any man speaks in company, it is to be supposed he does it for his hearers' sake, and not his own; so that common discretion will teach us not to force their attention, if they are not willing to lend it; nor, on the other side, to interrupt him who is in possession, because that is in the grossest manner to give the preference to our own good sense.

There are some people whose good manners will not suffer them to interrupt you, but, what is almost as bad, will discover an abundance of impatience, and lie upon the watch until you have done, because they have started something in their own thoughts, which they long to be delivered of. Meantime, they are so far from regarding what passes, that their imaginations are wholly turned upon what they have in reserve, for fear it should slip out of their memory; and thus they confine their invention, which might otherwise range over a hundred things full as good, and that might be much more naturally introduced.

There is a sort of rude familiarity, which some people, by practicing among their intimates, have introduced into their general conversation, and would have it pass for innocent freedom or humor; which is a dangerous experiment in our northern climate, where all the little decorum and politeness we have are purely forced by art, and are so ready to lapse into barbarity. This, among the Romans, was the raillery of slaves, of which we have many instances in Plautus. It seems to have been introduced among us by Cromwell, who, by preferring the scum of the people, made it a court entertainment, of which I have heard many particulars; and, considering all things were turned upside down, it was reasonable and judicious: although it was a piece of policy found out to ridicule a point of honor in the other extreme, when the smallest word misplaced among gentlemen ended in a duel.

There are some men excellent at telling a story, and provided with a plentiful stock of them, which they can draw out upon occasion in all companies; and, considering how low conversation runs now among us, it is subject to two unavoidable defects, frequent repetition, and being soon exhausted; so that, whoever values this gift in himself, has need of a good memory, and ought frequently to shift his company, that he may not discover the weakness of his fund; for those who are thus endued have seldom any other revenue, but live upon the main stock.

Great speakers in public are seldom agreeable in private conversation, whether their faculty be natural, or acquired by practice, and often venturing. Natural elocution, although it may seem a paradox, usually springs from a barrenness of invention, and of words; by which men who have only one stock of notions upon every subject, and one set of phrases to express them in, they swim upon the superficies, and offer themselves on every occasion; therefore men of much learning, and who know the compass of a language, are generally the worst talkers on a sudden, until much practice has inured and emboldened them; because they are confounded with plenty of matter, variety of notions and of words, which they cannot readily choose, but are perplexed and entangled by too great a choice; which is no disadvantage in private conversation; where, on the other side, the talent of haranguing is, of all others, most unsupportable.

Nothing has spoiled men more for conversation than the character of being wits; to support which they never fail of encouraging a number of followers and admirers, who list themselves in their service, wherein they find their accounts on both sides by pleasing their mutual vanity. This has given the former such an air of superiority, and made the latter so pragmatical, that neither of them are well to be endured. I say nothing here of the itch of dispute and contradiction, telling of lies, or of those who are troubled with the diseases called the wandering of the thoughts, so that they are never present in mind at what passes in discourse; for whoever labors under any of these possessions, is as unfit for conversation as a madman in Bedlam.

I think I have gone over most of the errors in conversation that have fallen under my notice or memory, except some that are merely personal, and others too gross to need exploding; such as lewd or profane talk; but I pretend only to treat the errors of conversation in general, and not the several subjects of discourse, which would be infinite. Thus we see how human nature is most debased, by the abuse of that faculty which is held the great distinction between men and brutes: and how little advantage we make of that, which might be the greatest, the most lasting, and the most innocent, as well as useful pleasure of life.

Considerations

1. Do you find yourself agreeing with Swift that "The two chief ends of conversation are to entertain and improve those we are among, or to receive those benefits ourselves"? Does this seem to hold true today? If not, why not? What "chief ends" may have replaced Swift's?

2. What evidence is there that this not only isn't a recipe, nor even a detached criticism of conversational faults, but that it may well be an attack on some actual individuals?

3. I find six conversational types delineated by Swift. How would you label those that you find? ("Egotist" seems to cover one type. Do you agree?)

Exercises

1. Respond to Swift's types with names, actual acquaintances, public figures, well-known fictional characters. Form a list, perhaps three or four for each category, of people with the irksome conversational habits Swift describes. Have other conversational types evolved since Swift's time? Label and describe them.

2. Develop a short piece with an intent similar to Swift's: to put in public form some aspect of human behavior that has long irked you. You may stick with Swift's subject, conversation and its despoilers. Most of us, though, have our own favorite sources of annoyance—mannerisms, habits, qualities of character that set our teeth on edge, whether it's the way certain people eat, behave at sports events, dress, act when they've drunk too much, etc.

ON THE PLEASURES OF PAINTING
William Hazlitt

Although Hazlitt here professes a love of painting and a distaste for writing, it was for the latter that he was best-known. Most often forcefully, Hazlitt brought to paper his beliefs about art and literature, as well as a multitude of other subjects. Yet he often expressed anger and despair about his involvement with the written word: "What abortions are these essays! What ... crooked reasons, what lame conclusions!" he exclaims in another piece. As you read "On the Pleasures of Painting," consider your own possibly negative experiences with writing and any art form that has given you special satisfaction, and compare your experiences with Hazlitt's.

"There is a pleasure in painting which none but painters know." In writing, you have to contend with the world; in painting, you have only to carry on a friendly strife with Nature. You sit down to your task, and are happy. From the moment that you take up the pencil, and look Nature in the face, you are at peace with your heart. No angry passions rise to disturb the silent progress of the work, to shake the hand, or dim the brow: no irritable humors are set afloat: you have no absurd opinions to combat, no point to strain, no adversary to crush, no fool to annoy—you are actuated by fear or favor to no man. There is "no juggling here," no sophistry, no intrigue, no tampering with the evidence, no attempt to make black white, or white black: but you resign yourself into the hands of a greater power, that of Nature, with the simplicity of a child, and the devotion of an enthusiast—"study with joy her manner, and with rapture taste her style." The mind is calm, and full at the same time. The hand and eye are equally employed. In tracing the commonest object, a plant or the stump of a tree, you learn something every moment. You perceive unexpected differences, and discover likenesses where you looked for no such thing. You try to set down what you see—find out your error, and correct it. You need not play tricks, or purposely mistake: with all your pains, you are still far short of the mark. Patience grows out of the endless pursuit, and turns it into a luxury. A streak in a flower, a wrinkle in a leaf, a tinge in a cloud, a stain in an old wall or ruin grey, are seized with avidity as the *spolia optima* of this sort of mental warfare, and furnish out labor for another half day. The hours pass away untold, without chagrin, and without weariness; nor would you ever wish to pass them otherwise. Innocence is joined with industry, pleasure with business; and the mind is satisfied, though it is not engaged in thinking or in doing harm.

I have not much pleasure in writing these Essays, or in reading them afterwards; though I own I now and then meet with a phrase that I like, or a thought that strikes me as a true one. But after I begin them, I am only anxious to get to the end of them, which I am not sure I shall do, for I seldom see my way a page or even a sentence beforehand; and when I have as by a miracle escaped, I trouble myself little more about them. I sometimes have to write them twice over: then it is necessary to read the *proof*, to prevent mistakes by the printer; so that by the time they appear in a tangible shape, and one can con them over with a conscious, sidelong glance to the public approbation, they have lost their gloss and relish, and become "more tedious than a twice-told tale." For a person to read his own works with any great delight, he ought first to forget that he ever wrote them. Familiarity naturally breeds contempt. It is, in fact, like poring fondly over a piece of blank paper: from repetition, the words convey no distinct meaning to the mind, are mere idle sounds, except that our vanity claims an interest and property in them. I have more satisfaction in my own thoughts than in dictating them to others: words are necessary to explain the impression of certain things upon me to the reader, but they rather weaken and draw a veil over than strengthen it to myself. However I might say with the poet, "My mind to me a kingdom is," yet I have little ambition "to set a throne or chair of state in the understandings of other men." The ideas we cherish most, exist best in a kind of shadowy abstraction,

"Pure in the last recesses of the mind;"

and derive neither force nor interest from being exposed to public view. They are old established acquaintance, and any change in them, arising from the adventitious ornaments of style or dress, is hardly to their advantage. After I have once written on a subject, it goes out of my mind: my feelings about it have been melted down into words, and *them* I forget. I have, as it were, discharged my memory of its old habitual reckoning, and rubbed out the score of real sentiment. In future, it exists only for the sake of others. But I cannot say, from my own experience, that the same process takes place in transferring our ideas to canvas; they gain more than they lose in the mechanical transformation. One is never tired of painting, because you have to set down not what you knew already, but what you have just discovered. In the former case, you translate feelings into words; in the latter, names into things. There is a continual creation out of nothing going on. With every stroke of the brush, a new field of inquiry is laid open; new difficulties arise, and new triumphs are prepared over them. By comparing the imitation with the original, you see what you have done, and how much you have still to do. The test of the senses is severer than that of fancy, and an over-match even for the delusions of our self-love. One part of a picture shames another, and you determine to paint up to yourself, if you cannot come up to nature. Every object becomes lustrous from the light thrown back upon it by the mirror of art: and by the aid of the pencil we may be said to touch and handle the objects of sight. The air-wove visions that hover on the verge of existence have a bodily presence given them on the canvas: the form of beauty is changed into a substance: the dream and the glory of the universe is made "palpable to feeling as to sight." And see! a rainbow starts from the canvas, with all its humid train of glory, as if it were drawn from its cloudy arch in heaven. The spangled landscape glitters with drops of dew after the shower. The "fleecy fools" show their coats in the gleams of the setting sun. The shepherds pipe their farewell notes in the fresh evening air. And is this bright vision made from a dead dull blank, like a bubble reflecting the mighty fabric of the universe? Who would think this miracle of Ruben's pencil possible to be performed? Who, having seen it, would not spend his life to do the like? See how the rich fallows, the bare stubble-field, the scanty harvest-home, drag in Rembrandt's landscapes! How often have I looked at them and nature, and tried to do the same, till the very "light thickened," and there was an earthiness in the feeling of the air! There is no end of the refinements of art and nature in this respect. One may look at the misty glimmering horizon till the eye dazzles and the imagination is lost, in hopes to transfer the whole interminable expanse at one blow upon the canvas. Wilson said he endeavored to paint the effect of the motes dancing in the setting sun. At another time, a friend coming into his painting-room, when he was sitting on the ground in a melancholy posture, observed that his picture looked like a landscape after a shower: he started up with the greatest delight, and said, "That is the effect I intended to represent, but thought I had failed." Wilson was neglected; and, by degrees, neglected his art to apply himself to brandy. His hand became unsteady, so that it was only by repeated attempts that he could reach the place, or produce the effect he aimed at; and when he had done a little to a picture, he would say to any acquaintance who chanced to drop in, "I have painted enough for one day: come, let us go somewhere." It was not so Claude left his pictures, or his studies on the banks of the Tiber, to go in search of other enjoyments, or ceased to gaze upon the glittering sunny vales and distant hills; and while his eye drank in the clear sparkling hues and lovely forms of nature, his hand stamped them on the lucid canvas to remain there for ever! One of the most delightful parts of my life was one fine summer, when I used to walk out of an evening to catch the last light of the sun, gemming the green slopes or russet lawns, and gilding tower or tree, while the blue sky gradually turning to purple and gold, or skirted with dusky grey, hung its broad marble pavement over all, as we see it in the great master of Italian landscape. But to come to a more particular explanation of the subject.

The first head I ever tried to paint was an old woman with the upper part of the face shaded by her bonnet, and I certainly labored it with great perseverance. It took me numberless sittings to do it. I have it by me still, and sometimes look at it with surprise, to think how much pains were thrown away to little purpose, yet not altogether in vain, if it taught me to see good in every thing, and to know that there is nothing vulgar in nature seen with the eye of science or of true art. Refinement creates beauty everywhere: it is the grossness of the spectator that discovers nothing but grossness in the object. Be this as it may, I spared no pains to do my best. If art was long, I thought that life was so too at that moment. I got in the general effect the first day; and pleased and surprised enough I was at my success. The rest was a work of time—of weeks and months (if need were) of patient toil and careful finishing. I had seen an old head by Rembrandt at Burleigh-House, and if I could produce a head at all like Rembrandt in a year, in my life-time, it would be glory and felicity and wealth and fame enough for me! The head I had seen at Burleigh was an exact and wonderful facsimile of nature, and I resolved to make mine (as nearly as I could) an exact facsimile of nature. I did not then, nor do I now believe with Sir Joshua, that the perfection of art consists in giving general appearances without individual details, but in giving general appearances with individual details. Otherwise, I had done my work the first day. But I saw something more in nature than general effect, and I thought it worth my while to give it in the picture. There was a gorgeous effect of light and shade: but there was a delicacy as well as depth in the *chiaroscuro,* which I was bound to follow into all its dim and scarce perceptible variety of tone and shadow. Then I had to make the transition from a strong light to as dark a shade, preserving the masses, but gradually softening off the intermediate parts. It was so in nature: the difficulty was to make it so in the copy. I tried, and failed again and again; I strove harder, and succeeded, as I thought. The wrinkles in Rembrandt were not hard lines; but broken and irregular. I saw the same appearance in nature, and strained every nerve to give it. If I could hit off this crumbling appearance, and insert the reflected light in the furrows of old age in half a morning, I did not think I had lost a day. Beneath the shrivelled yellow parchment look of the skin, there was here and there a streak of blood-color tinging the face; this I made a point of conveying, and did not cease to compare what I saw with what I did (with jealous, lynx-eyed watchfulness) till I succeeded to the best of my ability and judgment. How many revisions were there! How many attempts to catch an expression which I had seen the day before! How often did we strive to get the old position, and wait for the return of the same light! There was a puckering up of the lips, a cautious introversion of the eye under the shadow of the bonnet, indicative of the feebleness and suspicion of old age, which at last we managed, after many trials and some quarrels, to a tolerable nicety. The picture was never finished, and I might have gone on with it to the present hour.* I used to set it on the ground when my day's work was done, and saw revealed to me with swimming eyes the birth of new hopes, and of a new world of objects. The painter thus learns to look at nature with different eyes. He before saw her "as in a glass darkly, but now face to face." He understands the texture and meaning of the visible universe, and "sees into the life of things," not by the help of mechanical instruments, but of the improved exercise of his faculties, and an intimate sympathy with nature. The meanest thing is not lost upon him, for he looks at it with an eye to itself, not merely to his own vanity or interest, or the opinion of the world. Even where there is neither beauty nor use—if that ever were—still there is truth, and a sufficient source of gratification in the indulgence of curiosity and activity of mind. The humblest painter is a true scholar; and the best of scholars—the scholar of nature. For myself, and for the real comfort and satisfaction of the thing, I had rather have been Jan Steen, or Gerard Dow, than the greatest casuist or philologer that ever lived. The painter does not view things in clouds or "mist, the common gloss of theologians,"but applies the same standard of truth and disinterested spirit of inquiry, that influence his daily practice, to other subjects. He perceives form; he distinguishes character. He reads men and books with an intuitive glance. He is a critic as well as a connoisseur. The conclusions he draws are clear and convincing, because they are taken from actual experience. He is not a fanatic, a dupe, or a slave: for the habit of seeing for himself also disposes him to judge for himself. The most sensible men I know (taken as a class) are painters; that is, they are the most lively observers of what passes in the world about them, and the closest observers of what passes in their own minds. From their profession they in general mix more with the world than authors; and if they have not the same fund of acquired knowledge, are obliged to rely more on individual sagacity. I might mention the names of Opie, Fuseli, Northcote, as persons distinguished for striking description and acquaintance with the subtle traits of character.** Painters in ordinary society, or in obscure situations

---

*It is at present covered with a thick slough of oil and varnish (the perishable vehicle of the English school) like an envelope of goldbeaters' skin, so as to be hardly visible.

**Men in business, who are answerable with their fortunes for the consequences of their opinions, and are therefore accustomed to ascertain pretty accurately the grounds on which they act, before they commit themselves on the event, are often men of remarkably quick and sound judgments. Artists in like manner must know tolerably well what they are about, before they can bring the result of their observations to the test of ocular demonstration.

where their value is not known, and they are treated with neglect and indifference, have sometimes a forward self-sufficiency of manner: but this is not so much their fault as that of others. Perhaps their want of regular education may also be in fault in such cases. Richardson, who is very tenacious of the respect in which the profession ought to be held, tells a story of Michael Angelo, that after a quarrel between him and Pope Julius II. "upon account of a slight the artist conceived the pontiff had put upon him, Michael Angelo was introduced by a bishop, who, thinking to serve the artist by it, made it an argument that the Pope should be reconciled to him, because men of his profession were commonly ignorant, and of no consequence otherwise: his holiness, enraged at the bishop, struck him with his staff, and told him, it was he that was the blockhead, and affronted the man himself would not offend; the prelate was driven out of the chamber and Michael Angelo had the Pope's benediction accompanied with presents. This bishop had fallen into the vulgar error, and was rebuked accordingly."

Besides the employment of the mind, painting exercises the body. It is a mechanical as well as a liberal art. To do any thing, to dig a hole in the ground, to plant a cabbage, to hit a mark, to move a shuttle, to work a pattern,—in a word, to attempt to produce any effect, and to *succeed*, has something in it that gratifies the love of power, and carries off the restless activity of the mind of man. Indolence is a delightful but distressing state: we must be doing something to be happy. Action is no less necessary than thought to the instinctive tendencies of the human frame; and painting combines them both incessantly.* The hand furnishes a practical test of the correctness of the eye; and the eye, thus admonished, imposes fresh tasks of skill and industry upon the hand. Every stroke tells, as the verifying of a new truth; and every new observation, the instant it is made, passes into an act and emanation of the will. Every step is nearer what we wish, and yet there is always more to do. In spite of the facility, the fluttering grace, the evanescent hues, that play round the pencil of Rubens and Vandyke, however I may admire, I do not envy them this power so much as I do the slow, patient, laborious execution of Correggio, Leonardo da Vinci, and Andrea del Sarto, where every touch appears conscious of its charge, emulous of truth, and where the painful artist has so distinctly wrought.

"That you might also say his picture thought!"

In the one case, the colors seem breathed on the canvas as by magic, the work and the wonder of a moment: in the other, they seem inlaid in the body of the work, and as if it took the artist years of unremitting labor, and of delightful never-ending progress to perfection.** Who

---

*The famous Schiller used to say, that he found the great happiness of life, after all, to consist in the discharge of some mechanical duty.

**The rich *impasting* of Titian and Giorgione combines something of the advantages of both these styles, the felicity of the one with the carefulness of the other, and is perhaps to be preferred to either.

would not wish ever to come to the close of such works,—not to dwell on them, to return to them, to be wedded to them to the last? Rubens, with his florid, rapid style, complained that when he had just learned his art, he should be forced to die. Leonardo in the slow advances of his, had lived long enough!

Painting is not, like writing, what is properly understood by a sedentary employment. It requires not indeed a strong, but a continued and steady exertion of muscular power. The precision and delicacy of the manual operation makes up for the want of vehemence,—as to balance himself for any time in the same position the rope-dancer must strain every nerve. Painting for a whole morning gives one as excellent an appetite for one's dinner, as old Abraham Tucker acquired for his by riding over Banstead Downs. It is related of Sir Joshua Reynolds, that "he took no other exercise than what he used in his painting room,"—the writer means, in walking backwards and forwards to look at his picture; but the act of painting itself, of laying on the colors in the proper place and proper quantity, was a much harder exercise than this alternate receding from and returning to the picture. The last would be rather a relaxation and relief than an effort. It is not to be wondered at, that an artist like Sir Joshua, who delighted so much in the sensual and practical part of his art, should have found himself at a considerable loss when the decay of his sight precluded him, for the last year or two of his life, from the following up of his profession,—"the source," according to his own remark, "of thirty years uninterrupted enjoyment and prosperity to him." It is only those who never think at all, or else who have accustomed themselves to brood invariably on abstract ideas, that never feel *ennui*.

To give one instance more, and then I will have done with this rambling discourse. One of my first attempts was a picture of my father, who was then in a green old age, with strong-marked features, and scarred with the small-pox. I drew it with a broad light crossing the face, looking down, with spectacles on, reading. The book was Shaftesbury's Characteristics, in a fine old binding, with Gribelin's etchings. My father would as lief it had been any other book; but for him to read was to be content, was "riches fineless." The sketch promised well; and I set to work to finish it, determined to spare no time nor pains. My father was willing to sit as long as I pleased; for there is a natural desire in the mind of man to sit for one's picture, to be the object of continued attention, to have one's likeness multiplied; and besides his satisfaction in the picture, he had some pride in the artist, though he would rather I should have written a sermon than painted like Rembrandt or like Raphael! Those winter days, with the gleams of sunshine coming through the chapel-windows, and cheered by the notes of the robin-redbreast in our garden (that "ever in the haunch of winter sings")—as my afternoon's work drew to a close,—were among the happiest of my life. When I gave the effect I intended to any part of the picture for which I had prepared my colors, when I imitated the roughness of the skin by a lucky stroke of the pencil, when I hit the clear pearly tone of a vein, when I gave the ruddy complexion of health, the blood circulating under the broad shadows of one side of the face, I thought my fortune made; or rather it was already more than made, in my fancying that I might one day be able to say with Correggio, '*I also am a painter!*' It was an idle thought, a boy's conceit; but it did not make me less happy at the time. I used regularly to set my work in the chair to look at it through the long evenings; and many a time did I return to take leave of it, before I could go to bed at night. I remember sending it with a throbbing heart to the Exhibition, and seeing it hung up there by the side of one of the Honorable Mr Skeffington (now Sir George). There was nothing in common between them, but that they were the portraits of two very good-natured men. I think, but am not sure, that I finished this portrait (or another afterwards) on the same day that the news of the battle of Austerlitz came; I walked out in the afternoon, and, as I returned, saw the evening star set over a poor man's cottage with other thoughts and feelings than I shall ever have again. Oh for the revolution of the great Platonic year, that those times might come over again! I could sleep out the three hundred and sixty-five thousand intervening years very contentedly!

The picture is left: the table, the chair, the window where I learned to construe Livy, the chapel where my father preached, remain where they were; but he himself is gone to rest, full of years, of faith, of hope, and charity!

Considerations

1. Hazlitt favors painting over writing, but he nevertheless observes in another essay that "Words are the signs which . . . define the objects of the highest import to the human mind . . . ." Reflect on this statement before agreeing or disagreeing. What "objects" is Hazlitt possibly referring to? If you agree generally with the observation, generate a short list of your own "objects of the highest import" and explain why words define them better than any other symbolic system. If you disagree, explain how another system is more valuable than language for conveying the most important matters of mind.

2. What does Hazlitt mean by "In writing you have to contend with the world"? How contend? Does he refer only to people whose words are read by many, what we'd today call "professional writers"? As a writer, have you ever felt that you were *contending* with large, impersonal forces (or even a large, impersonal instructor)? Explain.

3. Interestingly, much that Hazlitt says about the experience of painting is applied by modern theorists to the act of *writing*. Which of these comments relates, if only figuratively, to any writing experience you can remember? Explain.

> . . . you take up the pencil, and look Nature in the face, [and] you are at peace. . . .

...no tampering with the evidence, no attempt to make black white....

The mind is calm, and full at the same time. The hand and eye are equally employed.

...you learn something every moment. You perceive unexpected differences, and discover likenesses where you looked for no such thing. You try to set down what you see—find out your error, and correct it.

He [the painter, but for our purposes, the writer] perceives form, he distinguishes character. He reads men and books with an intuitive eye.

I... did not cease to compare what I saw with what I did... till I succeeded to the best of my ability and judgment. How many revisions were there!

4. In the last long paragraph of this essay we may come closer to knowing William Hazlitt than is possible from most of his other works. What do you think of the man, and why? What clues about the self must a writer (you included) seemingly reveal, even without wishing to?

5. Without sneaking a look at an encyclopedia or other reference work, and mostly for fun, (a) place these authors in chronological order: Jonathan Swift, Lord Chesterfield, William Hazlitt, Francis Bacon; and (b) explain how you arrived at the ordering.

Exercise

There's little merit in asking that you imitate Hazlitt. His style is dated, and even back when it wasn't something about how and what he wrote often managed to infuriate nearly everyone. But you *can* write with his conviction, even passion, about something—some deeply gratifying spiritual or intellectual experience—that lends itself to comparison with some lesser experience. (One example offered by a student: running a good horse through a jump course compared to running a motorcycle over a motocross course.)

TOM PRY AND TOM PRY'S WIFE
Charles Lamb

It's unlikely that Charles Lamb ever walked in St. James's Park with Tom Pry, or ever accompanied Mrs. Pry to the Grimstones or Gubbinses. This amusing and somehow familiar couple are almost certainly fictions, concoctions of Lamb's sparkling imagination. He created hundreds of such people. In fact, he even invented a persona named *Elia* to write many of his essays. Yet Lamb's people vibrate with life; they are drawn with remarkable attention to the human model. We have no trouble agreeing with Lamb that "something answering to them has a being." Beyond the light amusement such pieces offer, Lamb would have us contemplate that "something"—the particular quality of being that, abstracted, describes mankind.

TOM PRY

My friend TOM PRY is a kind, warm-hearted fellow, with no one failing in the world but an excess of the passion of *Curiosity*. He knows everybody's name, face, and domestic affairs. He scents out a match three months before the parties themselves are quite agreed about it. Like the man in the play, *homo est* and no human interest escapes him. I have sometimes wondered how he gets all his information. Mere inquisitiveness would not do his business. Certainly the bodily make has much to do with the character. The auricular organs in my friend Tom do not lie flapping against his head as with common mortals, but they perk up like those of a hare at form. The lowest sound cannot elude him. Every parlor and drawing-room is to him a whispering gallery. His own name, pronounced in the utmost compression of susurration, they say, he catches at a quarter furlong interval. I suspect sometimes that the faculty of hearing with him is analogous to the scent in some animals. He seems hung round with ears, like the pagan emblem of Fame, and to imbibe sounds at every pore. You cannot take a walk of business or pleasure, but you are taxed with it by him next morning, with some shrewd guess at the purpose of it. You dread him as you would an inquisitor, or the ubiquitarian power of the old Secret Tribunal. He is the bird of the air, who sees the matter. He has lodgings at a corner house, which looks out four ways; and though you go a roundabout way to evade his investigation, you are somehow seen notwithstanding. He sees at multiplied angles. He is a sort of second memory to all his friends, an excellent refresher to a dull or oblivious conscience; for he can repeat to you at any given time all that ever you have done in your life. He should have been a death-bed confessor. His appetite for information is omnivorous. To get at the *name* only of a stranger whom he passes in the street, he counts a Godsend; what further he can pick up is a luxury. His friends joke with him about his innocent propensity, but the bent of nature is too deeply burned in to be removed with such forks. *Usque recurrit.* I myself in particular had been rallying him pretty sharply one day upon the foible, and it seemed to impress him a little. He asked no more questions that morning. But walking with him in St. James's Park in the evening, we met an old Gentleman unknown to him, who bowed to me. I could see that Tom kept his passion within with great struggles. Silence was observed for ten minutes, and I was congratulating myself on my friend's mastery over this inordinate appetite of knowing every thing, when we had not past the Queen's gate a pace of two, but the fire burnt within him, and he said, as if with indifference, "By the way, who was that friend of yours who bowed to you just now?" He has a place in the Post-office, which I think he chose for the pleasure of reading superscriptions. He is too honorable a man, I am sure, to get clandestinely at the contents of a letter not addressed to him, but the outside he cannot resist. It tickles him. He plays about the flame, as it were;

contents himself with a superficial caress, when he can get at nothing more substantial. He has a handsome seal, which he keeps to proffer to such of his friends as have not one in readiness, when they would fold up an epistle; nay, he will seal it for you, and pays himself by discovering the direction. As I have no directionary secrets, I generally humor him with pretending to have left my seal at home (though I carry a rich gold one, which was my grandfather's, always about me), to gratify his harmless inclination. He is the cleverest of sealing a letter of any man I ever knew, and turns out the cleanest impressions. It is a neat but slow operation with him—he has so much more time to drink in the direction. With all this curiosity, he is the finest tempered fellow in the world. You may banter him from morning to night, but never ruffle his temper. We sometimes raise reports to mislead him, as that such a one is going to be married next month, &c.; but he has an instinct, as I called it before, which prevents his yielding to the imposition. He distinguishes *at hearing* between giddy rumor and steady report. He listens with dignity, and his prying is without credulity.

TOM PRY'S WIFE

You say you were diverted with my description of the "Curious Man." Tom is in some respects an amusing character enough, but then it is by no means uncommon. But what power of words can paint Tom's wife? My pencil falters while I attempt it. But I am ambitious that the portraits should hang side by side: they may set off one another. Tom's passion for knowledge in the *pursuit* is intense and restless, but when satisfied it sits down and seeks no further. He must know all about every thing, but his desires terminate in mere science. Now as far as the *pure mathematics,* as they are called, transcend the *practical,* so far does Tom's curiosity, to my mind, in elegance and disinterestedness, soar above the craving, gnawing, *mercenary* (if I may so call it) inquisitiveness of his wife.

Mrs. Priscilla Pry must not only know all about your private concerns, but be as deeply concerned herself for them: she will pluck at the very heart of your mystery. She must anatomize and skin you, absolutely lay your feelings bare. Her passions are reducible to two, but those are stronger in her than in any human creature—*pity* and *envy.* I will try to illustrate it. She has intimacy with two families—the Grimstones and the Gubbinses. The former are sadly pinched to live, the latter are in splendid circumstances: the former tenant an obscure third floor in Devereux Court, the latter occupy a stately mansion in the Mayfair. I have accompanied her to both these domiciles. She will burst into the incommodious lodging of poor Grimstone and his wife at some unseasonable hour when they are at their meagre dinner, with a "Bless me! what a dark passage you have! I could hardly find my way upstairs! Isn't there a drain somewhere? Well, I like to see you at your *little* bit of mutton!" But her treat is to catch them at a meal of solitary potatoes. Then does her sympathy burgeon, and bud out into a thousand flowers of rhetorical pity and wonder; and it is trumpeted out afterwards to all her acquaintance, that the poor Grimstones were "making a dinner without flesh yesterday." The word *poor* is her favorite; the word (on my conscience) is endeared to her beyond any monosyllable in the language. Poverty, in the tone of her compassion, is somehow doubled; it is emphatically what a dramatist, with some license, has called *poor poverty*. It is a stark-naked *indigence* and never in her mind connected with any mitigating circumstances of self-respect and independence in the owner, which give to poverty a dignity. It is an object of pure pity, and nothing else. This is her first way. Change we the scene to Mayfair and the Gubbinses. Suppose it a morning call:

"Bless me! (for she equally blesses herself against want and abundance) what a style you *do* live in! what elegant curtains! You must have a great income to afford all these things. I wonder you can ever visit such poor folks as we!"—with more to the same purpose, which I must cut short, not to be tedious. She pumps all her friends to know the exact income of all her friends. Such a one must have a great salary. Do you think he has as much as eight hundred a year—seven hundred and fifty perhaps? A wag once told her I had fourteen hundred (Heaven knows we Bank Clerks, though with no reason to complain, in few cases realize that luxury) and the fury of her wonder, till I undeceived her, nearly worked her spirits to a fever. Now Pry is equally glad to get at his friends' circumstances; but his curiosity is disinterested, as I said, and passionless. No emotions are consequent upon the satisfaction of it. He is a philosopher who loves knowledge for its own sake; she is not content with a *lumen siccum* (dry knowledge, says Bacon, is best); the excess of her researches is nothing, but as it feeds the two main springs between which her soul is kept in perpetual conflict—Pity, and Envy.

Considerations

1. Perhaps you've been pressed too often in this text to respond not only to the form and content of a piece, but to the *writer* as a person. For nearly two centuries, however, readers have found Charles Lamb to be immensely likable, and it's worth discussing why, even given just these two small samples of his work. What is there about the voice in these pieces that puts its owner so squarely center-stage? Can it be reasonably argued that the narrator himself is part of the content here? If so, what's he like, and how do you know? Discuss what you were almost certainly taught somewhere along the line—that writers shouldn't let themselves show in their writing—that "being objective" is the thing—as opposed to the idea that you *should* show, *should* be part of the content in nearly anything you write, and "objectivity" be damned.

2. Find a place for Tom and Priscilla in Swift's "Hints Toward an Essay on Conversation." Within which conversational fault or type does each best fit? (If you can't find an existing slot, invent one in keeping with Swift.)

3. Although the Prys are busybodies, there are significant distinctions between their forms of prying. What are the differences? One thing that makes these character pieces so amusing is that it's nearly impossible to read them without having acquaintances pop into mind. We all know at least one Tom and one Priscilla. Which do you find more insufferable and why? Which is the more common type? Finally, how does Lamb save each of these poeple from being merely that, a *type*? Be specific; take a long look at what he actually *says*, as opposed to what you thought he said.

Exercise

According to Lamb, both Prys are flawed by "passions," Tom's "the passion of curiosity," Priscilla's, "pity and envy." You're invited to deal with any over-active passion as you have discovered it operating in an acquaintance. (Here let *passion* be defined as any obsessive behavior.) Keep your piece as short as Lamb's, not because you'd rather write less than more, but because you've attempted, as did Lamb, to pack much into each line.

FRA LIPPO LIPPI
Robert Browning

Brother Lippo Lippi is, like him or not, quite a fellow, a fast-talking, street-wise, pleasure-seeking, most unmonkish monk. But more than these: Lippi is passionately in love with life, committed to his art, disgusted with the hypocrisies and sillinesses that dictate its forms and subject matter. Despite the games he must play to survive, the "saints and saints/And saints again" that he's forced to paint, he is dedicated to the nonmystical, the beauty of the ordinary, to "this fair town's face, yonder river's line/The mountain round it and the sky above,/Much more the figures of man, woman, child/These are the frame to." Give yourself ample chance to get to know this man; he's well worth it.

"Fra Lippo Lippi" is a *dramatic monologue,* a form you may not be familiar with. When you've finished the poem—and read it *aloud*, more than once—define for yourself what's meant by the term.

>   I am poor brother Lippo, by your leave!
>   You need not clap your torches to my face.
>   Zooks, what's to blame? you think you see a monk!
>   What, 'tis past midnight, and you go the rounds,
> 5 And here you catch me at an alley's end
>   Where sportive ladies leave their doors ajar?
>   The Carmine's my cloister: hunt it up,
>   Do,—harry out, if you must show your zeal,
>   Whatever rat, there, haps on his wrong hole,
> 10 And nip each softling of a wee white mouse,
>   *Weke, weke,* that's crept to keep him company!
>   Aha, you know your betters! Then, you'll take
>   Your hand away that's fiddling on my throat,

And please to know me likewise. Who am I?
15 Why, one, sir, who is lodging with a friend
Three streets off—he's a certain . . . how d'ye call?
Master—a . . . Cosimo of the Medici,
I' the house that caps the corner. Boh! you were best!
Remember and tell me, the day you're hanged,
20 How you affected such a gullet's-gripe!
But you, sir, it concerns you that your knaves
Pick up a manner nor discredit you:
Zooks, are we pilchards, that they sweep the streets
And count fair prize what comes into their net?
25 He's Judas to a tittle, that man is!
Just such a face! Why, sir, you make amends.
Lord, I'm not angry! Bid your hangdogs go
Drink out this quarter-florin to the health
Of the munificent House that harbors me
30 (And many more beside, lads! more beside!)
And all's come square again. I'd like his face—
His, elbowing on his comrade in the door
With the pike and lantern,—for the slave that holds
John Baptist's head a-dangle by the hair
35 With one hand ("Look you, now," as who should say)
And his weapon in the other, yet unwiped!
It's not your chance to have a bit of chalk,
A wood-coal or the like? or you should see!
Yes, I'm the painter, since you style me so.
40 What, brother Lippo's doings, up and down,
You know them and they take you? like enough!
I saw the proper twinkle in your eye—
'Tell you, I liked your looks at very first.
Let's sit and set things straight now, hip to haunch.
45 Here's spring come, and the nights one makes up bands
To roam the town and sing out carnival,
And I've been three weeks shut within my mew,
A-painting for the great man, saints and saints
And saints again. I could not paint all night—
50 Ouf! I leaned out of window for fresh air.
There came a hurry of feet and little feet,
A sweep of lute-strings, laughs, and whiffs of song,—
Flower o' the broom,
Take away love, and our earth is a tomb!
55 *Flower o' the quince,*
I let Lisa go, and what good in life since?
Flower o' the thyme—and so on. Round they went.
Scarce had they turned the corner when a titter
Like the skipping of rabbits by moonlight,—three slim shapes,

60 And a face that looked up . . . zooks, sir, flesh and blood,
That's all I'm made of! Into shreds it went,
Curtain and counterpane and coverlet,
All the bed-furniture—a dozen knots,
There was a ladder! Down I let myself,
65 Hands and feet, scrambling somehow, and so dropped,
And after them. I came up with the fun
Hard by Saint Laurence, hail fellow, well met,—
Flower o' the rose,
If I've been merry, what matter who knows?
70 And so as I was stealing back again
To get to bed and have a bit of sleep
Ere I rise up to-morrow and go work
On Jerome knocking at his poor old breast
With his great round stone to subdue the flesh,
75 You snap me of the sudden. Ah, I see!
Though your eye twinkles still, you shake your head—
Mine's shaved—a monk, you say—the sting's in that!
If Master Cosimo announced himself,
Mum's the word naturally; but a monk!
80 Come, what am I a beast for? tell us, now!
I was a baby when my mother died
And father died and left me in the street.
I starved there, God knows how, a year or two
On fig-skins, melon-parings, rinds and shucks,
85 Refuse and rubbish. One fine frosty day,
My stomach being empty as your hat,
The wind doubled me up and down I went.
Old Aunt Lapaccia trussed me with one hand,
(Its fellow was a stinger as I knew)
90 And so along the wall, over the bridge,
By the straight cut to the convent. Six words there,
While I stood munching my first bread that month:
"So, boy, you're minded," quoth the good fat father
Wiping his own mouth, 'twas refection-time,—
95 "To quit this very miserable world?
Will you renounce" . . . "the mouthful of bread?" thought I;
By no means! Brief, they made a monk of me;
I did renounce the world, its pride and greed,
Palace, farm, villa, shop and banking-house,
100 Trash, such as these poor devils of Medici
Have given their hearts to—all at eight years old.
Well, sir, I found in time, you may be sure,
'Twas not for nothing—the good bellyful,
The warm serge and the rope that goes all round,
105 And day-long blessed idleness beside!

"Let's see what the urchin's fit for"—that came next.
Not overmuch their way, I must confess.
Such a to-do! They tried me with their books:
Lord, they'd have taught me Latin in pure waste!
110 *Flower o' the clove,*
All the Latin I construe is, "amo" I love!
But, mind you, when a boy starves in the streets
Eight years together, as my fortune was,
Watching folk's faces to know who will fling
115 The bit of half-stripped grape-bunch he desires,
And who will curse or kick him for his pains,—
Which gentleman processional and fine,
Holding a candle to the Sacrament,
Will wink and let him lift a plate and catch
120 The droppings of the wax to sell again,
Or holla for the Eight and have him whipped,—
How say I?—nay, which dog bites, which lets drop
His bone from the heap of offal in the street,—
Why, soul and sense of him grow sharp alike,
125 He learns the look of things, and none the less
For admonition from the hunger pinch.
I had a store of such remarks, be sure,
Which, after I found leisure, turned to use.
I drew men's faces on my copy-books,
130 Scrawled them within the antiphonary's marge,
Joined legs and arms to the long music-notes,
Found eyes and nose and chin for A's and B's,
And made a string of pictures of the world
Betwixt the ins and outs of verb and noun,
135 On the wall, the bench, the door. The monks looked black.
"Nay," quoth the Prior, "turn him out, d' ye say?
In no wise. Lose a crow and catch a lark.
What if at last we get our man of parts,
We Carmelites, like those Camaldolese
140 And Preaching Friars, to do our church up fine
And put the front on it that ought to be!"
And hereupon he bade me daub away.
Thank you! my head being crammed, the walls a blank,
Never was such prompt disemburdening.
145 First, every sort of monk, the black and white,
I drew them, fat and lean: then, folk at church,
From good old gossips waiting to confess
Their cribs of barrel-droppings, candle-ends,—
To the breathless fellow at the altar-foot,
150 Fresh from his murder, safe and sitting there
With the little children round him in a row

Of admiration, half for his beard and half
For that white anger of his victim's son
Shaking a fist at him with one fierce arm,
155 Signing himself with the other because of Christ
(Whose sad face on the cross sees only this
After the passion of a thousand years)
Till some poor girl, her apron o'er her head,
(Which the intense eyes looked through) came at eve
160 On tiptoe, said a word, dropped in a loaf,
Her pair of earrings and a bunch of flowers
(The brute took growling), prayed, and so was gone.
I painted all, then cried "'Tis ask and have;
Choose, for more's ready!"—laid the ladder flat,
165 And showed my covered bit of cloister-wall.
The monks closed in a circle and praised loud
Till checked, taught what to see and not to see,
Being simple bodies,—"That's the very man!
Look at the boy who stoops to pat the dog!
170 That woman's like the Prior's niece who comes
To care about his asthma: the life!"
But there my triumph's straw-fire flared and funked;
Their betters took their turn to see and say:
The Prior and the learned pulled a face
175 And stopped all that in no time. "How? what's here?
Quite from the mark of painting, bless us all!
Faces, arms, legs and bodies like the true
As much as pea and pea! it's devil's-game!
Your business is not to catch men with show,
180 With homage to the perishable clay,
But lift them over it, ignore it all,
Make them forget there's such a thing as flesh.
Your business is to paint the souls of men—
Man's soul, and it's a fire, smoke . . . no, it's not . . .
185 It's vapor done up like a new-born babe—
(In that shape when you die it leaves your mouth)
It's . . . well, what matters talking, it's the soul!
Give us no more of body than shows soul!
Here's Giotto, with his Saint a-praising God,
190 That sets us praising,—why not stop with him?
Why put all thoughts of praise out of our head
With wonder at lines, colors, and what not?
Paint the soul, never mind the legs and arms!
Rub all out, try at it a second time.
195 Oh, that white smallish female with the breasts,
She's just my niece . . . Herodias, I would say,—
Who went and danced and got men's heads cut off!
Have it all out!" Now, is this sense, I ask?

A fine way to paint soul, by painting body
200 So ill, the eye can't stop there, must go further
And can't fare worse! Thus, yellow does for white
When what you put for yellow's simply black,
And any sort of meaning looks intense
When all beside itself means and looks naught.
205 Why can't a painter lift each foot in turn,
Left foot and right foot, go a double step,
Make his flesh liker and his soul more like,
Both in their order? Take the prettiest face,
The Prior's niece . . . patron-saint—is it so pretty
210 You can't discover if it means hope, fear,
Sorrow or joy? won't beauty go with these?
Suppose I've made her eyes all right and blue,
Can't I take breath and try to add life's flash,
And then add soul and heighten them three-fold?
215 Or say there's beauty with no soul at all—
(I never say it—put the case the same—)
If you get simple beauty and naught else,
You get about the best thing God invents:
That's somewhat: and you'll find the soul you have missed,
220 Within yourself, when you return him thanks.
"Rub all out!" Well, well, there's my life, in short,
And so the thing has gone on ever since.
I'm grown a man no doubt, I've broken bounds:
You should not take a fellow eight years old
225 And make him swear to never kiss the girls.
I'm my own master, paint now as I please—
Having a friend, you see, in the Corner-house!
Lord, it's fast holding by the rings in front—
Those great rings serve more purposes than just
230 To paint a flag in, or tie up a horse!
And yet the old schooling sticks, the old grave eyes
Are peeping o'er my shoulder as I work,
The heads shake still—"It's art's decline, my son!
You're not of the true painters, great and old;
235 Brother Angelico's the man, you'll find;
Brother Lorenzo stands his single peer:
Fag on at flesh, you'll never make the third!"
Flower o' the pine,
You keep your mistr . . . manners, and I'll stick to mine!
240 I'm not the third, then: bless us, they must know!
Don't you think they're the likeliest to know,
They with their Latin? So, I swallow my rage,
Clench my teeth, suck my lips in tight, and paint
To please them—sometimes do and sometimes don't;

245   For, doing most, there's pretty sure to come
      A turn, some warm eve finds me at my saints—
      A laugh, a cry, the business of the world—
      (*Flower o' the peach,*
      Death for us all, and his own life for each!)
250   And my whole soul revolves, the cup runs over,
      The world and life's too big to pass for a dream,
      And I do these wild things in sheer despite,
      And play the fooleries you catch me at,
      In pure rage! The old mill-horse, out at grass
255   After hard years, throws up his stiff heels so,
      Although the miller does not preach to him
      The only good of grass is to make chaff.
      What would men have? Do they like grass or no—
      May they or mayn't they? all I want's the thing
260   Settled forever one way. As it is,
      You tell too many lies and hurt yourself:
      You don't like what you only like too much,
      You do like what, if given you at your word,
      You find abundantly detestable.
265   For me, I think I speak as I was taught;
      I always see the garden and God there
      A-making man's wife: and, my lesson learned,
      The value and significance of flesh,
      I can't unlearn ten minutes afterwards.

270   You understand me: I'm a beast, I know.
      But see, now—why, I see as certainly
      As that the morning-star's about to shine,
      What will hap some day. We've a youngster here
      Comes to our convent, studies what I do,
275   Slouches and stares and lets no atom drop:
      His name is Guidi—he'll not mind the monks—
      They call him Hulking Tom, he lets them talk—
      He picks my practice up— he'll paint apace,
      I hope so—though I never live so long,
280   I know what's sure to follow. You be judge!
      You speak no Latin more than I, belike;
      However, you're my man, you've seen the world
      —The beauty and the wonder and the power,
      The shapes of things, their colors, lights and shades,
285   Changes, surprises,—and God made it all!
      —For what? Do you feel thankful, ay or no,
      For this fair town's face, yonder river's line,
      The mountain round it and the sky above,
      Much more the figures of man, woman, child,

290 These are the frame to? What's it all about?
To be passed over, despised? or dwelt upon,
Wondered at? oh, this last of course!—you say.
But why not do as well as say,—paint these
Just as they are, careless what comes of it?
295 God's works—paint any one, and count it crime
To let a truth slip. Don't object, "His works
Are here already; nature is complete:
Suppose you reproduce her—(which you can't)
There's no advantage! you must beat her, then."
300 For, don't you mark? we're made so that we love
First when we see them painted, things we have passed
Perhaps a hundred times nor cared to see;
And so they are better, painted—better to us,
Which is the same thing. Art was given for that;
305 God uses us to help each other so,
Lending our minds out. Have you noticed, now,
Your cullion's hanging face? A bit of chalk,
And trust me but you should, though! How much more,
If I drew higher things with the same truth!
310 That were to take the Prior's pulpit-place,
Interpret God to all of you! Oh, oh,
It makes me mad to see what men shall do
And we in our graves! This world's no blot for us,
Nor blank; it means intensely, and means good:
315 To find its meaning is my meat and drink.
"Ay, but you don't so instigate to prayer!"
Strikes in the Prior: "when your meaning's plain
It does not say to folk—remember matins,
Or, mind you fast next Friday!" Why, for this
320 What need of art at all? A skull and bones,
Two bits of stick nailed crosswise, or, what's best,
A bell to chime the hour with, does as well.
I painted a Saint Laurence six months since
At Prato, splashed the fresco in fine style:
325 "How looks my painting, now the scaffold's down?"
I ask a brother' "Hugely," he returns—
"Already not one phiz of your three slaves
Who turn the Deacon off his toasted side,
But's scratched and prodded to our heart's content,
330 The pious people have so eased their own
With coming to say prayers there in a rage:
We get on fast to see the bricks beneath.
Expect another job this time next year,
For pity and religion grow i' the crowd—
335 Your painting serves its purpose!" Hang the fools!

   —That is—you'll not mistake an idle word
   Spoke in a huff by a poor monk, God wot,
   Tasting the air this spicy night which turns
   The unaccustomed head like Chianti wine!
340 Oh, the church knows! don't misreport me, now!
   It's natural a poor monk out of bounds
   Should have his apt word to excuse himself:
   And hearken how I plot to make amends.
   I have bethought me: I shall paint a piece
345 ... There's for you! Give me six months, then go, see
   Something in Sant' Ambrogio's! Bless the nuns!
   They want a cast o' my office. I shall paint
   God in the midst, Madonna and her babe,
   Ringed by a bowery flowery angel-brood,
350 Lilies and vestments and white faces, sweet
   As puff on puff of grated orris-root
   When ladies crowd to Church at midsummer.
   And then i' the front, of course a saint or two—
   Saint John, because he saves the Florentines,
355 Saint Ambrose, who puts down in black and white
   The convent's friends and gives them a long day,
   And Job, I must have him there past mistake,
   The man of Uz (and Us without the z,
   Painters who need his patience). Well, all these
360 Secured at their devotions, up shall come
   Out of a corner when you least expect,
   As one by a dark stair into a great light,
   Music and talking, who but Lippo! I!—
   Mazed, motionless and moonstruck—I'm the man!
365 Back I shrink—what is this I see and hear?
   I, caught up with my monk's-things by mistake,
   My old serge gown and rope that goes all round,
   I, in this presence, this pure company!
   Where's a hole, where's a corner for escape?
370 Then steps a sweet angelic slip of a thing
   Forward, puts out a soft palm—"Not so fast!"
   —Addresses the celestial presence, "nay—
   He made you and devised you, after all,
   Though he's none of you! Could Saint John there draw—
375 His camel-hair make up a painting-brush?
   We come to brother Lippo for all that,
   Iste perfecit opus!" So, all smile—
   I shuffle sideways with my blushing face
   Under the cover of a hundred wings
380 Thrown like a spread of kirtles when you're gay
   And play hot cockles, all the doors being shut,

Till, wholly unexpected, in there pops
The hothead husband! Thus I scuttle off
To some safe bench behind, not letting go
385 The palm of her, the little lily thing
That spoke the good word for me in the nick,
Like the Prior's niece . . . Saint Lucy, I would say.
And so all's saved for me, and for the church
A pretty picture gained. Go, six months hence!
390 Your hand, sir, and good-bye: no lights, no lights!
The street's hushed, and I know my own way back,
Don't fear me! There's the gray beginning. Zooks!

Considerations

1. Although I took a brief stab at summarizing Lippi in the headnote, *your* response to him is what counts. What kind of man do you understand him to be? Generalize at this point, the way you would if you'd actually met him and later tried to describe his nature to someone else.

2. Imagine a dialogue about art between Hazlitt and Lippi (who was, by the way, a real 15th-century painter, although Browning took poetic liberties in characterizing him). On what main point(s) would they be most likely to agree? Disagree? For Hazlitt, what were art's chief aims? For Lippi? Whose work would you probably be more drawn to? Why? What does the latter paint on the cloister wall, and why does it so rattle and anger the Prior? Why did it have a different effect on the monks?

3. What evidence is there that Brother Lippi is committed to the principle that the best defense is an offense? Detail your answer, and be certain to involve your sense of humor.

4. Lippi isn't talking to himself; he has an audience of one, and if you read carefully, you noted that his monologue is meant to have gone on for some hours. Who, sitting "hip to haunch" with him, listens so attentively? Is the audience you picture a truly appropriate one, given the nature of the subject? Why or why not?

5. Although the speaker may at first seem only to be attempting to wriggle out of a nasty situation (in fact, it sounds as if he has had to use the same strategies more than once before), it isn't long before some deeper concern takes over. Approximately where does this happen, and what form(s) does it take? How has Browning manipulated our sympathies, much as Lippi manipulates those of his listener toward the first?

6. How, according to the Prior, can the artist draw viewers' eyes away from the bodies of his subjects and hence draw their attention to their souls? What is the painter's argument in response?

7. Block out a passage that you particularly like (or dislike least) and after some rehearsal, give an oral interpretation to a group of your fellow students. Aim at bringing out your understanding of what kind of man Lippi really is.

Exercise

A man dressed strangely for the time and place has been accosted by police making late-night rounds, roughed up, and threatened with arrest. Nothing dated about *this* scenario; change the costumes, perhaps, and the setting—15th-century Florence—and what Browning introduces in the first few lines of this poem is transformed into the opening scene of last week's Tuesday Night Movie. Or next week's, the one you write. Kick some ideas around with three or four classmates. What's the character doing sneaking down an alley in the redlight district (and don't settle for the obvious)? Who is he? What will unfold? What larger story is he a part of? Who will you cast in the part? Will you begin where Browning does or earlier, perhaps with the character's hilarious descent from his room, or even, with flashbacks, to a much earlier point? Don't write out a full script; do rough up a fairly detailed scene-plot summary.

A MYSTERY OF HEROISM
Stephen Crane

Mahatma Gandhi once said, "Almost anything you do will be insignificant, but it is very important that you do it." It's easy enough to agree with the first part of this assertion; from a cosmic point of view we are ephemeral, all of our actions are inconsequential. How can it be, then, that doing something—*anything*—can have importance? Whether or not this is the central question in the following story, it is an inescapable one. Like Fred Collins of A Company, we've all confronted it.

> The dark uniforms of the men were so coated with dust from the incessant wrestling of the two armies that the regiment almost seemed a part of the clay bank which shielded them from the shells. On the top of the hill a battery was arguing in tremendous roars with some other guns, and to the eye of the infantry the artillerymen, the guns, the caissons, the horses, were distinctly outlined upon the blue sky. When a piece was fired, a red streak as round as a log flashed low in the heavens, like a monstrous bolt of lightning. The men of the battery wore white duck trousers, which somehow emphasized their legs; and when they ran and crowded in little groups at the bidding of the shouting officers, it was more impressive than usual to the infantry.
>
> Fred Collins, of A Company, was saying, "Thunder! I wisht I had a drink. Ain't there any water round here?" Then somebody yelled, "There goes th' bugler!"
>
> As the eyes of half the regiment swept in one machine-like movement, there was an instant's picture of a horse in a great, convulsive leap of a death wound and a rider leaning back with a crooked arm and spread fingers before his face. On the ground was the crimson terror of an exploding shell, with fibers of flame that seemed like lances. A glittering bugle swung clear of the rider's back as fell headlong the horse and the man. In the air was an odor as from a conflagration.

Sometimes they of the infantry looked down at a fair little meadow which spread at their feet. Its long, green grass was rippling gently in a breeze. Beyond it was the gray form of a house half torn to pieces by shells and by the busy axes of soldiers who had pursued firewood. The line of an old fence was now dimly marked by long weeds and by an occasional post. A shell had blown the well house to fragments. Little lines of gray smoke ribboning upward from some embers indicated the place where had stood the barn.

From beyond a curtain of green woods there came the sound of some stupendous scuffle, as if two animals of the size of islands were fighting. At a distance there were occasional appearances of swift-moving men, horses, batteries, flags, and with the crashing of infantry volleys were heard, often, wild and frenzied cheers. In the midst of it all Smith and Ferguson, two privates of A Company, were engaged in a heated discussion which involved the greatest questions of the national existence.

The battery on the hill presently engaged in a frightful duel. The white legs of the gunners scampered this way and that way, and the officers redoubled their shouts. The guns, with their demeanors of solidity and courage, were typical of something infinitely self-possessed in this clamor of death that swirled around the hill.

One of a "swing" team was suddenly smitten quivering to the ground, and his maddened brethren dragged his torn body in their struggle to escape from this turmoil and danger. A young soldier astride one of the leaders swore and fumed in his saddle and furiously jerked at the bridle. An officer screamed out an order so violently that his voice broke and ended the sentence in a falsetto shriek.

The leading company of the infantry regiment was somewhat exposed, and the colonel ordered it moved more fully under the shelter of the hill. There was the clank of steel against steel.

A lieutenant of the battery rode down and passed them, holding his right arm carefully in his left hand. And it was as if this arm was not at all a part of him, but belonged to another man. His sober and reflective charger went slowly. The officer's face was grimy and perspiring, and his uniform was tousled as if he had been in direct grapple with an enemy. He smiled grimly when the men stared at him. He turned his horse toward the meadow.

Collins, of A Company, said, "I wisht I had a drink. I bet there's water in that there ol' well yonder!"

"Yes; but how you goin' to git it?"

For the little meadow which intervened was now suffering a terrible onslaught of shells. Its green and beautiful calm had vanished utterly. Brown earth was being flung in monstrous handfuls. And there was a massacre of the young blades of grass. They were being torn, burned, obliterated. Some curious fortune of the battle had made this gentle little meadow the object of the red hate of the shells, and each one as it exploded seemed like an imprecation in the face of a maiden.

The wounded officer who was riding across this expanse said to himself: "Why, they couldn't shoot any harder if the whole army was massed here!"

A shell struck the gray ruins of the house, and as, after the roar, the shattered wall fell in fragments, there was a noise which resembled the flapping of shutters during a wild gale of winter. Indeed, the infantry paused in the shelter of the bank appeared as men standing upon a shore contemplating a madness of the sea. The angel of calamity had under its glance the battery upon the hill. Fewer white-legged men labored about the guns. A shell had smitten one of the pieces, and after the flare, the smoke, the dust, the wrath of this blow were gone, it was possible to see white legs stretched horizontally upon the ground. And at that interval, to the rear, where it is the business of battery horses to stand with their noses to the fight, awaiting the command to drag the guns out of the destruction, or into it, or wheresoever these incomprehensible humans demanded with whip and spur—in this line of passive and dumb spectators, whose fluttering hearts yet would not let them forget the iron laws of man's control of them—in this rank of brute-soldiers there had been relentless and hideous carnage. From the ruck of bleeding and prostrate horses, the men of the infantry could see one animal raising its stricken body with its forelegs and turning its nose with mystic and profound eloquence toward the sky.

Some comrades joked Collins about his thirst. "Well, if yeh want a drink so bad, why don't yeh go git it?"

"Well, I will in a minnet, if yeh don't shut up!"

A lieutenant of artillery floundered his horse straight down the hill with as little concern as if there were level ground. As he galloped past the colonel of the infantry, he threw up his hand in swift salute. "We've got to get out of that," he roared angrily. He was a black-bearded officer, and his eyes, which resembled beads, sparkled like those of an insane man. His jumping horse sped along the column of infantry.

The fat major, standing carelessly with his sword held horizontally behind him and with his legs far apart, looked after the receding horseman and laughed. "He wants to get back with orders pretty quick, or there'll be no batt'ry left," he observed.

The wise young captain of the second company hazarded to the lieutenant colonel that the enemy's infantry would probably soon attack the hill, and the lieutenant colonel snubbed him.

A private in one of the rear companies looked out over the meadow, and then turned to a companion and said, "Look there, Jim!" It was the wounded officer from the battery, who some time before had started to ride across the meadow, supporting his right arm carefully with his left hand. This man had encountered a shell, apparently, at a time when no one perceived him, and he could now be seen lying face downward with a stirruped foot stretched across the body of his dead horse. A leg of the charger extended slantingly upward, precisely as stiff as a stake. Around this motionless pair the shells still howled.

There was a quarrel in A Company. Collins was shaking his fist in the faces of some laughing comrades. "Dern yeh! I ain't afraid t' go. If yeh say much, I will go!"

"Of course, yeh will! You'll run through that there medder, won't yeh?"

Collins said, in a terrible voice, "You see now!"

At this ominous threat, his comrades broke into renewed jeers.

Collins gave them a dark scowl, and went to find his captain. The latter was conversing with the colonel of the regiment.

"Captain," said Collins, saluting and standing at attention—in those days all trousers bagged at the knees—"Captain, I want t' get permission to go git some water from that there well over yonder!"

The colonel and the captain swung about simultaneously and stared across the meadow. The captain laughed. "You must be pretty thirsty, Collins?"

"Yes, sir, I am."

"Well—ah," said the captain. After a moment, he asked, "Can't you wait?"

"No, sir."

The colonel was watching Collins's face. "Look here, my lad," he said, in a pious sort of voice, "look here, my lad"—Collins was not a lad—"don't you think that's taking pretty big risks for a little drink of water?"

"I dunno," said Collins uncomfortably. Some of the resentment toward his companions, which perhaps had forced him into this affair, was beginning to fade. "I dunno w'ether 'tis."

The colonel and the captain contemplated him for a time.

"Well," said the captain finally.

"Well," said the colonel, "if you want to go, why, go."

Collins saluted. "Much obliged t' yeh."

As he moved away, the colonel called after him. "Take some of the other boys' canteens with you, an' hurry back, now."

"Yes, sir, I will."

The colonel and the captain looked at each other then, for it had suddenly occurred that they could not for the life of them tell whether Collins wanted to go or whether he did not.

They turned to regard Collins, and as they perceived him surrounded by gesticulating comrades, the colonel said, "Well, by thunder! I guess he's going."

Collins appeared as a man dreaming. In the midst of the questions, the advice, the warnings, all the excited talk of his company mates, he maintained a curious silence.

They were very busy in preparing him for his ordeal. When they inspected him carefully, it was somewhat like the examination that grooms give a horse before a race; and they were amazed, staggered, by the whole affair. Their astonishment found vent in strange repetitions.

"Are yeh sure a-goin'?" they demanded again and again.

"Certainly I am," cried Collins at last, furiously.

He strode sullenly away from them. He was swinging five or six canteens by their cords. It seemed that his cap would not remain firmly on his head, and often he reached and pulled it down over his brow.

There was a general movement in the compact column. The long animal-like thing moved slightly. Its four hundred eyes were turned upon the figure of Collins.

"Well, sir, if that ain't th' derndest thing! I never thought Fred Collins had the blood in him for that kind of business."

"What's he goin' to do, anyhow?"

"He's goin' to that well there after water."

"We ain't dyin' of thirst, are we? That's foolishness."

"Well, somebody put him up to it, an' he's doin' it."

"Say, he must be a desperate cuss."

When Collins faced the meadow and walked away from the regiment, he was vaguely conscious that a chasm, the deep valley of all prides, was suddenly between him and his comrades. It was provisional, but the provision was that he return as a victor. He had blindly been led by quaint emotions, and laid himself under an obligation to walk squarely up to the face of death.

But he was not sure that he wished to make a retraction, even if he could do so without shame. As a matter of truth, he was sure of very little. He was mainly surprised.

It seemed to him supernaturally strange that he had allowed his mind to maneuver his body into such a situation. He understood that it might be called dramatically great.

However, he had no full appreciation of anything, excepting that he was actually conscious of being dazed. He could feel his dulled mind groping after the form and color of this incident. He wondered why he did not feel some keen agony of fear cutting his sense like a knife. He wondered at this, because human expression had said loudly for centuries that men should feel afraid of certain things, and that all men who did not feel this fear were phenomena—heroes.

He was, then, a hero. He suffered that disappointment which we would all have if we discovered that we were ourselves capable of those deeds which we most admire in history and legend. This, then, was a hero. After all, heroes were not much.

No, it could not be true. He was not a hero. Heroes had no shames in their lives, and as for him, he remembered borrowing fifteen dollars from a friend and promising to pay it back the next day, and then avoiding that friend for ten months. When, at home, his mother had aroused him for the early labor of his life on the farm, it had often been his fashion to be irritable, childish, diabolical; and his mother had died since he had come to the war.

He saw that in this matter of the well, the canteens, the shells, he was an intruder in the land of fine deeds.

He was now about thirty paces from his comrades. The regiment had just turned its many faces toward him.

From the forest of terrific noises there suddenly emerged a little uneven line of men. They fired fiercely and rapidly at distant foliage on which appeared little puffs of white smoke. The spatter of skirmish firing was added to the thunder of the guns on the hill. The little line of men ran forward. A color sergeant fell flat with his flag as if he had slipped on ice. There was hoarse cheering from this distant field.

Collins suddenly felt that two demon fingers were pressed into his ears. He could see nothing but flying arrows, flaming red. He lurched from the shock of this explosion, but he made a mad rush for the house, which he viewed as a man submerged to the neck in a boiling surf might view the shore. In the air little pieces of shell howled, and the earthquake explosions drove him insane with the menace of their roar. As he ran, the canteens knocked together with a rhythmical tinkling.

As he neared the house, each detail of the scene became vivid to him. He was aware of some bricks of the vanished chimney lying on the sod. There was a door which hung by one hinge.

Rifle bullets called forth by the insistent skirmishers came from the far-off bank of foliage. They mingled with the shells and the pieces of shells until the air was torn in all directions by hootings, yells, howls. The sky was full of fiends who directed all their wild rage at his head.

When he came to the well, he flung himself face downward and peered into its darkness. There were furtive silver glintings some feet from the surface. He grabbed one of the canteens, and unfastening its cap, swung it down by the cord. The water flowed slowly in with an indolent gurgle.

And now, as he lay with his face turned away, he was suddenly smitten with the terror. It came upon his heart like the grasp of claws. All that power faded from his muscles. For an instant he was no more than a dead man.

The canteen filled with a maddening slowness, in the manner of all bottles. Presently he recovered his strength and addressed a screaming oath to it. He leaned over until it seemed as if he intended to try to push water into it with his hands. His eyes as he gazed down into the well shone like two pieces of metal, and in their expression was a great appeal and a great curse. The stupid water derided him.

There was the blaring thunder of a shell. Crimson light shone through the swift-boiling smoke and made a pink reflection on part of the wall of the well. Collins jerked out his arm and canteen with the same motion that a man would use in withdrawing his head from a furnace.

He scrambled erect and glared and hesitated. On the ground near him lay the old well bucket, with a length of rusty chain. He lowered it swiftly into the well. The bucket struck the water and then, turning lazily over, sank. When, with hand reaching tremblingly over hand, he hauled it out, it knocked often against the walls of the well and spilled some of its contents.

In running with a filled bucket, a man can adopt but one kind of gait. So, through this terrible field over which screamed practical angels of death, Collins ran in the manner of a farmer chased out of a dairy by a bull.

His face went staring white with anticipation—anticipation of a blow that would whirl him around and down. He would fall as he had seen other men fall, the life knocked out of them so suddenly that their knees were no more quick to touch the ground than their heads. He saw the long blue line of the regiment, but his comrades were standing looking at him from the edge of an impossible star. He was aware of some deep wheel ruts and hoofprints in the sod beneath his feet.

The artillery officer who had fallen in this meadow had been making groans in the teeth of the tempest of sound. These futile cries, wrenched from him by his agony, were heard only by shells, bullets. When wild-eyed Collins came running, this officer raised himself. His face contorted and blanched from pain, he was about to utter some great beseeching cry. But suddenly his face straightened, and he called. "Say, young man, give me a drink of water, will you?"

Collins had no room amid his emotions for surprise. He was mad from the threats of destruction.

"I can't!" he screamed, and in his reply was a full description of his quaking apprehension. His cap was gone and his hair was riotous. His clothes made it appear that he had been dragged over the ground by the heels. He ran on.

The officer's head sank down, and one elbow crooked. His foot in its brass-bound stirrup still stretched over the body of his horse, and the other leg was under the steed.

But Collins turned. He came dashing back. His face had now turned grey, and in his eyes was all terror. "Here it is! Here it is!"

The officer was as a man gone in drink. His arm bent like a twig. His head dropped as if his neck were of willow. He was sinking to the ground, to lie face downward.

Collins grabbed him by the shoulder. "Here is is. Here's your drink. Turn over, man, for God's sake!"

With Collins hauling at his shoulder, the officer twisted his body and fell with his face turned toward that region where lived the unspeakable noises of the swirling missiles. There was the faintest shadow of a smile on his lips as he looked at Collins. He gave a sigh, a little primitive breath like that from a child.

Collins tried to hold the bucket steadily, but his shaking hands caused the water to splash all over the face of the dying man. Then he jerked it away and ran on.

The regiment gave him a welcoming roar. The grimed faces were wrinkled in laughter.

His captain waved the bucket away. "Give it to the men!"

The two genial, skylarking young lieutenants were the first to gain possession of it. They played over it in their fashion.

When one tried to drink, the other teasingly knocked his elbow. "Don't, Billie! You'll make me spill it," said the one. The other laughed.

Suddenly there was an oath, the thud of wood on the ground, and a swift murmur of astonishment among the ranks. The two lieutenants glared at each other. The bucket lay on the ground, empty.

Considerations

1. What is the "mystery" of heroism, according to Crane? Is it mysterious only because Collins isn't intelligent enough to comprehend the concept? Or is it a grander mystery, an unfathomable aspect of human nature? Bring your own thoughts on the matter into the discussion; beyond what Crane may be suggesting, what have your own life experiences provided in the way of answers?

2. Think back to Thoreau's description of the battle of the ants—the fierce intensity of the struggle between red and black insects over . . . over what? A few feet of dooryard? Certainly not over a principle. Only humans battle about such lofty, abstract matters as the integrity of the union of American states vs. the right to secede. Where, though, is this principle evident in the scene Crane creates? Are we meant to sense that it is significant? Why or why not?

3. The author uses distinct literary devices to depersonalize the fighting units. Although they're made up of men, Crane asks that we see them in other than strictly human terms. Cite examples of this, and comment on the overall effect. (What story elements *does* he describe in human terms?)

4. Collins is an unlikely hero, but then so is Pinocchio. From what you know about the hero figure and the heroic quest, cite other unlikely hero characters and situations. (Is Jonah a hero figure in the formal literary sense of the term?) Generalize about the possible meaning and importance of the hero story (by any measure, the most pervasive story in all of myth and literature). What are its central features? Its probable meaning? Does it matter whether the hero quests for a bucket of water or the dragon that threatens an entire kingdom? Is one kind of quest more "significant" than another? Or is any such quest essentially futile, silly?

5. Here is Crane's short poem "War Is Kind." In what respects does it touch on issues addressed in the story?

WAR IS KIND

Do not weep, maiden, for war is kind.
Because your lover threw wild hands toward the sky
And the affrighted steed ran on alone,
Do not weep.
5   War is kind.

Hoarse, booming drums of the regiment,
Little souls who thirst for fight,
These men were born to drill and die.
The unexplained glory lies above them,
10 Great is the battle-god, great, and his kingdom—
A field where a thousand corpses lie.

Do not weep, babe, for war is kind.
Because your father tumbled in the yellow trenches,
Raged at his breast, gulped and died,
15 Do not weep.
War is kind.

Swift blazing flag of the regiment,
Eagle with crest of red and gold,
These men were born to drill and die.
20 Point for them the virtue of slaughter,
Make plain to them the excellence of killing
And a field where a thousand corpses lie.

Mother whose heart hung humble as a button
On the bright splendid shroud of your son,
25 Do not weep.
War is kind.

TWO RUEFUL NOTES

Both of the following poems end on a rueful note. Housman and Yeats seem equally sensitive to what may be the most miserable of human experiences: falling deeply in love for the first time, only to suffer its loss. Probably you've gone through the same thing and have been filled with "sighs a plenty." That the speakers are able to address the subject at all is in itself cause for hope. They've survived it, and yet if I remember accurately this agonizing chapter in life, survival seemed most unlikely.

WHEN I WAS ONE-AND-TWENTY
A. E. Housman

When I was one-and-twenty
  I heard a wise man say,
'Give crowns and pounds and guineas
  But not your heart away;
5 Give pearls away and rubies
  But keep your fancy free.'
But I was one-and-twenty,
  No use to talk to me.

When I was one-and-twenty
10   I heard him say again,
'The heart out of the bosom

Was never given in vain;
'Tis paid with sighs a plenty
And sold for endless rue.'
15 And I am two-and-twenty,
And oh, 'tis true, 'tis true.

DOWN BY THE SALLEY GARDENS
William Butler Yeats

Down by the salley gardens my love and I did meet;
She passed the salley gardens with little snow-white feet.
She bid me take love easy, as the leaves grow on the tree;
But I, being young and foolish, with her would not agree.
In a field by the river my love and I did stand,
And on my leaning shoulder she laid her snow-white hand.
She bid me take life easy, as the grass grows on the weirs;
But I was young and foolish, and now am full of tears.

Considerations

1. Although it seems a basic human trait, romantic love is to some extent an acquired cultural characteristic; many societies don't understand the Western notion that relationships between the sexes are based on enflamed emotions, that somewhere is the predestined man or woman meant for us and no one else. Think about this for a minute: Wouldn't life be simpler, pleasanter if relationships and marriages were arranged by others? If we didn't have to worry sooner or later about finding the "perfect mate"? How many of your favorite books, movies, songs, even paintings, are somehow connected with the theme of frustrated romantic love?

2. Consider the advice offered to the speaker in each of the poems. Put both in your own words and comment on which makes the more sense, given what you believe about the human condition, the nature of love, the times in which you live.

3. Is there a chance, even an outside one, that either of these poems is partly humorous in tone? (You're supposed to answer Yes.) If so, which one, and what's humorous about it? Be specific.

4. Read any or all of these short, easy-to-find poems and contrast in writing and/or discussion their points of view as compared with the poems above: Thomas Hardy's "Neutral Tones," William Butler Yeats's "Ephemera," and Matthew Arnold's "Dover Beach."

Exercises

1. Write a "Dear Abby" response to one or both of these speakers.

2. Or take it seriously: reflect in writing on what wisdoms about love you've come to, either by observing others in such straits or by having gone through them yourself.

3. Or write whatever you want and in whatever form. Eighty-five percent of popular songs deal with the subject of love, mostly its miseries. Try a

lyric. Or a poem. Or even a short, silent film. Whatever, don't worry about sticking to the specifics of the selections you've just read and discussed; the content should come from you, and it will naturally seek the form that serves it best.

CORN-PONE OPINIONS
Mark Twain

Twain attempts to persuade us here that we don't think for ourselves, and that "public opinion" is actually an absence of any reasoned judgment, and is instead an eagerness to go along, to conform. Like it or not, there does seem to be a certain sheep-like quality to human behavior, a readiness to follow rather than to lead. As you read and annotate this piece, keep in mind the connections between hoop skirts and mini-skirts, the silver issue and the draft issue, the Smiths and Joneses then and the Smiths and Joneses now.

Fifty years ago, when I was a boy of fifteen and helping to inhabit a Missourian village on the banks of the Mississippi, I had a friend whose society was very dear to me because I was forbidden by my mother to partake of it. He was a gay and impudent and satirical and delightful young black man—a slave—who daily preached sermons from the top of his master's woodpile, with me for sole audience. He imitated the pulpit style of the several clergymen of the village, and did it well and with fine passion and energy. To me he was a wonder. I believed he was the greatest orator in the United States and would some day be heard from. But it did not happen; in the distribution of rewards he was overlooked. It is the way, in this world.

He interrupted his preaching now and then to saw a stick of wood, but the sawing was a pretense—he did it with his mouth, exactly imitating the sound the bucksaw makes in shrieking its way through the wood. But it served its purpose, it kept his master from coming out to see how the work was getting along. I listened to the sermons from the open window of a lumber room at the back of the house. One of his texts was this:

"You tell me whar a man gits his corn pone, en I'll tell you what his 'pinions is."

I can never forget it. It was deeply impressed upon me. By my mother. Not upon my memory, but elsewhere. She had slipped in upon me while I was absorbed and not watching. The black philosopher's idea was that a man is not independent and cannot afford views which might interfere with his bread and butter. If he would prosper, he must train with the majority; in matters of large moment, like politics and religion, he must think and feel with the bulk of his neighbors or suffer damage in his social standing and in his business prosperities. He must restrict himself to corn-pone opinions—at least on the surface. He must get his opinions from other people, he must reason out none for himself, he must have no first-hand views.

I think Jerry was right, in the main, but I think he did not go far enough.

1. It was his idea that a man conforms to the majority view of his locality by calculation and intention.

This happens, but I think it is not the rule.

2. It was his idea that there is such a thing as a first-hand opinion, an original opinion, an opinion which is coldly reasoned out in a man's head by a searching analysis of the facts involved, with the heart unconsulted and the jury room closed against outside influences. It may be that such an opinion has been born somewhere at some time or other, but I suppose it got away before they could catch it and stuff it and put it in the museum.

I am persuaded that a coldly-thought-out and independent verdict upon a fashion in clothes, or manners, or literature, or politics, or religion, or any other matter that is projected into the field of our notice and interest is a most rare thing—if it has indeed ever existed.

A new thing in costume appears—the flaring hoopskirt, for example—and the passers-by are shocked, and the irreverent laugh. Six months later everybody is reconciled; the fashion has established itself; it is admired now and no one laughs. Public opinion resented it before, public opinion accepts it now and is happy in it. Why? Was the resentment reasoned out? Was the acceptance reasoned out? No. The instinct that moves to conformity did the work. It is our nature to conform; it is a force which not many can successfully resist. What is its seat? The inborn requirement of self-approval. We all have to bow to that; there are no exceptions. Even the woman who refuses from first to last to wear the hoopskirt comes under that law and is its slave; she could not wear the skirt and have her own approval, and that she *must* have, she cannot help herself. But as a rule our self-approval has its source in but one place and not elsewhere—the approval of other people. A person of vast consequences can introduce any kind of novelty in dress and the general world will presently adopt it—moved to do it in the first place by the natural instinct to passively yield to that vague something recognized as authority, and in the second place by the human instinct to train with the multitude and have its approval. An empress introduced the hoopskirt and we know the result. A nobody introduced the bloomer and we know the result. If Eve should come again in her ripe renown, and reintroduce her quaint styles—well, we know what would happen. And we should be cruelly embarrassed, along at first.

The hoopskirt runs its course and disappears. Nobody reasons about it. One woman abandons the fashion, her neighbor notices this and follows her lead, this influences the next woman and so on and so on, and presently the skirt has vanished out of the world, no one knows how nor why; nor cares, for that matter. It will come again by and by, and in due course will go again.

Twenty-five years ago in England, six or eight wine glasses stood grouped by each person's plate at a dinner party, and they were used, not left idle and empty; to-day there are but three or four in the group and the average guest sparingly uses about two of them. We have not adopted this new fashion yet, but we shall do it presently. We shall not think it out, we shall merely conform and let it go at that. We get our notions and habits and opinions from outside influences; we do not have to study them out.

Our table manners and company manners and street manners change from time to time, but the changes are not reasoned out; we merely notice and conform. We are creatures of outside influences; as a rule we do not think, we only imitate. We cannot invent standards that will stick; what we mistake for standards are only fashions, and perishable. We may continue to admire them but we drop the use of them. We notice this in literature. Shakespeare is a standard, and fifty years ago we used to write tragedies which we couldn't tell from—from somebody else's, but we don't do it any more now. Our prose standard three quarters of a century ago was ornate and diffuse; some authority or other changed it in the direction of compactness and simplicity, and conformity followed without argument. The historical novel starts up suddenly and sweeps the land. Everybody writes one and the nation is glad. We had historical novels before; but nobody read them and the rest of us conformed—without reasoning it out. We are conforming in the other way now, because it is another case of everybody.

The outside influences are always pouring in upon us and we are always obeying their orders and accepting their verdicts. The Smiths like the new play, the Joneses go to see it and they copy the Smith verdict. Morals, religion, politics, get their following from surrounding influences and atmospheres almost entirely; not from study, not from thinking. A man must and will have his own approval first of all, in each and every moment and circumstance of his life—even if he must repent of a self-approved act the moment after its commission in order to get his self-approval *again*: but speaking in general terms, a man's self-approval in the large concerns of life has its source in the approval of the peoples about him, and not in a searching personal examination of the matter. Mohammedans are Mohammedans because they are born and reared among that sect, not because they have thought it out and can furnish sound reasons for being Mohammedans; we know why Catholics are Catholics, why Presbyterians are Presbyterians, why Baptists are Baptists, why Mormons are Mormons, why thieves are thieves, why monarchists are monarchists, why Republicans are Republicans and Democrats, Democrats. We know it is a matter of association and sympathy, not reasoning and examination; that hardly a man in the world has an opinion upon morals, politics, or religion which he got otherwise than through his associations and sympathies. Broadly speaking, there are none but corn-pone opinions. And broadly speaking, corn-pone stands for self-approval. Self-approval is acquired mainly from the approval of other people. The result is conformity. Sometimes conformity has a sordid business interest—the bread-and-butter interest—but not in most cases, I think. I think that in the majority of cases it is unconscious and not calculated, that it is born of the human being's natural yearning to stand well with his fellows and have their inspiring approval and praise— a yearning which is commonly so strong and so insistent that it cannot be effectually resisted and must have its way.

A political emergency brings out the corn-pone opinion in fine force in its two chief varieties—the pocketbook variety, which has its origin in self-interest, and the bigger variety, the sentimental variety—the one which can't bear to be outside the pale; can't bear to be in disfavor, can't endure the averted face and the cold shoulder, wants to stand well with his friends, wants to be smiled upon, wants to be welcome, wants to hear the precious words, *"He's* on the right track!" Uttered perhaps by an ass, but still an ass of high degree, an ass whose approval is gold and diamonds to a smaller ass, and confers glory and honor and happiness and membership in the herd. For these gauds many a man will dump his life-long principles into the street, and his conscience along with them. We have seen it happen. In some millions of instances.

Men think they think upon great political questions, and they do; but they think with their party, not independently; they read its literature but not that of the other side; they arrive at convictions but they are drawn from a partial view of the matter in hand and are of no particular value. They swarm with their party, they feel with their party, they are happy in their party's approval; and where the party leads they will follow, whether for right and honor or through blood and dirt and a mush of mutilated morals.

In our late canvass half of the nation passionately believed that in silver lay salvation, the other half as passionately believed that that way lay destruction. Do you believe that a tenth part of the people on either side had any rational excuse for having an opinion about the matter at all? I studied that mighty question to the bottom—came out empty. Half of our people passionately believe in high tariff, the other half believe otherwise. Does this mean study and examination or only feeling? The latter, I think. I have deeply studied that question, too—and didn't arrive. We all do no end of feeling and we mistake it for thinking. And out of it we get an aggregation which we consider a boon. It settles everything. Some think it the Voice of God.

Considerations

1. Is there any truth to Twain's observation that we hold public opinion "in reverence," that we take it for "the Voice of God"?

2. Name three or four contemporary personifications of this voice.

3. Mass media have altered the circumstances the author describes. Have they served to reduce or intensify our hunger to conform, our need for "self-approval"? Explain and cite examples to support your answer.

4. This isn't the best piece of writing Twain ever produced. What do you find wrong with it? As an editor, what would you argue that he should change, fix? What would happen to the work if the first eight paragraphs were yanked? (Don't try to get by with "It would be shorter.")

Exercises

1. At the end of the twelfth paragraph Twain uses short, nicely balanced sentences. Try an imitation of the following:

We have not adopted this new fashion yet, but we shall do it presently.

We shall not think it out, we shall merely conform and let it go at that.

We get our notions and habits and opinions from outside influences; we do not have to study them out.

2. In conformers (or self-approvers) you have the raw material for a Swiftian essay. Certainly you've discovered that such people tend to fit not only under the broad heading just above, but also that they divide into narrower types, from office "yes men" to fashion slaves to a host of other trendy types. Write them up.

3. Here are fragmentary notions that may provoke some fresh connections-making on paper:

A Conformist's Credo
Everybody Else Is a Conformist, Not Me
How Come All of a Sudden Everybody's . . . ?
I'm Not Such a Conformist That I Want To Write About the Same Thing Everyone Else Is Writing About.

THE ADVOCATE
Herman Melville

You should find this piece interesting, even fascinating. It's a chapter from Melville's great novel *Moby-Dick,* but it doesn't read like part of a novel, let alone that often quite difficult book. It's an argument, eloquent yet straightforward, that vibrates with pride and vigor.

> As Queequeg and I are now fairly embarked in this business of whaling; and as this business of whaling has somehow come to be regarded among landsmen as a rather unpoetical and disreputable pursuit; therefore, I am all anxiety to convince ye, ye landsmen, of the injustice hereby done to us hunters of whales.
>
> In the first place, it may be deemed almost superfluous to establish the fact, that among people at large, the business of whaling is not accounted on a level with what are called the liberal professions. If a stranger were introduced into any miscellaneous metropolitan society, it would but slightly advance the general opinion of his merits, were he presented to the company as a harpooneer, say; and if in emulation of

the naval officers he should append the initials S. W. F. (Sperm Whale Fishery) to his visiting card, such a procedure would be deemed pre-eminently presuming and ridiculous.

Doubtless one leading reason why the world declines honoring us whalemen, is this: they think that, at best, our vocation amounts to a butchering sort of business; and that when actively engaged therein, we are surrounded by all manner of defilements. Butchers we are, that is true. But butchers, also, and butchers of the bloodiest badge have been all Martial Commanders whom the world invariably delights to honor. And as for the matter of the alleged uncleanliness of our business, ye shall soon be initiated into certain facts hitherto pretty generally unknown, and which, upon the whole, will triumphantly plant the sperm whale-ship at least among the cleanliest things of this tidy earth. But even granting the charge in question to be true; what disordered slippery decks of a whale-ship are comparable to the unspeakable carrion of those battle-fields from which so many soldiers return to drink in all ladies' plaudits? And if the idea of peril so much enhances the popular conceit of the soldier's profession; let me assure ye that many a veteran who has freely marched up to a battery, would quickly recoil at the apparition of the sperm whale's vast tail, fanning into eddies the air over his head. For what are the comprehensible terrors of man compared with the interlinked terrors and wonders of God!

But, though the world scouts at us whale hunters, yet does it unwittingly pay us the profoundest homage; yes, an all-abounding adoration! for almost all the tapers, lamps, and candles that burn round the globe, burn, as before so many shrines, to our glory!

But look at this matter in other lights; weigh it in all sorts of scales; see what we whalemen are, and have been.

Why did the Dutch in De Witt's time have admirals of their whaling fleets? Why did Louis XVI of France, at his own personal expense, fit out whaling ships from Dunkirk, and politely invite to that town some score or two of families from our own island of Nantucket? Why did Britain between the years 1750 and 1788 pay to her whalemen in bounties upwards of £1,000,000? And lastly, how comes it that we whalemen of America now outnumber all the rest of the banded whalemen in the world; sail a navy of upwards of seven hundred vessels; manned by eighteen thousand men; yearly consuming 4,000,000 of dollars; the ships worth, at the time of sailing, $20,000,000; and every year importing into our harbors a well reaped harvest of $7,000,000. How comes all this, if there be not something puissant in whaling?

But this is not the half; look again.

I freely assert, that the cosmopolite philosopher cannot, for his life, point out one single peaceful influence, which within the last sixty years has operated more potentially upon the whole broad world, taken in one aggregate, than the high and mighty business of whaling. One way and another, it has begotten events so remarkable in themselves, and so continuously momentous in their sequential issues, that whaling may well be regarded as that Egyptian mother, who bore offspring themselves pregnant from her womb. It would be a hopeless, endless task to catalogue all these things. Let a handful suffice. For many years past the whale-ship has been the pioneer in ferreting out the remotest and least known parts of the earth. She has explored seas and archipelagoes which had no chart, where no Cook or Vancouver had ever sailed. If American and European men-of-war now peacefully ride in once savage harbors, let them fire salutes to the honor and the glory of the whaleship, which originally showed them the way, and first interpreted between them and the savages. They may celebrate as they will the heroes of Exploring Expeditions, your Cooks, your Krusensterns; but I say that scores of anonymous Captains have sailed out of Nantucket, that were as great, and greater than your Cook and your Krusenstern. For in their succorless empty-handedness, they, in the heathenish sharked waters, and by the beaches of unrecorded, javelin islands, battled with virgin wonders and terrors that Cook with all his marines and muskets would not willingly have dared. All that is made such a flourish of in the old South Sea Voyages, those things were but the lifetime commonplaces of our heroic Nantucketers. Often, adventures which Vancouver dedicates three chapters to, these men accounted unworthy of being set down in the ship's common log. Ah, the world! Oh, the world!

Until the whale fishery rounded Cape Horn, no commerce but colonial, scarcely any intercourse but colonial, was carried on between Europe and the long line of the opulent Spanish provinces on the Pacific coast. It was the whalemen who first broke through the jealous policy of the Spanish crown, touching those colonies; and, if space permitted, it might be distinctly shown how from those whalemen at last eventuated the liberation of Peru, Chili, and Bolivia from the yoke of Old Spain, and the establishment of the eternal democracy in those parts.

That great America on the other side of the sphere, Australia, was given to the enlightened world by the whalemen. After its first blunderborn discovery by a Dutchman, all other ships long shunned those shores as pestiferously barbarous; but the whale-ship touched there. The whale-ship is the true mother of that now mighty colony. Moreover, in the infancy of the first Australian settlement, the emigrants were several times saved from starvation by the benevolent biscuit of the whale-ship luckily dropping an anchor in their waters. The uncounted isles of all Polynesia confess the same truth, and do commercial homage to the whale-ship, that cleared the way for the missionary and the merchant, and in many cases carried the primitive missionaries to their first destinations. If that double-bolted land, Japan, is ever to become hospitable, it is the whale-ship alone to whom the credit will be due; for already she is on the threshold.

But if, in the face of all this, you still declare that whaling has no aesthetically noble associations connected with it, then am I ready to shiver fifty lances with you there, and unhorse you with a split helmet every time.

The whale has no famous author, and whaling no famous chronicler, you will say.

The whale no famous author, and whaling no famous chronicler? Who wrote the first account of our Leviathan? Who but mighty Job! And who composed the first narrative of a whaling-voyage? Who, but no less a prince than Alfred the Great, who, with his own royal pen, took down the words from Other, the Norwegian whale-hunter of those times! And who pronounced our glowing eulogy in Parliament? Who, but Edmund Burke!

True enough, but then whalemen themselves are poor devils; they have no good blood in their veins.

No good blood in their veins? They have something better than royal blood there. The grandmother of Benjamin Franklin was Mary Morrel; afterwards, by marriage, Mary Folger, one of the old settlers of Nantucket, and the ancestress to a long line of Folgers and harpooneers—all kith and kin to noble Benjamin—this day darting the barbed iron from one side of the world to the other.

Good again; but then all confess that somehow whaling is not respectable.

Whaling not respectable? Whaling is imperial! By old English statutory law, the whale is declared "a royal fish."

Oh, that's only nominal! The whale himself has never figured in any grand imposing way.

The whale never figured in any grand imposing way? In one of the mighty triumphs given to a Roman general upon his entering the world's capital, the bones of a whale, brought all the way from the Syrian coast, were the most conspicuous object in the cymballed procession.

Grant it, since you cite it; but, say what you will, there is no real dignity in whaling.

No dignity in whaling? The dignity of our calling the very heavens attest. Cetus is a constellation in the South! No more! Drive down your hat in presence of the Czar, and take it off to Queequeg! No more! I know a man that, in his lifetime, has taken three hundred and fifty whales. I account that man more honorable than that great captain of antiquity who boasted of taking as many walled towns.

And, as for me, if, by any possibility, there be any as yet undiscovered prime thing in me: if I shall ever deserve any real repute in that small but high hushed world which I might not be unreasonably ambitious of; if hereafter I shall do anything that, upon the whole, a man might rather have done than to have left undone; if, at my death, my executors, or more properly my creditors, find any precious MSS. in my deak, then here I prospectively ascribe all the honor and the glory to whaling; for a whale-ship was my Yale College and my Harvard.

Considerations

1. Melville makes clear that he would have people see whaling in a different light. How may we gather that it was viewed in Melville's time? What current businesses, professions, trades are viewed in generally the same way today?

2. Whaling has come under critical scrutiny in modern times for quite different reasons than were current in Melville's time. What are these reasons, and how might we expect Melville to respond to them, based on what he says here?

3. What evidence offered here suggests that whaling may have been partly the victim of the same "public opinion" that Twain comments on? (And, by implication, is it possible that today's harp seal business, for example, is to an extent a victim of the same force?)

4. How does Melville draw his readers into the argument? Try reading the latter section without heeding the italicized questions. What happens? Does the text gain strength, puzzle you, or simply weaken? Explain why.

5. "The Advocate" can be divided into either two or three distinct parts. Where are they, and what makes the divisions logical?

Exercise

In any vein and about any issue, pursuit, or cause, argue the matter's rightness by correcting popular misconceptions about it.

THREE POINTS OF DEPARTURE

The final three selections in this book got written because their writers happened to notice something they figured was worth writing down: something about their world occurred to them that hadn't occurred before. And even though none of these pieces amounts to a deeply significant contribution to human knowledge, they're all pretty good. They should provoke you to see and think and perhaps respond.

When something occurs to you that's worth writing down—something you might want to share with others—it's natural to want to make it pretty good, to make it worth another's reading. This isn't a "literary" urge; it's human nature. And while you may not be a journalist or a scientist like Goodman, Thomas, or Eiseley, you are something and someone that no one else is. This makes you uniquely qualified to read and think and write with an authority no one else possesses. You might as well begin now believing in the validity of your own way of seeing the world, and in your own way with language to say and write about what you see and think. Keep this in mind when you read the following essays.

BLAME THE VICTIM
Ellen Goodman

There is a sign I pass every day on the way to work which says in bold letters: Health Thyself. The sign is "A Friendly Message" from the Blue Cross/Blue Shield people, who have, I know, a vested interest in its meaning.

But the very tone of it, the sort of Eleventh Commandment, Thus Spake Blue Cross/Blue Shield attitude of it, sitting there above the highway, has slowly rubbed raw a small layer of my consciousness. I have begun to wonder whether the Self-Health movement—of which this sign is more symbol than substance—isn't another variation on our national theme song: Blame the Victim. How many measures, how many beats, how many half-notes is it from the order to Health Thyself to the attitude that blames the ill for their illness?

The titles on the bookshelf of my favorite store are a chorus stuck in this monotone: *Stay Out of the Hospital* instructs one; *The Anti-Cancer Diet* offers another; *You Can Stop* (smoking) cheerleads a third. They tell readers How To design their faces, control their migraines, lose weight, bear children without pain and psych themselves out of everything from back pain to heart disease.

Perhaps the most typical of them is one which touts *Preventing Cancer: What You Can Do to Cut Your Risks by Up to 50 Percent*. And another containing *Dr. Frank's No Aging Diet: Eat and Grow Younger*.

Now I am in favor—who is against it?—of proper diet and exercise. I am against—who is in favor of it?—smoking. I assume that a diet high in calories, cholesterol and cognac would eventually do me in. I think that self-consciousness about health, the desire to take responsibility for the shape of our lungs and calf muscles, is positive, and I agree that we are our own best screening system. But there is a risk. A risk that as we focus on the aspects of self-health we begin to look at all illness as self-inflicted and even regard death as a kind of personal folly.

There have been, among my acquaintances, the relatives of my relatives and friends of my friends, three heart attacks within the past year. One man, I was told, was, well, overweight. "He should have known better." Another woman was, her friends insist, a real "Type A." And the third man, I was assured by the most well-meaning of people, brought it on himself. "He was so out of shape."

Similarly, when people hear reports of cancer, how often do they inadvertently say that the victim should have stayed out of the sun, or off the pill, or away from nitrates?

Now maybe they are right and maybe they are wrong, but I fear that there are many who seek to know the cause of a disease not to cure it, but to judge its victims.

It is reassuring to hear that we can cut the risks of cancer by 50 percent. It is lovely to think that we can eat in special ways and grow younger. In a world of amorphous fears, where carcinogens are the new demons, it is very human to try to analyze illness in order to separate ourselves from it, to assure ourselves that we can be immune. There is a natural tendency to try to buy insurance packages—not of Blue Crosses and Blue Shields, but of diets and regimens and cautions.

But there is also something malignant about some of the extremists who make a public virtue of their health. It is the sort of self-righteousness that inspired a letter writer to suggest to me recently that we eliminate lung cancer research, because "smokers do it to themselves."

There is a judgmental attitude toward ill-health germinating in parts of the country and in parts of our minds that can be spread cruelly. It implies that those who do not "Health Thyself" are not only courting their own disasters, but are owed very little in the way of sympathy. It implies that illness is, at root, a punishment for foolishness.

This feeds into the hope, born of fear, that if we keep ourselves in shape and watch out, we can not only postpone death but prevent it. The notion that death is, in essence, suicide, and something we can avoid, is the most profound illusion of all.

AUTONOMY
Lewis Thomas

Working a typewriter by touch, like riding a bicycle or strolling on a path, is best done by not giving it a glancing thought. Once you do, your fingers fumble and hit the wrong keys. To do things involving practiced skills, you need to turn loose the systems of muscles and nerves responsible for each maneuver, place them on their own, and stay out of it. There is no real loss of authority in this, since you get to decide whether to do the thing or not, and you can intervene and embellish the technique any time you like; if you want to ride a bicycle backward, or walk with an eccentric loping gait giving a little skip every fourth step, whistling at the same time, you can do that. But if you concentrate your attention on the details, keeping in touch with each muscle, thrusting yourself into a free fall with each step and catching yourself at the last moment by sticking out the other foot in time to break the fall, you will end up immobilized, vibrating with fatigue.

It is a blessing to have options for choice and change in the learning of such unconsciously coordinated acts. If we were born with all these knacks inbuilt, automated like ants, we would surely miss the variety. It would be a less interesting world if we all walked and skipped alike, and never fell from bicycles. If we were all genetically programmed to play the piano deftly from birth, we might never learn to understand music.

The rules are different for the complicated, coordinated, fantastically skilled manipulations we perform with our insides. We do not have to learn anything. Our smooth-muscle cells are born with complete instructions, in need of no help from us, and they work away on their own schedules, modulating the lumen of blood vessels, moving things through intestines, opening and closing tubules according to the requirements of the entire system. Secretory cells elaborate their products in privacy; the heart contracts and relaxes; hormones are sent off to react silently with cell membranes, switching adenyl cyclase, prostaglandin, and other signals on and off; cells communicate with each other by simply touching; organelles send messages to other organelles; all this goes on continually, without ever a personal word from us. The arrangement is that of an ecosystem, with the operation of each part being governed by the state and function of all the other parts. When things are going well, as they generally are, it is an infallible mechanism.

But now the autonomy of this interior domain, long regarded as inviolate, is open to question. The experimental psychologists have recently found that visceral organs can be taught to do various things, as easily as a boy learns to ride a bicycle, by the instrumental techniques of operant conditioning. If a thing is done in the way the teacher wants, at a signal, and a suitable reward is given immediately to reinforce the action, it becomes learned. Rats, rewarded by stimulation of their cerebral "pleasure centers," have been instructed to speed up or slow down their hearts at a signal, or to alter their blood pressures, or switch off certain waves in their electroencephalograms and switch on others.

The same technology has been applied to human beings, with other kinds of rewards, and the results have been startling. It is claimed that you can teach your kidneys to change the rate of urine formation, raise or lower your blood pressure, change your heart rate, write different brain waves, at will.

There is already talk of a breakthrough in the prevention and treatment of human disease. According to proponents, when the technology is perfected and extended it will surely lead to new possibilities for therapy. If a rat can be trained to dilate the blood vessels of one of his ears more than those of the other, as has been reported, what rich experiences in self-control and self-operation may lie just ahead for man? There are already cryptic advertisements in the Personal columns of literary magazines, urging the purchase of electronic headsets for the training and regulation of one's own brain waves, according to one's taste.

You can have it.

Not to downgrade it. It is extremely important, I know, and one ought to feel elated by the prospect of taking personal charge, calling the shots, running one's cells around like toy trains. Now that we know that viscera can be taught, the thought comes naturally that we've been neglecting them all these years, and by judicious application of human intelligence, these primitive structures can be trained to whatever standards of behavior we wish to set for them.

My trouble, to be quite candid, is a lack of confidence in myself. If I were informed tomorrow that I was in direct communication with my liver, and could now take over, I would become deeply depressed. I'd sooner be told, forty thousand feet over Denver, that the 747 jet in which I had a coach seat was now mine to operate as I pleased; at least I would have the hope of bailing out, if I could find a parachute and discover quickly how to open a door. Nothing would save me and my liver, if I were in charge. For I am, to face the facts squarely, considerably less intelligent than my liver. I am, moreover, constitutionally unable to make hepatic decisions, and I prefer not be obliged to, ever. I would not be able to think of the first thing to do.

I have the same feeling about the rest of my working parts. They are all better off without my intervention, in whatever they do. It might be something of a temptation to take over my brain, on paper, but I cannot imagine doing so in real life. I would lose track, get things mixed up, turn on wrong cells at wrong times, drop things. I doubt if I would ever be able to think up my own thoughts. My cells were born, or differentiated anyway, knowing how to do this kind of thing together. If I moved in to organize them they would resent it, perhaps become frightened, perhaps swarm out into my ventricles like bees.

Although it is, as I say, a temptation. I have never really been satisfied with the operation of my brain, and it might be fun to try running it myself, just once. There are several things I would change, given the opportunity: certain memories that tend to slip away unrecorded, others I've had enough of and would prefer to delete, certain notions I'd just as soon didn't keep popping in, trains of thought that go round and round without getting anywhere, rather like this one. I've always suspected that some of the cells in there are fluffing off much of the time, and I'd like to see a little more attention and real work. Also, while I'm about it, I could do with a bit more respect.

On balance, however, I think it best to stay out of this business. Once you began, there would be no end to the responsibilities. I'd rather leave all my automatic functions with as much autonomy as they please, and hope for the best. Imagine having to worry about running leukocytes, keeping track, herding them here and there, listening for signals. After the first flush of pride in ownership, it would be exhausting and debilitating, and there would be no time for anything else.

What to do, then? It cannot simply be left there. If we have learned anything at all in this century, it is that all new technologies will be put to use, sooner or later, for better or worse, as it is in our nature to do. We cannot expect an exception for the instrumental conditioning of autonomic functions. We will be driven to make use of it, trying to communicate with our internal environment, to meddle, and it will consume so much of our energy that we will end up even more cut off from things outside, missing the main sources of the sensation of living.

I have a suggestion for a way out. Given the capacity to control autonomic functions, modulate brain waves, run cells, why shouldn't it be possible to employ exactly the same technology to go in precisely the opposite direction? Instead of getting in there and taking things over, couldn't we learn to disconnect altogether, uncouple, detach, and float free? You would only need to be careful, if you tried it, that you let go of the right end.

Of course, people have been trying to do this sort of thing for a long time, by other techniques and with varying degrees of luck. This is what Zen archery seems to be about, come to think of it. You learn, after long months of study under a master, to release the arrow without releasing it yourself. Your fingers must do the releasing, on their own, remotely, like the opening of a flower. When you have learned this, no matter where the arrow goes, you have it made. You can step outside for a look around.

THE FLOW OF THE RIVER
Loren Eiseley

If there is magic on this planet, it is contained in water. Its least stir even, as now in a rain pond on a flat roof opposite my office, is enough to bring me searching to the window. A wind ripple may be translating itself into life. I have a constant feeling that some time I may witness that momentous miracle on a city roof, see life veritably and suddenly boiling out of a heap of rusted pipes and old television aerials. I marvel at how suddenly a water beetle has come and is submarining there in a spatter of green algae. Thin vapors, rust, wet tar and sun are an alembic remarkably like the mind; they throw off odorous shadows that threaten to take real shape when no one is looking.

Once in a lifetime, perhaps, one escapes the actual confines of the flesh. Once in a lifetime, if one is lucky, one so merges with sunlight and air and running water that whole eons, the eons that mountains and deserts know, might pass in a single afternoon without discomfort. The mind has sunk away into its beginnings among old roots and the obscure tricklings and movings that stir inanimate things. Like the charmed fairy circle into which a man once stepped, and upon emergence learned that a whole century has passed in a single night, one can never quite define this secret; but it has something to do, I am sure, with common water. Its substance reaches everywhere: it touches the past and prepares the future; it moves under the poles and wanders thinly in the heights of air. It can assume forms of exquisite perfection in a snowflake, or strip the living to a single shining bone cast up by the sea.

Many years ago, in the course of some scientific investigations in a remote western county, I experienced, by chance, precisely this sort of curious absorption by water—the extension of shape by osmosis—at which I have been hinting. You have probably never experienced in yourself the meandering roots of a whole watershed or felt your outstretched fingers touching, by some kind of clairvoyant extension, the brooks of snow-line glaciers at the same time that you were flowing toward the Gulf over the eroded debris of worn-down mountains. A poet, MacKnight Black, has spoken of being "limbed . . . with waters gripping pole and pole." He had the idea, all right, and it is obvious that these sensations are not unique, but they are hard to come by; and the sort of extension of the senses that people will accept when they put their ear against a sea shell, they will smile at in the confessions of a bookish professor. What makes it worse is the fact that because of a traumatic experience in childhood, I am not a swimmer, and am inclined to be timid before any large body of water. Perhaps it was just this, in a way, that contributed to my experience.

As it leaves the Rockies and moves downward over the high plains towards the Missouri, the Platte River is a curious stream. In the spring floods, on occasion, it can be a mile-wide roaring torrent of destruction, gulping farms and bridges. Normally, however, it is a rambling, dispersed series of streamlets flowing erratically over great sand and gravel fans that are, in part, the remnants of a mightier Ice Age stream bed. Quicksands and shifting islands haunt its waters. Over it the prairie suns beat mercilessly throughout the summer. The Platte, "a mile wide and an inch deep," is a refuge for any heat-weary pilgrim along its shores. This is particularly true on the high plains before its long march by the cities begins.

The reason that I came upon it when I did, breaking through a willow thicket and stumbling out through ankle-deep water to a dune in the shade, is of no concern to this narrative. On various purposes of science I have ranged over a good bit of that country on foot, and I know the kinds of bones that come gurgling up through the gravel pumps, and the arrowheads of shining chalcedony that occasionally spill out of water-loosened sand. On that day, however, the sight of sky and willows and the weaving net of water murmuring a little in the shallows on its way to the Gulf stirred me, parched as I was with miles of walking, with a new idea: I was going to float. I was going to undergo a tremendous adventure.

The notion came to me, I suppose, by degrees. I had shed my clothes and was floundering pleasantly in a hole among some reeds when a great desire to stretch out and go with this gently insistent water began to pluck at me. Now to this bronzed, bold, modern generation, the struggle I waged with timidity while standing there in knee-deep water can only seem farcical; yet actually for me it was not so. A near-drowning accident in childhood had scarred my reactions; in addition to the fact that I was a nonswimmer, this "inch-deep river" was treacherous with holes and quicksands. Death was not precisely infrequent along its wandering and illusory channels. Like all broad wastes of this kind, where neither water nor land quite prevails, its thickets were lonely and untraversed. A man in trouble would cry out in vain.

I thought of all this, standing quietly in the water, feeling the sand shifting away under my toes. Then I lay back in the floating position that left my face to the sky, and shoved off. The sky wheeled over me. For an instant, as I bobbed into the main channel, I had the sensation of sliding down the vast tilted face of the continent. It was then that I felt the cold needles of the alpine springs at my fingertips, and the warmth of the Gulf pulling me southward. Moving with me, leaving its taste upon my mouth and spouting under me in dancing springs of sand, was the immense body of the continent itself, flowing like the river was flowing, grain by grain, mountain by mountain, down to the sea. I was streaming over ancient sea beds thrust aloft where giant reptiles had once sported; I was wearing down the face of time and trundling cloud-wreathed ranges into oblivion. I touched my margins with the delicacy of a crayfish's antennae, and felt great fishes glide about their work.

I drifted by stranded timber cut by beaver in mountain fastnesses; I slid over shallows that had buried the broken axles of prairie schooners and the mired bones of mammoth. I was streaming alive through the hot and working ferment of the sun, or oozing secretively through shady thickets. I *was* water and the unspeakable alchemies that gestate and take shape in water, the slimy jellies that under the enormous magnification of the sun writhe and whip upward as great barbeled fish mouths, or sink indistinctly back into the murk out of which they arose. Turtle and fish and the pinpoint chirpings of individual frogs are all watery projections, concentrations—as man himself is a concentration—of that indescribable and liquid brew which is compounded in varying proportions of salt and sun and time. It has appearances, but at its heart lies water, and as I was finally edged gently against a sand bar and dropped like any log, I tottered as I rose. I knew once more the body's revolt against emergence into the harsh and unsupporting air, its reluctance to break contact with that mother element which still, at this late point in time, shelters and brings into being nine tenths of everything alive.

As for men, those myriad little detached ponds with their own swarming corpuscular life, what were they but a way that water has of going about beyond the reach of rivers? I, too, was a microcosm of pouring rivulets and floating driftwood gnawed by the mysterious animalcules of my own creation. I was three fourths water, rising and subsiding according to the hollow knocking in my veins: a minute pulse like the eternal pulse that lifts Himalayas and which, in the following systole, will carry them away.

Thoreau, peering at the emerald pickerel in Walden Pond, called them "animalized water" in one of his moments of strange insight. If he had been possessed of the geological knowledge so laboriously accumulated since his time, he might have gone further and amusedly detected in the planetary rumblings and eructations which so delighted him in the gross habits of certain frogs, signs of that dark interior stress which has reared sea bottoms up to mountainous heights. He might have developed an acute inner ear for the sound of the surf on Cretaceous beaches where now the wheat of Kansas rolls. In any case, he would have seen, as the long trail of life was unfolded by the fossil hunters, that his animalized water had changed its shapes eon by eon to the beating of the earth's dark millennial heart. In the swamps of the low continents, the amphibians had flourished and had their day; and as the long skyward swing—the isostatic response of the crust—had come about, the era of the cooling grasslands and mammalian life had come into being.

A few winters ago, clothed heavily against the weather, I wandered several miles along one of the tributaries of that same Platte I had floated down years before. The land was stark and ice-locked. The rivulets were frozen, and over the marshlands the willow thickets made such an array of vertical lines against the snow that tramping through them produced strange optical illusions and dizziness. On the edge of a frozen backwater, I stopped and rubbed my eyes. At my feet a raw prairie wind had swept the ice clean of snow. A peculiar green object caught my eye; there was no mistaking it.

Staring up at me with all his barbels spread pathetically, frozen solidly in the wind-ruffled ice, was a huge familiar face. It was one of those catfish of the twisting channels, those dwellers in the yellow murk, who had been about me and beneath me on the day of my great voyage. Whatever sunny dream had kept him paddling there while the mercury plummeted downward and that Cheshire smile froze slowly, it would be hard to say. Or perhaps he was trapped in a blocked channel and had simply kept swimming until the tide contracted around him. At any rate, there he would lie till the spring thaw.

At that moment I started to turn away, but something in the bleak, whiskered face reproached me, or perhaps it was the river calling to her children. I termed it science, however—a convenient rational phrase I reserve for such occasions—and decided that I would cut the fish out of the ice and take him home. I had no intention of eating him. I was merely struck by a sudden impulse to test the survival qualities of high-plains fishes, particularly fishes of this type who get themselves immured in oxygenless ponds or in cut-off oxbows buried in winter drifts. I blocked him out as gently as possible and dropped him, ice and all, into a collecting can in the car. Then we set out for home.

Unfortunately, the first stages of what was to prove a remarkable resurrection escaped me. Cold and tired after a long drive, I deposited the can with its melting water and ice in the basement. The accompanying corpse I anticipated I would either dispose of or dissect on the following day. A hurried glance had revealed no signs of life.

To my astonishment, however, upon descending into the basement several hours later, I heard stirrings in the receptacle and peered in. The ice had melted. A vast pouting mouth ringed with sensitive feelers confronted me, and the creature's gills labored slowly. A thin stream of silver bubbles rose to the surface and popped. A fishy eye gazed up at me protestingly.

"A tank," it said. This was no Walden pickerel. This was a yellow-green, mud-grubbing, evil-tempered inhabitant of floods and droughts and cyclones. It was the selective product of the high continent and the waters that pour across it. It had outlasted the prairie blizzards that left cattle standing frozen upright in the drifts.

"I'll get the tank," I said respectfully.

He lived with me all that winter, and his departure was totally in keeping with his sturdy, independent character. In the spring a migratory impulse or perhaps sheer boredom struck him. Maybe, in some little lost corner of his brain, he felt, far off, the pouring of the mountain waters through the sandy coverts of the Platte. Anyhow, something called to him, and he went. One night when no one was about, he simply jumped out of his tank. I found him dead on the floor next morning. He had made his gamble like a man—or, I should say, a fish. In the proper place it would not have been a fool's gamble. Fishes in the drying shallows of intermittent prairie streams who feel their confinement and have the impulse to leap while there is yet time may regain the main channel and survive. A million ancestral years had gone into that jump, I thought as I looked at him, a million years of climbing through prairie sunflowers and twining in and out through the pillared legs of drinking mammoth.

"Some of your close relatives have been experimenting with air breathing," I remarked, apropos of nothing, as I gathered him up. "Suppose we meet again up there in the cottonwoods in a million years or so."

I missed him a little as I said it. He had for me the kind of lost archaic glory that comes from the water brotherhood. We were both projections out of that timeless ferment and locked as well in some greater unity that lay incalculably beyond us. In many a fin and reptile foot I have seen myself passing by—some part of myself, that is, some part that lies unrealized in the momentary shape I inhabit. People have occasionally written me harsh letters and castigated me for a lack of faith in man when I have ventured to speak of this matter in print. They distrust, it would seem, all shapes and thoughts but their own. They would bring God into the compass of a shopkeeper's understanding and confine Him to those limits, lest He proceed to some unimaginable and shocking act—create perhaps, as a casual afterthought, a being more beautiful than man. As for me, I believe nature capable of this, and having been part of the flow of the river, I feel no envy—any more than the frog envies the reptile or an ancestral ape should envy man.

Every spring in the wet meadows and ditches I hear a little shrilling chorus which sounds for all the world like an endlessly reiterated "We're here, we're here." And so they are, as frogs, of course. Confident little fellows. I suspect that to some greater ear than ours, man's optimistic pronouncements about his role and destiny may make a similar little ringing sound that travels a small way out into the night. It is only its nearness that is offensive. From the heights of a mountain, or a marsh at evening, it blends, not too badly, with all the other sleepy voices that, in croaks or chirrups, are saying the same thing.

After a while the skilled listener can distinguish man's noise from the katydid's rhythmic assertion, allow for the offbeat of a rabbit's thumping, pick up the autumnal monotone of crickets, and find in all of them a grave pleasure without admitting any to a place of preeminence in his thoughts. It is when all these voices cease and the waters are still, when along the frozen river nothing cries, screams or howls, that the enormous mindlessness of space settles down upon the soul. Somewhere out in that waste of crushed ice and reflected stars, the black waters may be running, but they appear to be running without life toward a destiny in which the whole of space may be locked in some silvery winter of dispersed radiation.

It is then, when the wind comes straitly across the barren marshes and the snow rises and beats in endless waves against the traveler, that I remember best, by some trick of the imagination, my summer voyage on the river. I remember my green extensions, my catfish nuzzlings and minnow wrigglings, my gelatinous materializations out of the mother ooze. And as I walk on through the white smother, it is the magic of water that leaves me a final sign.

Men talk much of matter and energy, of the struggle for existence that molds the shape of life. These things exist, it is true; but more delicate, elusive, quicker than the fins in water, is that mysterious principle known as "organization," which leaves all other mysteries concerned with life stale and insignificant by comparison. For that without organization life does not persist is obvious. Yet this organization itself is not strictly the product of life, nor of selection. Like some dark and passing shadow within matter, it cups out the eyes' small windows or spaces the notes of a meadow lark's song in the interior of a mottled egg. That principle—I am beginning to suspect—was there before the living in the deeps of water.

The temperature has risen. The little stinging needles have given way to huge flakes floating in like white leaves blown from some great tree in open space. In the car, switching on the lights, I examine one intricate crystal on my sleeve before it melts. No utilitarian philosophy explains a snow crystal, no doctrine of use or disuse. Water has merely leapt out of vapor and thin nothingness in the night sky to array itself in form. There is no logical reason for the existence of a snowflake any more than there is for evolution. It is an apparition from that mysterious shadow world beyond nature, that final world which contains—if anything contains—the explanation of men and catfish and green leaves.